THE LIBERAL WAY OF WAR

T0346787

The Liberal Way of War
Legal Perspectives

Edited by

ROBERT P. BARNIDGE, JR
OP Jindal Global University, India

LONDON AND NEW YORK

First published 2013 by Ashgate Publishing

2 Park Square, Milton Park, Abingdon, Oxon OX14 4RN
711 Third Avenue, New York, NY 10017, USA

Routledge is an imprint of the Taylor & Francis Group, an informa business

First issued in paperback 2016

Copyright © 2013 Robert P. Barnidge, Jr

Robert P. Barnidge, Jr has asserted his right under the Copyright, Designs and Patents Act, 1988, to be identified as the editor of this work.

All rights reserved. No part of this book may be reprinted or reproduced or utilised in any form or by any electronic, mechanical, or other means, now known or hereafter invented, including photocopying and recording, or in any information storage or retrieval system, without permission in writing from the publishers.

Notice:
Product or corporate names may be trademarks or registered trademarks, and are used only for identification and explanation without intent to infringe.

British Library Cataloguing in Publication Data
Barnidge, Robert P.
  The liberal way of war : legal perspectives.
  1. Humanitarian law. 2. International law and human rights.
  3. War (International law) 4. War (Islamic law) 5. War – Religious aspects – Islam.
  6. Human rights – Religious aspects – Islam.
  I. Title
  341.6'7–dc23

The Library of Congress has cataloged the printed edition as follows:
The liberal way of war : legal perspectives / edited by Robert P. Barnidge, Jr.
    pages cm
  Includes bibliographical references and index.
  ISBN 978-1-4094-6739-7 (hardback)
1. War (International law) 2. Humanitarian law. I.
Barnidge, Robert P., editor of compilation.
  KZ6385.L53 2013
  341.6–dc23

                                                                    2013002708

ISBN 978-1-4094-6739-7 (hbk)
ISBN 978-1-138-25467-1 (pbk)

Contents

List of Contributors

Louise Arimatsu, Associate Fellow, International Law, Chatham House

J. Craig Barker, Professor, Department of Law, University of Sussex

Robert P. Barnidge, Jr, Associate Professor, OP Jindal Global University; Lecturer, School of Law, University of Reading (2007–12)

Susan Breau, Professor, Law School, Flinders University

Kalliopi Chainoglou, Research Fellow, School of Law and Social Sciences, University of East London

Alan Cromartie, Professor, School of Politics and International Relations, University of Reading

Malcolm D. Evans, Professor, Law School, University of Bristol

Sandy Ghandhi, Professor, School of Law, University of Reading

Colin Harvey, Professor, School of Law, Queen's University Belfast

Noëlle Quénivet, Senior Lecturer, Department of Law, University of the West of England

Niaz A. Shah, Senior Lecturer, Law School, University of Hull

John Strawson, Reader, School of Law and Social Sciences, University of East London

David Turns, Senior Lecturer, Cranfield University, Defence Academy of the United Kingdom

Anicée Van Engeland, Lecturer, School of Law, School of Oriental and African Studies

List of Cases

List of Treaties and Conventions

Agreement for the Prosecution and Punishment of the Major War Criminals of the European Axis, and Charter of the International Military Tribunal (adopted 8 August 1945, entered into force 8 August 1945) (Nuremberg Charter)

Convention Against Torture and Other Cruel, Inhuman or Degrading Treatment or Punishment (adopted 10 December 1984, entered into force 26 June 1987)

Convention Concerning the Prohibition and Immediate Action for the Elimination of the Worst Forms of Child Labor (ILO No. 182) (adopted 17 June 1999, entered into force 19 November 2000)

Convention on the Elimination of All Forms of Discrimination Against Women (adopted 18 December 1979, entered into force 3 September 1981)

Convention on the Prevention and Punishment of the Crime of Genocide (adopted 9 December 1948, entered into force 12 January 1951)

Convention on the Rights of the Child (adopted 20 November 1989, entered into force 2 September 1990)

Convention Relating to the Status of Refugees (adopted 25 July 1951, entered into force 22 April 1954) (Refugee Convention)

European Convention on Human Rights (adopted 4 November 1950, entered into force 3 September 1953)

Geneva Convention for the Amelioration of the Condition of the Wounded and Sick in Armed Forces in the Field (adopted 12 August 1949, entered into force 21 October 1950) (First Geneva Convention)

Geneva Convention for the Amelioration of the Condition of the Wounded, Sick and Shipwrecked Members of the Armed Forces at Sea (adopted 12 August 1949, entered into force 21 October 1950) (Second Geneva Convention)

Geneva Convention Relative to the Treatment of Prisoners of War (adopted 12 August 1949, entered into force 21 October 1950) (Third Geneva Convention)

Geneva Convention Relative to the Protection of Civilian Persons in Time of War (adopted 12 August 1949, entered into force 21 October 1950) (Fourth Geneva Convention)

Guidelines and Measures for the Prohibition and Prevention of Torture, Cruel, Inhuman or Degrading Treatment or Punishment in Africa, Banjul (adopted 23 October 2002) (Robben Island Guidelines)

Geneva Declaration of the Rights of the Child (adopted 26 September 1924)

Hague Convention (IV) Respecting the Laws and Customs of War on Land and Its Annex: Regulations Concerning the Laws and Customs of War on Land (adopted 18 October 1907, entered into force 26 January 1910)

Acknowledgements

In June 2008, the University of Reading's 'The Liberal Way of War' application was successful in a national competition for a large-scale Leverhulme Trust Programme Award to study 'Security and Liberty' (2008–13). This project has involved interdisciplinary collaboration by over a dozen co-investigators and doctoral students from politics and international relations, law, history and modern languages and European studies at Reading over a number of years. The principal investigator, Alan Cromartie, has written the Foreword to this volume; Sandy Ghandhi and I, both co-investigators, have also contributed. We are grateful to the Leverhulme Trust's generosity in funding this important research, of which this volume forms but one part.

For their comments on my Introduction to this volume, I would like to thank Alan Cromartie, Sandy Ghandhi, Katja Samuel, Noëlle Quénivet and Ellen Owens. I am also grateful to Ellen Owens, a postgraduate student on Reading's Human Rights LLM programme, for her invaluable research assistance; her 'eagle eyes' and attention to detail are to be commended.

ROBERT P. BARNIDGE, JR
The Liberal Way of War Programme
University of Reading
1 December 2012

Foreword

Alan Cromartie

Whatever else is said about the attacks of 11 September 2001, they were surely an attack on legal order. Whatever else is said about George Bush's declaration that they 'were not acts of terror. They were acts of war', it was a considered description of what had just occurred that was meant to have some legal implications. It posed, as perhaps it was meant to pose, a challenge for legal discourse. If war as a cultural practice had changed, there would be implications for how war was discussed and how it would (perhaps) be regulated. If lawyers opted not to change the ways they spoke of war, they would be taking a political stand; they would also risk diminishing what influence they possessed on the realities of state violence.

The essays this volume assembles were written by lawyers as part of a larger project on 'The Liberal Way of War', for a conference that touched, from various angles, on connections between war, law and 'liberalism'. Liberalism was not defined: it was the object of enquiry. It was, however, taken to incorporate commitments to various kinds of individual freedom, including the rights to accumulate exclusive property, to live one's life in any way that did not cause a readily assignable harm to others and to choose (and then to practise) a religion. It was also taken for granted that societies that are 'liberal' give important roles to lawyers; on virtually any account of what it is to be a liberal, it is equality before the law – known laws openly applied through impartial procedures (see Locke 1988: 358–60) – that ultimately secures these privileges. But nothing in this framework could be taken to imply that ideas of law are static, or that the perceived relationship between the law and warfare is likely to be stable over time. Law is orderly; war is violent and chaotic. It is natural for observers – even lawyers – to doubt if the former can genuinely influence the latter. This collection offers a snapshot of various aspects of recent wars as understood by lawyers, at a moment at which the relationship between law, states and soldiers was under an unusual level of strain.

A 'Foreword' is a suitable place for two preliminary observations about that particular moment's unusual character (they should be read alongside the more sceptical remarks to be found in David Turns's 'Afterword'). One is concerned with the idea of 'war', and its derivative, the 'laws of war'. In the mainstream Western tradition of the last few centuries, not all collective violence counts as belligerence; we use the term 'war' to distinguish certain kinds of violence engaged in by a certain kind of agent. It has often been imagined as a kind of substitute for ordinary forms of litigation, in other words, as a technique of conflict resolution 'against those who cannot be coerced by laws' (Gentili 1933: I, 23). This did not mean, however, that belligerent behaviour was felt to take place in an absolute normative vacuum. The achievement of what might be called the 'litigation model' was to supply war with a guiding purpose – the settlement of disputes between supreme political powers – by reference to which the activities of soldiers could be both organised and regulated. It managed to make war susceptible of a degree of order, while separating it from moralism. Among other things, it did so by supplying a rationale for a combatant/non-combatant distinction: war settled disagreements between sovereigns through a contest between specialised employees. The idea of such a contest both justified and limited the activity in question. In time, it stimulated the rather fruitful notion that soldiers could do *all, but only*, the violent things that put their professional opponents out of action. But the more modern tendency has been to replace 'the laws of war' – rules that are generated by the nature of the contest – with regulations thought of as *humanitarian* laws, rules that are generated by considerations of humanity that stand apart from, and constrain, the needs of war itself. On the traditional view, the acceptability of war was a function of the wider acceptability of the emergent system of European states marked by so-called 'Westphalian' sovereignty. In the contemporary world, by contrast, the privileges of such states have been called into question.

The second observation has to do with liberalism, especially with the shifting liberal attitude to nations. Here the best point of reference is the best-known single statement ever composed by any liberal: John Stuart Mill's pronouncement that 'the only purpose for which power can rightfully be exercised over any member of a civilised community, against his will, is to prevent harm to others' (1974: 68). This principle limits legitimate coercion. It is not always noticed, however, that the privilege of freedom from paternalist coercion does not attach to individuals *qua* individuals, nor even to civilised individuals *qua* civilised individuals, but only to individuals (who may or may not be civilised themselves) who come from civilised *communities*. As Mill explained on the next page of his *On Liberty* (1859),

> we may leave out of consideration those backward states of society in which the race itself may be considered as in its nonage. The early difficulties in the way of spontaneous progress are so great that there is seldom any choice of means for overcoming them; and a ruler full of the spirit of improvement is warranted in the use of any expedients that will attain an end perhaps otherwise unattainable. (1974: 69)

Here, plainly, the value appealed to is 'progress', and 'civilisation' is valued because it is implicitly progressive. Underlying this view was the further unstated assumption that it is peoples organised as nations that are the natural vehicles of progress. In his fascinating essay 'A Few Words on Intervention' (a piece that was also first published in 1859), Mill claimed that the 'rules of ordinary international morality imply reciprocity. But barbarians will not reciprocate'; and also that 'nations which are still barbarous have not yet gone beyond the period during which it is likely to be for their benefit that they should be conquered and held in subjection by foreigners ... barbarians have no rights as a *nation*, except a right to such treatment as may, at the earliest possible period, fit them for becoming one' (1984: 118–19).

Mill's tough-mindedness was idiosyncratic, but the alternative that he represents does bring out the distinctiveness of the predominant strand in twenty-first-century liberal opinion. Contemporary liberalism's default assumptions are both humanitarian and universalist; they are extremely sensitive to *individual* pain; moreover, they treat *every* human being as the bearer of the same set of individual rights. The tendency of such ideas is cosmopolitan: they are hostile both to nationalism and state sovereignty and hospitable to such innovations as the 'responsibility to protect' and universal criminal jurisdiction. Where Mill's beliefs were founded in conceptions about progress that were (he believed) historically founded, these notions seem to rest in no clear view of history. Nonetheless, they have been deeply influential in the accelerating transformation of the United Nations Universal Declaration of Human Rights from a non-binding 'standard of achievement' into something much closer to the global Bill of Rights that Eleanor Roosevelt no doubt intended. In Colin Harvey's words in his contribution to this volume, they have 'bolted humanity onto legality in a way that is proving hard for even the most determined states to displace entirely' (p. 58). Their weakness is their pressure towards uniformity in a world that is losing its faith in the convergent form of progress implied, for Mill, by the concept of 'civilisation'.

The three parts of this volume address three aspects of the impact of more than a decade of military action. The first, which is concerned with international human rights law, considers four different expressions of universalist moral aspirations, starting from the stock example of a universal norm: the absolute prohibition upon torture. It then moves through discussions of migration and the 'responsibility to protect' to the first thorough survey of the United Nations Human Rights Committee's 'Concluding Observations' about security and liberty during the decade after the 2001 attacks.

The second looks at problems posed by the nature of recent wars for international humanitarian law. At its most abstract, in Louise Arimatsu's chapter, it considers the subversion of assumptions about war's territorial character; at its most concrete and specific, in Susan Breau's, it raises simple but intractable questions about the likely effects of new technologies of killing upon humanitarian principles; at its most disturbing, in Noëlle Quénivet's, it deals with the interplay between the tragic fact of child soldiers and liberal ideas of childhood. Kalliopi Chainoglou's chapter explores a number of challenging conundrums that cyber technologies pose for our inherited legal framework.

The last part gives a different perspective. An implication of the rights-based nature of modern liberal ideology is that political problems are experienced as legal; Islamic political thinking also appeals to legal thinking, in the form of a religious jurisprudence. The religion among whose adherents much of the 'war on terror' has actually been fought thus offers a comparative perspective. As Niaz

A. Shah's chapter shows, traditional Islam could generate restraints on war – such as proportionality, non-combatant immunity and prohibition of vindictiveness – that have some clear analogies in Christian Just War thinking; he prompts the depressing reflection that one of the main effects of modernisation, in this sphere, is to erode such genuinely civilised traditions. Anicée Van Engeland's and John Strawson's chapters describe the resources available to those Islamic thinkers who wish for an authentically Islamic modernisation that is, however, compatible with Western models of political order. Strawson's is noticeably more pessimistic, perhaps because it allows for the force of nationalism. But both offer hope of a world in which existing rights-based norms might come to be seen as genuinely global. In such a world, the abstractions that the West has long appealed to – the 'usages established among civilized peoples, from the laws of humanity, and the dictates of the public conscience' (Hague Convention IV 1907: pmbl.) – would lose their Eurocentric connotations, not least because the West would hold itself to its own standards when fighting against non-Western adversaries. We must all hope such a world comes into being.

ALAN CROMARTIE
The Liberal Way of War Programme
University of Reading
1 December 2012

References

Bush, George W. 2001. Act of War Statement. BBC News, 12 September. Available at: http://news.bbc.co.uk/1/hi/world/americas/1540544.stm [accessed: 22 July 2012].

Gentili, A. 1933. *De Jure Belli Libri Tres* (2 vols). Oxford: Clarendon.

Locke, J. 1988. *Two Treatises of Government*, ed. P. Laslett. Cambridge: Cambridge University Press.

Mill, J.S. 1974. *On Liberty*, ed. G. Himmelfarb. Harmondsworth: Penguin.

Mill, J.S. 1984. *The Collected Works of John Stuart Mill*, vol. 21. Toronto: University of Toronto Press.

Introduction

Robert P. Barnidge, Jr

The decade after 11 September 2001 is a relatively discrete period, with the terrorist attacks in New York City, Washington, DC and rural Pennsylvania at one end and the global financial crisis, revolutionary changes in the Middle East and North Africa and withdrawals from Iraq and Afghanistan at the other. These years saw military interventions by liberal states, primarily by the United States and the United Kingdom but also by North Atlantic Treaty Organization (NATO) states more generally, in the Arab and Muslim world. The legal implications of these military activities are myriad and complex and have demanded considerable intellectual work by international lawyers during this ten-year period. In addition to international human rights law and international humanitarian law, much of this work has involved an increasing focus on the interface between international law and Islamic law on matters of war and peace.

As Alan Cromartie's Foreword to this volume notes, there is a larger context to these developments. The role of lawyers has been shaped by a longer-term transition away from the assumption that sovereign nation-states are the indispensable building blocks of world order. This shift can be seen as internal to the intellectual world of people who can fairly be called 'liberal'. The authors of this volume have no shared definition of this contested term, but they would agree that a liberal state is one that is committed both to the rule of law and to the salience of human rights. Many of them would accept that international law is, at least in part, a liberal project and that it seeks to regulate the behaviour of states in accordance with a set of common values of generally liberal character. From this perspective, an international lawyer might define a liberal state as one that has a reasonable compliance record with the purposes and principles of the United Nations and with international law generally (see United Nations Charter 1945: arts. 1–2).

This volume examines some of the great challenges that liberal states faced in the ten years after 11 September as they sought to remain faithful to both liberal values and international law. It grapples with these challenges over the course of three parts: applying international human rights law; international humanitarian law and today's 'new wars'; and Islamic law and its interface with international law. The volume ends with an Afterword by David Turns.

Applying International Human Rights Law

Undoubtedly, one important aspect of liberalism in contemporary international law is the extent to which liberal states comply with international human rights law. Institutionally, there is an entire constellation of treaty bodies that supervises states' compliance with international human rights law, both internationally and regionally. In Chapter 4 Sandy Ghandhi looks at one of the oldest of these, the United Nations Human Rights Committee, and assesses how its Concluding Observations reflect the main security-related challenges that states have faced since 11 September. There are also, of course, human rights bodies, courts and other actors at municipal law level, as well as transnational actors. The International Court of Justice also seems to be paying greater attention to human rights issues in its jurisprudence.[1] To summarise, human rights has become a central feature in liberal discourse, and as it has become so, it has ever expanded past the state, to encompass also, according to some, non-state actors (see Ruggie 2011).

The United Nations Security Council, which article 24(1) of the United Nations Charter tasks with 'primary responsibility for the maintenance of international peace and security', has generally been slow to recognise the relevance of international human rights law to its mandate. The classic example of this in the post-11 September context is Resolution 1373, which, though truly sweeping in scope, only mentions international human rights law with regard to a very discrete aspect of fighting terrorism (see UNSC Res 1373 (2001): ¶ 3(f)). This aspect relates to refugee and asylum law, and as Colin Harvey suggests in Chapter 2, state and non-state actors have certainly struggled with a 'dance of legality and humanity' in this regard since 11 September. As United Nations Secretary-General Kofi Annan noted in the wake of Resolution 1373's adoption, human rights protection is 'not primarily the responsibility of the Council' (UNSC 2002: 3). Sir Jeremy Greenstock, speaking in his capacity as Chairman of the Counter-Terrorism Committee, noted in January 2002 that monitoring states' performance of their obligations under Resolution 1373 did not require inquiring into their compliance with international human rights treaties, though he did admit of some informal role for international human rights law (see UNSC 2002: 5). Indeed, as Sir Jeremy noted in his oral evidence before the Iraq Inquiry in London in November 2009, this view as to the (ir)relevance of human rights from the Security Council's perspective was the consensus view of states involved in the Security Council at the time (see Greenstock 2009: 14–15).

---

1   In his separate opinion appended to the International Court of Justice's 2010 judgment in *Ahmadou Sadio Diallo (Republic of Guinea* v. *Democratic Republic of the Congo)* [2010] ICJ Rep 639, for example, Judge Antônio Augusto Cançado Trindade noted that '[o]urs are the times of a new *jus gentium*, focused on the rights of the human person, individually or collectively, which the "*droit d'étatistes*" of the legal profession insist on refusing to reckon, or rather on refusing or failing to understand, willingly or not' (735).

One explanation for the Security Council's reluctance to situate human rights at the centre of its counter-terrorism strategy in the immediate aftermath of 11 September seems to have been a sense that international human rights law fell outside the Security Council's mandate or even that focusing on human rights would be counterproductive to or compromise the effective fighting of terror. From a legal perspective, it could be argued that the effect of articles 25 and 103 of the UN Charter meant that states were bound to comply with their Security Council obligations '[i]n the event of a conflict between the obligations of the Members of the United Nations under the present Charter and their obligations under any other international agreement' (UN Charter 1945: art. 103), international human rights treaties being, in this context, 'other international agreement[s]'. Human rights could still be said to play a formal legal role, however, through the interaction of the Security Council's counter-terrorism framework and both customary counter-terrorism law[2] and *jus cogens* norms.[3] In Chapter 1 Malcolm D. Evans reflects upon the 'direction of travel' of one of these intransgressible legal norms, the prohibition of torture, and reminds us that liberal states have not always lived up to liberal values.

Although the Security Council has since the adoption of Resolution 1373 consistently embedded states' counter-terrorism obligations within a legal framework that stresses the importance of complying with international human rights law, this express shift in language has raised other issues. What is the precise relationship between international human rights law and international humanitarian law? The relationship is a vexing one, both in theory and in practice, and it must be said that international law has not particularly been a beacon of clarity in this regard.[4] As the 2011 Report of the Secretary-General's Panel of Inquiry on the 31 May 2010 Flotilla Incident put it, 'it is difficult to make generalized statements on the exact nature of the relationship between human rights law and international humanitarian law ... [though] there is significant overlap between many of the protections provided under international humanitarian law and their counterparts under human rights law' (99). Have some manifestations of international human

---

2 See *Interlocutory Decision on the Applicable Law: Terrorism, Conspiracy, Homicide, Perpetration, Cumulative Charging* [2011], STL-11-01/I/AC/R176bis, Appeals Chamber, Special Tribunal for Lebanon: 65–6; *Armed Activities on the Territory of the Congo (Democratic Republic of the Congo v. Uganda)* [2005] ICJ Rep 168: 226–7.

3 See *Application of the Convention on the Prevention and Punishment of the Crime of Genocide (Bosnia and Herzegovina v. Serbia and Montenegro)* (Provisional Measures) [1993] ICJ Rep 325: 439–41 (J. Lauterpacht). Orakhelashvili (2008: 53–60) considers fundamental human rights to reflect *jus cogens*. The 1969 Vienna Convention on the Law of Treaties defines a *jus cogens* norm as a norm that is 'accepted and recognized by the international community of States as a whole as a norm from which no derogation is permitted and which can be modified only by a subsequent norm of general international law having the same character' (art. 53).

4 See *Legal Consequences of the Construction of a Wall in the Occupied Palestinian Territory* (Advisory Opinion) [2004] ICJ Rep 136: 178.

rights law proven themselves to be more 'effective' since 11 September than others? Has the law 'changed'?

Many of the fundamentals in this debate were already with us before 11 September, of course. What are the proper ends of the state, in particular the liberal state, in securing human rights, and how is the international community to make an accounting for the human rights of all in light of the classic Huberian notion of state sovereignty as *exclusion*[5] and article 2(7) of the UN Charter?[6] One reading of state sovereignty today would be that the state exists primarily to serve the needs of its people. One of the most powerful voices on the International Court of Justice for this view has been Judge Antônio Augusto Cançado Trindade. For him, there is a very clear notion of the state's territorial integrity as 'entitlement':[7] 'No State can, after perpetrating such heinous crimes, then invoke or pretend to avail itself of territorial integrity; the fact is that any State that acts this way ceases to behave like a State *vis-à-vis* the victimized population'.[8] Closely related to this, of course, is the notion of responsibility to protect, which burst to the fore in the (il)legality/(il)legitimacy debate during NATO's 1999 intervention in Kosovo. In Chapter 2 J. Craig Barker usefully locates the emergence of this concept within a liberal discourse that had previously focused on 'failed states' and humanitarian intervention. Barker does not dismiss responsibility to protect, but he is critical of its shortcomings, particularly in light of the contemporary examples of Libya and Syria.

---

5   In the *Island of Palmas* arbitration, arbitrator Max Huber famously defined state sovereignty as '[i]ndependence in regard to a portion of the globe ... the right to exercise therein, to the exclusion of any other State, the functions of a State' (*Island of Palmas (Netherlands/United States)* [1928] 2 Reports of International Arbitral Awards 829: 838). Similarly, as the United States Supreme Court put it over two centuries ago, '[t]he jurisdiction of the nation within its own territory is necessarily exclusive and absolute. It is susceptible of no limitation not imposed by itself. Any restriction upon it, deriving validity from an external source, would imply a diminution of its sovereignty to the extent of the restriction, and an investment of that sovereignty to the same extent in that power which could impose such restriction. All exceptions, therefore, to the full and complete power of a nation within its own territories, must be traced up to the consent of the nation itself. They can flow from no other legitimate source' (*The Schooner Exchange v. McFadden* [1812] 7 Cranch. 116: 136).

6   'Nothing contained in the present Charter shall authorize the United Nations to intervene in *matters which are essentially within the domestic jurisdiction of any state* or shall require the Members to submit such matters to settlement under the present Charter; but this principle shall not prejudice the application of enforcement measures under Chapter VII' (emphasis added). For a Third World perspective on sovereignty in international law today, see Nirmal 2006.

7   *Accordance with International Law of the Unilateral Declaration of Independence in Respect of Kosovo* (Advisory Opinion) [2010] ICJ Rep 403: 606 (J. Cançado Trindade).

8   *Accordance with International Law of the Unilateral Declaration of Independence in Respect of Kosovo* (Advisory Opinion) [2010] ICJ Rep 403: 605 (J. Cançado Trindade).

International Humanitarian Law and Today's 'New Wars'

Turning back more squarely to 11 September, it is clear that one of the main challenges that international humanitarian law has had to face since then has been how to reconcile the existing treaty framework with certain contemporary realities of warfare. The Four Geneva Conventions of 1949 were drafted to ameliorate the condition of the wounded and sick in the armed forces in the field and the wounded, sick and shipwrecked in the armed forces at sea and to regulate the treatment of prisoners of war and the protection of civilians in times of war. They were adopted, however, nearly seven decades ago, in the wake of the Second World War and in the early days of the United Nations, and their remit was meant to be profoundly inter-state (see Four Geneva Conventions 1949: art. 2), with only common article 3 applying to 'armed conflict[s] not of an international character occurring in the territory of one of the High Contracting Parties' (Four Geneva Conventions 1949: art. 3). To be sure, the Four Geneva Conventions were hardly without their own shortcomings even before 11 September. As Sir Hersch Lauterpacht put it in 1952, 'beneficent as they are, [they] abound in gaps, compromises, obscurities and somewhat nominal provisions resulting from the inability of the parties to achieve an agreed effective solution – occasionally to the point of the English and French texts laying down divergent rules' (380).

Less than thirty years after the adoption of the Four Geneva Conventions, two additional protocols were adopted, in 1977, to reflect realities that had not been anticipated in 1949. The first of these, the Protocol Additional to the Geneva Conventions of 12 August 1949, and Relating to the Protection of Victims of International Armed Conflicts, was drafted to further develop the law of international armed conflict by 'internationalising' wars of national liberation (see Additional Protocol I: art. 1(4)). The second, the Protocol Additional to the Geneva Conventions of 12 August 1949, and Relating to the Protection of Victims of Non-International Armed Conflicts, reflects the view that common article 3 alone does not suffice to regulate armed conflicts 'which take place in the territory of a High Contracting Party between its armed forces and dissident armed forces or other organized armed groups which, under responsible command, exercise such control over a part of its territory as to enable them to carry out sustained and concerted military operations and to implement this Protocol' (Additional Protocol II: art. 1(1)).[9]

Liberals and others have engaged in passionate debates about the adequacy and applicability of this treaty framework in the post-11 September context. Who, or what, are 'Parties to the Conflict'? *Where* are these conflicts? How are they to be geographically and temporally defined and delineated? How are they to be

_____

9 The Protocol Additional to the Geneva Conventions of 12 August 1949, and Relating to the Adoption of an Additional Distinctive Emblem, was adopted on 8 December 2005. It introduced the 'third Protocol emblem' and is of relatively minor significance to international humanitarian law generally.

classified? In an op-ed in the *New York Times* at the end of 2011, Goldstein and Pinker noted that '"War" is a fuzzy category, shading from global conflagrations to neighborhood turf battles, so the organizations that track the frequency and damage of war over time need a precise yardstick'. What role do such non-state actors as Al Qaeda play in the (re)formation of law in this area? How are these and related questions to be answered, and by whom, or what? Chapter 7, by Louise Arimatsu, adds to our understanding of these and other questions by arguing that today's transnational armed conflicts have resuscitated international law's traditional 'agnosticism towards boundaries' and shifted the focus to relationships and spatiality across borders.

To be sure, the Security Council has not been particularly helpful in clarifying this area of law. Resolution 1989 is typical in that it merely '[r]eaffirm[s] the need to combat by all means, in accordance with the Charter of the United Nations and international law, including applicable international human rights, refugee and humanitarian law, threats to international peace and security caused by terrorist acts' (UNSC Res 1989 (2011): pmbl.) and stops there. This statement of law may be welcome at some level, but to say that international (humanitarian) law 'applies' is actually not to say very much, or at least not to say 'enough' (cf. Bellinger 2007: 8).

Our internet age of new technologies and cyber warfare has also raised new questions, and Kalliopi Chainoglou addresses a number of these in Chapter 8 (see also Dunlap 2011). More generally, some frame access to the internet within the context of international human rights law and the right to freedom of opinion and expression (see La Rue 2011). Others, such as former Special Rapporteur of the United Nations Human Rights Council on Extrajudicial, Summary or Arbitrary Executions Philip Alston, argue that, '[a]lthough robotic or unmanned weapons technology has developed at astonishing rates, the public debate over the legal, ethical and moral issues arising from its use is at a very early stage, and very little consideration has been given to the international legal framework necessary for dealing with the resulting issues' (2010: 16).

It could be argued that Alston's concerns, while real, are somewhat exaggerated. First, many of the 'cardinal principles contained in the texts constituting the fabric of humanitarian law',[10] in particular the principles of distinction and proportionality, are themselves malleable enough to describe, and proscribe, almost anything, including technological innovations.[11] Second, the diverse interpretative possibilities that are inherent in many of these core principles mean that they necessarily update themselves in response to the felt needs of state and non-state actors.[12] Customary international humanitarian law, furthermore, with

---

10   *Legality of the Threat or Use of Nuclear Weapons* (Advisory Opinion) [1996] ICJ Rep 226: 257.

11   Of course, this is both an advantage and a disadvantage, as it facilitates both life and death, both risk and recrimination.

12   Within the context of Additional Protocol I, for example, there is the ever-present Martens Clause, with its focus on, *inter alia*, the 'principles of humanity and … dictates of

its undying commitment to the interplay between state practice and *opinio juris*,[13] is ever contested and open to organic change. Finally, many of these questions themselves involve ethical judgments that 'objective' analysis can never really definitively answer, even if international humanitarian law were to formally adopt new treaty language in response to the technological innovations of the twenty-first century.[14] Susan Breau makes a similar point in Chapter 5 when, in reflecting upon the somewhat stale debates as to whether particular drone attacks are or are not proportionate under international humanitarian law, she stresses that, at root, the 'true debate surely must be how many civilians should be sacrificed for the death of an important militant'. And in this she is surely correct.[15]

Given that international humanitarian law serves, at least in part, to protect and regulate the taking of life, it is interesting to consider the role that children play in contemporary armed conflicts. Chapter 6, by Noëlle Quénivet, radically critiques international law's construction of childhood and agency and can be seen as a general challenge to the universalist assumptions of a liberal discourse that seeks to rigidly categorise child soldiers as victims rather than appreciating their autonomy as agents of their own destinies. Hers is not so much a glorification of child soldiers – it is not – but, rather, a challenge to the universalistic 'human rights ideology' that, she argues, seeks to substitute its own vision of who should be protected from violence and be responsible for and entitled to engage in it. From her perspective, for international law to deny that children can be, at least to a degree, 'active agents' is to divest them of their autonomy. It is to depict child soldiers in a way not wholly unlike how Said famously contended Orientalist scholars depicted Arab Orientals, as 'that impossible creature whose libidinal energy drives him to paroxysms of overstimulation – and yet, he is as a puppet in the eyes of the world, staring vacantly out at a modern landscape he can neither understand nor cope with' (2003: 312). Yet one should perhaps be careful not to overstate the case. As Special Court for Sierra Leone Justice Geoffrey Robertson stated in his dissenting opinion appended to *Sam Hinga Norman*, what is 'voluntary' and 'consensual' is

---

public conscience' (art. 1(2)). Furthermore, according to article 36 of Additional Protocol I, which is specifically designed to deal with new weapons, '[i]n the study, development, acquisition or adoption of a new weapon, means or method of warfare, a High Contracting Party is under an obligation to determine whether its employment would, in some or all circumstances, be prohibited by this Protocol or by any other rule of international law applicable to the High Contracting Party.'

13 *Jurisdictional Immunities of the State (Germany v. Italy: Greece Intervening)* [2012] ICJ: ¶ 55.

14 On ethics in this regard, see *Public Committee Against Torture v. Government of Israel* [2006] HCJ 769/02: ¶ 45.

15 Breau builds upon important work that she has been doing as lead of a team of scholars in the Oxford Research Group's Every Casualty programme.

not always so clear-cut: 'Any organization which affords the opportunity to wield an AK47 will have a certain allure to the young'.[16]

Islamic Law and its Interface with International Law

In the decade after 11 September, liberal states also struggled to understand the role of Islam and how best to constructively engage with it. The relationship between Islam and international law, of course, is a complex and contested one. One explanation for this lies in the fact that Muhammad's birth in sixth-century Arabia presaged not simply the spread of a new understanding of religious devotion to faraway lands but also, with it, the emergence of a comprehensive system of law. Centuries before the 1648 Peace of Westphalia would consolidate the notion of the sovereign nation-state, Islam saw the development of an elaborate legal system that would govern relations between the Muslim and non-Muslim worlds. Classical Islamic law would emerge to mediate relations between not nation-states as such but, rather, between *Dar al-Islam*, the abode of Islam, and the 'other', in this case, *Dar al-Harb*, the abode of war (see Khadduri 1966: 10–14; Mahmassani 1966: 250–53, but see Ali and Rehman 2005: 333–5). This much is clear from Al-Shaybani's seminal work of Islamic international law, *Kitab Al-Siyar Al-Saghir* (1998), which puts forth intricate rules of law on matters of war and peace based largely upon the distinction between Muslims and non-Muslims. In a more contemporary context, this understanding is reflected in the recently-adopted Statute of the Organisation of Islamic Cooperation's Independent Permanent Human Rights Commission, which seeks to 'ensure consolidation of civil, political, economic, social and cultural rights in the Member States in accordance with the OIC Charter, *and to monitor observance of the human rights of Muslim communities and minorities*' (Cismas 2011: 1157, art. 10; emphasis added); in other words, an expression of a global Islamic law that distinguishes at its core between Muslims and non-Muslims.

   With the fall of the caliphate in the waning days of the Ottoman Empire, Islam would lose the 'protector of the Mussulman religion' (Ottoman Constitution 1908: 367, art. 4), the sultan as caliph, he who 'cause[d] to be executed the dispositions of the Sheri (sacred law) and the laws' (Ottoman Constitution 1908: 368, art. 7). The Ottoman Empire, of course, did not cover the entirety of the Muslim world; nor would it be correct to say that the caliphate functioned in the same way that the papacy has within the Catholic faith. What is clear, however, is that the caliph's influence and authority on matters of Islamic law and doctrine held sway for Muslims for well over a millennium and that, with the end of the Ottomans, it was no more.

---

16   *Prosecutor v. Sam Hinga Norman* 2004. SCSL. International Legal Materials, 43(5), 1129–65: 1150 (J. Robertson); cf. *Prosecutor v. Lubanga* (Judgment), ICC-01/04-01/06, T Ch (2012): ¶ 613.

This void is today filled with competing narratives about Islamic law and its role in the world. Is Islamic law compatible with contemporary international law, in whole or in part? In his Commentary to Al-Shaybani's *Kitab Al-Siyar Al-Saghir*, Ghazi notes that since the '*grundnorm* in Islamic law is the total submission and surrender before the revealed guidance brought by the Holy Prophet Muhammad (peace be on him), the *Sharī'ah* of the Prophet represents Good *par excellence*, Truth *par excellence*, and Justice *par excellence* and ensures the ultimate happiness both in this world and in the Hereafter' (Al-Shaybani 1998: 102, n. 119). Sheikh Yusuf Al-Qaradawi, one of the leading thinkers in Sunni Islam, contends that '[a]ll man-made laws are inherently defective and incomplete, since the law-makers, whether they be individuals, governments, or legislatures, limit themselves to dealing with material considerations, neglecting the demands of religion and morality' (1999: 348). Do the Islamic international law of *siyar* and contemporary international law reflect or challenge one another? Are they competing normative systems? How are conflicts, if and when they arise, to be mediated, by whom and on the basis of what, or whose, authority? How have revolutionary changes in the Middle East and North Africa, which have to date seen an increased role for Islam in political life, affected these discussions? How will they?

There is the view that Islam reflects and reinforces the purposes and principles of the United Nations. Egyptian author Naguib Mahfouz essentially conveyed this understanding of Islam in his 1988 Nobel Lecture:

> As for Islamic civilization I will not talk about its call for the establishment of a union between all Mankind under the guardianship of the Creator, based on freedom, equality and forgiveness. Nor will I talk about the greatness of its prophet. For among your thinkers there are those who regard him [as] the greatest man in history. I will not talk of its conquests which have planted thousands of minarets calling for worship, devoutness and good throughout great expanses of land from the environs of India and China to the boundaries of France. Nor will I talk of the fraternity between religions and races that has been achieved in its embrace in a spirit of tolerance unknown to Mankind neither before nor since.

The United Nations Alliance of Civilisations, an initiative that Spanish Prime Minister José Luis Rodríguez Zapatero and Turkish Prime Minister Recep Tayyip Erdoğan founded in 2005, also contends that Islam generally reflects and reinforces the purposes and principles of the United Nations. Chapters 9 and 10, by Niaz A. Shah and Anicée Van Engeland, respectively, the former from a Sunni tradition, the latter from a Shia tradition, make a similar argument as to the broad compatibility between Islamic law and international humanitarian law.

Competing with this view of Islam and its place in the world, of course, are the revolutionary agendas of radical Islam. These political projects, though not always consistent with one another or always manifesting themselves in violence, seek to upend secular legal norms, internationally, transnationally and within states themselves. Al Qaeda has come to embody radical Islamic terror, and the at least superficial 'rootedness' of its ideology within Islamic discourse and sources cannot be disputed, as even the most cursory examination of its many statements reveals.[17] This 'rootedness', in fact, explains some of its propaganda appeal. The eminent Middle East historian Bernard Lewis, for example, has referred to the seminal 1998 Declaration of the World Islamic Front for Jihad Against the Jews and the Crusaders as a 'magnificent piece of eloquent, at times even poetic Arabic prose' (1998: 14).

That Islamic law should struggle with the interpretation of language and tradition should not come as a surprise; to a greater or lesser extent, international law experiences a similar tension and indeterminacy. That the Islamic law of *qital* has certain 'grey areas' and 'blind spots', as Niaz A. Shah suggests in his chapter, or that, as John Strawson notes in Chapter 11, the Freedom and Justice Party in Egypt is struggling with how to give practical effect to its ideological commitments is perhaps to be expected. While many would object to the blanket statement that law is simply whatever those in power might wish it to be, it is clear that norms of Islamic law and international law embody what Koskenniemi has referred to as 'object[s] of interpretative controversy' (2009: 16) and subject themselves to negotiations of meaning (see Barnidge 2008).[18]

Afterword

In closing out this volume, David Turns's 'Afterword' examines the role that liberal commitments have played in influencing liberal states' engagements with the world beyond their borders. Like J. Craig Barker, he explores the recent NATO-led intervention in Libya and current anxiety about the deteriorating situation in Syria, but he does so by also drawing upon a particular historical tradition of liberal concern. With a keen eye to history, he shows how two centuries of 'benevolent aggression' reflect the insistence of many liberals that liberal values not cease at the 'water's edge'. Contemporary debates about humanitarian intervention and responsibility to protect must be understood within this context, and the reader will not be surprised to learn that both of these concepts are enormously controversial. When the Assembly of Heads of State and Government met at the United Nations Headquarters in September 2005 and adopted responsibility to protect in the World Summit Outcome (see UNGA Res 60/1 (2005): ¶¶ 138–40), significant cleavages

---

17   Two of the best collections of statements by Al Qaeda are Ibrahim 2007 and Lawrence 2005.

18   As an example, the 'threat', 'attack' and 'oppression' that Osama bin Laden's 2002 Letter to America identified and which he felt justified Al Qaeda's *jihad* against the United States do not easily square with the narrow parameters of contemporary international law's prohibition on the threat or use of force, or the law related to the conduct of hostilities (see bin Laden 2002).

arose along ideological lines. Cuba, for example, attacked responsibility to protect for 'run[ning] the risk of being invoked in the future as a pretext for aggression against our countries' (UNGA (2005), UN Doc A/60/PV.8: 47); the European Community representative in New York, by contrast, was much more positive, characterising responsibility to protect's inclusion in the final text as an 'important outcome' (UNGA (2005), UN Doc A/60/PV.8: 52). Apart from questions of policy, do the concepts of humanitarian intervention and responsibility to protect reflect customary international law, in whole or in part? Are they *lex lata* or *lex ferenda*? The praxis and interplay between liberal values and law that David Turns identifies helpfully bring together themes that permeate this entire volume: the anxieties that liberal states faced as they sought to bring their liberal values to bear in their engagements with international human rights law, international humanitarian law and Islamic law in the ten years after 11 September.

References

Al-Qaradawi, Y. 1999. *The Lawful and the Prohibited in Islam*, trans. K. El-Helbawy *et al.* Plainfield: American Trust.

Al-Shaybani, M.I.A.-H. 1998. *Kitab Al-Siyar Al-Saghir: The Shorter Book on Muslim International Law*, ed. M.A. Ghazi. Islamabad: Islamic Research Institute.

Ali, S.S. and Rehman, J. 2005. The Concept of *Jihad* in Islamic International Law. *Journal of Conflict and Security Law*, 10(3), 321–43.

Alston, P. 2010. Interim Report of the Special Rapporteur on Extrajudicial, Summary or Arbitrary Executions, UN Doc A/65/321.

Barnidge, R.P. Jr. 2008. War and Peace: Negotiating Meaning in Islam. *Critical Studies on Terrorism*, 1(2), 263–78.

Bellinger, J.B. III. 2007. Prisoners in War: Contemporary Challenges to the Geneva Conventions. Lecture at the University of Oxford, 10 December. Available at: http://insct.syr.edu/uploadedFiles/insct/uploadedfiles/PDFs/Bellinger%20Prisoners%20In%20War%20Contemporary%20Challenges%20to%20the%20Geneva%20Conventions.pdf [accessed: 22 November 2012].

bin Laden, O. 2002. Full Text: Bin Laden's 'Letter to America'. *Observer*, 24 November. Available at: http://www.guardian.co.uk/world/2002/nov/24/theobserver [accessed: 22 November 2012].

Cismas, I. 2011. Introductory Note to the Statute of the OIC Independent Permanent Human Rights Commission. *International Legal Materials*, 50(6), 1155–60.

Dunlap, C.J. Jr. 2011. Perspectives for Cyber Strategists on Law for Cyberwar. *Strategic Studies Quarterly*, 5(1), 81–99.

Goldstein, J.S. and Pinker, S. 2011. War Really is Going Out of Style. *New York Times*, 17 December.

Greenstock, J. 2009. Oral Evidence. Iraq Inquiry, 27 November. Available at: http://www.iraqinquiry.org.uk/media/40456/20091127am-final.pdf [accessed: 22 November 2012].

Ibrahim, R. (ed. and trans.) 2007. *The Al Qaeda Reader*. New York: Broadway Books.

Khadduri, M. 1966. Translator's Introduction, in *The Islamic Law of Nations: Shaybani's Siyar*. Baltimore: Johns Hopkins Press, 1–74.

Koskenniemi, M. 2009. The Politics of International Law – 20 Years Later. *European Journal of International Law*, 20(1), 7–19.

La Rue, F. 2011. Report of the Special Rapporteur on the Promotion and Protection of the Right to Freedom of Opinion and Expression, UN Doc A/HRC/17/27.

Lauterpacht, H. 1952. The Problem of the Revision of the Law of War. *British Year Book of International Law*, 29, 360–82.

Lawrence, B. (ed.) 2005. *Messages to the World: The Statements of Osama bin Laden*, trans. J. Howarth. London: Verso.

Lewis, B. 1998. License to Kill: Usama bin Ladin's Declaration of *Jihad*. *Foreign Affairs*, 77(6), 14–19.

Mahfouz, N. 1988. The Nobel Prize in Literature: Award Ceremony Speech. Available at: http://www.nobelprize.org/nobel_prizes/literature/laureates/1988/mahfouz-lecture.html?print=1 [accessed: 22 November 2012].

Mahmassani, S. 1966. The Principles of International Law in the Light of Islamic Doctrine, in *Collected Courses of The Hague Academy of International Law*, 117, 201–328.

Nirmal, B.C. 2006. Sovereignty in International Law. *Soochow Law Journal*, 3(2), 1–51.

Orakhelashvili, A. 2008. *Peremptory Norms in International Law*. Oxford: Oxford University Press.

Ottoman Constitution 1908. Promulgated the 7th Zilbridje, 1293 (11/23 December, 1876). *American Journal of International Law Supplement*, 2(4), 367–87.

Oxford Research Group. Every Casualty. Available at: http://www.oxfordresearchgroup.org.uk/rcac [accessed: 22 November 2012].

Report of the Secretary-General's Panel of Inquiry on the 31 May 2010 Flotilla Incident 2011. Available at: http://www.un.org/News/dh/infocus/middle_east/Gaza_Flotilla_Panel_Report.pdf [accessed: 22 November 2012].

Ruggie, J. 2011. Guiding Principles on Business and Human Rights: Implementing the United Nations 'Protect, Respect and Remedy' Framework, UN Doc A/HRC/17/31.

Said, E.W. 2003. *Orientalism*. New York: Vintage.

UNGA (2005), UN Doc A/60/PV.8.

UNGA Res 60/1 (2005), UN Doc A/RES/60/1.

United Nations Alliance of Civilisations. Available at: http://www.unaoc.org/ [accessed: 22 November 2012].

UNSC (2002), UN Doc S/PV.4453.

UNSC Res 1373 (2001), UN Doc S/RES/1373.

UNSC Res 1989 (2011), UN Doc S/RES/1989.

PART I
Applying International Human Rights Law

Chapter 1

How Has the Prohibition of Torture Survived 11 September 2001?

Malcolm D. Evans

Although it did not always seem so at the time, in some ways international action to prohibit and combat torture was approaching its zenith around the time of 11 September 2001, and the mood of those involved in international action against torture was, generally, optimistic. The absolute nature of the prohibition was entrenched in international human rights law and appeared to be unassailable. Just before the new millennium, the judgments of the House of Lords in the *Pinochet* cases had, perhaps for the first time, revealed the full potential of universal jurisdiction as a tool to hold those accused of torture to account.[1] Principles of individual criminal responsibility under international law were emerging, and at the domestic level, the barriers of immunity appeared to be on the verge of crumbling in the face of the *jus cogens* nature of the prohibition.[2] In Europe, the European Committee for the Prevention of Torture had established itself as a powerful force for change (see Cassese 1995; Evans and Morgan 1997) and the Guidelines and Measures for the Prohibition and Prevention of Torture, Cruel, Inhuman or Degrading Treatment or Punishment in Africa (Robben Island Guidelines) would shortly be drafted and adopted in Africa, ushering in a further wave of institutional activity against torture. At the United Nations, a new international instrument focusing on torture prevention, the Optional Protocol to the Convention Against Torture and Other Cruel, Inhuman or Degrading Treatment or Punishment, was in the final throes of being crafted.[3] Of course, there were grave challenges to be faced, but it seemed as if the general direction of travel was broadly positive, with the international community and international law continuing to bear down on those responsible for torture.

---

1   *R v. Bow Street Metropolitan Stipendiary Magistrate Ex parte Pinochet Ugarte (No. 1)* [1998] [2000] 1 AC 61; *R v. Bow Street Metropolitan Stipendiary Magistrate Ex parte Pinochet Ugarte (No. 2)* [1999] [2000] 1 AC 119; *R v. Bow Street Metropolitan Stipendiary Magistrate Ex parte Pinochet Ugarte (No. 3)* [1999] [2000] 1 AC 147.

2   See *Prosecutor v. Furundžija* (Judgment), IT-95-17/1-T, T Ch (1998): ¶¶ 153–7.

3   The major growth in torture prevention activities during the last ten years complements developments related to the prohibition of torture, but these developments lie outside the scope of this chapter. On the Optional Protocol to the Convention Against Torture and Other Cruel, Inhuman or Degrading Treatment or Punishment, see Murray *et al.* 2011.

Perhaps this is something of a caricature, but ten years on, and though many elements of this picture remain in place, many of the assumptions upon which this positive vision was based have been challenged, and the sense of there being an easy consensus around them has been broken. Some of these avenues have continued to develop apace, and other new avenues of accountability have been added, notably as regards individual criminal responsibility before international and hybrid tribunals. On the other hand, some areas of progressive development appear to have been closed down or, at least, the door to them narrowed. At the same time, a whole host of previously unaddressed issues has come to the fore, challenging the orthodox account of the inexorable rise of the absolute prohibition of torture.

What follows is a brief sketch of some of the more salient developments related to a number of key issues. This cannot be a comprehensive or exhaustive survey of so vast a field. Rather, taking its cue from the issues raised above, this chapter will offer some general thoughts on the 'direction of travel'. In doing so, particular attention will be paid to the way in which the United Nations General Assembly's annual Torture Resolutions have evolved because this offers interesting insights into the emergent issues and the extent of political consensus on a number of key issues. The conclusion will be that while the prohibition remains, and remains absolute in nature, it sits less easily than it did prior to 11 September and is vulnerable at the edges. The troubling question that still needs to be considered is whether it would be wise to draw the boundaries of the absolute prohibition more circumspectly in order to better preserve the inviolability of its central core, that is, whether it remains practical to be fully faithful to a maximalist vision of what the absolute prohibition entails in our post-11 September world.

The Ethical Dimension

As a preface to this discussion, it is worth stressing that in one vital respect the post-11 September world is irrevocably different from the world before 11 September. Put simply, indeed, put crudely, before 11 September torture was generally imagined to be the preserve of the 'bad'. It was what tyrants and dictators did; it was not what liberal, democratic societies did. In this imagining, if it came to be known that torture did occur in a liberal, democratic society, it was understood to be a wrong and would be treated as a wrong. The role of human rights law was to assist such states in doing so. The prohibition of torture was, therefore, a friend of democracy and the rule of law, not its foe (see Bingham 2010). Such perceptions were underscored by the judgment of the European Court of Human Rights in the *Greek Case* (1969) (European Commission of Human Rights 1972), which exposed the 'turn to torture' that had occurred in Greece following the overthrow of democratic government and the seizure of power by the military in 1967.

This idea that in a post-war human rights era democracies do not torture was, of course, never true. Any reader of Henri Alleg's *The Question* (2006), which exposes the reality of torture in Algeria during the 1950s, would know this, and to this might be added by way of example the alleged use of torture by British forces in Kenya during the Mau Mau rebellion, which has more recently come to the fore (see Anderson 2005).[4] But lest it be thought that these were 'merely' (if regrettable) colonial 'blindspots', the proceedings in the seminal case of *Ireland v. United Kingdom* before the European Commission on Human Rights (in 1976) and the European Court of Human Rights (in 1978) ought to have alerted us to the essential untruth of this myth.[5] The Commission had concluded that the use of interrogation techniques by British security forces in Northern Ireland amounted to torture, and although the Court ultimately disagreed, it found these techniques to have amounted to inhuman or degrading treatment, which, of course, still violated the absolute prohibition found in article 3 of the European Convention on Human Rights. The precise placement of the threshold was not as important as the essential fact that an international human rights court had found that functioning democracies do ill-treat detainees in ways that raise questions of torture (see Cobain 2012). Nevertheless, the myth that they did not (or, at least, did not as a matter of policy) was a useful myth since it assisted in the garnering of support for the anti-torture movement in the 1970s and 1980s, when the history of the use of torture in the 1950s and 1960s was slipping from view. Indeed, Darius Rejali has gone further, and in *Torture and Democracy* (2009), he argues that liberal democracy is in fact the ideal breeding ground for torture. Without necessarily wishing to go so far, this chapter does argue that the fundamental that has indeed changed is that torture is no longer automatically considered to be a mark of the outcast: it is claimed that 'good' people torture, too; or put perhaps more accurately, since people can torture in a good cause, then it may be that not all torture is necessarily 'bad' or, at least, wrong.[6]

One does not need to subscribe to this view in order to accept that the so-called 'torture debates' of the early to mid-2000s have had, and continue to have, a major impact upon the prohibition of torture.[7] At the time of 11 September, there was simply no real debate to be had. The closest that there had been to a debate concerned the 1987 Report of the Commission of Inquiry into the Methods of Investigation of the General Security Service Regarding Hostile Terrorist Activity

---

4　See also *Mutua and Others* v. *Foreign and Commonwealth Office* [2012] EWHC 2678.

5　*Ireland* v. *United Kingdom*, no. 5310/71 [1976]; *Ireland* v. *United Kingdom* [1978], ser. A, no. 25.

6　For wide-ranging discussions of the points raised, see Levinson 2004; Roth *et al.* 2005; and Greenberg 2006. For further contrasting views on the possibility of 'ethical' torture, see Ginbar 2008; Waldron 2010; and Greer 2011.

7　It is notable that the General Assembly's first annual Torture Resolution, in 2005, condemned 'any action or attempt by States or public officials to legalize, authorize or acquiesce' in torture or cruel, inhuman or degrading treatment or punishment (see UNGA Res 60/148 (2005): ¶ 3), a condemnation that has been repeated in all of the subsequent resolutions.

(Landau Report) in Israel, which had arisen out of concerns regarding the methods used by the Israeli General Security Service when interrogating Palestinian detainees. The Israeli Supreme Court, while not entirely unequivocal in its rejection of such forms of ill-treatment, did still condemn their use as a matter of official and approved practice, and the enduring statement of principle became Justice Aharon Barak's famous observation that '[a] democracy must sometimes fight with one hand tied behind its back. Even so, a democracy has the upper hand.'[8] Since 11 September, we have seen democracies attempting to loosen the knots that bind their hands when they consider that their most vital interests are at stake.[9] One might also ponder whether the 're-tightening of the restraints' in more recent years has had as much to do with the lessening of the risk or, perhaps, the emergence of alternatives than with the rekindling of conviction in the force of the absolute prohibition. It is the absolute prohibition that will now be considered.

The Absolute Prohibition

It is trite to say that the prohibition of torture is 'absolute'. Not only is it absolute in the sense of its not being subject to exception or restriction; it is also said to benefit from the higher normative status that flows from its being characterised as a *jus cogens* norm, a status that the General Assembly reflected for the first time in its 2008 Torture Resolution (see UNGA Res 63/166 (2008): pmbl.) and that the International Court of Justice confirmed in *Jurisdictional Immunities of the State*.[10] While it is equally trite to say that the prohibition of cruel, inhuman or degrading treatment or punishment is also 'absolute' as a matter of international human rights law, there is a sense in which it has always been the case that there has been a degree of relativity associated with the quality of absolutism attached to this. There is no need to dwell at length upon this: the origins of this perception are usually traced back to the consideration of article 3 of the European Convention on Human Rights in *Ireland*, in which, as already noted, the European Court of Human Rights considered interrogation practices that the European Commission on Human Rights had characterised as amounting to torture to amount 'only' to 'inhuman or degrading' treatment. As a result, although the 'threshold' at which forms of ill-treatment pass from 'only' being 'inhuman or degrading' to being acts of torture proper has come in for much comment and criticism, there is no gainsaying that there is a threshold here:

---

8   *Public Committee Against Torture* v. *State of Israel* [1999] HCJ 5100/94: ¶ 39.

9   One might pause at this point to recall the famous, or infamous, comment by the International Court of Justice in the 1996 *Legality of the Threat or Use of Nuclear Weapons* advisory opinion about the lengths to which a state might go in order to protect its vital interests.

10   *Jurisdictional Immunities of the State (Germany* v. *Italy: Greece Intervening)* [2012] ICJ: ¶ 99.

the question is more one of *when* and *how* it is crossed rather than *whether* it is crossed (see Evans 2002; Rodley 2009: 105–10).

At one extreme lie those who argue that it is the intensity of pain and suffering as experienced by the victim that causes ill-treatment to become a form of torture, whereas for others it is the purposive use of forms of ill-treatment by those exercising public authority that lies at the heart of the differentiation. The European Court of Human Rights has made it perfectly clear that, while both torture and inhuman or degrading treatment are prohibited in equal measure, a 'special stigma' attaches to those acts amounting to torture,[11] and for whatever reason this is, it is incontrovertibly true.

While this does not lessen the force of the absolute prohibition of torture or cruel, inhuman or degrading treatment or punishment as a matter of international human rights law, it does point to the reality that the consequences for perpetrators of having committed such acts are potentially very different. For example, the 1984 Convention Against Torture and Other Cruel, Inhuman or Degrading Treatment or Punishment (Convention Against Torture) clearly distinguishes between torture and cruel, inhuman or degrading treatment and permits the exercise of universal jurisdiction only in relation to the former. Similarly, there is a clear expectation that penalties for torture will be commensurate with the gravity of the offence, which means that they will, in principle, be more severe than the penalties for the 'other' absolutely prohibited forms of conduct. Indeed, the General Assembly's annual Torture Resolution, which, as has been said, provides an excellent barometer of political thinking on these issues, tends to drive a deeper cleavage: while emphasising that 'all acts of torture must be made offences under domestic criminal law', it merely 'encourages States to prohibit under domestic law acts constituting cruel, inhuman or degrading treatment or punishment' (UNGA Res 65/205 (2010): ¶ 2).[12]

There is nothing new here, but it is helpful to recall this when reflecting upon the debates concerning the 'definition' of torture, and so-called 'torture-lite'. For many, the most shocking element of the infamous 'Torture Memos' issued by the United States during the first years following 11 September was the claim that for an act to amount to torture it had to have the severity equivalent to the loss of a limb or organ failure. Later came the question of whether 'waterboarding', which, allegedly, 'simulates' drowning, was torturous in nature. While there can surely be little doubt that both claims, later recanted, did represent shameful attempts to permit the impermissible, the illegitimacy of such acts from a human rights perspective was never in doubt, and the focus on the question whether or not such practices did or did not amount to torture tended to obscure the more significant

---

11   See *Selmouni v. France*, no. 25803/94 [1999] ECHR: ¶ 96.

12   Even this, however, is a relatively recent development, first appearing in 2009, with previous resolutions referring only to the criminalisation of acts of torture.

question, which concerned the potential consequences of categorising an act as torture. This is an issue that remains as relevant today as it ever was.[13]

The legacy of the debate concerning the absolute prohibition of torture does not, then, lie in the effect that it has had upon the prohibition as such. Indeed, in many ways, the absolute nature of the prohibition has been strengthened by its being challenged, and by those challenges having been resisted. The real issues lie elsewhere. This finds reflection in the General Assembly's annual Torture Resolution in 2010, which, for the first time, added to its second preambular paragraph, which recalls the non-derogable and absolute nature of the prohibition, that 'legal and procedural safeguards against such acts must not be subject to measures that would circumvent this right' (UNGA Res 65/205 (2010)). So, what has been eroding the prohibition?

The Acquisition and Use of Information

The absolute nature of the prohibition means that it will always be a violation of international human rights law for one person to subject another person to torture, and any person doing so *should* find himself or herself subject to criminal liability. Few would now argue in favour of using forms of torture merely in order to acquire information needed to secure a conviction for the purposes of criminal prosecution. The arguments advanced in favour of torture tend to revolve around the need to acquire information in order to save the lives of others or to forestall some outrage or atrocity in one way or another, usually with reference to the so-called 'ticking bomb' scenario. While the absolute nature of the prohibition may require that the act of torture be criminalised, what of the information that might nevertheless be acquired as a result of such unlawful acts?

Article 15 of the Convention Against Torture provides that 'Each State Party shall ensure that any statement which is established to have been made as a result of torture shall not be invoked as evidence in any proceedings, except against a person accused of torture as evidence that the statement was made.'

This, it is argued, takes away the purpose of torture by rendering the information acquired through torture useless: if the product of torture cannot be used, then there is no point in torturing in the first place. This, of course, is quite untrue on various levels. First, from a textual perspective, article 15 refers to 'statements' and, in doing so, reflects the idea that people are 'tortured' in order to 'confess' to crimes, and that such confessions are inadmissible in judicial proceedings. It is interesting to note that the annual General Assembly Torture Resolutions continue to reflect the restrictive formula found in the text of the Convention Against Torture. The resolutions first addressed the subject in 2004, 'urging' that states

---

13   The 'Torture Memos' and the history surrounding them can be found in Danner 2004 and Greenberg and Datrel 2005. For an exploration of their background and practice related to them, see Sands 2008.

'ensure that any statement that is established to have been made as a result of torture shall not be invoked as evidence in any proceedings' (UNGA Res 59/182 (2004): ¶ 6). This remained unchanged until 2007, when the wording was changed in that it now 'strongly' urges states to do so (UNGA Res 62/148 (2007): ¶ 10), but the reference to 'statements' has remained unchanged throughout (see UNGA Res 66/150 (2011): ¶ 15).

It is generally accepted that the 'exclusionary rule' in article 15 relates not only to confessions but also to other forms of 'statements' that an accused might make that have probative value. There remains considerable uncertainty, however, over the extent to which evidence that was not itself acquired through torture but that was acquired as a result of information so acquired might be admissible in court proceedings, the so-called 'fruit of the poisoned tree' debate (see Pollard 2005).

Perhaps the most well-known case concerning the use of 'torture evidence' is *A and Others* v. *Secretary of State for the Home Department (No. 2)*,[14] in which the House of Lords determined, in 2005, that 'foreign torture evidence' was not admissible in proceedings before British courts. While this conclusion was warmly welcomed, the case also revealed some serious shortcomings in the judicial approach to the absolute prohibition. For example, the House of Lords made clear that the exclusionary rule only applied to evidence acquired as a result of torture, and also adopted a most onerous test in order to determine that it was indeed the product of torture.[15] The Convention Against Torture also distinguishes between statements acquired as a result of torture and information acquired as a result of inhuman or degrading treatment or punishment, with only the former being covered by the exclusionary rule in article 15. Similarly, the annual General

---

14   *A and Others* v. *Secretary of State for the Home Department (No. 2)* [2005] UKHL 71 (hereafter *A and Others (No. 2)*).

15   The majority of the House of Lords took the view that once the applicant had given plausible grounds for believing that evidence used against him or her had been the product of torture, it was for the Special Immigration Appeals Commission (SIAC) to make enquires, and if it was satisfied that, on the balance of probabilities, the evidence had indeed been the product of torture, then it should not be admissible. The minority would have excluded the evidence had it found there to be a 'real risk', this being a lower threshold, thus, in effect, rendering its exclusion more likely. In 2012, in *Othman (Abu Qatada)* v. *United Kingdom*, no. 8139/09 [2012], the European Court of Human Rights did not disapprove of the decision in *A and Others (No. 2)* as regards hearings before SIAC but took the view that while the burden of proof lay with the applicant in criminal cases that that burden would be met by showing there to be a 'real risk' (see ¶ 274). The enduring significance of this is perhaps best illustrated by the fact that it is now reflected in the guidance issued to Foreign Office officials for use when they have suspicions about the source of information received; this has been the subject of legal challenge by the Equality and Human Rights Commission. It might be noted that the United Nations Committee Against Torture appears to have used an even higher standard of proof, that 'in all probability' the statements were the product of torture (see *Sodupe* v. *Spain*, Communication No. 453/2011 (2012), UN Doc CAT/C/48/D/453/2011: ¶¶ 7.4–7.5).

Assembly Torture Resolutions only refer to the exclusion of statements established to have been made as a result of torture. This, perhaps unintentionally, was made very clear in 2009, when the General Assembly's annual Torture Resolution was amended to make the cautious suggestion that states might wish to 'consider extending that prohibition to statements made as a result of cruel, inhuman or degrading treatment or punishment' (UNGA Res 64/153 (2009): ¶ 13).

For others, however, the distinction is not so clear-cut, as was shown by the Grand Chamber of the European Court of Human Rights' 2010 decision in *Gäfgen* v. *Germany*.[16] In this case, the applicant challenged the fairness of his conviction, which he claimed had been based in part on evidence that had resulted from his having been threatened with ill-treatment. The Grand Chamber concluded that he had indeed been the victim of treatment that was 'inhuman or degrading' but that it did not amount to torture. The threats of ill-treatment had been motivated by the desire to discover the whereabouts of a young boy who had been kidnapped by the applicant but who, unbeknown to the police, had already been killed. Recalling the absolute nature of the prohibition of torture, inhuman or degrading treatment or punishment, the Court stressed that the motives of those responsible were completely immaterial, and there was no doubting that treatment in violation of article 3 had occurred. However, since the police officers who had been responsible for issuing the threats to the applicant had already been punished for having done so by the German courts, this was not at issue. The applicant was now claiming that his conviction had been the product of an unfair trial, thus in violation of article 6 of the European Convention on Human Rights, because evidence acquired as a result of ill-treatment had been admitted in court.

In *Gäfgen*, the European Court of Human Rights was clear that any confession or statement of guilt made as a result of treatment in violation of article 3 was inadmissible 'irrespective of the probative value of the statements and irrespective of whether their use was decisive in securing the defendant's conviction' (¶ 166). However, it noted that in previous cases it had left open the question of whether 'real evidence' that was the product of inhuman or degrading treatment also meant that a trial was necessarily unfair, noting that while the prohibition in article 3 was absolute, the right to a fair trial under article 6 was not (see ¶¶ 167, 178). The Court finally concluded that, although 'real evidence' that had been the product of impermissible treatment had indeed been admitted in evidence, this had not rendered the trial unfair since this evidence had not in the end proved critical to the outcome on the particular facts of the case. As such, the 'chain of causation' had been broken, and the trial was not unfair, even though evidence that had been presented during the proceedings was the product of ill-treatment. Irrespective of one's views about *Gäfgen*, the case does illustrate that the absolute nature of the prohibition of torture, inhuman or degrading treatment or punishment does not foreclose debate about whether, and under what circumstances, information derived from such forms of mistreatment

---

16   *Gäfgen* v. *Germany*, no. 22978/05 [2010].

might be used in judicial proceedings. It seems that the absolute prohibition does not make 'real evidence' absolutely inadmissible.

A substantially similar point can be made in the light of the 2012 judgement of the European Court of Human Rights in *Othman (Abu Qatada)* v. *United Kingdom*, in which, for the first time, it refused to permit the return of a suspect to a third state, Jordan, given that the result of any trial that he would face might amount to a 'flagrant denial of justice' because there were substantial grounds for believing there to be a real risk that evidence that had been the product of torture might be used against him. According to the European Court of Human Rights in *Othman*:

> the admission of torture evidence is manifestly contrary, not just to the provisions of Article 6, but to the most basic international standards of a fair trial. It would make the whole trial not only immoral and illegal, but also entirely unreliable in its outcome. It would, therefore, be a flagrant denial of justice if such evidence were admitted in a criminal trial. (¶ 267)[17]

However, the Court immediately went on to say that it 'does not exclude that similar considerations may apply in respect of evidence obtained by other forms of ill-treatment which fall short of torture. However, on the facts of the present case … it is not necessary to decide this question' (¶ 267). Thus, this leaves open the question whether a state might return a person to a third state when there is a real risk that evidence acquired as a result of inhuman or degrading treatment might be used against him or her during a subsequent trial, even if, following *Gäfgen*, that state might not itself be able to use such evidence before its own courts. Once again, the consequences of the absolute prohibition remain rather more opaque than might have been expected.

This all presupposes, of course, that the confession, statement, real evidence or information is being used in judicial proceedings. In *A and Others (No. 2)*, their Lordships made quite clear that while the exclusionary rule applied to 'torture evidence' presented in court, this did not prevent the executive branch of government from acting upon such information. In other words, while information acquired through torture might be inadmissible in court, it was not necessarily impermissible to use that information in other settings. This can be shortly stated, but its consequences are profound. As Lord Carswell said in *A and Others (No. 2)*, 'I should emphasise that my conclusion relates only to the process of proof before judicial tribunals … and is not intended to affect the very necessary ability of the Secretary of State to use a wide spectrum of material in order to take action to prevent danger to life and property' (¶ 149). Or, as Lord Brown put it, the 'functions and responsibilities of the executive and judiciary are entirely

---

17   In the subsequent case *El Haski* v. *Belgium*, no. 649/08 [2012], the European Court of Human Rights took the same approach as in *Othman*, ruling that Belgium had violated article 6 in that it had admitted evidence on the grounds that there was no 'concrete proof' that it had been the product of torture.

different', and in his view, article 15 of the Convention Against Torture 'creates no bar to the use of coerced statements as a basis for executive action' (¶ 162).

Removal from the Jurisdiction

Possibly the most 'visible' and often remarked upon issue in connection with the absolute prohibition of torture, and the issue that seems to have the most 'traction', concerns whether it is permissible to remove a person from the jurisdiction when that person is believed to pose a real risk to the security of the state. As is well-known, the European Court of Human Rights concluded in 1989 in *Soering* v. *United Kingdom*[18] that the absolute nature of the prohibition of torture, inhuman or degrading treatment or punishment meant that a state would be in breach of its obligation to return a person to a state if to do so would result in the person facing a real risk of such treatment. Then, in 1996, the Court confirmed in *Chahal* v. *United Kingdom*[19] that this was the case even if the presence of that person might pose a real risk to the security of the state itself. During the early years following 11 September, this became a source of considerable concern in policy circles, presumably because heightened surveillance of potential suspects resulted in heightened perceptions of potential threats. The United Kingdom, with others, sought to circumvent the effects of *Chahal* in a number of ways, most obviously by challenging the rule itself. In *Saadi* v. *Italy* (2008), however, the European Court of Human Rights declined to change its approach and upheld its previous jurisprudence on this point.[20] This continues to be its clear position.[21] Once again, the absolute nature of the prohibition seems to have been accorded priority.

Nevertheless, this is not the end of the matter, and other strategies have been employed to address the 'problem' posed by *non-refoulement* of terrorist suspects. One response, attempted but rejected by British courts, has been 'preventive detention', or detention without charge.[22] Falling short of this, there have been attempts to impose onerous and restrictive supervision regimes that, while not amounting to deprivation of liberty as such,[23] permit so close a control to be exercised that the person subject to them is barely able to exercise an autonomous existence. Such was the nature of the system of control orders provided for in the United Kingdom under the Prevention of Terrorism Act 2005. Control orders were replaced in 2011 by Terrorism Prevention and Investigation Measures (Tpims)

18　*Soering* v. *United Kingdom* [1989] ser. A, no. 161.

19　*Chahal* v. *United Kingdom* [1996] Reports of Judgments and Decisions V.

20　*Saadi* v. *Italy*, no. 37201/06 [2008] ECHR: ¶¶ 125, 138.

21　See *Othman*: ¶ 185; *Hirsi Jamaa and Others* v. *Italy*, no. 27765/09 [2012]: ¶ 122.

22　See *A and Others* v. *Secretary of State for the Home Department* [2004] UKHL 56; *A and Others* v. *United Kingdom*, no. 3455/05 [2009].

23　See *Austin and Others* v. *United Kingdom*, nos. 39692/09, 40713/09 and 41008/09 [2012].

as provided for by the Terrorism Prevention and Investigation Measures Act.[24] A Draft Enhanced Terrorism Prevention and Investigation Measures Bill has also been introduced, which would allow even greater restrictions to be imposed upon terrorist suspects in exceptional circumstances should this be thought necessary.[25]

Another approach is to 'recalibrate' the nature of the risks at stake. At the heart of the *Chahal* approach lies the belief that the risk posed by a foreign national cannot be balanced against the risk of torture or ill-treatment that the person will face upon his or her return. One potential 'solution' is to reduce the risk. Obviously, not returning the person at all is one way of reducing (or eliminating) the risk, but there are also others. One way is through the use of 'Deportations with Assurances', the idea that the risk can be reduced to an acceptable level by virtue of a combination of promises and guarantees offered by the state to which the person is to be deported. It is beyond the scope of this comment to explore this in depth, but two brief points can be made. First, the argument advanced by the then United Nations Special Rapporteur on Torture Manfred Nowak that such assurances can never reduce the risk to the point where a return would be acceptable has not found favour (see Nowak 2005a: 687; Nowak 2005b: ¶ 32; Nowak 2005c: ¶¶ 29–52). It is now generally accepted that such assurances can be effective when coupled with appropriate safeguards, in both principle and practice. This was reaffirmed by the European Court of Human Rights in *Othman*, in which it said:

> it [is] not for this Court to rule upon the propriety of seeking assurances, or to assess the long term consequences of doing so; its only task is to examine whether the assurances obtained in a particular case are sufficient to remove any real risk of ill-treatment ... assurances are not in themselves sufficient to ensure adequate protection against the risk of ill-treatment. There is an obligation to examine whether assurances provide, in their practical application, a sufficient guarantee that the applicant will be protected against the risk of ill-treatment. (¶¶ 186–7)

And, on the facts of the case, they were sufficient to reduce the risk to a sufficient degree (see *Othman*: ¶ 207).[26]

---

24 A total of fifty-two control orders were made during the life of the Prevention of Terrorism Act 2005, nine of which were still in force when it was repealed in December 2011, with those subject to them subsequently becoming subject to Tpims. For a summary of the experience of control orders and an overview of the system of Tpims, see Anderson 2012.

25 This was published in September 2011 and is due to be considered during the 2012–13 Parliamentary session.

26 For a list of the eleven factors that the European Court of Human Rights considered relevant to its assessment, see paragraph 189. For an examination of the factual situation in the light of them, see paragraphs 190–206.

Once again, it is also instructive to note how this has been reflected in the General Assembly's annual Torture Resolutions. Back in 2001, there was no mention of *non-refoulement* in the resolution. It was only in 2004 that the annual resolution first addressed this, '[r]ecall[ing]' that 'States shall not expel, return ("refouler") or extradite a person to another State where there are substantial grounds for believing that the person would be in danger of being subjected to torture' (UNGA Res 59/182 (2004): ¶ 8), following precisely the wording in article 3(1) of the Convention Against Torture. It was the very next year, however, in 2005, in which the General Assembly expanded the annual resolution by adding that it 'recognizes that diplomatic assurances, where used, do not release States from their obligations under international human rights, humanitarian and refugee law, in particular the principle of non-refoulement' (UNGA Res 60/148 (2005): ¶ 8). This wording has been repeated in all subsequent resolutions. Although in some sense a qualification or restraint upon diplomatic assurances, this is best seen as an endorsement of their use in the face of criticism being levelled against them at the time. It should also be noted that by following the wording of article 3 of the Convention Against Torture the resolutions only refer to *non-refoulement* as regards the risk of torture, rather than as regards the risk of cruel, inhuman or degrading treatment or punishment, a position that the United Nations Committee against Torture set out in its First General Comment in 1997 and to which it continues to adhere (see General Comment No. 1 (1997): ¶ 1). However, to the extent that the prohibition of cruel, inhuman or degrading treatment or punishment forms part of international human rights law more generally,[27] the change in wording in the 2005 resolution permits the conclusion that the General Assembly recognises the application of this principle to all such cases. This is certainly the view of the United Nations Human Rights Committee (cf. General Comment No. 20 (1992): ¶ 9) and the European Court of Human Rights.[28]

Complicity

One of the many worrying developments since 11 September has been not only the removal of persons to situations where they face a real risk of torture but so called 'extraordinary rendition', in which the very purpose of the movement is to facilitate the use of torture.[29] Although this is a topic of major concern, it can be dealt with quickly here as there is not the slightest possibility of such renditions

---

27 For a detailed consideration of this, see Rodley 2009: 45–81: 'International law prohibits every act of torture or other cruel, inhuman or degrading treatment or punishment' (81).

28 Beginning with *Soering*, the Court has never wavered in its view that the prohibition of *non-refoulement* applies to situations where the person being returned faces a real risk of inhuman or degrading treatment or punishment, not merely a real risk of torture.

29 That such renditions have occurred is clear (see Marty 2006, 2007; European Parliament 2007).

being anything other than in violation of international law, nor has it been claimed otherwise. To forcibly remove a person to another jurisdiction for the purposes of torture is to be complicit in the act of torture, engaging both state responsibility and individual criminal responsibility (see Convention Against Torture 1984: art. 4(1); Joint Committee on Human Rights 2009: ¶ 37). The challenge here is not so much to the absolute prohibition as such but, rather, raises the question of impunity. It is one thing to say that torture is absolutely prohibited, but it is quite another to ensure that those who are responsible for such acts are in fact held to account for what they have done.

A related question is, however, more difficult: to what extent can the participation in questioning or the receipt of information derived from such questioning constitute a form of 'acquiescence' so as to bring it within the scope of the prohibition set out in article 1 of the European Convention on Human Rights (see Joint Committee on Human Rights 2009: ¶¶ 38–43). This question lies at the heart of the Gibson Inquiry, which was established by Prime Minister David Cameron in July 2010 to look into allegations that British security and intelligence services had been complicit in the torture and ill-treatment of terror suspects in foreign custody in the wake of 11 September (see The Detainee Inquiry 2012).[30] Following the launch of police investigations into allegations of the rendition to Libya and the subsequent ill-treatment of two individuals, however, it was decided in January 2012 to cancel the Gibson Inquiry, the terms of reference of which had in any case been subject to intense criticism (see Amnesty International 2011). For current purposes, all that needs to be noted is that controversy surrounds the extent to which the security and intelligence services might be 'proximate' to torture. That there was such proximity is not itself in doubt. For current purposes, the mere fact that there is such a debate seems to suggest that there is a willingness to run the risk of collusion in the interests of national security and, in doing so, run the risk of breaching the absolute prohibition of torture.

The issue of complicity was also touched upon in *Equality and Human Rights Commission* v. *Prime Minister and Others*.[31] At its core, the debate in this 2011 case concerned whether the Consolidated Guidance to Intelligence Officers and Service Personnel on the Detention and Interviewing of Detainees Overseas, and on the

---

30   The Gibson Inquiry's Terms of Reference were, *inter alia*:
To examine whether, and if so to what extent, the UK Government and its security and intelligence agencies in the aftermath of 9/11:
 i) were involved in improper treatment, or rendition, of detainees held by other countries in counter terrorism operations overseas; and/or
 ii) were aware of improper treatment, or rendition, of detainees held by other countries in counter terrorism operations in which the UK was involved.
The primary focus of the Inquiry will be the cases involving the detention at Guantanamo Bay of UK nationals and former lawful UK residents.
31   *Equality and Human Rights Commission* v. *Prime Minister and Others* [2011] EWHC 2401 (Admin).

Passing and Receipt of Intelligence Relating to Detainees (2010; hereafter Official Guidance) referring to 'serious risk' should actually have referred to 'real risk', with the latter standard reflecting a lower threshold for engaging responsibility. The court concluded that there was no material difference between the two standards and that the Official Guidance made it clear that officers should not proceed unless there was no serious risk of torture or cruel, inhuman or degrading treatment or punishment occurring. What this judgment fails to dwell upon, for it was not the point before it, is that the Official Guidance implicitly permits ministers to authorise involvement in situations where there is a serious (or real) risk of torture provided that they have considered whether involvement by British agencies 'would increase or decrease the likelihood of torture or CIDT [i.e., cruel, inhuman or degrading treatment or punishment] occurring' (Official Guidance 2010: 6). Should British agencies be wrong in their assessment, then complicity would likely ensue. What needs to be stressed is just how fine a judgment call needs to be made under the Official Guidance. This illuminates just how narrow are the bands of the *cordon sanitaire* that is in place in respect of the acquisition of intelligence and, perhaps most critically, how close to the boundaries of the absolute prohibition authorities are prepared to navigate in order to acquire it.

Jurisdiction

Much attention has been given to the more general question of the extent to which human rights obligations, including the prohibition of torture, apply extraterritorially, particularly to armed forces serving overseas. It is fair to say that discovering that provisions of international human rights law apply to military forces acting overseas *in addition to* their obligations under international humanitarian law seems to have come as something of a surprise to many, and as Chapter 4 by Sandy Ghandhi shows, the United Nations human rights machinery has been particularly critical of states' failure to acknowledge this in practice since 11 September. Moving beyond this, another feature of the last ten years has been the extent to which the restraints upon the extraterritorial application of human rights commitments as regards the actions of a state's officers, organs or agencies overseas, which were ushered in by the 2001 decision of the European Court of Human Rights in *Banković and Others* v. *Belgium and 16 Other Contracting States*,[32] have been progressively eroded. This was made very clear by the European Court of Human Rights in 2011 in *Al-Skeini and Others* v. *United Kingdom*,[33] in which it was decided that the European Convention on Human Rights extended to situations in which state agents acting overseas exercised 'authority and control', a conclusion reaffirmed in 2012 in *Hirsi Jamaa*

---

32   *Banković and Others* v. *Belgium and 16 Other Contracting States*, no. 52207/99 [2001] ECHR XII.

33   *Al-Skeini and Others* v. *United Kingdom*, no. 55721/07 [2011] ECHR.

and Others v. *Italy*, which decided that irregular migrants at sea benefitted from European Convention on Human Rights protection when the naval forces of a State party attempted to prevent their entry into its territorial waters and return them to a risk of ill-treatment in Libya contrary to article 3. On such an approach, it is difficult to see how a state agent could ever not be subject to human rights commitments regarding the prohibition of torture, thus keeping open the possibility of state responsibility for any such acts. There would seem to be few, if any, jurisdictional vacuums as regards responsibility.

The problem, however, is less one of responsibility as of there being an appropriate mechanism for holding those responsible to account. Clearly, one of the major advances in recent years has been the growth of international criminal law, and to the extent that torture forms an element of an international crime, this offers a very real means of holding those responsible to account. However, torture is not in and of itself an international crime within the jurisdiction of the International Criminal Court, and this raises the problem of where, when and how it is possible to hold individuals to account.

This takes us to the question of the reach of domestic jurisdiction, a subject that has attracted much attention over the last ten years. The applicability of universal jurisdiction over the offence of torture under the Convention Against Torture is well understood and was recently affirmed by the International Court of Justice in a landmark 2012 case concerning the failure of Senegal to initiate domestic proceedings against Hissène Habré, the former President of Chad who had been resident in Senegal since 1991. In *Questions Relating to the Obligation to Prosecute or Extradite*,[34] which Belgium brought against Senegal, it was held that Senegal was in violation of its obligations under the Convention Against Torture for failing to submit the case to its prosecuting authorities.

Equally, if not more significantly, the International Court of Justice in *Belgium* stressed that the obligation to do so was owed *erga omnes*, meaning that any State party to the Convention Against Torture has standing to bring an international claim against any other State party that fails to initiate proceedings against someone suspected of being responsible for torture and who is within its jurisdiction (see ¶ 103). Whether this will lead to a spate of claims against States parties that harbour those responsible for torture remains to be seen, but it certainly suggests that states ought to be more assiduous in ensuring that such cases are promptly submitted to their prosecuting authorities if they are to avoid international liability. This might go some way towards addressing the general reluctance of states to resort to universal jurisdiction.

If, to date, relatively little use has been made of the extraterritorial criminal jurisdiction available to states with regard to individuals suspected of torture, there has been significantly greater interest in pursuing those responsible for human rights violations in civil proceedings. As with the assertion of extraterritorial

---

34 *Questions Relating to the Obligation to Prosecute or Extradite (Belgium* v. *Senegal)* [2012] ICJ (hereafter *Belgium*).

criminal jurisdiction, however, the ambitious arguments made in favour of extending extraterritorial civil liability have, so far, largely come to nothing. The model upon which such arguments have been built has been the application of the United States Alien Tort Claims Act of 1796 in the 1980 case *Filártiga* v. *Peña-Irala*.[35] While the actual decision in this case has never been called into question in subsequent decisions, attempts to expand the scope of this jurisdiction in the United States have been largely unsuccessful in recent times.[36] Nor has this model been adopted elsewhere. In the United Kingdom, for example, a Torture (Damages) Bill that would have lifted immunity in respect of proceedings against both states and individuals was given a first reading in the House of Lords in 2010 but has not progressed any further.[37] At one level, then, there are some signs of a more robust approach being taken to the assertion of criminal jurisdiction by states over those suspected of torture, though the direction of travel as regards the assertion of civil jurisdiction is rather less clear. As will be seen, however, whatever advances might have been made as regards the scope of jurisdictional competence have been more than negated by trends concerning the assertion of immunity from the jurisdiction of domestic courts.

Immunity

Perhaps the first area in which there appeared to be a weakening of the drive against torture concerned questions of immunity. It is one of the most well-established principles of international law that states enjoy immunity from process before the domestic courts of other states unless there is an express provision to the contrary. Thus, for example, under section 5(2) of the United Kingdom State Immunity Act, proceedings cannot be brought against another state in respect of an act of torture unless it has been committed within the jurisdiction of the United Kingdom. This position was challenged in 2001 before the European Court of Human Rights in *Al-Adsani* v. *United Kingdom*,[38] in which it was claimed that this was incompatible with the right to have access to a remedy and that as the prohibition of torture was a norm of *jus cogens*, the right to access a court in the context of proceedings related to torture took priority. The Court, by a majority of 8 to 7, rejected this argument, taking the view that principles of state immunity were of foundational

---

35   *Filártiga* v. *Peña-Irala* [1980] 630 F. 2d 876 (2d Cir.). In this landmark case, a Paraguayan defendant was successfully sued by a Paraguayan plaintiff in the United States federal court under the Alien Tort Claims Act in respect of the detention, torture and death of the applicant's brother in Paraguay. Both Paraguayans were present in the United States at the time of the suit.

36   See *Sosa* v. *Alvarez-Machain* [2004] 542 US 692; *Kiobel* v. *Royal Dutch Petroleum* [2010] 621 F. 3d 111.

37   For the text, background and details, see REDRESS.

38   *Al-Adsani* v. *United Kingdom*, no. 35763/97 [2001] ECHR XI.

importance to the international community. The International Court of Justice took a similar approach in its 2002 judgment in *Arrest Warrant of 11 April 2000*[39] and not only confirmed that the state itself was entitled to immunity before foreign courts in respect of alleged violations of crimes against humanity, and, *a fortiori*, acts of torture, but so also were serving 'high officials' of states.[40] In the United Kingdom, the House of Lords subsequently affirmed this approach in 2006 in *Jones* v. *Ministry of Interior Al-Mamlaka Al-Arabiya AS Saudiya (Saudi Arabia)*,[41] and the International Court of Justice has again reiterated its approach in terms which do not seem to admit of any uncertainty. In *Jurisdictional Immunities*, it said that, 'under customary international law as it presently stands, a State is not deprived of immunity by reason of the fact that it is accused of serious violations of international human rights law or the international law of armed conflict' (¶ 91). Lest there be any doubt, the International Court of Justice also made it known that, 'even on the assumption that the proceedings in the Italian courts involved violations of *jus cogens* rules, the applicability of the customary international law on State immunity was not affected' (¶ 97).

But what of the individual? In *R* v. *Bow Street Metropolitan Stipendiary Magistrate Ex parte Pinochet Ugarte (No. 3)* (hereafter *Pinochet (No 3)*), the House of Lords concluded that a former head of state did not enjoy immunity in respect of extradition to face criminal proceedings in respect of torture. The reasoning underpinning this outcome has eluded consensus ever since, and there is little to be gained by parsing the various judgments in a vain attempt to find what is not to be found. Nevertheless, the general gist seems to lie in the direction of equating the position of a former head of state with that of a serving diplomat, meaning that on the expiry of office personal immunities are lifted and there is no remaining immunity in respect of private, as opposed to official, acts. The nub of the issue, on this approach, is whether torture is to be seen as an official, even if illegal, act.

It is not necessary to resolve this question in order to contrast this approach with the approach that the House of Lords took in *Jones*, in which, in addition to a claim against the state itself, the applicants brought civil claims against a number of individual defendants who were not entitled to personal immunities on the basis of their status. They were 'just' employees of the state who were doing their jobs, albeit that from the perspective of international law theirs were wrongful jobs, or jobs done wrongfully. As there was no question of personal immunity, the House of Lords approached the issue from the perspective of state immunity and decided that individual functionaries of the state were entitled to benefit from the

---

39   *Arrest Warrant of 11 April 2000 (Democratic Republic of the Congo* v. *Belgium)* [2002] ICJ Rep 3.

40   The so-called 'big three', these being heads of state, heads of government and foreign ministers.

41   *Jones* v. *Ministry of Interior Al-Mamlaka Al-Arabiya AS Saudiya (Saudi Arabia)* [2006] UKHL 26.

same immunities as the state itself, meaning that if the state could not be sued for torture, then neither could its agents, provided only that the state chose to assert its immunity on their behalf. Doing otherwise, their Lordships thought, would have the practical effect of undermining state immunity since if the acts of individuals were attributable to, or were taken as being, the acts of the state itself, then a finding against an agent of the state would effectively amount to a finding against the state, the very thing that immunity from process is meant to prevent.

In the *Jurisdictional Immunities* case, the International Court of Justice seems to have endorsed this approach in relation to civil claims. It should be noted, however, that it has kept open the possibility that state functionaries who are not entitled to, or are no longer entitled to, personal immunity might be susceptible to the criminal jurisdiction of third states, stressing that it was 'addressing only the immunity of the State itself from the jurisdiction of other States; the question of whether, and if so to what extent, immunity might apply in criminal proceedings against an official of the State is not in issue in the present case' (¶ 91). This is something of a development from *Arrest Warrant*, in which the Court said that 'immunity' was not 'impunity' and pointed to a range of other procedural possibilities that did not include criminal prosecution before domestic courts of individuals suspected of torture.

All of this shows that while there have doubtless been numerous advances, the easy assumptions concerning the inevitable extension of liability and accountability before domestic courts held by many in the wake of *Pinochet (No. 3)* have been seriously retarded by the judicial restraints regarding immunities in the years that followed. Once again, none of this casts any doubt on the absolute nature of the prohibition of torture, which is more firmly entrenched now than ever before, but it does reflect the reality that the consequences of that prohibition have proven to be far less robust and effective than might have been expected a decade ago.

Conclusions

The overall picture is, then, mixed. After years of hesitancy, the International Court of Justice has finally broken its silence on the concept of *jus cogens* and has recognised the prohibition of torture as being of this nature. In determining that the obligation to criminalise and submit cases to prosecuting authorities under the Convention Against Torture is of an *erga omnes* nature, it has also recognised the community interest in the prohibition. On the other hand, it has refused to accept that states might be arraigned for torture before the courts of other states, has upheld the personal immunities of high officials and has suggested that more lowly state officers might be able to profit from assertions of state immunity. This would seem to point to a situation in which the preferred forum in which to pursue both individuals and states for violations of the prohibition of torture would be the forum of the international community itself. Little ink needs to be spilt in order to demonstrate the shortcomings of such an approach, but this does need to be placed in a somewhat broader context.

Although the International Court of Justice's credentials as a 'human rights court' appeared to have been dented by its refusal to accept jurisdiction in 2011 in *Case Concerning Application of the International Convention on the Elimination of All Forms of Racial Discrimination (Georgia* v. *Russia),*[42] that was hardly a typical 'human rights' case, and the attempt to frame it as such bore the hallmarks of a disingenuous attempt to find a semi-plausible basis upon which the court might exercise jurisdiction. What this did do, however, was shed light on the fact, surprisingly enough often overlooked, that many of the principle United Nations human rights treaties do have compromissory clauses that can be effective in providing the International Court of Justice with jurisdiction in exactly the type of 'inter-state cases' that are simply not brought before the specialist treaty bodies. Following *Belgium*, this is now very visible indeed. Moreover, and possibly in reaction to the negative signals given off in *Georgia*, the International Court of Justice chose to strike a rather unexpectedly ambitious note about its willingness to find violations of international human rights standards in its 2010 judgment in *Ahmadou Sadio Diallo.*[43] This appeared to be a quintessential case concerning diplomatic protection, yet the Court unexpectedly chose to characterise it as a case primarily concerning human rights and, arguably, went beyond existing understandings of the procedural obligations of states in relation to arbitrary detention.

Putting all these pieces of the jigsaw together, it might just be that the question of determining responsibility for violations of international standards concerning torture may yet take hold at the international level, and in truth, this may be a more amenable forum through which to project a robust assertion of the prohibition of torture and its practical consequences. This certainly seems to be the experience of the European Court of Human Rights, the approach of which stands in marked contrast to the patchwork of contradictions that has emerged from domestic jurisdictions. Of course, there is a reason for this. Domestic jurisdictions sit somewhat closer to the executive and the day-to-day pressures upon it. This is why international bodies must continue to take a strong and principled stance against torture and ill-treatment given that it is at the domestic level that the pressure to yield to the exigencies of the moment will be greatest. The practical outworking of the prohibition of torture after 11 September may remain precarious in practice, but there is some comfort to be drawn from the increasingly robust manner in which the prohibition is articulated and promulgated as a matter of international legal obligation on the international plane. At the same time, it is only by working

---

42   *Case Concerning Application of the International Convention on the Elimination of All Forms of Racial Discrimination (Georgia* v. *Russia)* (Preliminary Objections) [2011] ICJ (hereafter *Georgia*).

43   *Ahmadou Sadio Diallo (Republic of Guinea* v. *Democratic Republic of the Congo)* [2010] ICJ Rep 639.

in partnership with those exercising influence and authority at the domestic level that real change will come.

References

Alleg, H. 2006. *The Question*. Lincoln: University of Nebraska Press.

Amnesty International 2011. Public Statement, 4 August. AI Index: EUR 45/011/2011.

Anderson, D. 2005. *Histories of the Hanged: Britain's Dirty War in Kenya and the End of Empire*. Oxford: Oxford University Press.

Anderson, D. 2012. Control Orders in 2011: Final Report of the Independent Reviewer on the Prevention of Terrorism Act 2005.

Bingham, T. 2010. *The Rule of Law*. London: Penguin.

Cassese, A. 1995. *Inhuman States*. Cambridge: Polity Press.

Cobain, I. 2012. *Cruel Britannia: A Secret History of Torture*. London: Portobello Books.

Consolidated Guidance to Intelligence Officers and Service Personnel on the Detention and Interviewing of Detainees Overseas, and on the Passing and Receipt of Intelligence Relating to Detainees (July 2010). Available at: http://www.parliament.uk/deposits/depositedpapers/2011/DEP2011-1796.pdf [accessed: 6 November 2012].

Danner, M. 2004. *Torture and Truth: America, Abu Ghraib and the War on Terror*. London: Granta Books.

The Detainee Inquiry 2012. Available at: http://www.detaineeinquiry.org.uk/ [accessed: 22 October 2012] (Gibson Inquiry).

European Commission of Human Rights 1972. *The Greek Case, 1969*, Yearbook of the European Convention on Human Rights 12. The Hague: Martinus Nijhoff.

European Parliament Resolution on the Alleged Use of European Countries by the CIA for the Transportation and Illegal Detention of Prisoners (2007), Doc P6_TA(2007)0032.

Evans, M. 2002. Getting to Grips with Torture. *International and Comparative Law Quarterly*, 51(2), 365–83.

Evans, M. and Morgan, R. 1997. *Preventing Torture*. Oxford: Oxford University Press.

General Comment No. 1: Refoulement and Communications (Implementation of Article 3 in the Context of Article 22) (1997) (1998), UN Doc A/53/44, 52-53.

General Comment No. 20: Concerning Prohibition of Torture and Cruel Treatment or Punishment (Article 7) (1992), UN Doc HRI/GEN/1, 29-32.

Ginbar, Y. 2008. *Why Not Torture Terrorists? Moral, Practical and Legal Aspects of the 'Ticking Bomb' Justification for Torture*. Oxford: Oxford University Press.

Greenberg, K. 2006. *The Torture Debate in America*. New York: Cambridge University Press.

Greenberg, K. and Datrel, J. 2005. *The Torture Papers: The Road to Abu Ghraib*. New York: Cambridge University Press.

Greer, S. 2011. Should Police Threats to Torture Suspects Always be Severely Punished? Reflections on the *Gäfgen* Case. *Human Rights Law Review*, 11(1), 67–89.

Joint Committee on Human Rights 2009. Allegations of UK Complicity in Torture. HL Paper 152, HC 230.

Levinson, S. 2004. *Torture: A Collection*. New York: Oxford University Press.

Marty, D. 2006. Alleged Secret Detentions in Council of Europe Member States, Doc AS/Jur (2006) 03 rev.

Marty, D. 2007. Secret Detentions and Illegal Transfers of Detainees Involving Council of Europe Member States: Second Report, Doc. 11302 rev.

Murray, R., Steinerte, E, Evans, M. and Hallo de Wolf, A. 2011. *The Optional Protocol to the UN Convention Against Torture*. Oxford: Oxford University Press.

Nowak, M. 2005a. Challenges to the Absolute Nature of the Prohibition of Torture and Ill-Treatment. *Netherlands Quarterly of Human Rights*, 23(4), 674–88.

Nowak, M. 2005b. Torture and Other Cruel, Inhuman or Degrading Treatment, UN Doc E/CN.4/2006/6.

Nowak, M. 2005c. Torture and Other Cruel, Inhuman or Degrading Treatment or Punishment, UN Doc A/60/316.

Pollard, M. 2005. Rotten Fruit: State Solicitation, Acceptance, and the Use of Information Obtained Through Torture by Another State. *Netherlands Quarterly of Human Rights*, 23(3), 349–78.

REDRESS. The Torture (Damages) Bill in Parliament. Available at: http://www.redress.org/the-torture-bill/the-torture-bill-in-parliament [accessed: 22 October 2012].

Rejali, D. 2009. *Torture and Democracy*. Princeton: Princeton University Press. Report of the Commission of Inquiry into the Methods of Investigation of the General Security Service Regarding Hostile Terrorist Activity 1987. Available at: http://www.hamoked.org/files/2012/115020_eng.pdf [accessed: 6 November 2012] (Landau Report).

Rodley, N. 2009. *The Treatment of Prisoners under International Law*. 3rd edn. Oxford: Oxford University Press.

Roth, K. *et al.* 2005. *Torture: Does It Make Us Safer? Is it Ever OK? A Human Rights Perspective*. New York: Human Rights Watch.

Sands, P. 2008. *Torture Team: Deception, Cruelty and the Compromise of Law*. London: Allen Lane.

UNGA Res 59/182 (2004), UN Doc A/RES/59/182.

UNGA Res 60/148 (2005), UN Doc A/RES/60/148.

UNGA Res 62/148 (2007), UN Doc A/RES/62/148.

UNGA Res 63/166 (2008), UN Doc A/RES/63/166.

UNGA Res 64/153 (2009), UN Doc A/RES/64/153.

UNGA Res 65/205 (2010), UN Doc A/RES/65/205.
UNGA Res 66/150 (2011), UN Doc A/RES/66/150.
Waldron, J. 2010. *Torture, Terror and Trade-Offs*. Oxford: Oxford University Press.

Chapter 2

The 'Global Dance' of Humanity and Legality: Terror, Migration and Human Rights

Colin Harvey

The 'liberal way of war', as with any mode of conflict, will result in human displacement. War causes flight and produces refugee flows. Modern forms of terrorism are increasingly transnational, and state responses map the trend, whether defined as 'war' or not. Thus, the approach to migration offers one useful 'way in' to grasping the liberal approach.

Free movement is enjoyed by many persons, and the world can be a remarkably welcoming and open place. Developments in transport and technology impact upon our conceptions of time and space. The movement of particular individuals and particular communities, however, is often perceived as a risk to global, regional and national security. The cosmopolitan and borderless world order imagined in more elaborate accounts of the present era meets the harsh reality of intensified and innovative global regimes of regulation and control. This is not to discount or underplay the fact that credible threats do exist, or to underestimate the scale of violent conflict around the world, but it is to underline that the enjoyment of free movement rights will often depend upon who one is, where one is from and where one wants to go. A universal aspiration of humanitarianism, human rights and human dignity thus confronts grounded, situated and contextual realities.

The general trend of enhanced 'migration management' accelerated after 11 September 2001, but the patterns were there long before. The securitisation of migration is a common theme in practice, and in debates on, for example, European Union law and policy (see Brouwer 2003). The purpose of this chapter is to think about how a legal order that embraces the concept of humanity responds to the challenges posed as a result of heightened transnational security concerns. Law and policy have been shaped to draw migration firmly into global counter-terrorism practice, with an overriding ambition to ensure that there are no 'safe havens for terrorists' anywhere in the world. As one possible mechanism for movement, the institution of asylum thus becomes meshed with the desire to confront impunity, criminality and terrorism. This chapter focuses on the tensions between a law of humanity, human rights broadly understood and the pragmatics of a globalised practice of counter-terrorism. It uses selected aspects of refugee and asylum policy to explore what the interactions tell us about human rights and the ways that individuals and groups are constructed within, and mobilise around, law. The purpose is to understand how notions of humanity have become embedded within conceptions of legality, and to indicate what this might mean.

Human rights law, and human rights talk generally, are now centre stage in an internationalised network of individuals and groups seeking to confront abusive outcomes from the present regulatory regimes. This chapter, therefore, examines how human rights discourse is deployed, on the premise that the interpretative battles fought out across the world have genuine practical impacts in terms of justification, explanation, accountability and challenge. The engagements are transnational in scope, internationalised in their use of law and policy, and global in geographical reach.

Questions addressed in this chapter include: What does it mean to talk about humanity in 'rule of law'-style conversations? How does a globalised practice of counter-terrorism impact upon the rights of refugees and asylum seekers? How is human rights discourse used by participants in these global and local debates? What does the response of the 'human rights movement' and human rights law tell us? Is there an emerging global public sphere that is equipped to effectively respond to these questions, and what does this tell us about forms of 'liberal legalism' and political mobilisation around law? Is this a conversation without end? Will the tensions always be present? We first consider the relationship between humanity and legality and then proceed to reflect upon the interactions between counter-terrorism, rights and migration.

Humanity and Legality

There is now an international practice of rights that is securely nested within law and policy around the world. It is to be found at the national, regional and international levels. There are human rights standards reflected within normative orders to such an extent that it often stands as a defining ideology of our age. The story of the emergence of this 'international revolution' is well-known even if historical analysis is now casting doubt upon some of the more enthusiastic claims made about it (see Moyn 2010).

From the Universal Declaration on Human Rights in 1948 onwards, we have witnessed a proliferation of standard-setting, covering a vast range of subjects. Emerging in an expressly post-conflict context, this body of law created by states spoke to a new global order *beyond the state*. The focus was on the *human person* as the defining basis for entitlement, personhood as the way of thinking about rights. This emergent new law of humanity encountered a profound problem however, that has its roots in an old dilemma. While each person may well be 'born equal in dignity and rights', the reality is often more complicated and profoundly context-dependent. For one thing, securing the sort of life envisaged by human rights seems to involve an element of communal belonging, membership and practical organisation.

Hannah Arendt (1973) famously saw this early on in the development of the new world of human rights. She came to see the plight of refugees as symbolic of the age. All the talk about human rights could not disguise the fact that those who had to rely upon this status alone were most at risk. The human being stripped of statehood and the formal protections of belonging seemed lost. 'The very phrase "human rights" became for all concerned – victims, perpetrators, and onlookers alike – the evidence of hopeless idealism or fumbling feeble-minded hypocrisy' (Arendt 1973: 269). Arendt learned from experience just how hollow 'humanity' could sound. She experienced 'statelessness' and witnessed the consequences everywhere in her world, just as she knew how cruel and merciless organised political communities could become. When reliance rested upon the very thing that was said to be foundational, people always seemed most vulnerable. She was persuaded that:

> human dignity needs a new guarantee which can be found only in a new political principle, in a new law on earth, whose validity this time must comprehend the whole of humanity while its power must remain strictly limited, rooted in and controlled by newly defined territorial entities. (Arendt 1973: ix)[1]

For Arendt, and many of those within the republican tradition, the 'new guarantee' required anchorage in membership and belonging attached to organised communities committed to making a reality of principles. Nationality and citizenship, in their substantive senses (the 'right to have rights'), thus assumed fundamental significance as a way of embracing humanity properly.

The 'right to have rights' has subsequently attracted much attention (see Bhabha 2009; Kesby 2012). The jarring nature of the phrase still stands: people think that they have them 'as of right'. Arendt concluded that what really mattered was grounded political community for the purpose of rendering 'rights' meaningful, in the general project of building better and secure lives. Wherever she looked, 'humanity' ended up as a flimsy and inadequate basis for ensuring guarantees and protection.

Those compelled to fall back upon their 'humanity' still feel the divide between the sugary language (of which there is much) and the hardened realism of regulated and oppressive global and local spaces. Refugees, asylum seekers and displaced persons in general are particularly alive to the dilemma. When this is conflated with a globalised culture of suspicion and disbelief, attached to particularised communities of belonging, this becomes even more problematic. What mattered to Arendt (and remains pressing for those attracted to her thought) was having a safe 'place in the world'. The cosmopolitan new global order of freedom, based upon the universal international legal recognition of all human persons and their inherent human dignity, still exists with, and faces, an intensity

---

1 In this preface to the first edition, written in the summer of 1950, Arendt had in mind anti-Semitism, imperialism and totalitarianism (all broadly defined).

of focus on our situated nature (who we are, where we come from, where we belong, our status). The continuing collective march over all public and private space both makes freedom possible and reduces our world to a suffocating and tightly regulated sphere for many. However hopeless bureaucracies often are in realising the grand regulatory dreams (states can be *both* fierce and incompetent in the administration of migration and in tackling terrorism), the scale of the ambition is not in doubt. The cry of a common humanity can be mobilised, but it is often met with politico-legal systems within which membership, belonging, status and statehood determine outcomes. Carl Schmitt, for example, famously cast suspicion over its international deployment, seeing its tactical use everywhere as one way 'a particular state seeks to usurp a universal concept against its military opponent' (2007: 54).[2] For Schmitt, as for many agonistic thinkers, the use of humanity is part of an enduring liberal attempt to negate politics, undermine states and thus promote 'the utopian idea of total depoliticalization' (2007: 55). In this agonistic mode of thought, the liberal way is to drain the life from politics or pretend that conflict has been erased and overtaken by universalist categories and mindsets.

Human persons are thus 'thrown into' the world and depend upon others and social and human relations for basic survival. Proceeding to live a life of human dignity, then, requires structure and organisation, the mobilisation of a societal context. The human person will have an impressive range of characteristics, opinions and desires that will evolve in a relational way in interaction with others. The point is that the bland and blank canvas approach, which sometimes carried along with it the narrative of human rights, may not take us very far in thinking about securing practical protections. While this can be viewed as fatal, it is one reason why human rights is so successful as a 'universalist discourse': its malleable, flexible and contested nature contains enough ambiguity to keep productive tensions alive. It is why it retains its force and value for those individuals and groups that are rendered 'other' by dominant discourses in society. Its power, as a discourse for practical mobilisation in law and politics, will persist precisely because of its open texture.

This leads to further thought on mobilisation around human rights precisely because this approach will tend to focus upon how rights are used in context. Rights appear to retain strength as tools in counter-hegemonic struggles, and faith in their utility and potential has not been abandoned by those thinking critically about legality (see Hunt 1993; Williams 1993; Santos 2002: 280–83). In challenges to some of the most coercive dimensions of counter-terrorism policy, rights have been remarkably resilient in assisting the confrontation with state law, policy and practice. The 'global dance' of counter-terrorism strategy is followed by, and scrutinised through, a global rights regime that does not share the resources of many state actors but that can press hard for transparency and insist upon justification. Attempts by states to secure 'norm-free zones' and construct imaginative new normative categories can often be traced as one response to the

---

2   Schmitt also indicates that 'whoever invokes humanity wants to cheat' (2007: 54).

existence of this new law of humanity. There is an awareness 'in the world' of the normative and practical power of this mobilised community of human rights.

The starting point for this analysis is that the idea of rights that belong to persons, by that very fact alone, has become part of what it means to talk about the rule of law or humanity today. Through practical mobilisation, and the development of an international human rights movement, it has forced its way onto the agenda.

Legality as an ideal takes many forms. It is, however, difficult to conceive of the concept without acknowledging the notions of humanity, human dignity and human rights that are increasingly featuring within today's normative orders.[3] While it may appear easy to dismiss the ideal that underpins this as one based on a naive view of political, legal and societal contexts, there is no escape from the framing narrative that this implies: that whoever one is, however one behaves, one possesses certain rights and entitlements that derive from one's status as a human person alone. Perhaps even more significantly is the way that 'humanity' finds a basis within legality and also stands in persistent challenge to all forms of closure.[4] How this plays out in practice in the complex interactions between counter-terrorism, refugee, asylum and migration policies remains a source of contestation and debate.

Counter-Terrorism, Rights and Migration

States are concerned to protect their borders, and immigration law is an attempt to mark out territory by creating a system that defines who can enter, remain and be removed.[5] It is widely recognised in legal orders that states enjoy the collective right of regulation, within the constraints of legality.[6] In practice, this means that states exercise control within the limits of voluntarily assumed obligations that arise from membership and participation in the international community. It is in the interpretation of these obligations, and their practical use, that the tensions unfold: utterly norm-free zones are increasingly rare.

The ever-present risk in migration management, however, is the governmental temptation to nurture insecurity by constructing 'others' as a threat (see Huysmans

---

3　Human dignity, in particular, has enjoyed a resurgence as the underpinning rationale for the emergence of the new world order of international human rights (see Feldman 1999; McCrudden 2008).

4　According to Bosniak, 'the idea of personhood also contains the normative and rhetorical resources to challenge every context in which it is situated – including the national constitutional context itself' (2010: 29).

5　Dauvergne, for example, argues that '[m]igration law is constitutive of liberal states' (2007: 540). For a philosophical defence of the significance of membership, see Walzer 1983.

6　'[T]he State has the right to control the entry of non-nationals into its territory. This is hornbook law and requires no elaboration' (*R (Naik)* v. *Secretary of State for the Home Department* [2011] EWCA Civ 1546: 84 (LJ Gross)).

2006: 47). Internal cohesion is sought through the establishment of clear and precise external threats. Migration brings with it many benefits, but from the governmental perspective, it also carries potential risks. Immigration law has historically been used to limit these risks at the entry stage (often widely defined), and the state's enforcement and related national provisions are also applied against those considered a danger to public order or national security, which has included, for example, internment during times of war (see Cole 2003) and mass and individualised deportations;[7] those who had simply outstayed the terms of original entry also came under scrutiny.[8] It is a well-established area of legal regulation that vests formidable powers with the executive, and has done so for some time and in many states. Courts are often left to patrol the boundaries of this regulatory regime in instances in which adjudication is possible or even permissible. States may opt to adopt generous policies, and may enter regional or other agreements that permit free movement, but given that they generally view migration management as so fundamental to what it means to be a 'state', it is unlikely to wither away.

Refugees and asylum seekers generally require an effective form of international protection, as they are fleeing human rights abuses in their state of origin, where national protection has failed. They may even be escaping conflicts that they themselves were participants in, or became the targets of because of their beliefs or identity.[9] Refugees can thus be fleeing persecution as a result of seeking to exercise, in domestic contexts, internationally recognised human rights.[10] Refugee law provides an internationalised status that grants official recognition to a practical reality. If refugees and asylum seekers do secure a form of international protection, they may become politically active (perhaps renewing earlier commitments) or develop support for political movements overseas. Although they may be victims and survivors of conflict, this does not render refugees and asylum seekers empty of all the complex political and social human associations, allegiances and commitments to which everyone is party. Those seeking refuge may be both victims and perpetrators. It is when this activity begins to slide into the counter-terrorism frame, or the person concerned is simply a member of a 'suspect community' (see Hillyard 1993) as a result of the state that he or she

---

7   For an historical example on the deportation of Iraqis and Palestinians following the outbreak of the Gulf War in 1991, see *R* v. *Secretary of State for the Home Department, ex parte Cheblak* [1991] 2 All ER 319.

8   Nationality law can also be used, for example, in naturalisation proceedings. In *Secretary of State for the Home Department* v. *SK (Sri Lanka)* [2012] EWCA Civ 16, a failure to disclose membership of the Liberation Tigers of Tamil Eelam (LTTE) on an application form for naturalisation resulted in exclusion on grounds of 'good character'.

9   The 'terrorising violence' that they face can come from a state. Stafford Smith (2012) quite deliberately uses the terminology of terrorism to describe the use of drone warfare in Pakistan.

10   See *HJ (Iran)* v. *Secretary of State for the Home Department* [2011] 1 AC 596; *RT (Zimbabwe) and Others* v. *Secretary of State for the Home Department* [2012] UKSC 38.

is fleeing from, that problems can arise (in the sense that the person then gets entangled in the web of anti-terrorism measures).

In three broad areas of refugee law, the impact of the global anti-terrorism drive can become marked: first, in the determined attempts to exclude terrorists from refugee status and thus deny 'safe haven'; second, in the deployment by states of repressive internal measures to deal with established and emerging 'suspect communities' (which may include international protection seekers); and third, in attempts (ever more elaborate) to secure the removal of asylum seekers who pose a threat to national security (see Ramraj 2012). States such as the United Kingdom are increasingly uneasy about the risks that they face from transnational terrorist networks, and the scale and extent of the proactive and preventative responses demonstrate this clearly.

The events of 11 September (in the United States), 11 March 2004 (in Spain) and 7 July 2005 (in the United Kingdom) prompted a determined focus on the effectiveness of counter-terrorism policy, and the rapid international promotion of new and more proactive approaches. Expressing concern about the impact of such policies upon refugees, Martin and Martin note that '[t]he dilemma is that many of those seeking refugee status come from the countries that are defined as terrorist producing or harbouring' (2004: 343). As part of the general strategy, asylum, immigration and nationality law continue to be used in the 'global war against terror' (see Adelman 2002; Martin 2002; Gilbert 2003; Türks 2003; Federal Administrative Court 2009; Kidane 2010). The ease with which this body of law is deployed, as well as amended and enhanced, highlights the flexibility already embedded within this system of control. Immigration and asylum law appeared to allow states to achieve counter-terrorist aims but also contained enough constraints to generate significant and vocal governmental frustration. Legality, in its essentially dual nature, continued to both enable and limit the protection of rights.

One reason is that a connection between the national security obligations of states and their migration laws and policies is already present (see Moeckli 2010). Aspects of immigration and asylum law at the national level were put in place precisely because of security fears resulting from migration flows. To those engaged with immigration and asylum law, the new discourse of radical departures seemed misplaced. States had been thinking proactively and preventatively in a migration context for some time.

Refugee and asylum law was designed for the 'exceptional situation' of forced migration, where instability and insecurity are at the core of the human dilemma.[11] The law emerged in the aftermath of massive global conflict when war crimes, crimes against humanity and serious criminality were in the mind of the international community. The law is reflective of a world in which conflict and complexity are ever present. It is a regime that recognises that people may be

---

11   As Adelman notes, 'there is virtually no evidence linking *global* terrorism with refugees' (2002: 11).

involved in legitimate political struggle in their own societies and acknowledges that this might be the reason why they are seeking asylum elsewhere.[12] The dilemma arises when this activity takes a form that falls under an increasingly all-embracing counter-terrorism framework. If 'terrorism' is broadly defined, and the exclusion clauses are rendered a tool of counter-terrorism policy, then the real risk is of overly inclusive domestic standards that erode the protection of international obligations.

As noted, the 'security discourse' was evident well before 11 September, and this is now a familiar theme in the migration literature (see Huysmans 2006). The construction of the institution of asylum as a potential security threat has a history, with the last decade witnessing a further escalation. This is not to deny that potential security threats posed by global migration are credible: terrorists also make use of our interdependent world. Rather, it is to suggest that the new responses can be viewed as part of a pattern and to admit that there is a measure of continuity (see Shah 1999). Arguably, the pressures exerted in the national security context are more intense versions of the strain that the overall protection system is under, as it seeks to survive in the instrumentalised world of migration management (see Whitaker 2002). Refugee law is, however, not silent. The 1951 Convention Relating to the Status of Refugees (hereafter Refugee Convention) contains such express recognition of the concerns of states that at times it appears to privilege these over protection. One rights-based critique of refugee law is precisely that it lends excessive weight to the anxieties of states: it is to be recalled here that the Refugee Convention, in article 33, includes the now odd-sounding notion of permissible *refoulement*.

Legal provision in the United Kingdom for immigration and asylum law is extensive. An expansive statutory framework is in place.[13] Counter-terrorism legislation impacts nationals and non-nationals, though the adverse effects upon particular minority ethnic communities, refugees, asylum seekers and migrants remains marked.[14] The restrictive legal developments progressed alongside moves to further embed a culture of human rights – initiated by the Labour government from 1997 onwards. The Human Rights Act 1998 changed the human rights context by permitting localised access to rights guaranteed by the European Convention

---

12   In fact, individuals may be claiming to flee terrorism (see *R (Akram)* v. *Secretary of State for the Home Department* [2010] EWHC 3437 (Admin)).

13   The Immigration Act 1971 remains the governing legislation for entry and removal generally and sets the overall legal framework. In section 2A, the Home Secretary has the power to deprive a person of the right of abode in the United Kingdom if he or she thinks that it would be conducive to the public good for the person to be excluded or removed (a power subject to human rights and refugee convention obligations). The British Nationality Act 1981 is the principal legislation dealing with nationality and includes, in section 40, a power to deprive a person of British citizenship if the Home Secretary thinks that this would be conducive to the public good.

14   For example, see the Counter-Terrorism Act 2008, the Terrorism Act 2006, the Terrorism (Northern Ireland) Act 2006 and the Prevention of Terrorism Act 2005.

on Human Rights. The creation of human rights commissions (the Northern Ireland Human Rights Commission, the Scottish Human Rights Commission and the Equality and Human Rights Commission in particular), the establishment of a Joint Parliamentary Committee on Human Rights and the creation of a new United Kingdom Supreme Court are all notable trends in a steady constitutional transition. In the United Kingdom, the government opted to weave migration policy into a citizenship story that embraced the narrative of generalised security for all citizens, a trend also evident internationally in the actions of other states.

Concern about asylum, and the implications for counter-terrorism policy, reached the highest political levels and extended beyond national contexts. The United Nations Security Council, for example, stressed after 11 September that there should be no safe havens for terrorists and that refugee status should not be 'abused' by 'perpetrators, organizers or facilitators of terrorist acts' (UNSC Res 1373 (2001): 3(g); see also UNSC Res 1377 (2001)). This position was underlined further after 7 July, when the then British Prime Minister Tony Blair noted that the 'rules of the game are changing' (Blair 2005; see also UNSC Res 1624 (2005)). This international discourse continues and is still often closely aligned with an expressed commitment to enduring respect for international law, including human rights and refugee law. In other words, the result today is not the rhetorical abandonment of rights; in fact something of a resurgence took place as governments sought to justify their actions in precisely these terms. The contested nature of human rights was fought out within the dynamics of counter-terrorism strategy, with many states arguing, for example, that what they were doing was in defence of rights.

This pattern tends to confirm that the principle of legality continues to matter to states, and the practical impact of counter-terrorism policy upon the treatment of refugees and asylum seekers is evidence that constant vigilance is required. This prompts the suggestion that the values that give life to the principle need not be tied to any one institutional context and must become embedded within the wider (globalised) public sphere if the abuse of human rights is to be effectively confronted. There are few more challenging contexts than the collision of counter-terrorism, globalised conflict and migration, but there is evidence of a transnational public sphere rising to meet it.

The policy premise in the United Kingdom often reflects an embedded official view that the current system is being widely abused by those who are not in genuine need of international protection. This has also become the official grand narrative of Western democracies, who regard the humanitarian institution of asylum as a pathway into their states for those who they might generally rather exclude; these states can often have quite generous entry rules for selected and 'desirable migrants'. A 'culture of suspicion' remains evident, and the events of 11 September and 7 July, and what has followed, simply intensified an existing process of national deterrence and restriction. An overriding focus on the reduction in the number of applicants in general remains, combined with the persistent criminalisation, and securitisation, of the entire migration debate (see Huysmans

2006). Nevertheless, it is worth observing that the British government did not repeal its human rights and refugee law commitments, despite moments of evident irritation and frustration with particular judicial outcomes; this trend is once again evident beyond the United Kingdom. The arguments are intense, and remain so, but are largely conducted within the terms of human rights and refugee law: calls to repeal the Human Rights Act 1998 in the United Kingdom are couched in the language of human rights and civil liberties, and disagreements with Strasbourg tend to be interpretative in nature, on the meaning that the European Court of Human Rights places upon particular rights.

The refugee regime should primarily be concerned with the provision of protection to asylum seekers from return to another state where there is a real risk of sufficiently serious human rights abuse. Asylum is a humanitarian institution designed to offer surrogate protection to those in genuine need of it; a terrorist facing lawful and legitimate prosecution is, therefore, not someone who necessarily has a well-founded fear of being persecuted. Even that seemingly simple statement is, however, problematic. A terrorist may well have faced torture or other forms of mistreatment as part of the prosecution process in another state. Evidence obtained by the use of torture may have been used at his or her trial. A terrorist may have a well-founded expectation of similar treatment if returned; he or she may even be facing a trial at which evidence obtained by torture will be used against him or her. Malcolm D. Evans explores these and other issues related to the prohibition of torture in Chapter 1.

Permanent settlement may be the result of a grant of refugee status; however, the principal official purpose of the legal regime is to offer international protection as long as it is needed. Decision-making in asylum cases is particularly challenging because it involves judgments about future risk based upon the individual's testimony and available objective evidence about the applicant's state of origin; the outcome can have serious implications for each individual. The risks involved in getting this future-oriented assessment wrong are substantial, as are the challenges involved in getting it right.

The Boundaries of Exclusion

Refugee and asylum law provide for the exclusion of certain persons from protection, though they do not directly refer to terrorism (see Saul 2004; Universal Declaration of Human Rights 1948: art. 14(2); Refugee Convention 1951: arts. 1F, 32–3; Immigration Act 1971: sec. 3(5) and relevant Immigration Rules made under sec. 3(2); Asylum and Immigration Appeals Act 1993: secs. 1–2; Nationality, Immigration and Asylum Act 2002; Immigration, Asylum and Nationality Act 2006).[15] The exclusion clauses are part of international refugee

---

15   In the United Kingdom in particular, see United Kingdom Border Agency Asylum Policy Instructions 'Humanitarian Protection' and 'Discretionary Leave'; Immigration and Nationality Directorate Asylum Policy Unit Notice 1/2003 'Humanitarian Protection and Discretionary Leave'; and United Kingdom Border Agency Asylum Policy Unit Notice

law and in addition to being underlined internationally, they also now find a home within the European Union system.[16] The notion of exclusion from international protection for defined reasons is now embedded within a broader agenda that seeks to challenge criminality internationally. The clauses should be viewed within the context of counter-terrorism policy and attempts internationally to challenge impunity, particularly as this relates to those responsible for war crimes and crimes against humanity[17] but also within the context of globalised counter-terrorism policies. As noted, there is a determined global effort to ensure there are no safe havens for terrorists and as a direct result of this, the exclusion clauses risk being brought within the generalised counter-terrorism strategies of states, without adequate reference to this human rights-based framing narrative and practice.

The Office of the United Nations High Commissioner for Refugees (UNHCR) provides guidance on the Refugee Convention's interpretation and application (see UNHCR 2003). It suggests that the primary purpose of these clauses 'is to deprive those guilty of heinous acts, and serious common crimes, of international refugee protection and to ensure that such persons do not abuse the institution of asylum to avoid being held legally accountable for their acts' (UNHCR 2003: 2). The guidelines also address terrorism:

> Despite the lack of an ... agreed definition of **terrorism**, acts commonly considered to be terrorist in nature are likely to fall within the exclusion clauses even though Art. 1F is not to be equated with a simple anti-terrorism provision. Consideration of the exclusion clauses is, however, often unnecessary as suspected terrorists may not be eligible for refugee status in the first place, their fear being of legitimate prosecution as opposed to persecution for Convention reasons. (UNHCR 2003: 25)

The view is that each case requires individual consideration, and the fact that someone may be on a list of terrorist suspects might trigger assessment under the exclusion clauses but should not in and of itself justify exclusion (see UNHCR 2003: 26). In addition, the Office of the United Nations High Commissioner for Refugees suggests that the exclusion decision should, in principle, be addressed within the regular status determination process (see UNHCR 2003: 31).

'Exceptional Leave to Remain: Suspected War Criminals and Perpetrators of Crimes Against Humanity and Genocide'.

16   In the European Union, the exclusion clauses are now subject to a supranational forum of interpretation. See Council Directive 2004/83/EC: art. 12; *Germany* v. *B and D* (Joined Cases C-57/09 and C-101/09) [2011] Imm AR 190; *Abdulla and Others* v. *Germany* (Joined Cases C-175/08, C-176/08, C-178/08, C-179/08) [2010] CJEU; and *Germany* v. *Y and Z* (Joined Cases C-71/11, C-99/11) [2012] CJEU.

17   For a comparative analysis of relevant law in Australia, Canada, New Zealand, the United Kingdom and the United States, see Rikhof 2009.

In 1996, the Law Lords addressed the question of exclusion in *T* v. *Secretary of State for the Home Department*.[18] The appellant, an Algerian citizen whose claim for asylum was rejected, was involved in a bomb attack on Algiers airport, in which ten people were killed, and a raid on an army barracks, which resulted in another person being killed. The special adjudicator concluded that this brought him within the exclusion clause contained in article 1F(b) of the Refugee Convention[19] because, as provided in that provision, 'there were serious reasons for considering' that he had committed serious non-political crimes. The House of Lords dismissed the appeal. The ruling considers the meaning of 'serious non-political crime' within the context of refugee law, and provides a test to define a 'political crime' that has two conditions:

1. it is committed for a political purpose, i.e. with the object of overthrowing or subverting or changing the government of a state or inducing it to change its policy; and
2. there is a sufficiently close and direct link between the crime and the alleged political purpose (786–7).

In determining point 2., the majority stated that the means used should be examined, as well as the nature of the targets involved (governmental or civilian), and whether indiscriminate killing of members of the public was involved. It was held that point 2. had not been satisfied on the particular facts of the case, and the decision to exclude the applicant was upheld.

The position in the United Kingdom on the exclusion clauses has been further clarified (and expanded upon in the counter-terrorism context), with provision being made for a new immigration status in domestic law. The new legislation followed the events of 7 July in London and the then Prime Minister's twelve-point plan for tackling terrorism (see Blair 2005).[20] A plan was devised that heavily focused on foreign nationals even though, as Clive Walker (2007: 428) has emphasised, the bombings were carried out by British citizens. Section 54 of the Immigration, Asylum and Nationality Act 2006 specifically provides for an interpretation of article 1F(c) of the Refugee Convention that links the assessment of whether something is 'contrary to the purposes and principles of the United Nations' to acts of committing, preparing or instigating terrorism and acts of encouraging or inducing others to commit, prepare or instigate terrorism (see also Terrorism

---

18   *T* v. *Secretary of State for the Home Department* [1996] AC 742.

19   Article 1F provides: 'The provisions of this Convention shall not apply to a person with respect to whom there are serious reasons for considering that: ... (b.) he has committed a serious non-political crime outside the country of refuge prior to his admission to that country as a refugee.'

20   This plan included a commitment to automatically refuse asylum to anyone who had participated in terrorism.

Act 2000: sec. 1).[21] Following the European Union level approach, the domestic statutory provision, therefore, connects the exclusion clause directly to terrorism and is now widely drawn. This statutory theme is mapped onto the appeal process through a system of certification according to which the Asylum and Immigration Tribunal, or Special Immigration Appeals Commission, must begin substantive consideration of the appeal on the basis of the Secretary of State's certification that the individual is not entitled to article 33(1) protection because articles 1F or 33(2) apply. In other words, exclusion is to be considered as a preliminary issue, meaning that application of the clause arguably widens.

Other matters addressed in the Immigration, Asylum and Nationality Act 2006 include, for example, the removal of British citizenship if this would be 'conducive to the public good', and again, this has been meshed with the general national security context (secs. 56–57).[22] At European Union level, article 12 of the Council Directive 2011/95/EU on Standards for the Qualification of Third-Country Nationals or Stateless Persons as Beneficiaries of International Protection, for a Uniform Status for Refugees or for Persons Eligible for Subsidiary Protection, and for the Content of the Protection Granted (Council Directive 2011/95/EU (hereafter Qualification Directive (recast)); see also Council Directive 2004/83/EC (hereafter Qualification Directive)) addresses exclusion (see Gilbert 2004; Storey 2008). It follows the language of the 1951 Convention with some notable additions. For example, particularly cruel actions, even if committed with an alleged political objective, may be classed as 'non-political'. The Qualification Directive (recast) also makes clear that the exclusion clauses apply to those who instigate or otherwise participate in the commission of crimes or other relevant acts, and trends in the United Kingdom are now intertwined with European Union level advances.

The British case *R (JS (Sri Lanka))* v. *Secretary of State for the Home Department*[23] is instructive, and involved the question of the correct interpretation of article 1F(a) of the Refugee Convention.[24] This 2010 case hinged upon membership of an organisation that had been involved in war crimes and precisely what more than simple membership was required to determine personal responsibility and exclude a person from refugee status. The respondent in the case was a Tamil and member of the Liberation Tigers of Tamil Eelam, an organisation

---

21   For a domestic application of article 1F(c), see *SS (Libya)* v. *Secretary of State for the Home Department* [2011] EWCA 1547 and now *Al-Sirri* v. *Secretary of State for the Home Department; DD (Afghanistan)* v. *Secretary of State for the Home Department* [2012] UKSC 54.

22   The twelve-point plan also included a commitment to stripping citizens of citizenship (see *Secretary of State for the Home Department* v. *Hicks* [2006] EWCA Civ 400; *R (GI)* v. *Secretary of State for the Home Department* [2011] EWHC 1875 (Admin)).

23   *R (JS (Sri Lanka))* v. *Secretary of State for the Home Department* [2010] UKSC 15.

24   For Canadian practice, see Simeon 2009 (concluding that post-11 September fears about enhanced use of the exclusion clauses has not come to pass in Canada).

that the court acknowledged was not exclusively terrorist in nature, and held a variety of positions. His application for asylum and humanitarian protection was refused by the Home Secretary on article 1F(a) grounds.[25]

In the Supreme Court, Lord Brown stated:

> Put simply, I would hold an accused disqualified under article 1F if there are serious reasons for considering him voluntarily to have contributed in a significant way to the organisation's ability to pursue its purpose of committing war crimes, aware that his assistance will in fact further that purpose. (*R (JS (Sri Lanka))*: 38)[26]

The judgment attempts to shift the exclusive focus away from the nature of the organisation[27] to carve out subcategories among organisations engaged in terrorism[28]– in this, Lord Brown was critical of the Immigration Appeal Tribunal's decision in *Gurung* v. *Secretary of State for the Home Department*[29]– and presumptions of individual liability to an assessment of the war crimes and crimes against humanity alleged to have been committed. It also reflects a concern not to narrow notions of responsibility in an excessively restrictive way. In its approach, the Supreme Court drew heavily upon the 1998 Rome Statute of the International Criminal Court, as well as guidance from the Office of the United Nations High Commissioner for Refugees (see UNHCR 2001) and the Qualification Directive.

This reliance on UNHCR guidance was further evident in the 2012 judgment of the Supreme Court in *Al-Sirri* v. *Secretary of State for the Home Department; DD (Afghanistan)* v. *Secretary of State for the Home Department*. Here, the Court had an opportunity to clarify the approach to article 1F(c) in particular, but also to the standard of proof generally in exclusion cases. The conclusions underline the significance of the requirement of an international character/dimension, express

---

25   Following the Court of Appeal judgment in *KJ (Sri Lanka)* v. *Secretary of State for the Home Department* [2009] EWCA Civ 292, the application of article 1F(c) to cases from Sri Lanka involving the Liberation Tigers of Tamil Eelam had become less straightforward.

26   Lord Hope stated: 'Lord Brown puts the test for complicity very simply at the end of para 38 of his judgment. I would respectfully endorse that approach. The words "serious reasons for considering" are, of course, taken from article 1F itself. The words "in a significant way" and "will in fact further that purpose" provide the key to the exercise. Those are the essential elements that must be satisfied to fix the applicant with personal responsibility. The words "made a substantial contribution" were used by the German Administrative Court, and they are to the same effect. The focus is on the facts of each case and not on any presumption that may be invited by mere membership' (49).

27   'War crimes are war crimes however benevolent and estimable may be the long-term aims of those concerned. And actions which would not otherwise constitute war crimes do not become so merely because they are taken pursuant to policies abhorrent to western liberal democracies' (*R (JS (Sri Lanka))*: 32).

28   Lord Brown did, however, provide a seven-point guide to assessing complicity with reference to membership (see 30).

29   *Gurung* v. *Secretary of State for the Home Department* [2012] EWCA Civ 62.

caution about any automatic or blanket approach to 1F(c), but strongly suggest that it is likely, given the 'essence of terrorism', that there will be international repercussions (that is, 'terrorism' appropriately understood is likely to come within 1F(c)). The strong preference is for detailed assessment of the facts of particular cases, and on the standard of proof ('serious reasons for considering'), the Supreme Court supported interpretation of the words on their own terms, rather than the simple adoption of the domestic criminal or civil standard.

The British approach is part of a general international trend of drawing attention to actions engaged in individually and corporately, as a way of avoiding the definitional complexity often encountered in attempts to capture 'terrorism' as a conceptual category in blanket terms. It confirms the 'case by case view' that these clauses should be interpreted narrowly and restrictively and applied with caution. Exclusion will thus involve detailed and individualised assessment of personal circumstances, past actions and the wider objective context. Such an approach should erode inappropriate and abusive uses of these provisions of refugee law, and the real risk that an overly inclusive understanding of 'terrorism' will underline protection principles.

In contexts in which, for example, the European Convention on Human Rights applies, exclusion from refugee status may not mean return. To the evident irritation of successive British governments, deportation may not be permitted for human rights reasons. Of course, this is hardly ideal for the individual concerned either, who may then continue to exist in a form of legal limbo.

The International 'Dance of Legality': Deportation, Assurances and Human Rights

The transnational interaction between rights, counter-terrorism strategies, states and non-governmental actors often resembles an 'international dance of legality' in which mobilisation across borders, which increasingly avails of new technology, maps normative standards onto all spaces and zones. The practical implications of these debates, and the precise interactions between humanity and legality, are played out in cases such as *A and Others* v. *Secretary of State for the Home Department* (2002 and 2004).[30] Here, the dilemma surrounds individuals who must not be deported for 'human rights' reasons but who are designated as suspected terrorists. British legislation introduced after the terrorist attacks of 11 September empowered the Home Secretary to issue a certificate if he reasonably believed that an individual's continuing presence in the United Kingdom was a risk to national security and suspected that the person was a terrorist. Suspected international terrorists could, therefore, effectively be detained indefinitely. There was a right of appeal to the Special Immigration Appeals Commission (see Barder 2004;

---

30   *A and Others* v. *Secretary of State for the Home Department* [2002] EWCA Civ 1502; *A and Others* v. *Secretary of State for the Home Department* [2004] UKHL 56.

Tomkins 2010).[31] A challenge was brought against the provisions. The Special Immigration Appeals Commission held that the measures were discriminatory and contrary to articles 5 and 14 of the European Convention on Human Rights, as they did not apply equally to British nationals.

On appeal against the Special Immigration Appeals Commission decision, the Court of Appeal reached a different conclusion. Following an approach with echoes of *Secretary of State for the Home Department* v. *Rehman*,[32] Lord Woolf stated:

> Decisions as to what is required in the interest of national security are self-evidently within the category of decisions in relation to which the court is required to show considerable deference to the Secretary of State because he is better qualified to make an assessment as to what action is called for. (*A and Others* 2002: 40).

British nationals were not in the same position as foreign nationals in this context. According to Lord Woolf, the non-nationals involved in this case no longer had a right to remain, only a right not to be removed (see *A and Others* 2002: 47). This distinguished their plight from that of nationals. He also relied upon a distinction in international law between the treatment of nationals and the treatment of non-nationals. Parliament was entitled to limit application to foreign nationals on the basis that article 15 of the European Convention on Human Rights permitted measures that derogate only 'to the extent strictly required by the exigencies of the situation'. The tension between articles 14 and 15 had, Lord Woolf argued, an important impact. The Secretary of State was obliged to derogate only to the extent necessary, and widening the powers of indefinite detention would conflict with this objective.

The case subsequently progressed to the House of Lords (*A and Others* 2004; see Feldman 2005; Campbell 2009; cf. Finnis 2007), and the issues were also tested eventually before the Grand Chamber of the European Court of Human Rights (*A and Others* v. *United Kingdom* 2009).[33] In one of the leading judgments under the Human Rights Act 1998, the majority of the Law Lords concluded that there was a public emergency threatening the life of the nation (article 15(1)) but, unlike the Court of Appeal, were willing to quash the derogation order and declare section 23 of the Anti-Terrorism, Crime and Security Act 2001 incompatible with the European Convention on Human Rights on the basis of the (dis)proportionate nature of discriminatory detention of suspected international terrorists who were non-nationals. The judgments question and probe the notion of executive detention, with Lord Hoffmann being particularly scathing in his comments about the Anti-Terrorism, Crime and Security Act 2001, Lord Nicholls expressing his

---

31   See also *W and Others (Algeria)* v. *Secretary of State for the Home Department* [2012] UKSC 8.

32   *Secretary of State for the Home Department* v. *Rehman* [2001] UKHL 47.

33   *A and Others* v. *United Kingdom*, no. 3455/05 [2009]. See also *Charkaoui* v. *Canada* [2007] SCC 9.

concern about the idea of indefinite detention and Lord Bingham making pointed comments about the nature and significance of judicial decision-making in these cases. In foregrounding constitutional principle in the face of executive detention, the case did not herald the end of deference. As is clear in the judgment of Lord Bingham, it underlines notions of 'degrees of deference' and, in confirming the role of the Home Secretary in determining when there is a public emergency, endorsed the concept of variable institutional competencies.

Strasbourg's judgment largely followed the conclusions reached by the House of Lords (an example of 'judicial dialogue'); however, in the operation of the Special Immigration Appeals Commission process (on the issue of reliance on closed material and the lack of disclosure of sufficient information), the European Court of Human Rights found a violation of article 5(4).

While the significance of such individual cases should never be exaggerated, what remains relevant for the purpose of this chapter is just how problematic the distinction drawn between nationals and non-nationals was found to be for these purposes. All human persons, nationals or non-nationals, have the capacity to fall under the category 'suspected terrorist'. For these purposes, the complexity of humanity takes on an added dimension since the court recognises that terrorism is something that can be practised by citizens and non-citizens alike.

The procedures used by the Special Immigration Appeals Commission were also questioned in the other *A and Others* case to reach the House of Lords (*A and Others (No. 2)* 2005).[34] *A and Others* v. *Secretary of State for the Home Department (No. 2)* addressed the admissibility of evidence by the Special Immigration Appeals Commission that may have been procured by torture inflicted by officials of other states without the complicity of British authorities. The value and importance of the rule of law was once again underlined, here with Lord Bingham stressing the constitutional principles at stake, and the House of Lords concluded that evidence obtained in this way should not be admissible, though the majority disagreed with Lord Bingham on the burden of proof. The two *A and Others* cases demonstrate the role that courts might have in setting out a view of what the rule of law is, even when national security is raised and indicating that the *humanity* in rights-based legality can have genuine and substantial meaning (in all its senses) in domestic contexts.

But in the determined response adopted by the United Kingdom do we not see the institutional 'dance' in operation once again? Following the first *A and Others* judgment, new measures were enacted under the Prevention of Terrorism Act 2005,[35] providing for the much criticised 'control orders' abolished as a result of a Review conducted in 2011 (see Review of Counter-Terrorism and Security

---

34 *A and Others* v. *Secretary of State for the Home Department (No. 2)* [2005] UKHL 71.

35 The long title states: 'to provide for the making against individuals involved in terrorism-related activity of orders imposing obligations on them for purposes connected with preventing or restricting their further involvement in such activity'. See Counter-Terrorism Act 2008; Crime and Security Act 2010.

Powers 2011), which then led to the enactment of the Terrorism Prevention and Investigation Measures Act 2011, a new regime that was operationalised in January 2012. One version of executive detention was, therefore, replaced by a more carefully engineered form of control and restraint ('control orders'), which was then also overtaken by an even more intricate mechanism in 2012.

The Prevention of Terrorism Act 2005, it will be recalled, established an elaborate form of individualised monitoring and explicitly applied to both British nationals and non-nationals alike. The system again attracted considerable judicial scrutiny, where the terms of particular control orders were assessed with reference to obligations under the European Convention on Human Rights,[36] as was the procedure for making and challenging them.[37] In these cases, the Law Lords, and the Supreme Court, gave careful, close and anxious scrutiny to their use, with human rights concerns noted (taking into account developments in the Strasbourg jurisprudence) on the nature of the repressive restrictions imposed (holding that they have in specific contexts amounted to a deprivation of liberty) and on aspects of the procedure (the disclosure of information, the use of special advocates and the need, stressed by the Grand Chamber of the European Court of Human Rights, for the provision of sufficient information to a 'controllee' to permit effective instruction to his or her special advocate). The case law that has emerged suggests a determined executive placing ever more 'sophisticated', complex and oppressive processes in place, with judges attempting to ensure that the correct level of scrutiny and careful assessment is applied and, ultimately, challenging their severity through the use of human rights standards. The replacement of 'control orders' in 2012 indicates that the 'dance' continues, the regulatory regimes of counter-terrorism strategy evolve further and the 'dialogue' between branches of government continues.

Despite the best efforts of the British government, the Grand Chamber of the European Court of Human Rights, in *Saadi* v. *Italy*,[38] confirmed the absolute nature of the prohibition against return in article 3. The British government continues to argue internationally that there should be a balancing element injected into article 3 assessments, namely the risk of return balanced against the national security threat, a test similar to the approach adopted by the Canadian Supreme Court in 2002 in *Suresh* v. *Canada*.[39] The European Court of Human Rights has consistently held to its established jurisprudence, much to the vocal and evident frustration of

---

36   See *Secretary of State for the Home Department* v. *E* [2007] UKHL 47; *Secretary of State for the Home Department* v. *JJ* [2007] UKHL 45; and *Secretary of State for the Home Department* v. *AP* [2010] UKSC 24.

37   Cf. *Secretary of State for the Home Department* v. *MB* [2007] UKHL 46 and *Secretary of State for the Home Department* v. *AF* [2009] UKHL 28.

38   *Saadi* v. *Italy*, no. 37201/06 [2008] ECHR.

39   *Suresh* v. *Canada* [2002] 1 SCR 3.

the British government.[40] In effect, this means that no balancing is involved or permitted (*Saadi* v. *Italy* 2008; see Bruin and Wouters 2003) and that the 'conduct of the person concerned, however undesirable or dangerous, cannot be taken into account' (*Saadi* v. *Italy* 2008: 138).

The government did not, however, avoid tackling related concerns and seeking parliamentary approval for its approach. For example, and following the Court of Appeal's judgment in *S and Others* v. *Secretary of State for the Home Department*, it decided in the Criminal Justice and Immigration Act 2008, in part 10, to provide for a special immigration status to attach to 'foreign criminals' who have committed terrorist or other serious criminal offences but who cannot be removed for Human Rights Act 1998 reasons. The impact is that a person so designated does not have leave to enter or remain in the United Kingdom (under section 132), and a range of conditions may be imposed upon residence, employment, reporting and monitoring (in relation to the police, the Secretary of State or an immigration officer) (under section 133), and particular arrangements have been put in place to limit existing support (under section 134). While these provisions can be read as a particularised governmental response to a particular judicial outcome, they are also illustrative of a mindset and a pervasive approach. Once again, they demonstrate the 'dance of legality and humanity', of response and reaction, and how executives, parliaments and courts interact in seeking to achieve policy objectives while showing respect for the culture of human rights that has emerged (see Rawlings 2005).

In addition to further promoting a targeted internal regime through legislative and other mechanisms, the British government has also worked hard to secure assurances from other states to facilitate the process of removal.[41] This is additional evidence of a government seeking to achieve its counter-terrorism objectives, and doing so, again, through legal argumentation and often in human rights terms. The normative and practical hold of an argument from humanity does seem to be in play here, as governments seek to achieve objectives within the interpretative field of human rights.

The British government has had more success in agreeing diplomatic assurances than it has in persuading the European Court of Human Rights to abandon its

---

40   See also the government's response to the Afghan hijackers' case, *S and Others* v. *Secretary of State for the Home Department* [2006] EWCA Civ 1157. 'We commend the judge for an impeccable judgment … Judges and adjudicators have to apply the law as they find it, and not as they wish it to be' (*S and Others* 2006: 50). Then Prime Minister Blair had described the first instance judgment of Mr Justice Sullivan as 'an abuse of common sense' (BBC News 2006).

41   For concerns about their use, see Human Rights Watch 2004; Human Rights Watch 2005; and UNHCR 2006. For instances in which rights violations occurred despite assurances from Egypt, see *Agizav v. Sweden*, Communication No. 233/2003 [2005], UN Doc. CAT/C/34/D/233/2003 and *Alzery v. Sweden*, Communication No. 1416/2005 [2006], UN Doc. CCPR/C/88/D/1416/2005.

decision in *Chahal* v. *United Kingdom*.[42] Diplomatic assurances have been secured with a number of North African and Middle Eastern States.

What, then, has been the response when the counter-terrorism measure adopted is deportation to a state from which assurances have been received? The protection of refugee law can indeed be limited, as the Refugee Convention provides for the concept of permissible return and the distinct and separate question of exclusion from status. The European Convention on Human Rights, however, contains a strong prohibition on return, a position that Strasbourg has consistently confirmed and upheld.[43] The European Court of Human Rights does not rule out the notion of an effective assurance, but the conditions have been clearly described. The hard questions here will, therefore, often arise around how effective these assurances are in practice. Will they prove robust enough to permit human rights-compliant deportation? Seeking them in the first place is an open acknowledgement of risk, but can there be sufficient certainty around their application in practice? Detailed tests have been developed to determine compliance with human rights obligations, but the British government has no absolute guarantee that even where an assurance has been concluded that it will be upheld. In *RB (Algeria) and Another and OO Jordan (Jordan)* v. *Secretary of State for the Home Department* (2009),[44] precisely this question arose (see Walker 2007: 441–50; Tooze 2010). The absolute prohibition under article 3 of the European Convention is clear, but the European Court of Human Rights has established that assurances may provide a basis for safe return with the adequacy of the assurance determined on a case-by-case basis (see *Saadi* v. *Italy* 2008). The result has been the development by the Special Immigration Appeals Commission of a set of tests to determine if it is permissible to rely upon particular assurances.

The Law Lords unanimously held that reliance by the Special Immigration Appeals Commission on the assurances given by Algeria and Jordan could not be regarded as irrational, and for a range of additional reasons, the practical result was that the Law Lords agreed with the Special Immigration Appeals Commission that Abu Qatada could be deported to Jordan. This judgment, therefore, confirmed the potential legality of deportation with diplomatic assurances as one tool in a counter-terrorism policy that includes removal from the United Kingdom.[45]

---

42   *Chahal* v. *United Kingdom* [1996] Reports of Judgments and Decisions V. 'The Court notes first of all that States face immense difficulties in modern times in protecting their communities from terrorist violence. It cannot therefore underestimate the scale of the danger of terrorism today and the threat it presents to the community. That must not, however, call into question the absolute nature of Article 3' (*Saadi* v. *Italy* 2008: 137).

43   See *A* v. *The Netherlands*, no. 4900/06 [2010]; *Al Husin* v. *Bosnia and Herzegovina*, no. 3727/08 [2012]; and *Auad* v. *Bulgaria*, no. 46390 [2012].

44   *RB (Algeria) and Another and OO Jordan (Jordan)* v. *Secretary of State for the Home Department* [2009] UKHL 10.

45   See, for example, *XX (Ethiopia)* v. *Secretary of State for the Home Department* [2012] EWCA Civ 742, in which an appeal from a Special Immigration Appeals Commission

British governmental frustration arose, however, following Abu Qatada's success at Strasbourg.[46] The result has been an extensive national conversation, at times intense, about the role of the European Court of Human Rights, counter-terrorism policy and the powers of removal from the United Kingdom to countries with poor human rights records. This has even included an official visit by the Home Secretary to Jordan in order to ensure a removal that would comply with the European Convention on Human Rights. As with the previous government, a direct collision arose between an insistence on rights-based reasons preventing removal with an executive desire (effectively endorsed by the domestic judiciary) to secure deportation. This area will remain a source of contention.

The exchanges in these areas are evidence of constitutionalised tensions between the different branches of government, often played out in the media.[47] The reasons are not hard to explain and can be witnessed in global and local conversations on the principle of legality. Governments view public protection and the 'security of the nation' as fundamental and core. Executives will see this as a key duty and responsibility. When there are risks of sufficient gravity, law, policy and practice will move to address them. The courts, as guardians of the rule of law, become the official institutional reminder of the enabling and constraining functions of legality. In these divisive areas, this may mean insisting that determined executive action has strayed beyond the confines of legality or infringed upon the rights of individuals. Judges are not the only people in democratic life who can give voice to this, but they are often the ones who have this official role. In the United Kingdom's dialogic model of constitutionalism, this will always be an arena poised and ripe for constitutional conflict. And this is precisely how it should be.

The notion that the executive must be excessively deferred to because of its democratic legitimacy and expertise in times of crisis is one that is often advanced. It cannot be lightly dismissed in contexts in which judicial expertise and factual knowledge may be limited and given the fact that executives are politically accountable for their security failures. However, there are crucial distinctions to be drawn between the constitutional roles of the executive and the judiciary, and one essential function of courts and judges is precisely to test justifications and rationales in order to ensure that the principle of legality is being complied with in all contexts. In national security cases, the rule of law

---

decision to uphold the deportation of an Ethiopian citizen on national security grounds was dismissed. The Court of Appeal judgment reflects a measure of unease about some of the verification gaps that existed on return but nevertheless was satisfied that the assurances were compliant.

46 See *Othman (Abu Qatada)* v. *United Kingdom*, no. 8139/09 [2012] and *R (Othman)* v. *Special Immigration Appeals Commission, Secretary of State for the Home Department and Governor of HMP Long Lartin* [2012] EWHC 2349 (Admin).

47 The media can also be a participant in creating this climate (see Barrett and Ensor 2012).

is tested, both in the sense of protecting individual rights and in ensuring that an effective regulatory framework exists. By according decisive weight to the views of the executive, judges are not discharging their responsibility to take a view on the meaning of law. If and when the courts do this, they risk abandoning one of the values of the rule of law: the defence of the person against arbitrary power through an established legal framework properly interpreted and applied. The more disturbing implication would seem to be that there are norm-free zones of executive action; there is evidence from the response of courts in the United Kingdom and elsewhere that such an approach has not been endorsed. The 'liberal way' seems to remain one of operating within self-limiting protocols that cannot be dismissed as mere pretence and facade. Legality seems to retain some purchase even in the most testing times.

Conclusions

This chapter has had a basic and simple aim. The suggestion is that the 'dance of legality and humanity' is evidence of a globalised practice of rights mobilisation in action in historical and contemporary terms. It is 'historical' in the sense that a practice of human rights has bolted humanity onto legality in a way that is proving hard for even the most determined states to displace entirely. This is a process that continues. While it remains possible to exaggerate both the spread and the effectiveness of this pattern, it is hard to dismiss it as an explanation for the way participants in the international legal and political orders operate. Normative footholds provide a basis for seeking transparency, accountability and justifications for how human persons are treated anywhere. It is a discourse and an approach that is increasingly being deployed against power-centres however configured (state, non-state, individual and collective) to hold them to account. It remains a way to draw us back to our common humanity, even when we face each other in conflict and war.

The challenge for a human rights movement that retains emancipatory ambitions is to enable this performance to continue. A democratised global order will, of necessity, always hold the multiple elements in tension, and different configurations will emerge over time. There is clear evidence that legality has absorbed an argument from humanity to the extent that rights hold and are effectively deployed even in harsh and difficult periods. The principle of legality seems to have attached itself, however insecurely, to the 'liberal way of war'.

References

Adelman, H. 2002. Refugees and Border Security Post-September 11. *Refuge*, 20(4), 5–14.

Arendt, H. 1973. *The Origins of Totalitarianism*. New edn. New York and London: Harvest/Harcourt, Brace, Jovanovich.

Barder, B. 2004. On SIAC. *London Review of Books*, 26(6), 40–41.

Barrett, D. and Ensor, J. 2012. Judges Who Allow Foreign Criminals to Stay in Britain. *Sunday Telegraph*, 16 June.

BBC News 2006. Blair Dismay Over Hijack Afghans, 10 May.

Bhabha, J. 2009. Arendt's Children: Do Today's Migrant Children Have a Right to Have Rights? *Human Rights Quarterly*, 31(2), 410–51.

Blair, Tony. 2005. Full Text: The Prime Minister's Statement on Anti-Terror Measures. *Guardian*, 5 August.

Bosniak, L. 2010. Persons and Citizens in Constitutional Thought. *International Journal of Constitutional Law*, 8(1), 9–29.

Brouwer, E. 2003. Immigration, Asylum and Terrorism: A Changing Dynamic Legal and Practical Developments in the EU in Response to the Terrorist Attacks of 11.09. *European Journal of Migration and Law*, 4(4), 399–424.

Bruin, R. and Wouters, K. 2003. Terrorism and the Non-Derogability of *Non-Refoulement*. *International Journal of Refugee Law*, 15(1), 5–29.

Campbell, D. 2009. The Threat of Terror and the Plausibility of Positivism. *Public Law*, July, 501–18.

Cole, D. 2003. *Enemy Aliens*. New York: The New Press.

Council Directive 2004/83/EC on Minimum Standards for the Qualification and Status of Third Country Nationals or Stateless Persons as Refugees or as Persons Who Otherwise Need International Protection and the Content of the Protection Granted, 29 April 2004, *Official Journal L.* 304, 30/09/2004, 12–23 (Qualification Directive).

Council Directive 2011/95/EU on Standards for the Qualification of Third-Country Nationals or Stateless Persons as Beneficiaries of International Protection, for a Uniform Status for Refugees or for Persons Eligible for Subsidiary Protection, and for the Content of the Protection Granted of 13 December 2011, *Official Journal L.* 337, 20/12/2011, 9–27 (Qualification Directive (recast)).

Dauvergne, C. 2007. Security and Migration Law in the Less Brave New World. *Social and Legal Studies*, 16(4), 533–49.

Federal Administrative Court. 2009. Decision, BVerwG 10 C 48.07, OVG 8 A 2632/06.A [2008]. *International Journal of Refugee Law*, 21(3), 592–611.

Feldman, D. 1999. Human Dignity as a Legal Value: Part I. *Public Law*, Winter, 682–702.

Feldman, D. 2005. Proportionality and Discrimination in Anti-Terrorism Legislation. *Cambridge Law Journal*, 64(2), 271–3.

Finnis, J. 2007. Nationality, Alienage and Constitutional Principle. *Law Quarterly Review*, 123(July), 417–45.

Gilbert, G. 2003. Protection after September 11th. *International Journal of Refugee Law*, 15(1), 1–4.

Gilbert, G. 2004. Is Europe Living Up to its Obligations to Refugees? *European Journal of International Law*, 15(5), 963–87.

Hillyard, P. 1993. *Suspect Community: People's Experience of the Prevention of Terrorism Acts in Britain*. London: Pluto Press.

Human Rights Watch 2004. *Empty Promises: Diplomatic Assurances No Safeguard Against Torture*. April 16(4).

Human Rights Watch 2005. *Still at Risk: Diplomatic Assurances No Safeguard Against Torture*. April 17(4).

Hunt, A. 1993. *Explorations in Law and Society: Towards a Constitutive Theory of Law*. London: Routledge.

Huysmans, J. 2006. *The Politics of Insecurity: Fear, Migration and Asylum in the EU*. Abingdon: Routledge.

Immigration and Nationality Directorate Asylum Policy Unit Notice 1/2003 'Humanitarian Protection and Discretionary Leave'.

Kesby, A. 2012. *The Right to Have Rights: Citizenship, Humanity, and International Law*. Oxford: Oxford University Press.

Kidane, W. 2010. The Terrorism Bar to Asylum in Australia, Canada, the United Kingdom, and the United States: Transporting Best Practices. *Fordham International Law Journal*, 33(2), 300–71.

McCrudden, C. 2008. Human Dignity and Judicial Interpretation of Human Rights. *European Journal of International Law*, 19(4), 655–724.

Martin, K. 2002. Preventive Detention of Immigrants and Non-Citizens in the United States Since September 11th. *Refuge*, 20(4), 23–8.

Martin, S. and Martin, P. 2004. International Migration and Terrorism: Prevention, Prosecution and Protection. *Georgetown Immigration Law Journal*, 18(2), 329–44.

Moeckli, D. 2010. Immigration Law Enforcement after 9/11 and Human Rights, in *Human Security and Non-Citizens: Law, Policy and International Affairs*, ed. A. Edwards and C. Ferstman. Cambridge: Cambridge University Press, 459–94.

Moyn, S. 2010. *The Last Utopia: Human Rights in History*. Cambridge, MA: Harvard University Press.

Ramraj, V.V. 2012. The Impossibility of Global Anti-Terrorism Law?, in *Global Anti-Terrorism Law and Policy*, ed. V.V. Ramraj, M. Hor, K. Roach and G. Williams. 2nd edn. Cambridge: Cambridge University Press, 44–66.

Rawlings, R. 2005. Review, Revenge and Retreat. *Modern Law Review*, 68(3), 378–410.

Review of Counter-Terrorism and Security Powers: A Report by Lord Macdonald of River Glaven QC 2011. Cm 8004, 26 January.

Rikhof, J. 2009. War Criminals Now Welcome: How Common Law Countries Approach the Phenomenon of International Crimes in the Immigration and Refugee Context. *International Journal of Refugee Law*, 21(3), 453–507.

Santos, B.d.S. 2002. *Toward a New Legal Common Sense*. 2nd edn. London: Reed Elsevier.

Saul, B. 2004. Exclusion of Suspected Terrorists from Asylum: Trends in International and European Refugee Law. Institute for International Integration Studies Discussion Paper, No. 26, July.

Schmitt, C. 2007. *The Concept of the Political*, in *The Concept of the Political: Expanded Edition*, trans. G. Schwab. Chicago and London: University of Chicago Press, 19–79.

Shah, P. 1999. Taking the 'Political' Out of Asylum: The Legal Containment of Refugees' Political Activism, in *Refugee Rights and Realities: Evolving International Concepts and Regimes*, ed. F. Nicholson and P. Twomey. Cambridge: Cambridge University Press, 119–35.

Simeon, J.C. 2009. Exclusion Under Article 1F(a) of the 1951 Convention in Canada. *International Journal of Refugee Law*, 21(2), 193–217.

Stafford Smith, C. 2012. Our Terror Campaign. *Guardian*, 25 September.

Storey, H. 2008. EU Refugee Qualification Directive: A Brave New World? *International Journal of Refugee Law*, 20(1), 1–49.

Tomkins, A. 2010. National Security and the Role of the Court: A Changed Landscape? *Law Quarterly Review*, 126 (October), 543–67.

Tooze, J. 2010. Deportation with Assurances: The Approach of the UK Courts. *Public Law*, April, 362–86.

Türk, V. 2003. Forced Migration and Security. *International Journal of Refugee Law*, 15(1), 113–25.

UNGA Res 217(III)(A) (1948), Universal Declaration of Human Rights, UN Doc A/RES/217(III)A.

UNHCR 2001. Addressing Security Concerns Without Undermining Refugee Protection: UNHCR's Perspective.

UNHCR 2003. Guidelines on International Protection No. 5: Application of the Exclusion Clauses: Article 1F of the 1951 Convention Relating to the Status of Refugees. HCR/GIP/03/05.

UNHCR 2006. Note on Diplomatic Assurances and International Refugee Protection.

United Kingdom Border Agency. Asylum Policy Instructions. Available at: http://www.ukba.homeoffice.gov.uk/sitecontent/documents/policyandlaw/asylumpolicyinstructions/ [accessed: 24 October 2012].

United Kingdom Border Agency. Asylum Policy Unit Notice 'Exceptional Leave to Remain: Suspected War Criminals and Perpetrators of Crimes Against Humanity and Genocide'.

United Kingdom Border Agency. Immigration Rules. Available at: http://www.ukba.homeoffice.gov.uk/policyandlaw/immigrationlaw/immigrationrules/ [accessed: 24 October 2012].

UNSC Res 1373 (2001), UN Doc S/RES/1373.

UNSC Res 1377 (2001), UN Doc S/RES/1377.

UNSC Res 1624 (2005), UN Doc S/RES/1624.

Walker, C. 2007. The Treatment of Foreign Terror Suspects. *Modern Law Review*, 70(3), 427–57.

Walzer, M. 1983. *Spheres of Justice*. New York: Basic Books.

Whitaker, R. 2002. Refugee Policy after September 11: Not Much New. *Refuge*, 20(4), 29–33.

Williams, P.J. 1993. *The Alchemy of Race and Rights*. London: Virago Press.

Chapter 3

The Responsibility to Protect: Lessons from Libya and Syria

J. Craig Barker

The United Nations Security Council authorised intervention by the North Atlantic Treaty Organization (NATO) in Libya, which began on 19 March 2011 and ended on 31 October 2011.[1] The International Coalition for the Responsibility to Protect (2012) hailed Operation Unified Protector as 'a turning point in the response to mass atrocities' that marked the solidification of responsibility to protect as an actionable norm in international law.[2] However, at the time of writing, the Security Council has repeatedly failed to authorise intervention in Syria in the face of ongoing bombardment of civilian targets across that state.[3] If Libya (arguably) represents the zenith of responsibility to protect, then the international community's failure to protect civilian targets in Syria surely represents its nadir.

The purpose of this chapter is not to condemn responsibility to protect as a concept. There are many facets of it that should be developed and built upon. Rather, this chapter seeks to explore its limitations in light of the Libyan and Syrian conflicts. In particular, consideration is given to the genealogy of responsibility to protect as the latest manifestation of a post-Cold War process of liberal interventionism. The situations in Libya and Syria provide the backdrop for a critical analysis of the concept and a prognosis for its implementation in future conflicts.

---

1   The intervention was authorised by Security Council Resolution 1973 on 17 March 2011.

2   According to Powell, 'the Security Council's invocation of RtoP in the midst of the Libyan crisis significantly deepens the broader, ongoing transformation in the international law system's approach to sovereignty and civilian protection. This transformation away from the traditional Westphalian notion of sovereignty has been unfolding for decades, but the Libyan case represents a further normative shift from sovereignty as a right to sovereignty as a responsibility' (2012: 298).

3   On 4 October 2011, the Security Council voted on draft resolution S/2011/612. This was vetoed by China and Russia, and Brazil, India, Lebanon and South Africa abstained. On 4 February 2012, the Security Council voted on draft resolution S/2012/77. The vote took place at the time of the attack on the city of Homs and was vetoed by China and Russia, with all of the other members of the Security Council voting in favour of the resolution. On 19 July 2012, the Security Council voted on draft resolution S/2012/538. This was vetoed by China and Russia, and Pakistan and South Africa abstained.

Responsibility to Protect: The Genealogy of an Idea

Responsibility to protect is one of the most controversial ideas to emerge in international legal and political discourse in the twenty-first century. Simply stated, it seeks to allocate responsibility for the protection of civilians between the territorial state, with whom primary responsibility for protection resides, and the international community, whose residual responsibility applies should the territorial state fail in its primary responsibility. The concept of responsibility to protect is most commonly dated back to the Report of the International Commission on Intervention and State Sovereignty (hereafter Commission Report) in 2001. However, the genealogy of the idea can be traced back at least as far as the policy initiatives and writings of Dag Hammarskjöld, the second United Nations Secretary-General. Although not using the word 'responsibility', Hammarskjöld, in 1957, identified the protection of basic human rights as being a matter of shared concern:

> the work for peace is basically a work for the most elementary of human rights: the right of everyone to security and to freedom from fear. We therefore recognise it as one of the first duties of a government to take measures in order to safeguard for its citizens this very right. But we also recognise it as an obligation for the emerging world community to assist governments in safeguarding this elementary human right without having to lock themselves behind the wall of arms. (Wilder Foote 1962: 127)

Hammarskjöld primarily focused upon the United Nations' emerging role in questions of international peace and security, particularly in the colonised world. He is credited with developing the United Nations' peacekeeping capabilities and expanding the Secretariat's role from a mere administrator to an important political actor within the United Nations system, thereby creating an international executive authority capable of responding to the needs of both individuals and states (see Orford 2011: 3–7). Hammarskjöld was no idealist, and he abundantly recognised the limits of international law, particularly given the importance of state sovereignty. His terminology, particularly in relation to the responsibility of the international community, focused upon the provision of assistance as opposed to intervention. Indeed, it is interesting that Hammarskjöld spoke rarely, if ever, of the concept of sovereignty. Yet it is sovereignty that has, at least since the end of the Cold War, provided the greatest obstacle to the international community's ability to enforce human rights and humanitarian norms. It is not surprising, therefore, that since the end of the Cold War the liberal discourse around the development and enforcement of human rights has focused upon the notion of state sovereignty.

The Failed States Discourse

One significant discourse has focused upon the concept of failed states. According to Helman and Ratner, 'civil strife, government breakdown and economic privation' led in the early 1990s to a 'disturbing new phenomenon: the failed nation-state, utterly incapable of sustaining itself as a member of the international community' (1992–93: 3). Helman and Ratner's analysis (1992–93: 7) recognises the importance of Hammarskjöld's 'assistance-based' approach, as well as subsequent developments in relation to the responsibility of the United Nations and other international organisations, including the World Bank, the International Monetary Fund, the United Nations High Commissioner for Refugees and the Organisation for Economic Co-operation and Development. In particular, they highlight the work of United Nations Secretary-General Boutros Boutros-Ghali's 'An Agenda for Peace: Preventive Diplomacy, Peacemaking and Peacekeeping' (1992), which 'set forth the concept of post-conflict peace-building' that envisaged the United Nations' direct involvement in the internal affairs of failed or failing states (Helman and Ratner 1992–93: 7). Nevertheless, 'deeply rooted political obstacles have tended to prevent extensive U.N. direction of a country's internal matters and even stifled debate about the appropriateness of such involvement. Those barriers stem from the talisman of "sovereignty"' (Helman and Ratner 1992–93: 9). In addition, Helman and Ratner point to the legal obstacle of article 2(7) of the United Nations Charter, which limits the power of the United Nations to interfere 'in matters which are essentially within the domestic jurisdiction of any state' to actions authorised by the Security Council under Chapter VII of the Charter (1992–93: 9).

The solution, according to Helman and Ratner, is the development of United Nations conservatorship, akin to domestic law notions of trusteeship or guardianship, that would operate at three levels: for *failing* states, which 'still maintain some type of minimal governmental structure', the United Nations could provide what they refer to as 'governance assistance'; for *failed* states, a second level would involve the delegation of certain governmental functions to the United Nations; the third level, the 'most radical option', is direct United Nations trusteeship (1992–93: 13, 14, 16). This final level of assistance would require amendment of the existing, though now inoperative, United Nations international trusteeship system provided for by articles 77 and 78 of the UN Charter. Although they acknowledge that their proposals would have practical limitations and not overcome the political and legal objections to United Nations assistance outlined above, Helman and Ratner argue that the idea of conservatorship is consistent with sovereignty insofar as its purpose would be 'to enable the state to resume responsibility for itself' (1992–93: 16).

A number of points can be made about Helman and Ratner's analysis. First, inherent within this discourse are the two fundamental notions that form the foundation of responsibility to protect, that is, the primary responsibility of the territorial state and the residual responsibility of the international community (in the form of the United Nations). Second, the discourse is explicitly linked to the 'central Charter values: human rights for all and stability in international relations' (Helman and Ratner 1992–93: 12). Finally, Helman and Ratner emphasise that their failed states discourse is not about removing sovereignty but, rather, about understanding the limits of sovereignty as a concept, especially when faced with widespread violations of human rights. It is worth highlighting the conclusion that 'the irreducible minimum of sovereignty requires some form of consent from the host state' (Helman and Ratner 1992–93: 13).

The failed states discourse has been criticised for being too simplistic and overstating the 'sovereignty problem'. Richardson (1996: 2) notes that the involvement of international financial institutions in setting conditions for financial assistance diminishes sovereignty, as does the delivery of humanitarian assistance. Thürer (1999: 731–2) has criticised the term 'failed state' for being too broad, and its French equivalent, 'Etats sans gouvernement', or 'states without government', for being too narrow. Wilde's is the most interesting critique of the discourse and, in focusing upon the question of responsibility, pre-empts some of the later debates about responsibility to protect. For him, the responsibilities discourse in relation to 'failed states' is misplaced. He argues that the label 'suggests that when governmental infrastructure collapses, the state, its people, and its leaders are solely responsible' (Wilde 2003: 426). While he accepts that indigenous factors such as 'civil conflict or corrupt leadership' often contribute, to a significant degree, to state collapse, 'the involvement of foreign states, international financial institutions such as the International Monetary Fund and the World Bank, multinational corporations, and the like often plays a major role in mediating the state of local conditions, thereby affecting the viability of the economy and governmental infrastructure' (Wilde 2003: 426). As will be shown below, the responsibilities discourse is much narrower than its equivalent in relation to 'failed states', focusing as it does exclusively upon the protection of civilians from massive human rights abuses. Wilde's primary assertion that responsibility cannot be seen as a simple question of singular fault is important to bear in mind, however, when considering the prospects of responsibility to protect. Responsibility turns out to be a considerably more complex notion than the 'failed states' discourse would suggest.

The 'failed states' discourse achieved some purchase in the academic literature and policy prescriptions during the immediate post-Cold War era. The Fund for Peace, a United States-based non-governmental organisation, continues to publish an annual 'Failed States Index', which it uses to analyse and support weak and 'failing' states. It provides policy advice to governments in relation to conflict, early warning and assessment, which is an important element in the potential success and development of the responsibility to protect process. However, the 'failed states' idea has not provided the basis for development of institutional and normative change in the way suggested by Helman and Ratner. In particular, the establishment of conservatorship and the reinvigoration of the United Nations' international trusteeship system have not happened.

Humanitarian Intervention

A second major discourse of liberal interventionism focuses upon humanitarian intervention. The academic literature on this is vast, reflecting its contemporary and historical significance. The importance of the discourse and practice of humanitarian intervention to the present discussion focuses upon the impact that it has had upon the development of responsibility to protect. To some extent, responsibility to protect can be seen as a direct response to the critiques of humanitarian intervention, particularly as applied to NATO's 1999 intervention in Kosovo (see Commission Report 2001: ¶ 1.2).

The ethnic cleansing of Kosovar Albanians from Kosovo by Serb forces in 1998–99 resulted, ultimately, in a sustained bombing attack on Belgrade by NATO forces over a seventy-eight-day period during the spring and early summer of 1999. In light of the significant breaches of international law attributable to Serbia in relation to the plight of Kosovar Albanians, Bruno Simma has argued that the international community had an obligation to intervene to stop massive human rights violations and possible genocide, not least because 'the obligation on states to respect and protect the basic rights of all human persons is the concern of all states, that is, they are owed *erga omnes*. Consequently, in the event of material breaches of such obligations, every other state may lawfully consider itself legally "injured" and is thus entitled to resort to countermeasures' (1999: 2). However, where such countermeasures involve the use of force, the only mechanism to ensure the legality of such an intervention would be through Security Council authorisation under article 42 of the UN Charter. As Simma notes, in such circumstances 'a "humanitarian intervention" by military means is permissible' (1999: 5).

In the context of Kosovo, there is general agreement that the NATO intervention constituted a prima facie violation of international law. Nevertheless, it has been consistently asserted that, in spite of this, it was a legitimate response to the horrors that were unfolding in Kosovo. Thus, for example, the Independent International Commission on Kosovo (2000: 186) concluded that the intervention was illegal yet legitimate. For Simma, political and moral considerations left NATO with 'no choice but to act outside the law' (1999: 22). However, he was wary of the potential 'boomerang effect' of such instances and 'their potential to erode the precepts of international law' (Simma 1999: 22). Others went further and asserted the development of a new right of humanitarian intervention outside the parameters of the UN Charter. In direct response to Simma's analysis, for example, Antonio Cassese, while warning of the possibility of opening a Pandora's box, nevertheless challenged international lawyers to address two fundamental questions:

First, was the NATO armed intervention at least rooted in and partially justified by contemporary trends of the international community? Second, were some parameters set in this particular instance of the use of force that might lead to

> a gradual legitimation of forcible humanitarian countermeasures by a group of
> states outside any authorization by the Security Council? (1999: 25)

More than ten years after Kosovo, Cassese's calls have been the subject of
considerable discussion but little concrete action. As Brunée and Toope recently
put it, 'humanitarian intervention never achieved the solidity that its promoters
sought' (2010: 324). This might be partly due to the shift of focus away from
humanitarian intervention to intervention in response to global terrorism in the
aftermath of 11 September 2001. It has been argued by some that the United
States-led invasions of Afghanistan and Iraq were undertaken, at least in part, on
humanitarian grounds. However, in neither case did humanitarian concerns provide
the primary justification for intervention. In fact, to a greater or lesser extent,
both interventions have solidified public opinion against military intervention,
whatever the justification. Consequently, the failure to develop a more systematic
legal basis for unauthorised humanitarian intervention is also due to the strength
of the shared understanding that buttresses the collective security regime of the
UN Charter (see Brunée and Toope 2010: 323). More importantly, the failure to
develop the discourse of humanitarian intervention into an actionable international
legal process can be put down to the development of the concept of responsibility
to protect, which, as will be shown in the following section, rapidly emerged from
a simple idea put forward in an unofficial report into a 'candidate norm' aimed at
regulating international intervention in the face of massive human rights violations
(Brunée and Toope 2010: 324).

Responsibility to Protect: The Crystallisation of an Idea

As noted previously, Kosovo provided the impetus for a fundamental
reassessment of the relationship between state sovereignty and the possibility
of intervention in the face of massive human rights violations. Inspired by the
call of the then United Nations Secretary-General Kofi Annan to find a new
consensus on humanitarian intervention,[4] Canada, supported by a number of major
funders, created the Commission. The Commission, which consisted of twelve
independent commissioners under the co-chairmanship of Gareth Evans and
Muhammad Sahnoun, was asked to consider legal, moral, operational and political
questions relevant to the relationship between humanitarian intervention and state
sovereignty and, in particular, to respond to Secretary-General Annan's call. The
Commission Report devised a concept of responsibility to protect that was built
upon two basic principles: first, that 'State sovereignty implies responsibility,

---

4   As Secretary-General Annan put it in his 2000 Millennium Report, 'if humanitarian
intervention is, indeed, an unacceptable assault on sovereignty, how *should* we respond to
a Rwanda, to a Srebrenica – to gross and systematic violations of human rights that offend
every precept of our common humanity?' (¶ 217).

and the primary responsibility for the protection of its people lies with the state itself'; and second, 'Where a population is suffering serious harm, as a result of internal war, insurgency, repression or state failure, and the state in question is unwilling or unable to halt or avert it, the principle of non-intervention yields to the international responsibility to protect' (Commission Report 2001: XI). The Commission recognised state sovereignty but also, crucially, the obligations that sovereignty implies. The Commission Report placed significant emphasis on the Security Council's responsibility and explicitly sought to enhance specific legal obligations under international human rights law and international humanitarian law (see Commission Report 2001: XI).

Responsibility to protect, according to the Commission, comprises three specific responsibilities: the responsibility to prevent, the responsibility to react and the responsibility to rebuild (Commission Report 2001: XI). The 'single most important' of these is prevention, and 'less intrusive and coercive measures ... [should be] considered before more coercive and intrusive ones are applied' (Commission Report 2001: XI). Nevertheless, the Commission Report laid down a number of principles for military intervention including a 'just cause threshold' requiring large-scale loss of life or large-scale ethnic cleansing, as well as four 'precautionary principles': right intention (to halt or avert human suffering), last resort (according to which every non-military option has been explored), proportional means ('the minimum necessary to secure the defined human protection objectives') and reasonable prospects (including a reasonable chance of success that is 'not likely to be worse than the consequences of inaction') (Commission Report 2001: XII). Finally, and importantly in light of the prima facie illegality of the Kosovo intervention, the Commission identified right authority as an essential element for military intervention. That authority should come from the Security Council, whose permanent members should agree not to apply their veto powers but whose inaction within a reasonable time could allow a use of force to be authorised by 'the General Assembly in Emergency Special Session acting under the Uniting for Peace procedure' and 'action within area of jurisdiction by regional or sub-regional organisations under Chapter VIII of the Charter, subject to their seeking subsequent authorisation from the Security Council' (Commission Report 2001: XII–XIII).

The notion of shared responsibility between territorial states and the international community was taken up in the 2004 report of the United Nations Secretary-General's High-Level Panel on Threats, Challenges and Change, 'A More Secure World: Our Shared Responsibility', which endorsed the idea of responsibility to protect and identified it as an emerging norm to be embraced and acted upon (2004: ¶¶ 201–2). Further endorsement of the principle was provided by Secretary-General Annan in his 2005 report, 'In Larger Freedom: Towards Development, Security and Human Rights for All' (2005: ¶¶ 16–22). The 2005 World Summit Outcome's adoption of the idea of responsibility to protect represented a major breakthrough, though there were two significant restrictions. First, its application was restricted to four situations: genocide, war crimes, ethnic cleansing and crimes against humanity (see UNGA Res 60/1 (2005): ¶¶ 138–9). United Nations Secretary-General Ban Ki-moon explained this restriction on the basis that the four 'situations' were those upon which consensus was achievable at the World Summit (see Verdirame 2011: 152). Second, and perhaps more problematically, the World Summit Outcome did not refer to a potential role for the United Nations General Assembly or regional organisations providing appropriate authority for military intervention. With regard to regional organisations, paragraph 139 of the World Summit Outcome mentions Chapter VII of the UN Charter but only does so in relation to 'diplomatic, humanitarian and other *peaceful* purposes'. Paragraph 13 endorses the willingness of the General Assembly 'to take collective action, in a timely and decisive manner, through the Security Council, in accordance with Chapter VII, on a case-by-case basis *and in cooperation with regional organisations as appropriate*'. With reference to the General Assembly, the World Summit Outcome refers only to 'the need for the General Assembly to continue consideration of the responsibility to protect populations from genocide, war crimes, ethnic cleansing and crimes against humanity and its implications, bearing in mind the principles of the Charter and international law' (UNGA Res 60/1 (2005): ¶ 139). It is not surprising, therefore, that this somewhat diluted version of responsibility to protect was itself unanimously endorsed by the Security Council in 2006 in Resolution 1674 on the protection of civilians in armed conflict (see ¶ 4).[5] Further endorsement came from states across the world, both developed and developing, and from regional organisations, including the African Union and the African Commission on Human and Peoples' Rights (see Orford 2011: 17–20).

With these, albeit conditional, endorsements secured, the now modified concept of responsibility to protect took on a new momentum within the United Nations under the enthusiastic leadership of Secretary-General Ban (see Orford 2011: 17). In 2007, he created the position of United Nations Special Adviser on the Prevention of Genocide, and a further new role of Special Adviser on the Responsibility to Protect was introduced in 2008. Both positions were created within the newly established Office on Genocide Prevention and Responsibility to Protect. Building upon this, the Secretary-General published a detailed report in January 2009 entitled 'Implementing the Responsibility to Protect' (hereafter 'Implementing Responsibility'). This thirty-page document advances a three-pillar strategy focused upon the responsibilities of the state, the responsibilities of the international community in providing assistance and capacity-building, and the need for a timely and decisive response.

What is clearly apparent from 'Implementing Responsibility' is that responsibility to protect is not a short-term process. The report recognises that responsibility to protect is, 'first and foremost, a matter of state responsibility' (Ban 2009: ¶ 14) and identifies 'respect for human rights' as 'an essential element of responsible sovereignty' (Ban 2009: ¶ 16). It identifies a number of ways

---

5   For a detailed analysis of each of these endorsements of responsibility to protect, see Stahn 2007: 99–100.

in which states can review and enhance what they can do in relation to human rights protection and cooperation with the United Nations, including by assisting the United Nations Human Rights Council, especially through the universal periodic review mechanism and by becoming parties 'to the relevant international instruments on human rights, international humanitarian law and refugee law as well as to the Rome Statute of the International Criminal Court', by embodying these in national law and, where necessary, by criminalising international human rights law and international humanitarian law abuses within domestic law (Ban 2009: ¶ 17). 'Implementing Responsibility' further calls upon states to undertake a process of self-reflection to ensure that gross violations do not occur, and to engage in state-to-state cooperation, favourably citing the African Peer Review Mechanism and the New Partnership for Africa's Development in this regard (Ban 2009: ¶ 22). The report also encourages new training and education processes, particularly of 'critical actors in society, such as the police, soldiers, the judiciary and legislators' (Ban 2009: ¶ 25).

The second pillar in 'Implementing Responsibility' aims at a lengthy process of building state capacity to avoid genocide, war crimes, ethnic cleansing and crimes against humanity based upon 'active partnership between the international community and the state' and working through 'persuasive measures and positive incentives' (Ban 2009: ¶¶ 28, 29). Suggested measures to facilitate such partnership include 'dialogue, education and training on human rights and humanitarian standards and norms', the provision of direct country-based human rights assistance through the United Nations and its partners, increased support from regional and sub-regional bodies, the creation of rapid-response civilian and police capacity, and military assistance with the consent of the host government within the context of preventive deployment (Ban 2009: ¶¶ 33–42).[6] However, the report explicitly admits that such measures should not be undertaken without the consent of the target state. Where such consent is not forthcoming, then timely and decisive action would be required:

> If the political leadership of the state is determined to commit crimes and violations relating to the responsibility to protect, then assistance measures under pillar two would be of little use and the international community would be better advised to begin assembling the capacity and will for a 'timely and decisive' response, as stipulated under paragraph 139 of the Summit Outcome. (Ban 2009: ¶ 29)

'Implementing Responsibility' makes clear that measures under the third pillar need not depend upon measures having been taken under pillar two (Ban 2009: ¶ 50). The primary objective of the report remains the peaceful settlement of disputes under Chapters VI and VIII of the UN Charter, through the work of the Secretary-General, the General Assembly and the Security Council and,

---

6 On preventive deployment, see also Boutros-Ghali 1992.

where appropriate, other intergovernmental bodies, including the International Criminal Court (Ban 2009: ¶¶ 51–5). Nevertheless, 'Implementing Responsibility' recognises that 'there should be no hesitation to seek authorization for more robust measures', including articles 41 and 42 of the Charter (Ban 2009: ¶ 56). Furthermore, despite their omission from paragraphs 138 and 139 of the 2005 World Summit Outcome, 'Implementing Responsibility' does specifically mention the possibility of enforcement measures authorised by the General Assembly and regional organisations acting under article 53 of the UN Charter (Ban 2009: ¶¶ 56, 63). Nevertheless, the primary responsibility for a 'timely and decisive' response lies with the five permanent members of the Security Council 'because of the privileges of tenure and the veto power they have been granted under the Charter' (Ban 2009: ¶ 61). In the view of the Secretary-General:

> I would urge them to refrain from employing or threatening to employ the veto in situations of manifest failure to meet the obligations relating to the responsibility to protect, as defined in paragraph 139 of the Summit Outcome, and to reach a mutual understanding to that effect. (Ban 2009: ¶ 61)

What is apparent from this brief survey of the crystallisation of responsibility to protect is that, though arguably providing a more holistic approach to United Nations intervention, the concept does little to change the existing provision of international law related not only to military intervention but also more generally to the capacity-building, preventive diplomacy role of the United Nations. Indeed, 'Implementing Responsibility' is replete with examples of how the United Nations has successfully acted under pillars two and three in the past. For many, responsibility to protect constitutes, accordingly, little more than 'old wine in new bottles' (Stahn 2007: 111).

On the other hand, the concept of responsibility to protect was presented in the original Commission Report as 'a new approach' (Commission Report 2001: 11–19). According to one of the report's primary authors, Gareth Evans, '[w]hat we have seen over the last five years is the emergence, almost in real time, of a new international norm, one that may ultimately become a new rule of customary international law with really quite fundamental ethical importance and novelty in the international system' (2006–2007: 704). In a similar vein, Thomas Weiss has asserted that by conceptualising the 'new approach' to massive human rights violations as responsibility to protect, 'the ICISS sought to drive a stake through the heart of "humanitarian intervention"' (2007: 102). Weiss argues that the new terminology avoids the assertion of 'the moral high ground' that is inherent in the concept of 'humanitarianism' and contends that 'it overlooks the self-interested dynamics of the strong to impose their will on the weak in the name of the so-called universal principles of the day … An honest debate about motivations and likely costs and benefits is required, not visceral accolades because of a qualifying adjective' (2007: 102–3).

In spite of this powerful rhetoric, it will be argued in the forthcoming section that the discourse of responsibility to protect has failed, particularly in the cases of Libya and Syria, to provide a new ethical or practical framework for dealing with mass atrocities. In particular, the concepts of 'responsibility' and 'protection' are both flawed as foundational principles for a 'new approach' to intervention to prevent massive human rights abuses in the face of state sovereignty.

Responsibility to Protect as a Normative Discourse

Evans and Weiss both accept that responsibility to protect has yet to emerge as a legally binding norm. It is merely a 'moral injunction' that provides the basis for moral responsibility. However, both consider that it is only a matter of time before the concept achieves customary international law status. The question remains how this normative development is to be achieved. According to Peter Cane, 'moral *responsibility* is often distinguished from legal *liability*' insofar as 'liability refers primarily to formal institutionalised imposts, sanctions and penalties, which are characteristic of law and legal systems but not of morality' (2002: 1). However, he identifies an important role for law in the 'reinforcement of morality'. Thus, he notes that, '[p]roductive and fulfilling social interaction is possible only within an agreed framework of agreed norms and behaviours. When people disagree … about the norms according to which social life ought to be conducted, law provides a mechanism for making and enforcing choices amongst competing views' (2002: 15).

Within legal discourse, responsibility is perceived of, most commonly, as an historic notion of answerability for past events, deriving as it does from the Latin *respondeo*, meaning 'I answer' (Lucas 1993: 5). This is particularly the case within the context of international law. Thus, a leading commentator on the law of state responsibility, Alain Pellet (2010: 6), though describing responsibility as a multi-faceted notion, considers responsibility to be an exclusively historic process. Having described the move away from 'the traditional definition of international responsibility', he concludes, nevertheless, that responsibility in international law 'is now also, and perhaps principally, a mechanism having as its function the condemnation of *breaches* by subjects of international law of their legal obligations and the restoration of international legality, respect for international law being a matter in which the international community as a whole has an interest' (Pellet 2010: 15). In terms of obligations of prevention, it should be noted that article 14(3) of the International Law Commission's 2001 Articles on the Responsibility of States for Internationally Wrongful Acts only provides for responsibility 'when the event occurs' (see Haffner and Buffard 2010).

Cane argues that the focus on 'historic responsibility' in accounts of legal responsibility operates at the expense of 'prospective responsibility' (2002: 31). He notes that 'the prime aim of "the legal system of responsibility" is maximisation of the incidence of responsible (law-compliant) behaviour, not the imposition of liability for irresponsible (law-breaking) behaviour' (Cane 2002: 60). He continues:

> Legal responsibility practices and concepts are concerned not only with imposing penalties and obligations of repair in relation to the past, but also, and primarily, with establishing norms of behaviour – 'responsibilities' – for the future. It is the failure to fulfil such responsibilities that ground historic responsibility. Legal rules and principles distribute responsibilities within society. (Cane 2002: 187–8)

Furthermore, 'historic responsibility finds its role and meaning only in responding to non-fulfilment of prospective responsibilities; and in this sense, it is subsidiary and parasitic' (Cane 2002: 35). Turning this analysis on its head, historic responsibility or legal liability cannot exist without the prior existence of prospective responsibility in the form of legal rules and principles.

As indicated above, the first principle upon which responsibility to protect is based is the notion of sovereignty as responsibility. The development of this notion is most commonly attributed to the work of Francis Deng and his co-investigators at the Brookings Institution. In *Sovereignty as Responsibility: Conflict Management in Africa*, Deng *et al.* assert that 'sovereignty carries with it certain responsibilities for which governments must be held accountable' (1996: 1). This assertion is based upon a detailed analysis of the concept of state sovereignty, particularly during the 'fourth phase' of the development of sovereignty, which consists of 'the contemporary pragmatic attempt at reconciling state sovereignty with responsibility' (Deng *et al.* 1996: 2).

Deng *et al.* conclude that 'responsible sovereignty' is based upon four principles. First, it asserts that the legitimacy of a government derives from acceptance of the responsibility of a state towards its population. Second, 'in many countries in which armed conflict and communal violence cause massive internal displacement ... the validity of sovereignty must be judged by reasonable standards of how much of the population is represented, marginalized or excluded' (Deng *et al.* 1996: 32). Third, responsibility implies the existence of a higher authority capable of holding the supposed sovereign accountable. Fourth, 'the dominant authority or power must assume responsibility that transcends parochialism or exclusive national interests' (Deng *et al.* 1996: 32–3). Ultimately, responsible sovereignty depends upon good governance (Deng *et al.* 1996: 34–6), 'the management of identities based on race, ethnicity, culture, language and religion' (Deng *et al.* 1996: 61–92) and 'economic well-being or welfare of demand-bearing groups in a society' (Deng *et al.* 1996: 93–130).

The idea of sovereignty being conditional and, as a result, removable reflects some of the ideas put forward in the 'failed states' discourse referred to above and can be subjected to some of the same criticisms. However, the primary criticism concerns accountability, which Deng *et al.* identify as being central to the success of the idea of sovereignty as responsibility. It appears that accountability here is more a moral and political accountability than a legal accountability. Deng *et al.* ultimately accept that sovereignty as responsibility is a moral endeavour in that 'international concern and involvement become moral imperatives essentially to fill the vacuum of moral responsibility' (1996: 223). The question of legal responsibility is not addressed.

International law seeks to distribute responsibility within international society primarily through the recognised sources of international law: treaties, customary international law and general principles of law. The body of positive obligations for states (prospective responsibilities) in relation to international human rights law and international humanitarian law is considerable. However, although highlighting the considerable progress that has taken place in relation to the enforcement of international human rights law and international humanitarian law in the past several decades, Deng *et al.* admit that 'mechanisms and procedures of implementation of the wide array of human rights and humanitarian standards remain underdeveloped and grossly inadequate' (1996: 10). Without further developing mechanisms, such as treaty monitoring and reporting bodies, the international community is severely limited in what it can do to ensure that states comply with their legal obligations. Indeed, as will be argued below, even those mechanisms that do function to ensure compliance with international human rights law and international humanitarian law have singularly failed, over decades, to hold Libya and Syria to account even before armed conflict broke out in those two states, thereby raising further questions about the relevance of both the responsibility to protect and the sovereignty as responsibility concepts.

It is worth considering Anne Orford's assertion that 'the responsibility to protect concept has been carefully couched so as not to impose legal duties upon states or international organisations to take particular actions in specific circumstances' (2011: 24). Nonetheless, Orford argues that responsibility to protect 'raises fundamentally important legal questions' not by imposing new duties but rather by conferring powers '"of a public or official nature" and that allocates jurisdiction' (2011: 25). Thus, 'the [responsibility to protect] concept is not primarily concerned with the distribution of jurisdiction and authority between sovereign states, but rather with the distribution of jurisdiction and authority between states and international actors' (Orford 2011: 27). She ultimately concludes that:

> The significant feature of the responsibility to protect concept ... lies not only in its relation to humanitarian intervention, but also in its relation to the practices of international executive action that have been developed to displace humanitarian intervention. The responsibility to protect concept makes those practices intelligible in new ways and seeks to strengthen and consolidate them to ends defined by the international community. It is the resulting form of international executive rule that should be the focus of critical engagement with the responsibility to protect concept. (Orford 2011: 34)

This conclusion is innovative and persuasive. It certainly chimes with the overarching theme in 'Implementing Responsibility'. Nevertheless, with respect to Libya and Syria, the international community's level of engagement with these two states prior to and during the atrocities committed against civilian populations was minimal. In the case of Libya, the Security Council did eventually authorise an intervention under Chapter VII of the UN Charter. Therefore, the overall legality of this intervention cannot be doubted, though some questions remain as to the legality of certain aspects of the intervention. To this extent, the intervention in Libya differs significantly from the *prima facie* illegal humanitarian intervention in Kosovo, which was also undertaken by NATO. However, the Security Council's inability to agree to a resolution even for a non-military intervention in Syria calls into question significant elements of the responsibility to protect concept. It is to a consideration of these two conflicts that this chapter now turns.

The Responsibility to Protect in Libya and Syria

Contrary to the assertion of the International Coalition for the Responsibility to Protect that the intervention in Libya crystallised responsibility to protect as an actionable norm in international law, both Libya and Syria actually represent the failure of responsibility to protect, both as a moral concept and in terms of independent legal authority for international executive action. This conclusion does not immediately call into question the importance and value of the concept itself. Rather, it provides a framework for lessons learned in relation to future crises and for reappraising responsibility to protect in light of two closely linked conflicts that represent the precise type of conflict that responsibility to protect was explicitly meant to resolve.

Lesson 1: The Limitations of Prevention and the Concept of Sovereignty as Responsibility

In an address to the Stanley Foundation on the Responsibility to Protect on 18 January 2012 marking the first decade in the life of responsibility to protect, Secretary-General Ban called for 2012 to be made the 'Year of Prevention'. It is clear from the above analysis that prevention lies at the heart of responsibility to protect. Yet in neither Libya nor Syria was the international community able to prevent widespread attacks on civilian populations. While it is certainly true that at least in the case of Libya the result of Security Council Resolution 1973 was to prevent an overwhelming attack on the city of Benghazi, in the period leading up to the Libyan civil war and, indeed, for many decades before, Libya's engagement with the international community was problematic to say the least. Indeed, it is fair to say that Libya's record of engagement in international relations is replete with examples of illegality and non-conformity with international standards.

Libya's sponsorship of international terrorism is well-documented. This includes the direct funding of such terrorist organisations as the Irish Republican Army and directly engaging in acts of terrorism itself, such as the bombing of a discotheque in Berlin in 1986, which ultimately resulted in a reprisal attack by the United States on targets in Tripoli and Benghazi later that year. Libya was also held responsible for the bombing of Pan Am flight 103 over Lockerbie in 1988. Furthermore, Libya regularly breached key foundational rules of international law, including the Vienna Convention on Diplomatic Relations 1961. Thus, the bullet that killed WPC Yvonne Fletcher in London in April 1984 was fired from inside the self-styled Libyan People's Bureau, which served as the Libyan diplomatic embassy.

Similar problems exist in relation to Syria's historic engagement with international relations. Syria has regularly engaged in armed conflicts with a number of its neighbours, including Israel and Lebanon. It has been directly implicated in a number of terrorist attacks (see Dobson and Payne 1987) and has been accused of sponsoring Hezbollah-led attacks, for example on United States Marines stationed in Beirut in 1983 and at the United States Embassy there the next year.

In terms of their engagement with international human rights law, Libya and Syria are both parties to all of the key international human rights treaties. In relation to international humanitarian law, Libya and Syria are both parties to the 1949 Four Geneva Conventions and their two Additional Protocols from 1977, but they are not parties to the treaties dealing with conventional weapons. Neither state is party to the main refugee treaties. In terms of the enforcement of its international human rights law obligations, particularly in relation to civil and political rights, it should be noted that Libya has submitted four periodic reports to the United Nations Human Rights Committee.[7] In response to Libya's most recent report (of 10 May 2007), the Committee noted a number of concerns, particularly in relation to Libya's failure to implement previous recommendations of the Committee. Syria presented its third periodic report to the Committee in 2004, and similarly, the Committee highlighted a number of concerns. Both states have been the subject of repeated condemnatory reports from such human rights non-governmental organisations as Human Rights Watch and Amnesty International.

Given this level of condemnation, one can question the degree of responsibility that both Libya and Syria have shown in terms of the concept of sovereignty as responsibility. While their membership of various treaty regimes and engagement with relevant treaty-monitoring bodies is to be welcomed, their overt breaching of the obligations contained within these regimes and failure to comply with the recommendations of treaty monitoring bodies is problematic. Yet the level of United Nations engagement in both Libya and Syria was singularly lacking prior to the outbreak of violence in the two states. Within the context of the 'Arab Spring', it might, of course, be argued that the level of popular uprising in these states was unpredictable given the context of the rapid spread of revolution across North

---

7 The work of the Human Rights Committee since 11 September 2001 is covered in detail by Sandy Ghandhi in Chapter 4.

Africa and the Middle East.[8] However, the lack of United Nations engagement with Libya and Syria before these uprisings can, to a considerable degree, be put down to a common belief that both states were gradually developing human rights and were not considered to be 'irresponsible' sovereigns. The concept of responsibility to protect, particularly as envisaged in 'Implementing Responsibility', should have provided an opportunity for the United Nations to become more directly involved in both states, but the opportunity was not taken. If this failure was the result of concerns about being seen to overly criticise the two regimes as such, then the concept of responsibility to protect would have shown itself to be nothing more than a rhetorical and deeply unconvincing statement of purpose. If lessons can be learned about the importance of identifying and acting upon emerging threats to civilian populations, even in the face of strong central governments, then there is hope that the concept can emerge into an 'age of prevention'.

Lesson 2: The Use and Abuse of the Concept of Protection

The apparent strength of the central governments in Libya and Syria raises another concern and points to a second potential lesson to emerge from the international community's engagement with these two states. In her analysis of responsibility to protect, Orford (2011: 109) has welcomed the so-called 'turn to protection', which, she argues, can be used in the name of peace. On the other hand, she is acutely aware of the origins of the appeal to protection, which 'has often emerged in times of civil war or revolution' (Orford 2011: 109). Referencing Thomas Hobbes's *Leviathan*, Orford notes that, '[a]ccording to Hobbes, the lawful authority is recognisable as the one who achieved protection in the broad sense of bringing into being a condition in which the safety of the people can be achieved' (2011: 36).[9] This argument was revived, according to Orford, by Carl Schmitt in the twentieth century, though Schmitt used the idea of protection to justify authoritarian government. Thus, 'Schmitt was concerned with conjuring up the figure of an all-powerful sovereign who could restore order and issue commands that would be obeyed' (Orford 2011: 132). Such a figure would function on the basis of its 'capacity to represent the will of an "indivisibly similar, entire, unified people"' (Orford 2011: 37) against 'enemies both within and beyond the state' (Orford 2011: 130). In the words of Schmitt, '[d]emocracy requires ... first homogeneity and second – if the need arises – elimination or eradication of heterogeneity ... A democracy demonstrates its political power by knowing how to refuse or keep at bay something foreign and an equal that threatens its homogeneity' (1988: 9).

---

8   For further on these revolutions, with particular reference to Egypt, see Chapter 11 by John Strawson.

9   For a full discussion of Hobbes's analysis of protection as the basis of authority during civil or religious war, see Orford 2011: 112–25.

This defence of totalitarianism 'was realised in the fascist states of 20th-century Europe' (Orford 2011: 37).[10]

Therefore, Orford is clearly well aware of the paradox of the 'turn to protection' within the context of the responsibility to protect, which challenges the tyranny of states and insurgents by providing an authority to protect to someone or something. In the case of the responsibility to protect, that something is the rather ephemeral and unidentified 'international community'.[11] The power of the international community is, therefore, to secure protection, ultimately through the potentially tyrannical power to distinguish between friend and enemy. It is at this point that Orford makes clear her primary concern with the concept of responsibility to protect: 'The history of attempts to ground authority upon protection shows that much will depend upon who interprets what protection or [what] the safety of the people means in a particular time and place, and who decides whether and how it will be achieved' (2011: 137). Thus, according to Orford, '[i]t is to that question of limits that those who are institutionalising the responsibility to protect must turn if the authoritarian tendencies inherent in the appeal to de facto protective authority are to be avoided' (2011: 137).

Orford is undoubtedly correct in her analysis, and she certainly presents an optimistic assessment of the potential for responsibility to protect. The irony, of course, is that in seeking to identify and give a normative framework to the concept the way has been opened for states such as Libya and Syria to utilise the turn to protection to justify attacks on civilians. The words of the Syrian representative to the United Nations after the Security Council had failed to pass a resolution condemning Syria on 4 October 2011 are telling:

> the unprecedented, aggressive language used against the leaders of his country underscored what he had previously said – that the country was targeted, not because of any humanitarian concerns, but because of its independent political positions. Syria did need reform, he acknowledged, but the needs of the masses were being misused by the external opposition that was paving the way for external intervention. He said that terrorist groups were responsible for the violence, and maintained that the country was in the process of enacting reforms. (Press Release 2011)

The Syrian representative expressed similar sentiments after the failure to adopt a second draft resolution on 4 February 2012 (see Press Release 2012).

---

10 For a fuller discussion of Schmitt's analysis of 'protection as war,' see Orford 2011: 125–33.

11 On the existence of the 'international community' and the development of the principle of solidarity as a principle of international law, see Wellens 2010.

Lesson 3: The 'Irresponsibility' of the United Nations Security Council?

The most critical problem with applying responsibility to protect within the context of Libya and Syria remains, as it always has, the Security Council. Responsibility to protect ultimately depends upon the ability of the Security Council to live up to its stated responsibilities. The Commission Report, as well as the other developmental documents referred to above and, indeed, also the World Summit Outcome, all mention the Security Council's responsibility to act in cases of genocide, war crimes, ethnic cleansing and crimes against humanity in order to protect civilian populations. Indeed, the Commission Report calls upon the five permanent members to agree not to apply their veto power in cases involving such atrocities (Commission Report 2001: XIII). As noted above, 'Implementing Responsibility' makes clear that 'the five permanent members bear particular responsibility because of the privileges of tenure and the veto power they have been granted under the Charter' and urges them to refrain from employing or even from threatening to employ the veto 'in situations of manifest failure to meet obligations relating to the responsibility to protect, as defined in paragraph 139 of the Summit Outcome, and to reach a mutual understanding to that effect' (Ban 2009: ¶ 61).

Of course, the Security Council did not shirk its responsibilities in relation to Libya. In Resolution 1970, it referred the situation to the International Criminal Court and imposed an arms embargo, travel ban and assets freeze. In Resolution 1973, it ultimately authorised the use of force against Libya specifically for the protection of the civilian population. The language of both resolutions is couched squarely in the language of responsibility to protect and does seem to clearly endorse the concept. For some, the invocation of responsibility to protect in Libya built upon earlier precedents in Côte D'Ivoire, the Democratic Republic of the Congo and Darfur (see Powell 2012: 305), though it is difficult to see how any of these situations could be argued to be great successes for the concept of responsibility to protect.

It is important, therefore, to point out the specifics of the Libyan situation that may limit its usefulness as a precedent for responsibility to protect. First, Libya's position did not garner widespread international support. Second, Libya was not able to call upon the support of any of the permanent members of the Security Council. Finally, its actions had met with widespread condemnation not only from the West but also from the League of Arab States, the African Union and the Organization of the Islamic Conference (as it was then known) (see UNSC Res 1973 (2011): pmbl.). Ultimately, the straw that broke the camel's back as far as the possibility of military intervention was concerned was Muammar Gaddafi's promise to hunt down like dogs and kill everyone in Benghazi. It is unlikely that this level of condemnation of a state will be repeated anytime soon. This is particularly so given the subsequent condemnation by Russia, as well as the Arab League, of NATO's role in the intervention, which, coming after its unlawful intervention in Kosovo and continued operations in Afghanistan, arguably has the potential to provide an excuse for states to turn against responsibility to protect. It would certainly appear that NATO's role in Libya is one of the reasons that the opinions of, at least, Russia and China have galvanised against the military intervention element of responsibility to protect. Taking all of this on board, it is asserted that the authorisation of military intervention in Libya might come to be seen as the exception that proved the rule.

The Security Council's response to Syria would certainly seem to support this assertion. In many ways, the Syrian situation is worse than it was in Libya, given the international community's failure to prevent the attacks on Homs in the same way that the attacks on Benghazi were averted. The situation in the two beleaguered cities was not very different. Yet the repeated failure of the Security Council to secure a resolution on Syria, not least on 4 February 2012, immediately after the bloody siege of Homs in January 2012, represents a return to the geopolitical deadlock that has for so long blighted the Security Council. Even draft resolutions that fell short of authorising military action and, instead, called for the resignation of the Head of State have been vetoed by Russia and China, and as indicated above, it is likely that the conduct of the intervention in Libya had something to do with this, as has the consequence of military intervention in Libya, that is, regime change. Even calls for Syrian President Bashar Assad to step down in favour of his deputy have been classified as regime change by Russia. But regime change is, almost by definition, an inevitable consequence of responsibility to protect in cases where there is a manifest failure by the government of a state to protect its citizens. In spite of Secretary-General Ban's condemnation of the Security Council's failure to adopt the draft resolution of 4 February 2012, it is hard to avoid the conclusion that responsibility to protect has failed at every level in Syria.

For many (see Powell 2012: 309), the Syrian situation can be distinguished from Libya on the basis that one of the precautionary principles of responsibility to protect was not met in relation to the former state, that is, that 'there must be a reasonable chance of success in halting or averting the suffering which has justified the intervention, with the consequences of action not likely to be worse than the consequences of inaction' (Commission Report 2001: XXII). In many ways, this provides the ultimate 'get-out' clause for the permanent members of the Security Council. However, the question remains whether these states need a get-out clause at all. Attempts to modify the composition of the Security Council and, in particular, the permanent membership have led nowhere, and initiatives to impose some form of legal limitation on the use of the veto have, similarly, floundered. In one of the most interesting and compelling discussions of sovereignty and responsibility to protect, Anne Peters argues that the use of the veto might be illegal in certain circumstances. She propounds a teleological interpretation of article 27(3) of the UN Charter, but still, she has to admit that exactly this 'blocking option' was 'part of the deliberate institutional design of the organization' (Peters 2009: 539). No broad interpretations of the UN Charter can, it seems, overcome the clear and legitimate actions of Russia and China in blocking the relevant resolutions. No matter one's moral indignation, the legal outcome is that this has had the effect of blocking any authorised intervention in Syria. Notably, within the context of the broader context of liberal interventionism, the unforeseen consequence of seeking to persuade and cajole the Security Council to act responsibly has the effect of firmly establishing, in all cases where a Security Council resolution authorising military intervention is not obtained, the illegality of any military intervention in the target state. Thus, any assertion that a military intervention in Syria might have been 'unlawful but legitimate' must surely be squashed. To this extent, responsibility to protect may very well represent the final nail in the coffin of 'unauthorised' humanitarian intervention.

Conclusions

In spite of many reservations about the conceptual and practical basis for responsibility to protect, particularly in relation to the (non-)interventions in Libya and Syria, the concept should not be abandoned. Orford's designation of responsibility to protect as a normative grounding for the practices of international executive action is accurate and should give rise to further endeavours by the United Nations to intervene in crisis-torn states. In light of the first lesson highlighted above, such interventions should be early and avoid the use of force. This is perhaps the strongest aspect of responsibility to protect, and the failings of the concept in relation to Libya and Syria should not serve to undermine the use of international executive action as envisaged by Orford. 'Implementing Responsibility' is replete with examples, and challenges, as to how this might be achieved.

In light of the second lesson, it should be stressed that greater care must be taken to more precisely conceptualise and define still further the concepts of both 'responsibility' and 'protection'. None of the official documentation emanating from the United Nations or the Commission adequately does this. It is particularly important that the United Nations, or the international community more broadly, defines 'protection' in a way that sets its legal limits but avoids its authoritarian tendencies and clarifies the concept of 'responsibility'.

Finally, an analysis of the genealogy of liberal interventionism through its various manifestations of failed states discourse, humanitarian intervention and, ultimately, responsibility to protect once again highlights that the current legal framework for the authorisation of military intervention to prevent widespread human rights abuses is controlled, as it always has been, by the Security Council in general and its permanent members in particular. The option still remains through a combination of article 2(7) and Chapter VII of the UN Charter for collective security measures to be taken in the form of authorised interventions. However, the final lesson of Libya and Syria is that such authorised interventions will continue to be the exception rather than the rule, and they are, in themselves, no guarantee of a successful outcome.

References

Annan, K. 2000. Millennium Report of the Secretary-General of the United Nations, UN Doc DPI/2083/Rev.1.

Annan, K. 2005. In Larger Freedom: Towards Development, Security and Human Rights for All, UN Doc A/59/2005.

Ban, K.-M. 2009. Implementing the Responsibility to Protect, UN Doc A/63/677.

Ban, K.-M. 2012. Address to the Stanley Foundation Conference on the Responsibility to Protect, 18 January. Available at: http://www.un.org/apps/news/infocus/sgspeeches/statments_full.asp?statID=1433 [accessed: 16 November 2012].

Boutros-Ghali, B. 1992. An Agenda for Peace: Preventive Diplomacy, Peacemaking and Peacekeeping, UN Doc A/47/277.

Brunée, J. and Toope, S. 2010. *Legitimacy and Legality in International Law*. Cambridge: Cambridge University Press.

Cane, P. 2002. *Responsibility in Law and Morality*. Oxford: Hart.

Cassese, A. 1999. *Ex Injuris Ius Oritur:* Are We Moving Towards International Legitimation of Forcible Humanitarian Countermeasures in the World Community? *European Journal of International Law*, 10(1), 23–30.

Consideration of Reports Submitted by States Parties under Article 40 of the Covenant: Concluding Observations of the Human Rights Committee: Libyan Arab Jamahiriya (2007), UN Doc CCPR/C/LBY/CO/4.

Consideration of Reports Submitted by States Parties under Article 40 of the Covenant: Concluding Observations of the Human Rights Committee: Syrian Arab Republic (2005), UN Doc CCPR/CO/84/SYR.

Consideration of Reports Submitted by States Parties under Article 40 of the Covenant: Fourth Periodic Reports of States Parties Due in 2002: Libyan Arab Jamahiriya (2007), UN Doc CCPR/C/LBY/4.

Consideration of Reports Submitted by States Parties under Article 40 of the Covenant: Third Periodic Report: Syria (2004), UN Doc CCPR/C/SYR/2004/3.

Deng, F.M., Kimaro, S., Lyons, T., Rothchild, D. and Zartman, I.W. 1996. *Sovereignty as Responsibility: Conflict Management in Africa*. Washington, DC: Brookings Institution.

Dobson, C. and Payne, R. 1987. *The Never-Ending War on Terrorism in the 1980s*. New York: Facts on File.

Evans, G. 2006–2007. From Humanitarian Intervention to Responsibility to Protect. *Wisconsin International Law Journal*, 24(3), 703–22.

Fund for Peace. Available at: http://www.fundforpeace.org/global/ [accessed: 13 November 2012].

Haffner, G. and Buffard, I. 2010. Obligations of Prevention and the Precautionary Principle, in *The Law of International Responsibility*, ed. J. Crawford, A. Pellet and S. Olleson. Oxford: Oxford University Press, 521–34.

Helman, G.B. and Ratner, S.R. 1992–93. Saving Failed States. *Foreign Policy*, 89, 3–20.

Independent International Commission on Kosovo 2000. *The Kosovo Report: Conflict, International Response, Lessons Learned*. Oxford: Oxford University Press.

International Coalition for the Responsibility to Protect 2012. The Crisis in Libya. Available at: http://www.responsibilitytoprotect.org/index.php/crises/crisis-in-libya [accessed: 14 November 2012].

International Commission on Intervention and State Sovereignty 2001. The Responsibility to Protect. Available at: http://responsibilitytoprotect.org/ICISS%20Report.pdf [accessed: 14 November 2012].

International Law Commission 2001. *Articles on Responsibility of States for Internationally Wrongful Acts*. Yearbook of the International Law Commission, 2(2), UN Doc A/CN.4/SER.A/2001/Add.1 (Part 2).

Lucas, J.R. 1993. *Responsibility*. Oxford: Clarendon Press.

Orford, A. 2011. *International Authority and the Responsibility to Protect*. Cambridge: Cambridge University Press.

Pellet, A. 2010. The Definition of Responsibility in International Law, in *The Law of International Responsibility*, ed. J. Crawford, A. Pellet and S. Olleson. Oxford: Oxford University Press, 3–16.

Peters, A. 2009. Humanity as the A and Ω of Sovereignty. *European Journal of International Law*, 20(3), 513–44.

Powell, C. 2012. Libya: A Multilateral Constitutional Moment? *American Journal of International Law*, 106(2), 298–315.

Press Release 2011. Security Council Fails to Adopt Draft Resolution Condemning Syria's Crackdown on Anti-Government Protestors, Owing to Veto by Russian Federation, China (4 October), UN Doc SC/10403.

Press Release 2012. Security Council Fails to Adopt Draft Resolution on Syria as Russian Federation, China Veto Text Supporting Arab League's Proposed Peace Plan (4 February), UN Doc SC/10536.

Richardson, H.J. 1996. 'Failed States,' Self-Determination and Preventative Diplomacy: Colonialist Nostalgia and Democratic Expectations. *Temple International and Comparative Law Journal*, 10(1), 1–78.

Schmitt, C. 1988. *The Crisis of Parliamentary Democracy*, trans. E. Kennedy. Boston: MIT Press.

Simma, B. 1999. NATO, the UN and the Use of Force: Legal Aspects. *European Journal of International Law*, 10(1), 1–22.

Stahn, C. 2007. Responsibility to Protect: Political Rhetoric or Emerging Legal Norm? *American Journal of International Law*, 101(1), 99–120.

Thürer, D. 1999. The 'Failed State' in International Law. *International Review of the Red Cross*, 81(836), 731–61.

UNGA Res 60/1 (2005), UN Doc A/RES/60/1 (World Summit Outcome).

UN High-Level Panel on Threats, Challenges and Change 2004. A More Secure World: Our Shared Responsibility, UN Doc A/59/565.

UNSC Draft Resolution [On Cessation of Violence and Implementation of the Six-Point Plan of the Joint Special Envoy of the United Nations and the League of Arab States on the Syrian Arab Republic] (2012), UN Doc S/2012/538.

UNSC Draft Resolution [On Situation of Human Rights in the Syrian Arab Republic] (2011), UN Doc S/2011/612.

UNSC Draft Resolution [On Situation of Human Rights in the Syrian Arab Republic] (2012), UN Doc S/2012/77.

UNSC Res 1674 (2006), UN Doc S/RES/1674.

UNSC Res 1970 (2011), UN Doc S/RES/1970.

UNSC Res 1973 (2011), UN Doc S/RES/1973.

Verdirame, G. 2011. *The UN and Human Rights: Who Guards the Guardians?* Cambridge: Cambridge University Press.

Weiss, T.G. 2007. *Humanitarian Intervention*. Cambridge: Polity Press.

Wellens, K. 2010. Revisiting Solidarity as a (Re-)Emerging Constitutional Principle: Some Further Reflections, in *Solidarity: A Structural Principle of International Law*, ed. R. Wolfrum and C. Kojima. Heidelberg: Springer, 3–14.

Wilde, R. 2003. The Skewed Responsibility Narrative of the 'Failed States' Concept. *ILSA Journal of International and Comparative Law*, 9(2), 425–30.

Wilder Foote, H. (ed.) 1962. *The Servant of Peace: A Selection of the Speeches and Statements of Dag Hammarskjöld*. London: Bodley Head.

Chapter 4

The United Nations Human Rights Committee and Counter-Terrorism Measures of States Parties to the International Covenant on Civil and Political Rights after 11 September 2001

Sandy Ghandhi

The seventy-third session of the United Nations Human Rights Committee opened in Geneva on 15 October 2001 in the long, dark shadow cast by the terrorist attacks of 11 September 2001. The opening address was given by Mary Robinson, the then United Nations High Commissioner for Human Rights. The High Commissioner described the attacks as 'tragic' and 'unprecedented' and stated that the 'consequences are still fresh in our minds'. She commented that 'the attack was aimed at one nation and wounded an entire world; it was an attack on all humanity, and all humanity has a stake in defeating the forces behind it' (UNHCHR 2001). It was an attack, in other words, that required a response from the international community, and from international law.

The High Commissioner welcomed the contribution that the United Nations human rights treaty bodies could make to the 'global strategy to combat international terrorism'. She suggested that the 'treaty bodies contribute to the fight against terrorism as forcefully as they can, within the confines of their respective mandates'. Mary Robinson also welcomed the adoption of General Comment No. 29 on states of emergency. The High Commissioner pointed out that the Comment had been 'well received, not least by our colleagues in the field, where the General Comment will be a very useful reference document', and remarked that '[r]espect for the non-derogable provisions of the Covenant must remain an essential consideration for all States parties – and that includes the measures they adopt, as necessary and timely as they are – to fight terrorism'. Mary Robinson described General Comment No. 29 as being an 'indispensable guide to my Office in developing our own analysis of the present crisis'. Finally, she sought the views of the human rights treaty bodies through a letter to the chairpersons of the treaty bodies soliciting their reflections on 'how the global community may ensure that the right balance is struck between the security and human rights concerns' (UNHCHR 2001).

While it is not possible to detail the Committee's responses to all reports of States parties during the ten years since 11 September, this chapter will focus on the Concluding Observations to the Periodic Reports of the Permanent Members of the United Nations Security Council, specifically the United Kingdom, the United States, France and the Russian Federation, that were the driving force behind the adoption of Security Council Resolution 1373 (2001).[1] The Concluding Observations on major contributors to North Atlantic Treaty Organization (NATO) actions overseas, such as Germany, Belgium and Canada, will also be examined. Further, the Concluding Observations on North African and Middle Eastern States that have witnessed serious terrorist activities or rebellion, civil unrest and transitions to democratic rule, such as Tunisia, Egypt, Libya, Syria and Yemen, will be reviewed and, of necessity, Israel, which is at the forefront of combating international terrorism. Such a detailed analysis of the Committee's Concluding Observations in the security context has not been attempted before in the existing literature. The chapter will conclude with some final comments.

The Concluding Observations of the United Nations Human Rights Committee on the Reports of States Parties

The Committee was established in 1976 as the principal international organ of implementation of the 1966 International Covenant on Civil and Political Rights (art. 28).

The Covenant and the (First) Optional Protocol 1966 provide for various distinct procedures as measures of implementation. In each of these procedures, the Committee plays a central role. First, the Committee's function is to study the reports submitted by States parties in accordance with article 40 of the Covenant and then to deliver its Concluding Observations.[2] Second, the Committee receives and considers individual communications submitted under the (First) Optional Protocol and then delivers its Views. Third, the Committee may make General Comments. Each of these procedures has played its part in the response of the Committee to the events of 11 September.

---

1   China signed the Covenant on 5 October 1998 but, despite suggestions to the contrary, has as yet shown no inclination to ratify it. For the single pertinent issue that has arisen in respect of the Hong Kong Special Administrative Region, see Report of the Human Rights Committee: Volume 1 (2006): 50.

2   Michael O'Flaherty (2006), himself a member of the Committee, provides the most detailed analysis of Concluding Observations. The inescapable conclusion from his examination of the contours of Concluding Observations is that they are not, *stricto sensu*, binding in any formal legal sense, though they do possess some unspecified authority for States parties where violations of the Covenant are pronounced upon or where provisions of the Covenant are interpreted.

The Security Council, acting under Chapter VII of the UN Charter, adopted Resolution 1373 on 28 September 2001, which introduced wide-ranging prescriptions designed to reduce and eliminate all facets of terrorism, such as financing, political support and safe havens or sanctuaries. All Member States were given ninety days to report on their implementation of the resolution. In all of its Concluding Observations since then, the Committee has had the opportunity to consider the anti-terrorism measures adopted by States parties pursuant to this resolution. More generally, it has also had the opportunity to consider the derogation provisions under article 4 of the Covenant during states of emergency, the use of torture and cruel, inhuman or degrading treatment or punishment of detainees by law enforcement officials (which can also occur outside the security context),[3] renditions, the extra-territorial application of the Covenant, *refoulement* to states where the returnee would face treatment contrary to article 7 of the Covenant,[4] targeted killings of suspected terrorists and reparation for human rights violations.[5] These are certainly the themes that permeate all of the pronouncements of the Committee.

Permanent Members of the Security Council

In its consideration of the United Kingdom's Fifth Periodic Report, the Committee noted with concern that the State party, in seeking to give effect to its obligations under Resolution 1373, was considering the adoption of legislative measures which might have 'potentially very far-reaching effects on rights guaranteed under the Covenant' and which the State party had conceded would require derogations from human rights obligations. The Committee warned that '[t]he State party should ensure that any measures it undertakes in this regard are in full compliance with the provisions of the Covenant, including, where applicable, the provisions on derogation contained in article 4 of the Covenant' (Report of the Human Rights Committee: Volume I (2002): 37).

Of course, as is well-known, the United Kingdom subsequently notified other States parties to the Covenant through the Secretary-General of the United Nations on 18 December 2001 that it reserved the right to derogate from its obligations under article 9 of the Covenant by virtue of the extended powers of arrest and detention that it had taken under the Anti-Terrorism, Crime and Security Act 2001 (ATCSA). This legislation was adopted by the United Kingdom in response to the events of 11 September and was stated to be strictly required by the exigencies of the situation as required by the Covenant. It was a temporary measure, which came into force for an initial period of fifteen months, which would then expire unless

---

3 On the *jus cogens* nature of the prohibition of torture, see *Prosecutor* v. *Furundžija* (Judgment), IT-95-17/1-T, T Ch (1998): 58–61. For an overview of this prohibition's 'direction of travel' since 11 September, see Chapter 1 in this volume by Malcolm D. Evans.

4 On *non-refoulement* and *jus cogens*, see Allain 2001.

5 On reparations for human rights violations, see UNGA Res 60/147 (2005).

renewed by parliament. This legislation was thereafter regularly renewed until replaced by subsequent legislation. The notice of derogation stated that where British authorities wished to remove or deport a suspected terrorist on national security grounds, continued detention might not always be compatible with article 9 of the Covenant. The government had considered carefully whether the measure to detain for an extended period might infringe the stipulations of article 9 and decided to avail itself of the right of derogation under article 4(1).

Unfortunately for the government, in 2004 in *A and Others v. Secretary of State for the Home Department*,[6] the Appellate Committee of the House of Lords declared that Section 23, the offending provision of Part IV of the ATCSA, was incompatible with the European Convention on Human Rights because it was disproportionate and also discriminatory given that it applied only to foreign suspected terrorists. This eventually prompted the government to allow the provisions in ATCSA to expire on 14 March 2005, when the Prevention of Terrorism Act 2005 (PTA) came into force introducing the derogating and non-derogating Control Order regime to replace the detention without trial provisions under Part IV of the ATCSA.

Many of the issues raised with the United Kingdom in respect of its previous report to the Committee arose again in its Sixth Periodic Report. The Committee was critical of the United Kingdom's established policy of concluding Memorandums of Understanding on Deportations with Assurances on the ground that they did not always in practice ensure that the affected individuals would not be subject to treatment contrary to article 7 of the Covenant. The Committee advised that the United Kingdom should ensure that all individuals, including persons suspected of terrorism, were not returned to other states if there were substantial reasons for fearing that they would be subject to torture or to cruel, inhuman or degrading treatment or punishment. The United Kingdom was asked to recognise that the more systematic the practice of torture and ill treatment was, the less likely it would be that a real risk of the offending treatment could be avoided by diplomatic assurances, however stringent any agreed follow-up procedure might be. Furthermore, the United Kingdom was requested to use the utmost care in the conclusion of such agreements and adopt clear and transparent procedures allowing adequate judicial review before individuals were deported in addition to effective post-return monitoring mechanisms (see Report of the Human Rights Committee: Volume I (2008): 66–7).

The second issue concerned the policy of sending, or assisting in the sending of, suspected terrorists to third states (rendition). The Committee was rather concerned that the State party had permitted the use of British Indian Ocean Territory as a transit point on at least two occasions for rendition flights of persons to states where they were at risk of treatment contrary to article 7 of the Covenant. The Committee recommended that the United Kingdom investigate such alleged occurrences and implement an inspection system to ensure that

---

6   *A and Others* v. *Secretary of State for the Home Department* [2004] UKHL 56.

its airports were not used for such purposes (see Report of the Human Rights Committee: Volume I (2008): 67).

The Committee again criticised the United Kingdom for its limited acceptance of the extra-territorial ambit of the Covenant, inasmuch as the United Kingdom recognised that its obligations under the Covenant applied only to persons taken into custody by the armed forces and held in British-run military detention facilities outside the United Kingdom and then only exceptionally. There was also criticism of the United Kingdom's failure to provide details of prosecutions, sentences and reparation granted to victims of torture or other forms of mistreatment in detention abroad. The Committee commented that the United Kingdom should state clearly that the Covenant applied to all individuals who are subject to its jurisdiction or control. The Committee detailed that all allegations concerning suspicious deaths, torture or mistreatment inflicted by its personnel (including commanders) in detention facilities in Afghanistan and Iraq should be fully investigated, prosecutions launched and punishment imposed; everything should be done to prevent such occurrences, including proper training and guidance to all ranks (see Report of the Human Rights Committee: Volume I (2008): 67).

The final issue of concern in respect of this chapter was the Committee's criticism of the Control Order regime introduced by the PTA, which imposed a wide range of restrictions including sixteen hour curfews on individuals suspected of being involved in terrorism but who had not been charged with any criminal offence. The Committee also criticised the fact that the court could consider secret material in closed session. The Committee recommended that the United Kingdom review the Control Order system to ensure its compliance with the provisions of the Covenant (see Report of the Human Rights Committee: Volume I (2008): 68).[7]

It is hardly surprising that the consolidated Second and Third Periodic Reports of the United States, which were delivered seven years late, produced much detailed critical appraisal by the Committee. As a general preliminary matter, the Committee regretted that the State party had not integrated into its Report information on the implementation of the Covenant with respect to individuals under its jurisdiction and *outside its territory*, but had only provided this information 'out of courtesy' (Report of the Human Rights Committee: Volume I (2006): 57).

Accordingly, the Committee addressed the issue of the extra-territorial reach of the Covenant at the outset of its Principal Subjects of Concern and Recommendations, while linking it with two other elements of critique. The Committee noted with concern the restrictive interpretation made by the State party of its obligations under the Covenant, in particular as a result of (1) its position that the Covenant did not apply with respect to individuals under its jurisdiction but outside its territory, nor in time of war, despite the contrary opinion and established jurisprudence of the Committee and the International Court of Justice; (2) its

---

7   As an example, the Committee recommended that the judicial review procedure should be conducted on the basis of equality of arms and access to the evidence on which the Control Order was made by the controlee and counsel of his or her own choosing.

failure to take fully into consideration its obligation under the Covenant not only to respect, but also to ensure respect for, the rights prescribed by the Covenant; and (3) its restrictive approach to some substantive provisions of the Covenant, which was not in conformity with the interpretation made by the Committee before and after the State party's ratification of the Covenant. Generally, the Committee suggested that the State party should review its approach and interpret the Covenant in good faith, in accordance with the ordinary meaning to be given to its terms in their context, including subsequent practice, and in the light of its object and purpose. In particular, the United States was asked to (1) acknowledge the applicability of the Covenant to individuals within its jurisdiction but outside its territory, as well as its applicability in time of war; (2) take positive steps, where necessary, to ensure the full implementation of rights enshrined in the Covenant; and (3) consider in good faith the interpretation of the Covenant provided by the Committee pursuant to its mandate (see Report of the Human Rights Committee: Volume I (2006): 58).

The Committee then addressed the issue of anti-terrorism legislation. The Committee was concerned about the potentially overbroad reach of the definitions of terrorism under domestic law, in particular under 8 USC paragraph 1182(a)(3) (B) and Executive Order 13224, which seemed to extend to conduct, for example in the context of political dissent, which, though unlawful, should not be understood as constituting terrorism. The Committee recommended that the State party should ensure that its anti-terrorism measures fully conformed to the Covenant and that the legislation adopted in this context was limited to crimes that would justify being assimilated with terrorism and the grave consequences associated with it (see Report of the Human Rights Committee: Volume I (2006): 58).

The Committee then turned its attention to clandestine interrogation facilities that the State party had established. The Committee was seriously concerned about the credible and uncontested information that the State party had engaged in the practice of detaining persons secretly and in secret places for months and years on end, without keeping the International Committee of the Red Cross informed. The Committee pointed out that in such cases the rights of the families of the detainees were also being violated. Furthermore, the Committee was concerned that even when such persons may have had their detention acknowledged, they had still been held incommunicado for months or even years, a practice that violated articles 7 and 9 of the Covenant. Indeed, the Committee was critical of the fact that persons were detained in places where they could not benefit from the protection of either domestic or international law or where that protection was substantially curtailed, a practice that could not be justified by the stated need to remove them from the battlefield. The Committee recommended that the United States immediately cease its practice of secret detention and close all secret detention facilities and grant the International Committee of the Red Cross prompt access to any person detained in connection with an armed conflict. In general, the Committee stated that the United States should ensure that all detainees, regardless of their place of detention, always benefited from the full protection of the law (see Report of the Human Rights Committee: Volume I (2006): 58–9).

The Committee then turned its attention to the interrogation techniques deployed by the United States in its self-styled 'war on terror'. The Committee turned its fire on the use of enhanced interrogation techniques, such as prolonged stress positions and isolation, sensory deprivation, hooding, exposure to heat and cold, sleep and dietary adjustments, twenty hour interrogations, the removal of clothing and deprivation of all comfort and religious items, forced grooming and exploitation of detainees' individual phobias. The Committee made no explicit reference to water-boarding. The Committee welcomed the assurance that, according to the Detainee Treatment Act 2005, such interrogation techniques were prohibited by the present Army Field Manual on Intelligence Interrogation but was perturbed that (1) the State party refused to acknowledge that such techniques, several of which were allegedly applied, either individually or in combination, over a protracted period of time, violated the prohibition enshrined by article 7 of the Covenant; (2) no sentence had been imposed on any member of the armed forces whatsoever or other agent of the government for using harsh interrogation techniques that had been approved; (3) these interrogation techniques might still be authorised or used by other agencies, including intelligence agencies and private contractors; and (4) the State party had provided no information on the fact that oversight systems of such agencies had been established to ensure compliance with article 7 of the Covenant. The Committee recommended that (1) any revision of the Army Field Manual only provide for interrogation techniques in conformity with the international understanding of the scope of the prohibition under article 7 of the Covenant; (2) the United States should ensure that the current interrogation techniques or any revised techniques were binding on all agencies of the United States government and any others acting on its behalf; (3) the State party should ensure that there were effective means to deal with abuses committed by agencies operating outside the military structure and that appropriate sanctions be imposed on its personnel who used or approved the use of the now prohibited techniques; (4) the United States should ensure that the right of reparation of the victims of such practices be accepted; and (5) it should inform the Committee of any amendments to the interrogation techniques approved by the Army Field Manual (see Report of the Human Rights Committee: Volume I (2006): 59).

The Committee then voiced serious concerns about the investigations into torture and ill-treatment conducted by the United States. In particular, the Committee was very concerned about shortcomings concerning the independence, impartiality and effectiveness of investigations into allegations of torture and mistreatment inflicted by American military and non-military personnel or contract employees in detention facilities in Guantanámo Bay, Cuba, Afghanistan, Iraq and other overseas locations and also about alleged cases of suspicious deaths in custody in these locations. The Committee criticised the lack of information regarding details of prosecutions, sentences passed, which appeared excessively light for offences of such gravity, and reparation granted to victims. The Committee recommended (1) prompt and independent investigations into all allegations concerning suspicious deaths, torture and cruel, inhuman or degrading treatment or punishment inflicted by its personnel, including commanders, and contract employees at detention facilities in Guantánamo Bay, Afghanistan, Iraq and other overseas locations; (2) that those responsible should be prosecuted and punished in accordance with the gravity of the crime; (3) that all necessary measures should be taken to prevent the recurrence of such behaviour by providing adequate training and clear guidance to all actors on the parameters of articles 7 and 10 of the Covenant; and (4) that the United States notify the Committee about measures taken to ensure that victims received reparation (see Report of the Human Rights Committee: Volume I (2006): 59–60).

The Committee gave separate treatment to a further issue in relation to detainee treatment. The Committee objected to section 1005(e) of the Detainee Treatment Act, which barred detainees in Guantánamo Bay from seeking judicial review of their treatment or poor conditions of detention. The Committee recommended that the relevant section of the legislation be amended to allow such detainees to seek review before a court (see Report of the Human Rights Committee: Volume I (2006): 60).

The Committee then proceeded to deal with a raft of issues in relation to the parameters of article 7 of the Covenant. The Committee deplored the State party's restrictive interpretation of article 7 of the Covenant, according to which (1) the obligation not to subject anyone to treatment in breach of article 7 did not extend to an obligation not to expose them to such treatment by means of transfer, rendition, extradition, expulsion or *refoulement*; (2) in any case, it was not under any obligation not to deport an individual who might undergo cruel, inhuman or degrading treatment or punishment short of torture, as the State party understood the term; and (3) it was not under any international obligation to respect a *non-refoulement* rule in relation to persons it detained outside its territory. In addition, the Committee was concerned that in practice the State party appeared to have adopted a policy of rendition of suspected terrorists from American territory or territories of other states for the purposes of detention and interrogation without the appropriate safeguards to prevent treatment in breach of article 7 of the Covenant. This was rendered more serious by the fact that there were numerous well-publicised and documented cases of persons who had been sent to third states in this way and who had indeed been subjected to treatment that grossly violated article 7 of the Covenant. The Committee's concern was heightened further by the successful plea of state secrecy in cases where the victims of these practices had sought a remedy before the State party's courts.[8]

The Committee declared that the State party should review its position in the light of General Comments Nos. 20 (1992) on Article 7 and 31 (2004) on the Nature of the General Legal Obligation Imposed on States parties. In particular, the Committee urged the United States to take all necessary steps to ensure that

---

8   See *Arar* v. *Ashcroft* [2006] F. Supp. 2d., 2006 WL 346439 (E.D.N.Y.); *El-Masri* v. *Tenet* [2006] 437 F. Supp. 2d. 530 (E.D.Va.).

individuals, including those whom it had detained outside its own territory, were not returned to other states by way, *inter alia*, of their transfer, rendition, extradition, expulsion or *refoulement* if there were substantial grounds for believing that they would be in danger of being subjected to treatment contrary to article 7 of the Covenant. The State party was also asked to conduct thorough and independent investigations into allegations that persons had been sent to third states where they had suffered treatment contrary to article 7 of the Covenant, modify its legislation and policies to ensure that such situations would never be repeated and afford an appropriate remedy to victims. Furthermore, the Committee recommended that the United States exercise the utmost care in the use of diplomatic assurances and adopt clear and transparent procedures with adequate judicial mechanisms for review before any individuals were deported, as well as effective mechanisms to monitor the fate of those removed, bearing in mind that the more systematic the use of torture was, the less likely it would be that a real risk of such treatment could be avoided by monitoring procedures, however stringent (see Report of the Human Rights Committee: Volume I (2006): 60–61).

The next issue dealt with by the Committee concerned the procedure before Combatant Status Review Tribunals and Administrative Review Boards, which were mandated, respectively, to determine and review the status of detainees following the United States Supreme Court's ruling in 2004 in *Rasul v. Bush*.[9] The Committee was concerned that these bodies might not offer adequate safeguards of due process, in particular due to (1) their lack of independence from the executive branch and the military; (2) restrictions on the right of detainees to have access to all proceedings and evidence; (3) inevitable difficulties in summoning witnesses; and (4) the possibility given to Combatant Status Review Tribunals and Administrative Review Boards to weigh evidence obtained through coercion for its probative value. The Committee expressed its regret that the procedures for reviewing detentions in other locations, such as Iraq and Afghanistan, provided even fewer guarantees. The Committee recommended that the United States should ensure that persons detained in Guantánamo Bay were entitled to proceedings before a court to decide without delay the lawfulness of their detention, or to order their release, in accordance with the terms of article 9(4) of the Covenant. Due process, independence of the reviewing courts from the executive branch and the military, and access of detainees to counsel of their choice and to all proceedings and evidence should be guaranteed (see Report of the Human Rights Committee: Volume I (2006): 61).

The penultimate issue of concern for the Committee was the post-11 September long periods of detention of many non-American citizens suspected to have committed terrorism-related offences pursuant to immigration laws with fewer guarantees than in the context of ordinary criminal proceedings or on the basis of

---

9   *Rasul v. Bush* [2004] 542 US 466.

the Material Witness Statute only.[10] The Committee was also concerned with the compatibility of the Material Witness Statute with the Covenant since it could be applied to both upcoming trials and to investigations or proposed investigations. The Committee requested the United States to review its practice with a view to ensuring that the Material Witness Statute and immigration laws were not used to detain persons suspected of terrorism or any other criminal offences with fewer guarantees than in ordinary criminal proceedings. Those improperly detained should receive appropriate compensation (see Report of the Human Rights Committee: Volume I (2006): 61–2).

Finally, the Committee acknowledged the United States Supreme Court's 2006 decision in *Hamdan v. Rumsfeld*,[11] according to which Guantanámo Bay detainees were to be judged by a regularly constituted court affording all the judicial guarantees required by common article 3 of the Four Geneva Conventions of 1949, but noted that it remained to be fulfilled. The Committee requested information on the implementation of the decision (see Report of the Human Rights Committee: Volume I (2006): 62).[12]

It should be noted that in its Fourth Periodic Report to the Committee of 30 December 2011, the United States provided detailed responses to the concerns expressed by the Committee in its Concluding Observations on its Second and Third Periodic Reports (see Consideration of Reports (2012)). These will be discussed by the Committee at the oral examination of the report at Geneva in October 2013.

The main issue in the case of France's Fourth Periodic Report involved the removal of persons to states where they faced a real risk of treatment contrary to article 7 of the Covenant. Although France stated that it sought to honour the rule of *non-refoulement* in such circumstances, the Committee was concerned at reported incidences of such returns occurring, including allegations that foreign persons were often not properly informed of their rights, including the right to seek asylum, and lacked access to legal assistance. Issues about a number of other procedural safeguards were raised by the Committee, for example asylum applications to be lodged within five days in the French language without translation assistance in some cases. The Committee observed that France needed to adopt a fair process that excluded the return of persons to states where they

---

10   The Material Witness Statute (18 USC 3144) provides for the arrest and detention of *witnesses* only when absolutely necessary and for the limited purpose of securing their testimony when material to a criminal proceeding. The statute does not provide for the detention of persons *suspected* of criminal conduct, but against whom there is insufficient proof to meet constitutional requirements for arresting or charging as criminal suspects (according to the Fourth Amendment to the United States Constitution) in order to conduct further investigation.

11   *Hamdan* v. *Rumsfeld* [2006] 126 S. Ct. 2749.

12   Subsequent to the Supreme Court decision, Congress passed the United States Military Commission Act 2006, *inter alia*, embracing the application of common article 3 to the conflict between the United States and Al Qaeda.

might face violations of article 7 of the Covenant. France was also advised to recognise that the more systematic the practice of torture, the less likely it would be that such practices could be avoided by the extraction of diplomatic assurances, however stringent the follow-up procedure. Accordingly, the utmost care needed to be used when accepting such assurances and embracing procedures allowing review by competent judicial mechanisms before deportation, in addition to the adoption of post-return safeguards (see Report of the Human Rights Committee: Volume I (2008): 76).

Leaving aside Chechnya, in respect of Russia's Fifth Periodic Report the Committee concerned itself with two main issues within the scope of this chapter. First, the Committee was concerned at the reported occurrence of torture or ill-treatment, particularly during informal interrogations at police stations, during which the presence of a lawyer was not mandatory. In this regard, the Committee recommended that the State party should ensure that members of law enforcement agencies who had acted contrary to article 7 of the Covenant were prosecuted and that the charges brought corresponded to the gravity of the crime (see Report of the Human Rights Committee: Volume I (2004): 22). Second, the Committee was concerned that the proposed amendments to the Law on Combating Terrorism (and, incidentally, the Law on Mass Media) that the State Duma had adopted in 2001 in the aftermath of the events of 11 September were incompatible with the requirements of article 19 of the Covenant. The Committee noted that the President had vetoed the amendments in November 2002. The Committee recommended that these amendments, which had been put on hold in November 2002 but were due to be debated again by a Parliamentary Commission, needed to conform to the Russian obligations under the Covenant (see Report of the Human Rights Committee: Volume I (2004): 24).

In Russia's Sixth Periodic Report, once again leaving aside Chechnya, there were two main matters of concern to the Committee. First, the Committee was concerned about several aspects of the 2006 Federal Law on Counteracting Terrorism, which imposed a wide range of restrictions on Covenant rights that, in the Committee's view, were comparable to those permitted only under a state of emergency under the State party's Constitution and the State of Emergency Law. In particular, the Committee drew attention to (1) the lack of precision in the very broad definitions of terrorism and terrorist activity; (2) the fact that the counter-terrorism regime that the 2006 law had established was not subject to the requirement of justification on grounds of necessity or proportionality, or to procedural safeguards or judicial or parliamentary oversight; and (3) the lack of limitations in the federal law on derogations that could be made from the provisions of the Covenant and the fact that it did not take into account the obligations imposed by article 4 of the Covenant. The Committee also regretted that the federal law lacked a provision explicitly outlining the obligation of the authorities to respect and protect human rights in the context of anti-terrorist operations. Accordingly, the Committee proposed that the State party should review the relevant provisions of the 2006 Federal Law on Counteracting Terrorism to bring it into compliance with article 4 of the Covenant, taking into account the Committee's General Comments Nos. 29 and 31. In particular, the State party should (1) adopt a narrower definition of crimes of terrorism limited to offences that could be justifiably equated with terrorism and its serious consequences and ensure that the procedural guarantees under the Covenant were complied with; (2) consider establishing an independent mechanism to review and report on laws related to terrorism; and (3) provide the Committee with information on which Covenant rights could be suspended during an anti-terrorist operation and under what conditions (see Report of the Human Rights Committee: Volume I (2010): 35–6).

Another matter of concern earlier raised in the Concluding Observations to the previous report was the continuing substantiated reports of acts of torture and mistreatment committed by law enforcement personnel and other state agents. The Committee recommended that (1) the Criminal Code be amended to criminalise torture; (2) while welcoming the adoption of the 2008 Federal Law on the Public Control of Monitoring of Human Rights in Places of Detention, the State party take all necessary measures for a fully functioning independent human rights monitoring body to review all places of detention and cases of alleged abuse of persons while in custody, ensuring regular, independent, unannounced and unrestricted visits to places of detention, and initiate criminal and disciplinary proceedings against all those found responsible; and (3) the State party should ensure that all cases of alleged torture and mistreatment by law enforcement personnel be fully and promptly investigated by an authority independent of ordinary prosecutorial and police organs, that those found guilty be punished by sentences commensurate with the gravity of the offences and that compensation be paid to victims or their families (see Report of the Human Rights Committee: Volume I (2010): 38–9).

Member States of the North Atlantic Treaty Organization

The first issue of concern to the Committee in Germany's Fifth Periodic Report was the extra-territorial application of the Covenant. The Committee was concerned that Germany had not yet taken a position regarding the applicability of the Covenant to persons subject to its jurisdiction in situations where German troops or police forces operate abroad, in particular within the context of peace missions. The Committee reaffirmed its view that the application of international humanitarian law does not preclude the accountability of States parties under article 2(1) of the Covenant for the actions of its agents outside of their own territories. The Committee requested that Germany clarify its position and provide relevant training in this regard for members of its security forces deployed internationally (see Report of the Human Rights Committee: Volume I (2004): 40–41). Germany responded to the Committee's concern as follows:

> Pursuant to article 2, paragraph 1, Germany ensures the rights recognized in the Covenant to all individuals within its territory and subject to its jurisdiction. Wherever its police or armed services are deployed abroad, in particular when

participating in peace missions, Germany ensures to all persons that they will be granted the rights recognized in the Covenant, insofar as they are subject to its jurisdiction. Germany's international duties and obligations, in particular those assumed in fulfilment of obligations stemming from the Charter of the United Nations, remain unaffected. The training it gives its security forces for international missions includes tailor-made instruction in the provisions of the Covenant. (Comments by the Government of Germany to the Concluding Observations (2005): 3)

The second issue of concern to the Committee in Germany's Fifth Periodic Report was connected with the adoption of anti-terrorism legislation. While recognising Germany's firm stance in respecting human rights within the context of the anti-terrorism legislation that it had adopted after 11 September, the Committee expressed concern about the effect that those measures might have on certain persons of foreign extraction because of an atmosphere of latent suspicion towards them. The Committee requested that Germany should (1) ensure that anti-terrorism measures were in full conformity with the Covenant; (2) ensure that concern over terrorism was not a source of abuse, in particular for persons of foreign extraction, including asylum seekers; and (3) undertake an educational campaign through the media to protect persons of foreign extraction, in particular Arabs and Muslims, from stereotypes associating them with terrorism, extremism and fanaticism (see Report of the Human Rights Committee: Volume I (2004): 42–3).

The Committee's first substantial issue of concern in Belgium's Fourth Periodic Report was the extra-territorial application of the Covenant. The Committee expressed its concern at the fact that Belgium was unable to confirm, in the absence of a finding by an international body, that it had failed to honour its obligations or that the Covenant applied automatically when it exercised power or effective control over a person outside its territory regardless of the circumstances in which such power or effective control was obtained, such as forces constituting a national contingent assigned to an international peace-keeping or peace-enforcement action. The Committee recommended that Belgium should respect the safeguards established by the Covenant, not only in its own territory, but also when it exercises its jurisdiction abroad, as, for example, in the case of peace-keeping missions or NATO military missions, and should train the members of such missions appropriately (see Report of the Human Rights Committee: Volume I (2004): 57).

The Committee was also concerned that Belgium's Act of 19 December 2003 on terrorist offences gave a definition of terrorism that, in referring to the degree of severity of offences and the perpetrators' intended purpose, did not entirely satisfy the principle of offences and penalties established by law in accordance with article 15 of the Covenant. The Committee recommended that Belgium should produce a more precise definition of terrorist offences (see Report of the Human Rights Committee: Volume I (2004): 60).

Somewhat surprisingly perhaps, the Committee was seriously concerned with several aspects of Canada's Fifth Periodic Report. The Committee criticised the wide definition of terrorism in the state's Anti-Terrorism Act and suggested that Canada needed to adopt a more precise definition of terrorist offences to ensure that individuals would not be targeted on the basis of political, religious or ideological convictions in connection with measures of prevention, investigation or detention (see Report of the Human Rights Committee: Volume I (2006): 22).

The Committee was also concerned about amendments to the Canada Evidence Act introduced by Section 38 of the Anti-Terrorism Act. These related to the non-disclosure of information in connection with or during the course of proceedings, including criminal proceedings, which would cause injury to international relations, national defence or national security. The Committee considered that such provisions did not fully conform to the requirements of article 14 of the Covenant. The Committee advised Canada to review its legislation to guarantee the right of all persons to a fair trial and, in particular, to ensure that individuals would not be condemned on the basis of evidence to which they or their legal representatives did not have full access. The Committee reminded Canada that in the light of General Comment No. 29, it should not invoke exceptional circumstances as a justification for deviating from fundamental principles of fair trial (see Report of the Human Rights Committee: Volume I (2006): 22).

The Committee was substantially concerned by the State party's policy that, in exceptional circumstances, persons could be deported to a state where they would face the risk of torture or cruel, inhuman or degrading treatment in violation of article 7 of the Covenant. Undoubtedly, the Committee here was thinking of cases such as *Ahani* (2004), in which Canada had done just this in defiance of a Rule 92 request (interim measures of relief). The Committee recommended that Canada should recognise the absolute and non-derogable nature of the prohibition on torture. The Committee remarked that such treatment could never be justified on the basis of a balance between society's interests and the individual's rights under article 7 of the Covenant. No person, without exception, even those suspected of presenting a real danger to national security and even during a state of emergency, could be deported to a state where he or she would run the risk of being subjected to torture. The Committee advised that this principle must be enacted into Canadian law (see Report of the Human Rights Committee: Volume I (2006): 23).

Closely related to this issue was the Committee's concern, which Canada firmly denied during the dialogue, that it may have colluded with foreign agencies known to resort to torture with the aim of extracting information. The Committee noted that a public enquiry was under way regarding the role of Canadian officials in *Arar v. Ashcroft*.[13] The Committee regretted that insufficient information had been furnished as to whether similar cases were the subject of that or any other inquiry. The Committee stated that a public and independent inquiry needed to review all such cases and determine whether Canadian officials had directly or

---

13   In this case, a Canadian citizen who had been arrested in the United States and deported to Syria was reportedly tortured.

indirectly facilitated or tolerated any such arrests and detentions (see Report of the Human Rights Committee: Volume I (2006): 23).

North African and Middle Eastern States

It is interesting to read the Committee's Observations on Tunisia's Fifth Periodic Report in the light of its largely peaceful transition from authoritarian government to democratic rule in the spring of 2011.

The Committee expressed its concern that despite the conviction of certain public officials for torture and inhuman and degrading treatment or punishment, and the fact that reparations had been made to victims, there were serious and substantiated reports that torture and other forms of ill-treatment were still being committed by the State party, that judges were unwilling to register related complaints and that some superiors responsible for the conduct of their agents were not being investigated or prosecuted. In now fairly standard terms, the Committee insisted that all such allegations be investigated by an independent authority and that perpetrators, including their superiors, be brought to justice and that victims receive reparation (see Report of the Human Rights Committee: Volume I (2008): 47).

The Committee noted that although Article 101 bis of the Tunisian Criminal Code prohibited torture, confessions obtained through torture were not excluded in evidence at trial and were not expressly prohibited in the legislation. The Committee recommended that the use of confessions obtained by torture be completely prohibited and that the burden of proof should not rest on the victim to prove that he or she had been tortured (see Report of the Human Rights Committee: Volume I (2008): 47).

In addition, the Committee was concerned at the lack of precision in the particularly broad definition of terrorist acts in the Terrorism and Money-Laundering Act (Act No. 2003-75). The Committee insisted that all anti-terrorism provisions should conform to Covenant norms and that the definition of terrorist acts should not curtail the legitimate expression of rights contained in the Covenant (see Report of the Human Rights Committee: Volume I (2008): 48).

Given the largely peaceful revolution overthrowing President Hosni Mubarak in 2011, the attention given to various matters in the Third and Fourth Periodic Reports of Egypt by the Committee and its Concluding Observations is clearly of interest. The Committee expressed considerable concern that the state of emergency that Egypt had proclaimed in 1981 was still in effect at the date that it examined the report, leaving the state in a semi-permanent state of emergency for over twenty years. The Committee suggested that the State party should consider lifting the state of emergency.

The Committee also expressed serious disquiet about the persistence of torture and cruel, inhuman or degrading treatment at the hands of law enforcement personnel, in particular the security services, whose recourse to such practices appeared to display a systematic pattern. There was equal disquiet expressed at a general lack of investigation of such practices, as well as the lack of an independent investigatory body, punishment of those responsible and reparation for victims. The Committee recommended that all violations of articles 6 and 7 of the Covenant be investigated and that appropriate action be taken against those responsible and reparation be made to victims; it also suggested the creation of an independent body to investigate such complaints (see Report of the Human Rights Committee: Volume I (2003): 32–3).

In relation specifically to anti-terrorism measures, the Committee remarked that (1) the effect of the very broad and general definition given to terrorism in Act No. 97 of 1992 was such as to increase the number of offences attracting the death penalty, which clearly ran counter to the requirements of article 6(2) of the Covenant; (2) it was concerned that the military courts and state security courts had jurisdiction to try civilians accused of terrorism offences, despite the fact that there were neither guarantees of judicial independence nor rights of appeal to a higher tribunal; and (3) Egyptian nationals suspected or convicted of terrorist offences abroad and expelled to Egypt had been subjected to ill-treatment, particularly by being held incommunicado for periods of over one month (see Report of the Human Rights Committee: Volume I (2003): 34).

Given the civil war in Libya during 2011, leading to the overthrow of the Muammar Gaddafi regime, the observations of the Committee on Libya's Fourth Periodic Report in 2008 reveal some valuable insights indeed.

The Committee noted the State party's assurance that all anti-terrorism measures taken by the State party complied with international law but was nevertheless concerned that the terrorism-related elements in the draft penal code did not fully comply with the Covenant and that the draft law lacked a clear definition of terrorism. The Committee was also concerned at the lack of information regarding the safeguards detailed in article 4 in times of public emergency. It further deplored the lack of information on the alleged rendition to Libya by other states of Libyan nationals accused of terrorist crimes.

The Committee recommended that both the presently applicable anti-terrorism measures and the draft penal code measures on anti-terrorism conform fully to the Covenant. It also requested information regarding the whereabouts of Libyan nationals who had been subject to rendition to Libya (see Report of the Human Rights Committee: Volume I (2008): 25).

The Committee reiterated its concern about the large number of forced disappearances and cases of extra-judicial, summary or arbitrary executions and the lack of information from the State party in this regard. It recommended that Libya should urgently investigate all such occurrences and prosecute and punish the perpetrators and grant effective reparation, including compensation, to victims and families (see Report of the Human Rights Committee: Volume I (2008): 25–6).

The next issue for Libya concerned the systematic use of torture and other forms of ill-treatment in Libyan detention facilities and the lack of information regarding prosecutions for such offences. The Committee's recommendations were urgent: effective measures to stop such institutionalised ill-treatment and to ensure prompt, thorough and impartial investigations by an independent mechanism, as well as the prosecution and punishment of perpetrators and effective remedies to victims, were needed (see Report of the Human Rights Committee: Volume I (2008): 26).

The final issue for Libya concerned the routine and even collective rendition of persons to states where they might be subject to torture and ill-treatment in detention centres before rendition. The Committee recommended that the State party adopt immediate measures to prevent any form of return of such persons to states where they might face violation of article 7, and that an appeal procedure be made available to such persons before rendition (see Report of the Human Rights Committee: Volume I (2008): 26–7).

It is interesting to observe the Committee's responses to Syria's Third Periodic Report in the light of evidence of the extremely grave human rights atrocities being committed by the Syrian Arab Republic against its own people beginning in the summer of 2011 and continuing to the time of writing in late 2012.[14]

The major concern for the Committee was the issue of derogations. It was alarmed that a state of emergency that was declared more than forty years previously still remained in force and provided for many derogations in law or practice from rights guaranteed under, *inter alia*, articles 9, 14, 19 and 22 of the Covenant without any convincing explanation being given in respect of the relevance of these derogations to the conflict with Israel or the necessity for these derogations to meet the exigencies of the situation claimed to have been created by the conflict. The Committee also noted that Syria had failed in its obligation, as required by article 4(3) of the Covenant, to notify other States parties of the derogations that it had made and also the reasons for the derogations. The Committee also acknowledged the statement made by the delegation during examination that in June 2005 the Baath Party Congress had decided that emergency provisions would be limited to activities that threatened state security, but noted that it had received no information that this resolution had been adopted into law. The Committee recommended that the State party should ensure that (1) its derogation measures taken in a time of public emergency were strictly required by the exigencies of the situation, guided by General Comment No. 24; (2) the rights provided for in article 4(2) of the Covenant were made non-derogable in law and practice; and (3)

---

14   The United Nations Human Rights Council concluded its Fourth Special Session on Syria by adopting Resolution A/HRC/RES/S-19/1 on 1 June 2012 (adopted by a recorded vote of forty-nine in favour, three against (China, Cuba and the Russian Federation) and two abstentions (Ecuador and Uganda), condemning in the strongest possible terms the outrageous use of force resulting in the killing of 108 civilians, including thirty-four women, and in the harshest terms the outrageous killing of forty-nine children all under the age of 10 years and requesting the Independent International Commission of Inquiry to Syria, established at the end of the Second Special Session on Syria on 22 August 2011, to conduct a Special Inquiry into the killings at El-Houleh.

the notification procedures detailed in article 4(3) were adhered to in respect of both derogation and any subsequent termination (see Report of the Human Rights Committee: Volume I (2005): 79).

The Committee's second main issue of concern was the continuing reports of torture and mistreatment of detainees at the hands of law enforcement personnel, exacerbated by resort to prolonged incommunicado detention, especially in cases of concern to the Supreme State Security Court and the Security and Intelligence Services. The Committee determined that the State party should take firm steps to remove the use of incommunicado detention, eradicate all forms of torture and mistreatment by law enforcement officials and ensure prompt, thorough, independent and impartial investigations of such allegations leading to prosecution and punishment of perpetrators and compensation to victims (see Report of the Human Rights Committee: Volume I (2005): 80).

Given the present status of Yemen as a state verging on being a failed state, with Al Qaeda franchises, in particular Al Qaeda in the Arabian Peninsula, committing serious terrorist atrocities, the Committee's examination of the Yemeni Third Periodic Report and adoption of its Concluding Observations make interesting reading for its prescient remarks.

The Committee criticised (1) the lack of clarity in the legal provisions permitting the declaration of a state of emergency and derogation from the obligations established in the Covenant; (2) the continued existence of cases of torture and cruel, inhuman or degrading treatment for which law enforcement officers were responsible, as well as a general lack of investigations into such practices and punishment of perpetrators and the lack of any independent body to investigate reports of mistreatment; and (3) the attitude of the Security Services, including Political Security, which arrested and detained anyone suspected of links with terrorism, in violation of the guarantees established in article 9 of the Covenant, together with the expulsion of suspected terrorists without any possibility of legal challenge and without any consideration of the potential for mistreatment upon return to their states of origin (see Report of the Human Rights Committee: Volume I (2002): 74–5).

Given the continuing state of terrorist activity in Yemen since its Third Periodic Report, it is not surprising that the main issue of concern for the Committee during its examination of Yemen's Fourth Periodic Report was the State party's continuing efforts to combat terrorism. The Committee was concerned about grave violations of articles 6, 7, 9 and 14 of the Covenant that were committed in the name of the anti-terrorism campaign, especially extra-judicial killings, enforced disappearances, arbitrary arrests, indefinite detention without charge or trial, torture and ill-treatment and the deportation of aliens to states where they were in danger of being subjected to torture or ill-treatment. The Committee instructed that the utmost consideration should be given to the principle of proportionality in the State party's responses to terrorism and the non-derogable character of specified rights under the Covenant. Furthermore, the Committee expressed its wish to receive information on the findings and recommendations of the parliamentary committee established to monitor the situation of those detained on terrorism-related charges (see Report of the Human Rights Committee: Volume I (2005): 67).

In its discussion of Israel's Second Periodic Report, the Committee acknowledged that Israel had serious security concerns in the context of its presence in the West Bank and the Gaza Strip, as well as difficult human rights issues related to a resurgence of suicide bombings that had targeted Israel's civilian population since the start of the second intifada in September 2000. The Committee raised four issues of relevance to this chapter.

(1) The extra-territorial scope of the Covenant: The Committee noted the State party's position that the Covenant does not apply beyond its territory, notably in the West Bank and Gaza, particularly as long as there is a situation of armed conflict in these areas. The Committee reiterated the view, which it had previously articulated in paragraph 10 of its Concluding Observations on Israel's Initial Report (see Consideration of Reports (1998): 3), that the applicability of the regime of international humanitarian law does not preclude the applicability of the Covenant, including article 4, which covers situations of public emergency threatening the life of the nation. The Committee also stated that the applicability of the regime of international humanitarian law does not preclude the responsibility of States parties under article 2(1) of the Covenant for actions of their authorities outside of their own territories, including in occupied territories. Thus, the Committee emphasised that, in the current circumstances, the provisions of the Covenant apply to the Occupied Territories and that Israel's failure to comply with its obligations in this regard would involve state responsibility. The Committee requested the State party to review its position and include in its Third Periodic Report all relevant information regarding the application of the Covenant to the Occupied Territories (see Report of the Human Rights Committee: Volume I (2003): 66).

(2) The issue of derogation: The Committee welcomed Israel's decision to review its declared state of emergency and to prolong it on a yearly basis rather than indefinitely. Nevertheless, the Committee remained concerned about the sweeping nature of measures during the state of emergency that appeared to derogate from provisions other than article 9 of the Covenant. The Committee's opinion was that these derogations extended far beyond what would be permissible under those provisions of the Covenant that allow for the limitation of rights, such as articles 12(3), 19(3) and 21 of the Covenant. As far as measures derogating from article 9 of the Covenant itself, the Committee was very concerned at the frequent use of various forms of administrative detention, particularly for Palestinians from the Occupied Territories, which involved restrictions on access to counsel and on the full disclosure of the reasons for detention. The Committee remarked that these features limited the scope and effectiveness of judicial review and, thus, endangered the protection against torture and other inhuman treatment prohibited under article 7 of the Covenant; they also represented a derogation from article 9 of the Covenant more extensive than what in the Committee's view was permissible

under article 4 of the Covenant. The Committee referred to its earlier Concluding Observations on Israel and General Comment No. 24 in this respect.

The Committee recommended that Israel conclude as quickly as possible the review of legislation governing states of emergency that the Ministry of Justice had initiated. Pending the adoption of appropriate legislation, Israel was asked to review the modalities governing renewal of the state of emergency and to specify the provisions of the Covenant from which it sought to derogate to the extent strictly required by the exigencies of the situation (see Report of the Human Rights Committee: Volume I (2003): 66).

(3) Anti-terrorism measures: The Committee was highly critical of definitional vagueness in Israeli anti-terrorism law, which, though subject to judicial review, 'appear to run counter to the principle of legality in several respects owing to the ambiguous wording of the provisions in several aspects and the use of several evidentiary presumptions to the detriment of the defendant'. This had adverse consequences for the rights protected by article 15 of the Covenant, which, of course, is non-derogable under article 4(2) of the Covenant. The Committee stated that Israel should ensure that anti-terrorism measures, whether adopted in conformity with Resolution 1373 or within the context of the ongoing armed conflict in the West Bank and Gaza, fully conformed to the terms of the Covenant (see Report of the Human Rights Committee: Volume I (2003): 67).

(4) Targeted killings: The Committee was somewhat alarmed at what the State party called targeted killings of suspected terrorists in the Occupied Territories. The Committee commented that the practice seemed to be used as a deterrent or punishment and, thus, raised issues under article 6 of the Covenant. The Committee noted the delegation's observations about respect for the principle of proportionality in any response to terrorist activities and affirmation that only persons directly participating in hostilities had been targeted. However, the Committee was still concerned about the nature and extent of the responses by the Israeli Defence Force to Palestinian terrorist attacks.

The Committee recommended that Israel should not use targeted killings as a deterrent or punishment. Furthermore, the Committee requested that Israel give the utmost consideration to the principle of proportionality in its responses to terrorism and that state policy be sufficiently clear and conveyed to regional military commanders. Further still, complaints about the disproportionate use of force should be investigated promptly by an independent body. Finally, the Committee reiterated that all measures to arrest a person suspected of being in the process of committing an act of terrorism must be exhausted before lethal force could be used (see Report of the Human Rights Committee: Volume I (2003): 67).

In its Comments on the Concluding Observations of the Committee, Israel addressed the issue of targeted killings. The Comment involves ten paragraphs of observations, including the following statement:

Without prejudice to Israel's position regarding the non-applicability of the ICCPR to the present armed conflict against Palestinian terrorism, Israel confirms that it *does not* use 'targeted killings' as a means of deterrence or punishment. (Comments by the Government of Israel on the Concluding Observations (2007): 4)[15]

As it had done in respect of Israel's Second Periodic Report, the Committee, in examining its Third Periodic Report once again recognised Israel's security concerns in the context of its present conflict in the West Bank and Gaza, but nevertheless reiterated the need to observe and guarantee human rights in accordance with the provisions of the Covenant (see Report of the Human Rights Committee: Volume I (2010): 76).

The Committee raised a number of issues, including many of its concerns with Israel's previous Periodic Report.

(1) The extra-territorial scope of the Covenant: The Committee reiterated its previous stance that the Covenant was applicable in respect of acts done by a state in the exercise of its jurisdiction outside its own territory and cited in support the 2004 advisory opinion of the International Court of Justice in *Legal Consequences of the Construction of a Wall in the Occupied Palestinian Territory*.[16] Furthermore, the applicability of the regime of international humanitarian law did not preclude the accountability of States parties under article 2(1) of the Covenant for the actions of their authorities or agents outside their own territories. Thus, the provisions of the Covenant applied for the benefit of the population of the Occupied Territories with regard to all conduct by the State party's authorities or agents in those territories affecting the enjoyment of Covenant rights. Accordingly, Israel should ensure the full application of the Covenant in Israel, the Occupied Territories, including the West Bank, Gaza, East Jerusalem and the occupied Syrian Golan Heights. In accordance with General Comment No. 31, Israel should ensure that all persons under its jurisdiction and effective control were afforded the full enjoyment of the rights enshrined in the Covenant (see Report of the Human Rights Committee: Volume I (2010): 77).

(2) The issue of derogation and states of emergency: The Committee restated its concern at the State party's prolonged process of review regarding the need to maintain the state of emergency that it had declared in 1948. While noting the

---

15 On targeted killings, see, in particular, the Alston Report, in which a targeted killing is defined as the 'intentional, premeditated and deliberate use of lethal force, by States or their agents acting under colour of law, or by an organized armed group in armed conflict, against a specific individual who is not in the physical custody of the perpetrator' (Alston 2010: 3).

16 *Legal Consequences of the Construction of a Wall in the Occupied Palestinian Territory* (Advisory Opinion) [2004] ICJ Rep 136.

State party's declaration under article 4 with respect to derogations from article 9, the Committee expressed serious disquiet at the extensive use of administrative detention, including for children. Referring to General Comment No. 29, the Committee reminded Israel that derogation measures must be of an exceptional and temporary nature and limited to the extent strictly required by the exigencies of the situation. Furthermore, Israel should refrain from the use of administrative detention, especially for children, and swiftly complete its review of legislation governing states of emergency (see Report of the Human Rights Committee: Volume I (2010): 77–8).

(3) Targeted killings: Israel should end its practice of targeted killings of individuals suspected of involvement in terrorist activities; all its agents should uphold the principle of proportionality in their responses to terrorist threats and activities; utmost care should be taken to protect every civilian's right to life; all other measures should be exhausted for the arrest and detention of terrorist suspects before resorting to the use of deadly force; and an independent body should be established to promptly and thoroughly investigate claims about the disproportionate use of force (see Report of the Human Rights Committee: Volume I (2010): 79).

(4) Torture: The Committee noted that the crime of torture (as defined in article 1 of the 1984 Convention Against Torture and Other Cruel, Inhuman or Degrading Treatment or Punishment and article 7 of the Covenant) had not yet been incorporated into the State party's domestic legislation. The Committee expressed concern at constant allegations of the use of torture and other forms of mistreatment against Palestinian detainees suspected of security-related offences. The Committee also noted that although allegations of torture were factually denied or justified on the basis of necessity or the 'ticking bomb' scenario, the ban on torture was absolute and could never be derogated from. Thus, Israel was exhorted to define torture appropriately in its domestic legislation and remove the notion of necessity as a possible justification for the crime (see Report of the Human Rights Committee: Volume I (2010): 79). The Committee went on to state that Israel should ensure that all alleged cases of torture, mistreatment and disproportionate uses of force by all varieties of security personnel be promptly investigated by an independent body, that appropriate punishment be meted out to guilty parties and that compensation be paid to victims and families (see Report of the Human Rights Committee: Volume I (2010): 79–80).

(5) Anti-terrorism measures: The Committee noted that the State party was presently reviewing its definition of terrorism and related offences. The Committee reinforced its previous recommendation that measures designed to counter terrorism, whether adopted in compliance with Resolution 1373 or in the context of the ongoing conflict in the Occupied Territories, should fully conform to the Covenant. In particular, definitions of terrorism should be precise and limited

to countering terrorism and the maintenance of national security and must be in conformity with the Covenant (see Report of the Human Rights Committee: Volume I (2010): 80).

The following conclusions may be drawn from the above analysis of the Concluding Observations on the three groups of states examined above: (1) the Committee has noted that many States parties have derogations in place, whether long-standing or introduced as a result of the events of 11 September or Resolution 1373, and, accordingly, has been zealous in reminding States parties that their derogations must strictly comply with the requirements of article 4 of the Covenant and that derogation by definition is a departure from a state of normality and should not extend for an indefinite period; (2) the Committee has advised States parties to be particularly careful in adopting Memorandums of Understanding to return suspected terrorists to their states of origin to face trial where those proceedings could be tainted by violations of article 7; (3) on several occasions, the Committee has found it necessary to warn States parties of possible breaches of article 7 of the Covenant in cases of rendition, *refoulement*, transfer, extradition or expulsion of suspected terrorists; (4) the Committee has reaffirmed its long-standing view that the Covenant extends extra-territorially to all those persons within the State party's control or jurisdiction; (5) the Committee has frequently commented on the need for States parties to ensure that any anti-terrorism legislation fully and strictly conforms to the stipulations of the Covenant and, in particular, that the definition of terrorism adopted is sufficiently precise and closely drawn so as to comply with Covenant norms; and (6) the Committee has repeatedly reminded States parties of the need to ensure that all interrogation techniques in the case of detainees, including suspected terrorists, strictly conform to the requirements of article 7. Furthermore, States parties have been constantly reminded to conduct serious and independent inquiries into allegations of detainee mistreatment by law enforcement officers and similar officials, and that perpetrators must be brought to justice and reparation paid to victims of such conduct.

Final Comments

It is difficult to gauge the success of the Committee in monitoring and ensuring that States parties comply with their obligations under the Covenant. This is particularly the case in respect of anti-terrorism legislation that states have adopted in order to comply with Resolution 1373 and their declarations of states of emergency.

Any evaluation of the Committee's success in this regard must be premised on the inherent limitations of the Committee's powers. Leaving aside the notorious and egregious delays by many States parties in fulfilling their reporting obligations under article 40 of the Covenant, the nature of Concluding Observations, as described by O'Flaherty above,[17] does not admit of any compulsory enforcement procedure (notwithstanding the Sessional Reports by the Special Rapporteur for Follow-Up on Concluding Observations) because these are not, *stricto sensu*, binding in any formal legal sense. Indeed, there is nothing in the Replies of States parties to Concluding Observations to suggest that they do anything other than cherry-pick the recommendations that they are willing to implement.

In conclusion, it cannot be claimed that the pronouncements of the Committee have made a significant difference to States parties' compliance with their obligations under the Covenant in respect of their actions since 11 September. This is not the fault of the Committee, however: it can go no further and no faster than the limitations on its powers permit. Unfortunately, the record of States parties' compliance revealed by the Sessional Reports of the Special Rapporteur for Follow-Up on Concluding Observations is not striking for its degree of compliance. Despite all of the congratulatory comments on the occasion of the one hundredth session of the Committee in October 2010 (see Celebration 2011), there are serious dangers ahead for the Committee: it must do more to carry States parties with it if it is not to lose its credibility and authority in the future.

References

Ahani. Views: Communication No. 1051/2002 (2004), UN Doc CCPR/C/80/D/1051/2002.

Allain, J. 2001. The *Jus Cogens* Nature of *Non-Refoulement*. *International Journal of Refugee Law*, 13(4), 533–58.

Alston, P. 2010. Report of the Special Rapporteur on Extrajudicial, Summary or Arbitrary Executions, UN Doc A/HRC/14/24/Add.6.

Celebration of the 100th Session of the Human Rights Committee (2011), UN Doc CCPR/C/SR.2771.

Comments by the Government of Germany to the Concluding Observations of the Human Rights Committee (2005), UN Doc CCPR/CO/80/DEU/Add.1.

Comments by the Government of Israel on the Concluding Observations of the Human Rights Committee (2007), UN Doc CCPR/CO/78/ISR/Add.1.

Consideration of Reports Submitted by States Parties under Article 40 of the Covenant: Concluding Observations of the Human Rights Committee: Israel (1998), UN Doc CCPR/C/79/Add.93.

Consideration of Reports Submitted by States Parties under Article 40 of the Covenant: Fourth Periodic Report: United States of America (2012), UN Doc CCPR/C/USA/4.

General Comment No. 20: Concerning Prohibition of Torture and Cruel Treatment or Punishment (Article 7) (1992), UN Doc HRI/GEN/1, 29–32.

---

17   See note 2.

General Comment No. 24: Issues Relating to Reservations Made upon Ratification or Accession to the Covenant or the Optional Protocols Thereto, or in Relation to Declarations under Article 41 of the Covenant (1994), UN Doc CCPR/C/21/Rev.1/Add.6.

General Comment No. 29: States of Emergency (Article 4) (2001), UN Doc CCPR/C/21/Rev.1/Add.11.

General Comment No. 31: The Nature of the General Legal Obligation Imposed on States Parties to the Covenant (2004), UN CCPR/C/21/Rev.1/Add. 13.

O'Flaherty, M. 2006. The Concluding Observations of United Nations Human Rights Treaty Bodies. *Human Rights Law Review*, 6(1), 27–52.

Report of the Human Rights Committee: Volume I (2002), UN Doc A/57/40.

Report of the Human Rights Committee: Volume I (2003), UN Doc A/58/40.

Report of the Human Rights Committee: Volume I (2004), UN Doc A/59/40.

Report of the Human Rights Committee: Volume I (2005), UN Doc A/60/40.

Report of the Human Rights Committee: Volume I (2006), UN Doc A/61/40.

Report of the Human Rights Committee: Volume I (2008), UN Doc A/63/40.

Report of the Human Rights Committee: Volume I (2010), UN Doc A/65/40.

UNGA Res 60/147 (2005), UN Doc A/RES/60/147.

UNHCHR. 2001. Press Release, 20 November.

UNHRC Res S-19/1 (2012), UN Doc A/HRC/RES/S-19/1.

UNSC Res 1373 (2001), UN Doc S/RES/1373.

PART II
International Humanitarian Law and Today's 'New Wars'

Chapter 5

Civilian Casualties and Drone Attacks: Issues in International Humanitarian Law

Susan Breau

One of the most significant ways in which warfare has changed since 11 September 2001 has been the use of unmanned drones[1] to kill combatants rather than using conventional ground forces to do so.[2] The first reported Central Intelligence Agency drone attack occurred on 3 November 2002, when a Predator drone fired a missile at a car in Yemen that killed Qaed Senyan al-Harithi, an Al Qaeda leader who had allegedly been responsible for the *USS Cole* bombing in 2000 (BBC News 2002). Under the Administration of United States President Barack Obama, the Central Intelligence Agency's use of drones to target terrorists, particularly in Pakistan and Yemen, has greatly increased, and drones are also being used by the Central Intelligence Agency in the conflict in Afghanistan (O'Connell 2010: 5–6).[3] Although it is the leader in the use of drones, the United States is not alone. The Israelis, for example, are known to use them in the Gaza Strip (Wilson 2011).

This chapter focuses on the rules of international humanitarian law that regulate civilian casualties that result from drone attacks. It agrees with the position advanced by Louise Arimatsu in Chapter 7 of this volume that the attacks of 11 September 2001 do not warrant new laws to capture a new type of war, and that drone attacks must be viewed through 'the fundamental rules and principles that comprise the law of armed conflict' (p. 167). Given the number of drone attacks that are taking place in various locations throughout the greater Middle East, this discussion is both timely and appropriate. There are a myriad of other international legal issues that are involved when drones are used. First, there are important *jus ad bellum* issues with respect to the prohibition of the threat or

---

1　According to the United States Department of Defense's *Dictionary of Military and Associated Terms*, a drone is a 'powered, aerial vehicle that does not carry a human operator, uses aerodynamic forces to provide vehicle lift, can fly autonomously or be piloted remotely, can be expendable or recoverable, and can carry a lethal or nonlethal payload. Ballistic or semiballistic vehicles, cruise missiles, and artillery projectiles are not considered unmanned aerial vehicles' (Department of Defense 2008: 579).

2　'Combatants' is not a term that is used in non-international armed conflicts. The significance of this term will be discussed at length in the next section of this chapter.

3　The United States has also used drones in Iraq and Somalia.

use of force. Much of the academic scholarship on this issue is divided as to whether the current drone campaign violates article 2(4) of the United Nations Charter, is covered by the law of self-defence or is otherwise permissible on the basis of state consent (see Paust 2010; Shah 2010). This chapter only concerns itself with drones within the context of international humanitarian law and, thus, the legality of the overall use of force has no bearing here. Second, there is the important issue of whether these attacks occur within the context of an armed conflict at all, which would obviously be the condition predicate for engaging international humanitarian law in the first place. For the purposes of this chapter, it will be assumed that the drone attacks considered here occur within an armed conflict, with particular emphasis being given to the non-international armed conflict in Afghanistan that has 'spilled over' into the tribal areas of north-west Pakistan (see Ojeda 2009: 360). Arguably, there is also a non-international armed conflict in Gaza, though this is complicated by issues of occupation.[4] Third, there is also the debate about the legality of drone weaponry itself, but for the purposes of this discussion, it will be assumed that the weapon itself is not, at least not yet, unlawful in terms of the various weapons conventions and the international humanitarian law prohibition of unnecessary suffering.[5]

In addressing the rules of international humanitarian law that regulate civilian casualties that often accompany the use of drones, this chapter proceeds in three parts. The first section highlights the controversy over how many of these casualties have actually been uninvolved civilians, which engages the thorny issue of direct participation in hostilities. This portion of the chapter reviews the International Committee of the Red Cross (ICRC)'s newly released Interpretive Guidance on the Notion of Direct Participation in Hostilities under International Humanitarian Law (Melzer 2008a) (hereafter Interpretive Guidance), which was adopted by the Assembly of the International Committee of the Red Cross on 26 February 2009, and assesses whether it provides sufficient clarity in this area. The second section of this chapter briefly reviews issues of targeting and the cardinal principle of proportionality.[6] The third and pivotal section of this chapter introduces the little discussed but very real obligations in international humanitarian law towards missing and dead civilians. Regardless of whether or not the rules of international humanitarian law are complied with, civilians who are killed in these attacks are entitled to a dignified burial.

---

4   For an extensive discussion of the controversy concerning classification of this conflict, see Report of the Secretary-General's Panel of Inquiry on the 31 May 2010 Flotilla Incident 2011: 41–4.

5   For an example of such a convention, see the 1980 United Nations Convention on Prohibitions or Restrictions on the Use of Certain Conventional Weapons Which May Be Deemed to Be Excessively Injurious or to Have Indiscriminate Effects.

6   See Legality of the Threat or Use of Nuclear Weapons (Advisory Opinion) [1996] ICJ Rep 226 (hereafter *Nuclear Weapons*): 257.

Civilian Casualties of Drones Attacks

Most of the civilian casualties of drone attacks have been located in the tribal areas of north-west Pakistan. O'Connell (2010: 6) asserts that the use of drones in this area has resulted in a large number of uninvolved civilians being killed along with the intended targets. Regrettably, due to the secrecy involved, there are inconsistent accounts of the number of drone attacks that have taken place and about the precise number of casualties involved in these attacks. It is estimated that 316 drone strikes have occurred on Pakistani territory since 2004 and that 306 of these have taken place since January 2008 (see Roggio and Mayer 2012). There are eight separate studies on casualties in Pakistan for the year 2010 alone (see Beswick 2011). The most conservative study, commissioned by the New America Foundation (2012), estimates that through 11 October 2012, drone attacks launched by the United States caused between 1,907 and 3,220 deaths, with a range of between 1,618 and 2,765 of these deaths being 'militants'. It has to be noted that the label 'militant' is not one that is recognised by international humanitarian law, and careful analysis must be conducted regarding the status of those killed. A less conservative estimate conducted by the Bureau of Investigative Journalism (2012) indicates that as of 20 October 2012 a total of between 2,593 and 3,365 persons have been killed and of those, it is estimated that between 474 and 884 were civilians, including 176 children.

One of the cardinal principles of international humanitarian law is the requirement to distinguish between civilians and combatants (see ICRC Study on Customary International Humanitarian Law: Rule 1; Protocol Additional to the Geneva Conventions of 12 August 1949, and Relating to the Protection of Victims of International Armed Conflicts (hereafter Additional Protocol I): arts. 43(2), 51(3)). According to this principle, combatants can be targeted at any time and at any place, whereas civilians are immune from attack unless and for such time as they directly participate in hostilities (see Additional Protocol I: arts. 48, 51(2) (defining lawful targets)).[7] In a report on terrorism that it published in 2002, the Inter-American Commission on Human Rights (IACmHR) stated that 'the combatant's privilege ... is in essence a licence to kill or wound enemy combatants and destroy other enemy military objectives' (¶ 68). This means that a combatant cannot be prosecuted for killing or wounding an enemy combatant but is subject to prosecution for war crimes if a civilian is intentionally killed (see Dörmann 2003).

Within the context of an international armed conflict, combatants are broadly defined in article 43 of Additional Protocol I as 'all organized armed forces, groups and units which are under a command responsible to that Party for the conduct of its subordinates'. Civilians are defined in article 50(1) of the same instrument as:

---

7   The term 'combatant' is not defined in international humanitarian law, but it can be extrapolated from article 4(A) of the Third Geneva Convention of 1949 (see Goodman 2009: 51).

any person who does not belong to one of the categories of persons referred to in Article 4(A)(1), (2), (3) and (6) of the Third Convention and in Article 43 of this Protocol. In case of doubt whether a person is a civilian, that person shall be considered to be a civilian.

This definition is fairly straightforward in traditional warfare, but the involvement of irregular armed forces in the recent international armed conflicts in Iraq and Afghanistan has meant that the issue of combatant status has emerged as a major debate in international humanitarian law (see Garraway 2007). At various times after 11 September (during the Presidency of George W. Bush but abandoned by President Obama), the United States argued that both Al Qaeda and Taliban fighters were 'unlawful combatants', a highly disputed category in international humanitarian law (see Dörmann 2003: 45; see also Reply of the Government of the United States 2006). The authority that it relied upon for this was the 1942 United States Supreme Court case *Ex parte Quirin*,[8] in which the Court labelled German army saboteurs who had discarded their uniforms as unlawful combatants subject to trial and punishment in addition to capture and detention. The reason for this finding was that they did not seem to have the level of organisation and command necessary to comply with the definition above. Eventually, the United States recognised Taliban fighters as combatants, but Al Qaeda's loosely organised members have not been so recognised given that they do not conform to the conditions set out in customary international humanitarian law.[9]

O'Connell (2010: 22) argues that civilians who do not have a right to directly participate in hostilities are unlawful combatants and can be tried and prosecuted and that this could apply to Al Qaeda members participating in the conflict in Afghanistan and north-west Pakistan. It is clear that if such persons are captured on the battlefield that article 5 of the Geneva Convention Relative to the Treatment of Prisoners of War of 12 August 1949 (Third Geneva Convention) and article 45 of Additional Protocol I provide for a special procedure, a competent tribunal, to determine the captive's status (see Dörmann 2003: 47). The United States established Combatant Status Review Tribunals to assess the status of detainees in Guantánamo Bay, Cuba.[10] For the purposes of immunity from attack, Dörmann (2003: 72–3) asserts that international humanitarian law does not recognise a right to target unlawful combatants because they are civilians. The rule is that for such time as civilians directly participate in hostilities they are lawful targets of attack; when they do not do so or are no longer doing so, however, they enjoy civilian immunity and may not be targeted (see Dörmann 2003: 72–3). As such, it is critical to determine the issue of direct participation in hostilities, and this is

---

8   *Ex parte Quirin* [1942] 317 US 1.

9   There are many academic articles that have considered this issue. See, for example, Matheson 1987 and Goldman and Tittemore 2002. The United States is not a party to Additional Protocol I.

10   See Detainee Treatment Act [2005] 10 USC 801. See also Corn *et al.* 2007.

even more so the case in a non-international armed conflict: although only persons who are members of armed forces or dissident armed groups or those taking an active (direct) part in hostilities can be targeted (see International Institute of Humanitarian Law 2006: 4), those in the last two groups may not wear uniforms and may be difficult to distinguish in such conflicts.

In a non-international armed conflict, the rules are not nearly as clear as they are in an international armed conflict because at least one of the parties to the conflict is generally not a national armed force but, rather, a guerrilla group. The provisions for non-international armed conflict in common article 3 of the 1949 Four Geneva Conventions and in the Protocol Additional to the Geneva Conventions of 12 August 1949, and Relating to the Protection of Victims of Non-International Armed Conflicts (hereafter Additional Protocol II) contain only meagre provisions. Neither common article 3 nor Additional Protocol II contains any provisions dealing with prisoners of war or expressly recognises the nomenclature of combatant. Article 13 of Additional Protocol II, which is entitled 'Protection of the Civilian Population', specifies the protections due to the civilian population as follows:

> 1. The civilian population and individual civilians shall enjoy general protection against the dangers arising from military operations. To give effect to this protection, the following rules shall be observed in all circumstances.
> 2. The civilian population as such, as well as individual civilians, shall not be the object of attack. Acts or threats of violence the primary purpose of which is to spread terror among the civilian population are prohibited.
> 3. Civilians shall enjoy the protection afforded by this part, unless and for such time as they take a direct part in hostilities.

Despite the rudimentary nature of the international humanitarian law treaty regime in this area for non-international armed conflict, most important rules have attained the status of customary international law. The cardinal principle of distinction (see *Nuclear Weapons*: 257) also applies to non-international armed conflict and includes the word 'combatant'. Although this terminology is not used in non-international armed conflicts, it is a necessary part of the discussion given the imperative to distinguish between the various participants in the conflict. As O'Connell argues, citing Henckaerts and Doswald-Beck:

> Persons taking a direct part in hostilities in non-international armed conflicts are sometimes labelled 'combatants.' For example, in a resolution on respect for human rights in armed conflict adopted in 1970, the UN General Assembly speaks of 'combatants in all armed conflicts.' More recently, the term 'combatant' was used in the Cairo Declaration and Cairo Plan of Action for both types of conflicts. However, this designation is only used in its generic meaning and indicates that these persons do not enjoy the protection against attack accorded to civilians, but does not imply a right to combatant status or prisoner-of-war

status, as applicable in international armed conflicts. Nor does there appear to be any reason to restrict the term 'combatant' to international armed conflicts, as the 'direct participation' definition appears in Additional Protocol II to the Geneva Conventions relative to non-international armed conflict. (2009: 852)

According to Melzer (2008b: 311), the concept of direct participation in hostilities describes persons who do not enjoy civilian immunity but does not imply a right to the combatant's privilege or prisoner of war status. He continues by asserting that categories of persons protected against attack include uninvolved civilians, medical and religious personnel and persons *hors de combat*, that is, those who have surrendered or are wounded and are unable to continue to directly participate in hostilities (Melzer 2008b: 311–12).

A critical issue within the context of any armed conflict, of course, is to determine who can be targeted and who is immune from attack. Melzer argues that those who belong to armed forces or armed groups can be targeted at any time. A group of international humanitarian lawyers at the International Institute of Humanitarian Law in San Remo published the *Manual on the Law of Non-International Armed Conflict* in 2006, and that manual defines members of armed groups as 'fighters' (International Institute of Humanitarian Law 2006: 4–5). Consider the following:

1.1.2 Fighters
a. For the purposes of this Manual, fighters are members of armed forces and dissident armed forces or other organized armed groups, or taking an active (direct) part in hostilities.
b. Medical and religious personnel of armed forces or groups, however, are not regarded as fighters and are subject to special protection unless they take an active (direct) part in hostilities. (International Institute of Humanitarian Law 2006: 4)

It has to be noted that 'fighters' is not a word that is associated with either the treaty or customary law of non-international armed conflict. The more sensible view would seem to be O'Connell's, namely that the phrase 'combatant' can be applied to any conflict. Of course, in either case, the term is just as arbitrary.

With respect to terrorists or, as they are often labelled, 'militants', therefore, the issue in both international and non-international armed conflicts is whether they should be considered civilians who 'directly participate in hostilities' or as combatants who can be targeted at any time. The Interpretive Guidance provides some assistance in that persons who perform a 'continuous combat function' are members of organized armed groups, a notion equivalent to combatants, who can be targeted at any time (Melzer 2008a: 1002). The Interpretive Guidance further states that 'all armed actors showing a sufficient degree of military organization and belonging to a party to the conflict must be regarded as part of the armed forces of that party' (Melzer 2008a: 999). In contrast, articles 1 of the 1907 Hague

Convention (IV) Respecting the Laws and Customs of War on Land and Its Annex: Regulations Concerning the Laws and Customs of War on Land and 4(A)(2) of the Third Geneva Convention note four criteria for the classic category of prisoners of war that also effectively set forth the criteria for combatants: (a) being commanded by a person responsible for his or her subordinates; (b) having a fixed distinctive sign recognisable at a distance; (c) carrying arms openly; and (d) conducting their operations in accordance with the laws and customs of war.

Neither the Taliban nor Al Qaeda would qualify as prisoners of war under these four criteria, but they might well meet the definition in the Interpretive Guidance of directly participating in hostilities by virtue of a continuous combat function and, thus, be lawfully targeted by drone attacks (see Melzer 2008a: 995). While it is difficult to delineate precisely who is a party to the armed conflict, it is clear that some Al Qaeda splinter group members are fighting in Afghanistan. The difficulty arises when the United States attempts to classify the conflict, which it commonly did under the Bush Administration, as a 'war on terror' because this allows the parties to be understood more broadly and conceivably extends to Al Qaeda members regardless of where they live. This is not the position of the International Committee of the Red Cross or this chapter. Surely, the party to the conflict has to be a group that actually participates in the armed conflict in Afghanistan: the idea of a war on a concept has no validity in international law.

Another difficulty relates to Al Qaeda's 'support personnel', that is, those who might support the group to a greater or lesser degree but who do not carry arms. According to Watkin (2010: 644), the Interpretive Guidance suggests that persons who carry out substantial and continuing integrated support functions for Al Qaeda and other such groups should be considered civilians who are immune from attack even though the functions that they perform are the same ones on the basis of which members of a state's regular armed forces can be attacked. This effectively means that these persons enjoy a form of immunity from attack that is not provided to similarly situated persons serving in a state's armed forces. The Interpretive Guidance further indicates that such supporting civilians only lose their protection from attack if they perform acts that fall within a very narrow interpretation of what constitutes direct participation in hostilities. Watkin argues that 'in assessing direct participation in hostilities, the Interpretive Guidance's focus on the tactical level of war does not match the realities of how warfare is conducted' and that 'there is an emphasis placed on the "bearing of arms" which fails to fully recognize how armed groups are organized or how they fight' (2010: 644).

It is clear that civilians who benefit from protection against attack will lose their immunity for such time as they directly participate in hostilities (see Melzer 2008b: 313). Regrettably, there is no commonly accepted definition of direct participation in hostilities (see Alston 2010: 19). The Interpretive Guidance provides a degree of clarity as to when a civilian who directly participates in hostilities can be targeted, but these guidelines are not legally binding (see Melzer 2008a: 991; Fenrick 2009:

288).[11] Nonetheless, there is agreement that direct participation in hostilities may only include conduct that approximates that of a fighter or that directly supports combat (see Alston 2010: 19).

According to the Interpretive Guidance, civilians who have a continuous combat function can be targeted at all times and in all places (Melzer 2008a: 1007 and throughout). Furthermore, each specific act by a civilian must meet three cumulative requirements to constitute direct participation in hostilities:

> 1. the act must be likely to adversely affect the military operations or military capacity of a party to an armed conflict or, alternatively, to inflict death, injury, or destruction on persons or objects protected against direct attack (threshold of harm);
> 2. there must be a direct causal link between the act and the harm likely to result either from that act, or from a coordinated military operation of which that act constitutes an integral part (direct causation);
> 3. the act must be specifically designed to directly cause the required threshold of harm in support of a party to the conflict and to the detriment of another (belligerent nexus). (Melzer 2008a: 995–6)

To reiterate, the Interpretive Guidance remains highly controversial, with academics lining up to comment upon what they perceive to be its flaws. The basic objection for some is that the Interpretive Guidance's notion of direct participation in hostilities seems to be temporarily limited. When someone is 'off duty', the criticism goes, they cannot be targeted, and this is unreasonable (see Schmitt 2010: 739).[12]

In his May 2010 report on targeted killings, the then United Nations Special Rapporteur on Extrajudicial, Summary or Arbitrary Executions Philip Alston maintained the view that the Interpretive Guidance's three cumulative requirements for direct participation in hostilities do not include acts of 'one-off' terrorism, stating that, 'although illegal activities, e.g. terrorism may cause harm, they do not meet the criteria for direct participation *in hostilities*' (Alston 2010: 20). Although defensible, however, Alston's view is not the only one. There are arguably circumstances in which those who may be classified as civilians and who are also terrorists do indeed take a direct part in hostilities (see Fenrick 2009).

Civilians lose their immunity from attack when they directly participate in hostilities, and they can be targeted for so long as they do so (see Goodman 2009: 51). As a way of distinguishing between various participants in an armed conflict, Goodman argues that civilians do not lose their immunity if they 'merely' indirectly participate in hostilities or, of course, if they are non-participants. Indirect participants could be those such as 'supply contractors [and] members of labour units or of services responsible for the welfare of armed forces' (Goodman

---

11   Fenrick and Melzer specifically state that the Interpretive Guidance reflects the International Committee of the Red Cross's position on how existing international humanitarian law should be interpreted.

12   Schmitt describes this as 'clos[ing] the revolving door of participation' (2010: 739).

2009: 52 (referring to Third Geneva Convention: art. 4(A)(4))). These also include political and religious leaders, financial contributors, informants, collaborators and other service providers without a combat function (see Goodman 2009: 52–3). Goodman distinguishes direct from indirect participation on the grounds that the latter does not have a direct causal relationship between the individual's activity and any damage inflicted on the enemy. It may not occur on a battlefield (see Goodman 2009: 54). When one contemplates the label 'militants' being applied to those targeted in drone attacks, however, it seems that this might be a broader category of persons than fighters and those who directly participate in hostilities. At the very least, it is not clear that any of the statistical studies that deal with the civilian casualties of drone attacks understand militants as the equivalent of fighters or those who directly participate in hostilities (see Barnidge 2012: 420).

Thus, one can conclude that international humanitarian law only permits the targeting of civilians in non-international armed conflicts who are members of organised armed groups, that is, those who have a continuous combat function or otherwise directly participate in hostilities. This does not include past participation in a completed terrorist attack unless the person is a member of an organised armed group. As O'Connell points out, '[s]uspected militant leaders wear civilian clothes' (2010: 23). Thus, the issue of which targets are actually fighters, direct participants or immune civilians remains unresolved. The statistics of persons killed in drone attacks probably includes all three categories, and it is because of this that the issue of targeting becomes relevant.

Targeting Issues: The Second 'Cardinal Principle' of Proportionality

There is much discussion over whether drone operators thousands of miles from the battlefield can actually comply with the international humanitarian law obligation of proportionality. The rhetoric surrounding the various drone attacks has focused on the large number of civilian casualties that has been caused, but has this actually been the case? In fact, it will be argued here that drones, by and large, are weapons that *can* fulfil the international humanitarian law obligations of distinction and proportionality, and it is the issue of *who* constitutes a combatant that is the key area of international humanitarian law that is sometimes violated, not the law of targeting as such.

In its 1996 *Legality of the Threat or Use of Nuclear Weapons* advisory opinion, the International Court of Justice considered international humanitarian law and ruled that the principles of distinction, proportionality and the Martens Clause constituted the 'cardinal principles contained in the texts constituting the fabric of humanitarian law' (*Nuclear Weapons*: 257). It was not until Additional Protocol I was adopted in 1977, however, that proper treaty-based rules were set forth with respect to distinction and proportionality. Article 51(4) of that treaty sets out the general definition of indiscriminate attacks as:

(a) those which are not directed at a specific military objective;

(b) those which employ a method or means of combat which cannot be directed at a specific military objective; or

(c) those which employ a method or means of combat the effects of which cannot be limited as required by this Protocol; and consequently, in each such case, are of a nature to strike military objectives and civilians or civilian objects without distinction.

Article 51(5)(b) of Additional Protocol I articulates the principle of proportionality as:

an attack which may be expected to cause incidental loss of civilian life, injury to civilians, damage to civilian objects, or a combination thereof, which would be excessive in relation to the concrete and direct military advantage anticipated. (see also Additional Protocol I: arts. 57(2)(a)(iii), 57(2)(b))

Rule 14 of the International Committee of the Red Cross's Study on Customary International Humanitarian Law confirms the customary status of the principle of proportionality (see Schmitt 2007).

The United States, though not a party to Additional Protocol I, is bound by its customary rules and has specifically accepted the proportionality principle as custom (see Matheson 1987: 426–7). Therefore, an American commander of a drone attack is obliged to weigh up the relevant factors in a proportionality calculation, but nowhere does international law specify how many civilians can lawfully be killed for a single high-value target, such as an Al Qaeda leader.

With respect to the difficulty involved in calculating proportionality, Barnidge and O'Connell examine the killing of Tehrik-e-Taliban leader Hakimullah Mehsud in north-west Pakistan in August 2009 (see O'Connell 2010; Barnidge 2012). It was reported that a Hellfire missile from a Predator drone killed him but also killed his wife, mother- and father-in-law, seven bodyguards and a Tehrik-e-Taliban lieutenant (see Mayer 2009).[13] Mehsud arguably played a key role in supporting the insurgency across the Durand Line in Afghanistan and in numerous acts of terrorism inside Pakistan itself, including the Marriott Hotel bombing in Islamabad in September 2008 and the assassination of Prime Minister Benazir Bhutto a year earlier (see Mayer 2009). Barnidge concludes that '[g]iven Mehsud's leadership position in the TTP and the crucial role he played in the ongoing armed conflict in AfPak, opposing both the United States and Pakistan, the drone attack seems to have been proportionate despite the reasonable foreseeability of collateral damage' (2012: 441). On the other hand, O'Connell (2010: 24–5) argues that the drone attack on Mehsud likely violated international humanitarian law because he had been receiving an intravenous transfusion at the time of the attack and, as such, was an enemy person *hors de combat*. This particular attack may be mired in controversy, but the true debate surely must be how many civilians should be

---

13   Callam (2010) reports that Mehsud's uncle also died in the attack.

sacrificed for the death of an important militant. This consideration is neither discussed nor made clear.

The only other possible argument from a targeting perspective could be that drones are not capable of being directed against a single military objective and, thus, are more likely to result in disproportionate damage, but this does not seem to be the prevailing opinion (see Downes 2004: 285). Drones are used precisely because they can be directed against specific targets. In fact, in his assessment of the first drone attack, Downes (2004: 285) argues that it was both highly effective and proportionate. Drones are capable of being directed against a single military objective, which in the case of the Yemeni attack was a car in which al-Harathi had been travelling that contained arms and explosives (see Downes 2004: 284). In opposition to this view, Alston has expressed concern that '[i]t is not possible for the international community to verify the legality of a killing, to confirm the authenticity or otherwise of intelligence relied upon, or to ensure that unlawful targeted killings do not result in impunity' (2010: 27). This point of view relates to the earlier point of distinction between civilians and combatants and does not relate to the weapon system as such.

As a general proposition, therefore, international humanitarian law does not forbid launching a drone attack simply because it may cause civilian casualties. If an attack is disproportionate, then illegality will arise. Although drone operations are steeped in secrecy, there is nothing to suggest that these proportionality calculations are not taking place. In fact, it is likely that they are. It is also likely that there is a material disagreement about who is a civilian immune from attack and who is a member of an organised armed group or a civilian directly participating in hostilities. Simply classifying individuals as militants does not in and of itself reflect compliance with international law. While there is nothing at this point to suggest that drones as such are indiscriminate or that as such they are unable to comply with such rules of international humanitarian law as proportionality, there is a vital need for the United States to provide further information as to the status of persons being targeted rather than simply giving the sometimes flippant description of them as 'militants' or 'terrorists'.[14]

---

14 In a speech given to the Wilson Center in April 2012, for example, Assistant to President Obama for Homeland Security and Counterterrorism John O. Brennan stated that counterterrorism efforts were strengthened by 'adherence to the law, including the legal authorities that allow us to pursue members of al-Qaida ... and to do so using technologically advanced weapons' (2012). Nowhere in his speech, however, did Brennan discuss how American authorities were ensuring that uninvolved civilians were not being targeted, and he used, in response to questions, the terms 'militants' and 'terrorists'.

Obligations to Record Civilian Casualties within an Armed Conflict

This section introduces the legal regime for the recording of civilian casualties within an armed conflict. Notwithstanding the problem of classifying casualties as civilians, combatants or civilians directly participating in hostilities, this section will argue for identical treatment regardless of status, and it is in this respect that drone operators are violating their international law obligations towards civilian casualties. State responsibility follows from this, including an obligation to compensate victims' families for not providing details of the identity of the victims and the cause of death or recording the location of their graves.

Although it is clear that at least some of the people who have been killed in American drone attacks can be classified as fighters or direct participants in hostilities as international humanitarian law understands these concepts, it is equally certain that there have been other civilian casualties, both persons within the vicinity of the attacks and those who sympathise with one of the various terrorist organisations but who do not directly participate in hostilities. International law has been slow to develop a system of obligations associated with the civilian casualties of armed conflict, but this has changed dramatically as a result of the Study on Customary International Humanitarian Law. This is particularly important within the context of drone attacks because unless casualties can be identified and recorded, classifying the victims as fighters, direct participants or uninvolved civilians is impossible. What follows is a review of the limited treaty regime and customary international humanitarian law related to obligations to record civilian casualties within the context of an armed conflict.

The International Humanitarian Law Treaty Regime

The main treaty provision that deals with the collection of civilian casualties is article 16 of the 1949 Geneva Convention Relative to the Protection of Civilian Persons in Time of War (Fourth Geneva Convention), which states:

> The wounded and sick, as well as the infirm, and expectant mothers, shall be the object of particular protection and respect.
> As far as military considerations allow, each Party to the conflict shall facilitate the steps taken to search for the killed and wounded, to assist the shipwrecked and other persons exposed to grave danger, and to protect them against pillage and ill-treatment.

An important limitation within this provision, of course, is that searching for civilian persons can only be conducted *as far as military considerations allow*. The implications of this are significant. There is no obligation to arrange for a ceasefire to collect casualties, for example, and the extensive obligation that is contained in the other three Geneva Conventions of 1949 to identify, record and bury with dignity military casualties does not exist for civilian casualties (see First

Geneva Convention 1949: arts. 15–17; Second Geneva Convention 1949: arts. 18–21; Third Geneva Convention 1949: arts. 120–21).

It was not until Additional Protocol I was adopted in 1977 – and one should recall that some key states within the conflicts being discussed in this chapter, including the United States and Pakistan, are not parties to Additional Protocol I – that detailed treaty provisions for missing persons required the recording of information, a point that will be discussed later in this section. The relevant provisions in Additional Protocol I are preceded by a general statement, in article 32, of the 'right of families to know the fate of their relatives'. There is a specific provision that deals with searching for the missing and recording deaths (see Additional Protocol I: art. 33; see also Additional Protocol I: art. 34). Once again, the provision contains a limitation clause, 'as soon as circumstances permit', but importantly, there is a proviso according to which the search for the missing and the recording of the dead should begin at the very latest 'from the end of active hostilities'.

These provisions in Additional Protocol I markedly improve upon the Fourth Geneva Convention, but sadly, this is not repeated for non-international armed conflicts. Article 8 of Additional Protocol II states:

> Whenever circumstances permit and particularly after an engagement, all possible measures shall be taken, without delay, to search for and collect the wounded, sick and shipwrecked, to protect them against pillage and ill-treatment, to ensure their adequate care, and to search for the dead, prevent their being despoiled, and decently dispose of them.

This provision does not contain 'at the latest from the end of active hostilities' language or require that the parties shall endeavour to agree on arrangements to locate the casualties (see Additional Protocol I: art. 33). This general provision is very similar to the one in the Fourth Geneva Convention.

Because Additional Protocols I and II do not apply to the drone attacks in Pakistan or Israel given that the United States, Pakistan and Israel are not parties to these treaties, and, even if they were, Additional Protocol II contains such limited obligations, it is necessary to determine the customary international law in this field. Customary international law is universally binding except upon persistent objector states, but there do not seem to be such states in the case of the rules on the missing and the dead.[15]

Customary International Humanitarian Law

The Study on Customary International Humanitarian Law concludes that many of the treaty provisions in Additional Protocols I and II have emerged as customary

---

15 For an excellent discussion of customary international law and the theory of persistent objector states, see International Law Association 2000.

rules since the treaties' adoption in 1977. The study was originally published in book form by Henckaerts and Doswald-Beck (2005, 2009), and in it they focus particular attention on the state practice of those states that are not parties to Additional Protocols I and II because this shows the existence of legal norms that operate outside of the treaty context alone. Since the release of the study in book form, the International Committee of the Red Cross has established the Customary International Humanitarian Law database, which outlines the supporting practice and is added to on a regular basis. Its aim is to view the practice in many states rather than use the (by necessity) selective method used in the original Study on Customary International Humanitarian Law. The most recent update integrates national practice up to the end of 2007 for a set of twenty-seven additional states. The materials are gathered by a network of International Committee of the Red Cross delegations and Red Cross and Red Crescent societies around the world and are incorporated by a research team based at the Lauterpacht Centre for International Law at the University of Cambridge.

This section outlines the rules in the Study on Customary International Humanitarian Law that deal with civilian casualties because these rules are clearly relevant to the drone attacks that are taking place in Afghanistan, Iraq, Pakistan and Yemen. These rules are reviewed in the same way that the other rules in the Study on Customary International Humanitarian Law were examined by a group of international humanitarian law experts in a 2007 collection edited by Wilmshurst and the present author entitled *Perspectives on the ICRC Study on Customary International Humanitarian Law*. The only part of the Study on Customary International Humanitarian Law's rules that that work did not examine were the rules with respect to the missing and the dead. This section takes a similar approach as a 'constructive comment' upon the methodology of the study and the rules formed as a result of that methodology with respect to the missing and the dead, with a view to assessing their customary status (see Wilmshurst and Breau 2007: viii).

In Chapter 35 on 'The Dead' and Chapter 36 on 'Missing Persons', the Study on Customary International Humanitarian Law states that the essence of the extensive treaty provisions in Additional Protocol I reflect custom and that almost all of these provisions also apply as a matter of customary obligation to non-international armed conflicts. Importantly, the study clarifies the scope of these obligations.

The first rule of relevance to this discussion is Rule 112. According to it:

> Whenever circumstances permit, and particularly after an engagement, each party to the conflict must, without delay, take all possible measures to search for, collect and evacuate the dead without adverse distinction.

One of the unique aspects of drone attacks is that they are not usually part of a series of attacks. The effect of this is that parties must take all possible measures to search for, collect and evacuate the dead once a particular drone attack has ended. This could include permitting humanitarian organisations or the civilian population to assume this task. Permission for either of these options must not be denied arbitrarily.

The Study on Customary International Humanitarian Law indicates that Rule 112 applies to all the dead, without adverse distinction. This means that it applies no matter which side the dead are from and irrespective of their status. Support for this rule is found in the Israel High Court of Justice's judgment in *Barake* v. *Minister of Defense*,[16] which Rule 112 cites. In that 2002 case, the Court stated that the obligation to search for and collect the dead derived from 'respect for all dead' (¶ 9). The Court also held that locating the dead was an 'important humanitarian act' and that the 'respondents are responsible for the location, identification, evacuation, and burial of the bodies. This is their obligation under international law' (¶¶ 7, 9). This is legally very important given that Israel is not a party to Additional Protocol I, and therefore, its practice has a special significance as a non-party state.

Further support is found in the United States Navy's *Annotated Supplement to the Naval Handbook*, which states that, '[a]s far as military exigencies permit, after each engagement all possible measures should be taken without delay to search for and collect the shipwrecked, wounded, and sick and to recover the dead' (United States 1997: 8.8). Again, as with the Israeli example above, this is legally very important given that the United States is not a party to Additional Protocol I and, therefore, its practice has a special significance as a non-party state.

According to Rule 112 of the Study on Customary International Humanitarian Law, best practice involves using humanitarian organisations such as the International Committee of the Red Cross to search for, collect and document missing and deceased persons. The study notes numerous examples of practice in which such humanitarian organisations have searched for and collected the dead. The use of humanitarian organisations cannot be said to be part and parcel of the rule; rather, it is a logical conclusion as to how a party might adhere to the rule.

It seems reasonable to conclude from this extensive practice that compliance with Rule 112 is a customary obligation in both international and non-international armed conflicts.

Given the customary status of this rule, the Afghan, American, Israeli, Iraqi, Pakistani and Yemeni governments must put in place civilian casualty mechanisms that comply with this obligation. This can be done by funding organisations that already perform this task on a voluntary basis or by establishing an international organisation to assume coordination.

Rule 113, the next rule in the Study on Customary International Humanitarian Law, is surely part and parcel of the first obligation. According to Rule 113:

> Each party to the conflict must take all possible measures to prevent the dead from being despoiled. Mutilation of dead bodies is prohibited.

---

16 *Barake* v. *Minister of Defense* [2002] Israel HCJ (hereafter *Jenin (Mortal Remains)*).

Given that all drone attacks take place in parts of the world where Muslims form a majority, one of the distressing parts of this rule as applied in practice arises out of the necessity under the Islamic faith to bury the dead as soon as possible (see Siala n.d.). Notwithstanding this fact, coroners or medical examiners must ensure that the bodies are identified and that the cause of death is determined before burial, and this might take longer than twenty-four hours. Sadly, drone attacks often result in difficulties in identifying the remains of the dead. Still, this does not relieve the parties involved of their obligations under this rule of customary international humanitarian law, and mechanisms must be put in place to swiftly respond to drone attacks in this respect.

An example of best practice and one that applies to every one of these customary rules dealing with civilian casualties is the practice that the City of New York adopted following the World Trade Center attacks of 11 September. Although it may be debateable whether or not these attacks were a criminal act or part of an armed conflict, or possibly both, the efforts to identify every casualty were truly heroic, even though many of the bodies could never be found or identified. Relatives of the victims of the attacks were left in no doubt as to the good faith efforts of the rescuers and the forensic scientists on their behalf. As the situation in New York clearly revealed, being attacked regrettably often requires DNA analysis to actually identify the remains of the dead in order to return them to their families. Establishing a civilian casualty recording mechanism will require a forensic capability in order to ensure compliance with this international legal obligation.

There is one rule in the Study on Customary International Humanitarian Law that would only apply if drone attacks took place within the context of an international armed conflict. This rule, Rule 114, contains important obligations with respect to the bodies of the deceased and their property. According to it:

> Parties to the conflict must endeavour to facilitate the return of the remains of the deceased upon request of the party to which they belong or upon the request of their next of kin. They must return their personal effects to them.

Regrettably, this does not apply as a matter of customary international humanitarian law to non-international armed conflicts. This is confirmed by the practice examined in the Study on Customary International Humanitarian Law: there simply is not the volume or consistency of practice to support this rule's applicability in a non-international armed conflict. Therefore, this rule does not apply to the drone attacks being discussed in this chapter.

One of the rules of direct relevance to attacks by drones is the next rule in the Study on Customary International Humanitarian Law, Rule 115, which deals with respectful burial and tending of graves. One difficulty of attacks from the air, of whatever nature, is that there is often a shattering of the bodies of those directly hit and, on occasion, no family members are left to tend to their fallen relatives. According to Rule 115:

> The dead must be disposed of in a respectful manner and their graves respected
> and properly maintained.

The Study on Customary International Humanitarian Law states that this rule applies in both international and non-international armed conflicts. This obligation was upheld in the *Jenin (Mortal Remains)* case, which held that burials must be performed with respect, in a timely manner and according to religious custom, and if at all possible, the remains must be returned to the families of the deceased (see *Jenin (Mortal Remains)*: ¶ 10).

The requirement to protect and maintain gravesites is laid down in numerous military manuals, which the Study on Customary International Humanitarian Law covers, though, in truth, an examination of these manuals seems to be more relevant to military casualties than to civilian casualties. The commentary to Rule 115 states that the dead must be buried, if possible according to the rites of the religion to which the deceased belonged, and that the dead should only be cremated in exceptional circumstances, namely when imperative reasons of hygiene so dictate or on account of the religion of the deceased based upon an express wish. Burial should also be in individual graves, with collective graves only being permitted in circumstances that do not allow for the use of individual graves or in cases of burial of prisoners of war or civilian internees. If possible, according to Rule 115, graves should be grouped according to nationality. An example that the Study on Customary International Humanitarian Law gives of state practice in a non-international armed conflict is the Columbia Council of State's decision that the deceased must be buried individually and not in mass graves.

Once again, state practice with respect to Rule 115 is extensive and the practice, particularly in non-international armed conflicts such as Columbia, seems to reflect the customary nature of the rule. However, the actual implementation of this rule in the situation of drone attacks will need further study and consultation.

The Study on Customary International Humanitarian Law continues, with Rule 116, as follows:

> With a view to the identification of the dead, each party to the conflict must record
> all available information prior to disposal and mark the location of the graves.

This rule is reinforced by the international human rights law requirement dealing with respect for family life, which would arguably include the right of relatives to know the fate of their relatives (see International Covenant on Civil and Political Rights 1966: art. 23). Case law in the European Court of Human Rights includes within the right to life (see European Convention on Human Rights 1950: art. 2) an investigation obligation.[17] The International Committee of the Red Cross

---

17   See *Osman v. United Kingdom* (2000). European Human Rights Reports, 29, 245–327 (requiring the State to determine in certain circumstances whether the right has been 'arbitrarily deprived').

maintains a Central Tracing Agency, but this does not include a record of the location of civilian graves. The role of the Central Tracing Agency is to trace people, exchange family messages, reunite families and clarify the fate of those who remain missing as a result of armed conflict. The best model to be found is the practice of military organisations such as the Commonwealth War Graves Commission, which identifies the graves of all soldiers who have been killed in battle and contains a list of missing soldiers. There is not, however, a comparable service for civilians.

State practice supports Rule 116 in both international and non-international armed conflicts. According to the commentary to Rule 116, for example, the case law of Argentina and Columbia holds that the dead must be examined with a view to identifying them and establishing the circumstances of death prior to disposal.[18] Furthermore, in December 1991, when the armed conflict in the former Yugoslavia was characterised as non-international in nature, the parties to the conflict reached an agreement with respect to the exchange of information about the identities of the deceased (Plan of Operation 1991: prop. 1.1). Another important example of practice is the 1974 United Nations General Assembly Resolution, Resolution 3220, which called upon parties to cooperate 'in providing information on the missing and dead in armed conflicts' (UNGA Res 3220 (1974): ¶ 4).[19] The compilation of practice is impressive and establishes this rule as binding in both international and non-international armed conflicts.

The final rule to be considered is located in the chapter in the Study on Customary International Humanitarian Law entitled 'Missing Persons'. This chapter contains only one rule, Rule 117, and it is entitled 'Accounting for Missing Persons'. According to Rule 117:

> Each party to the conflict must take all feasible measures to account for persons reported missing and as a result of armed conflict and must provide their family members with any information it has on their fate.

General Assembly Resolution 3220 supports this rule in that it calls upon parties involved in armed conflicts to provide information on the missing. The United Nations Commission on Human Rights passed a resolution in 2002 that affirmed that each party to an armed conflict 'shall search for the persons who have been reported missing by an adverse party' (UNCHR Res 2002/60: 254).

The practice in the Study on Customary International Humanitarian Law suggests that exhumation may be an appropriate method for establishing the fate of missing persons. Practice also indicates that possible ways of accounting for missing persons include the setting up of special commissions or other tracing mechanisms. Croatia's Commission for Tracing Persons Missing in War Activities

---

18   See *Military Juntas* case (1986): sec. 563; *Case No. 10941*, Columbia Council of State, Judgment, 6 September 1995: sec. 564.

19   Resolution 3220 was adopted by 95 votes in favour, none against and 32 abstentions.

in the Republic of Croatia is one example. The United Nations Secretary-General's Bulletin on Observance by United Nations Forces of International Humanitarian Law provides that United Nations forces shall facilitate the work of the Central Tracing Agency (Secretary-General's Bulletin 1999: 3). States and international organisations have on many occasions requested that an accounting be made for persons missing as a result of conflicts in, *inter alia,* Cyprus, East Timor, Guatemala, Kosovo and the former Yugoslavia. As another example of state practice, the Study on Customary International Humanitarian Law points out that the position of Expert for the Special Process on Missing Persons in the Territory of the Former Yugoslavia was created in the Yugoslav conflict to address this need (see Nowak Report 1995).

Rule 117 is further supported by practice as set forth in a number of military manuals. It is also reflected in some national legislation and supported by official statements. In remarks that he made in 1987, for example, Deputy Legal Adviser to the United States Department of State M.J. Matheson supported the rule that the search for missing persons must be carried out 'when circumstances permit, and at the latest from the end of hostilities' (1987: 424). Because, as indicated above, drone attacks typically do not take place within the context of continuing attacks, searching for the missing must take place shortly after each of these attacks.

The following conclusions can be drawn from this examination of Rules 112–17 of the Study on Customary International Humanitarian Law:

1. There are binding international legal obligations upon the parties to an armed conflict to:
    a. search for all civilians missing due to hostilities, occupation or detention
    b. collect all of the casualties of armed conflict from the area of hostilities as soon as circumstances permit
    c. if at all possible, the remains of those killed are to be returned to the relatives of the deceased
    d. the remains of the dead should not to be despoiled
    e. any property found with the bodies of the dead must be returned to the relatives of the deceased
    f. the dead are to be buried with dignity and in accordance with their religious or cultural beliefs
    g. the dead are to be buried individually and, except in exceptional circumstance, not in mass graves
    h. graves are to be maintained and protected
    i. the exhumation of bodies is only permitted in circumstances of public necessity, which will include identifying cause of death
    j. the location of the place of burial is to be recorded by the party to the conflict in control of that territory
    k. in the case of civilian casualties, an official graves registration service should be established.

2. Taken together, these international legal obligations bind each party to an armed conflict, be the armed conflict international or non-international in nature, to record every civilian casualty.

Although these obligations directly apply to states that are involved in drone attacks, there is little evidence to suggest that they are complying with any of them. These obligations might be complied with by establishing a civilian casualty retrieval and recording mechanism. Governments should consult with the Every Casualty campaign in London, which coordinates a group of non-governmental organisations that are involved in the recording of civilian casualties, to determine the resourcing needs to best accomplish these tasks.[20]

Conclusions

Aside from the *jus ad bellum*, classification of conflict issues and international human rights law, which this chapter did not discuss, the main controversy with drone attacks relates to disputes over the number of casualties and the number and proportion of these who have and have not been legitimate targets. What should be equally troubling to the international community, however, is the lack of attention that has been given to those who have perished in these attacks. Simply because the status of a victim of a drone attack is undetermined, or because the victim may have been directly participating in hostilities at the time that he or she was attacked, does not relieve the parties to the conflict of their legal obligations to record every casualty. As with the position advanced by Kalliopi Chainoglou in Chapter 8 of this volume with respect to cyber warfare, it is not that public international law frameworks do not exist; rather, it is that the legal obligations that exist must be respected.

The responsibility properly to record casualties is a requirement jointly held by those who launch and control drones and those who authorise or agree to their use. In the case of drone attacks, this responsibility is held by, *inter alia*, Afghanistan, Iraq, Israel, Pakistan, the United States and Yemen. Non-state actors also have a specific and very real responsibility to comply with their obligations to record civilian casualties with respect to areas under their control. This would include the terrorist groups in the tribal areas of north-west Pakistan and Hamas and the Palestine Liberation Organization in the Occupied Palestinian Territories.

While efforts to disinter and identify the remains of drone victims may be daunting, as with any high-explosive attack, this in no way absolves parties from their responsibility to record every casualty. And to reiterate what has already been said above, the fact that drone attacks typically do not take place within the context

---

20   For a list of non-governmental organisations that are involved in casualty recording and for the Every Casualty campaign's recommendations for establishing proper recording for casualties, see http://everycasualty.org/ [accessed: 15 September 2012].

of continuing attacks means that there is no need to delay until the cessation of hostilities before taking measures to search for, collect and evacuate the dead.

The obvious question is how this legal obligation might best be complied with in practice. States must discuss how their extensive obligations with respect to civilian casualties might be implemented, either through national or international mechanisms. It seems clear that those who are fighting in such conflicts are in many cases not able to comply with their obligations towards civilian casualties and that the responsibility could be delegated to an agency tasked with this specific responsibility. However, the precise methods of compliance demand further study and negotiation between the parties involved in today's armed conflicts, the International Committee of the Red Cross and the agencies involved in humanitarian and human rights within the context of the United Nations.

References

Alston, P. 2010. Report of the Special Rapporteur on Extrajudicial, Summary or Arbitrary Executions, UN Doc A/HRC/14/24/Add.6.

Barnidge, R.P. Jr. 2012. A Qualified Defense of American Drone Attacks in Northwest Pakistan under International Humanitarian Law. *Boston University International Law Journal*, 30(2), 409–48.

BBC News 2002. CIA 'Killed Al-Qaeda Suspects' in Yemen, 5 November. Available at: http://news.bbc.co.uk/2/hi/2402479.stm [accessed: 6 October 2012].

Beswick, J. 2011. Working Paper: The Drone Wars and Pakistan's Conflict Casualties 2010. Oxford Research Group. Available at: http://www.oxfordresearchgroup.org.uk/sites/default/files/Working%20Paper%20Pakistan2010-SecondVersion.pdf [accessed: 29 September 2012].

Brennan, J.O. 2012. The Ethics and Efficacy of the President's Counterterrorism Strategy. Wilson Center, 30 April. Available at: http://www.wilsoncenter.org/event/the-efficacy-and-ethics-us-counterterrorism-strategy [accessed: 19 October 2012].

Bureau of Investigative Journalism 2012. CIA Drone Strikes in Pakistan. Available at: http://www.thebureauinvestigates.com/2011/08/10/most-complete-picture-yet-of-cia-drone-strikes/ [accessed: 20 October 2012].

Callam, A. 2010. Drone Wars: Armed Unmanned Aerial Vehicles. *International Affairs Review*, 18(3). Available at: http://www.iar-gwu.org/node/144 [accessed: 1 October 2012].

Corn, G., Jensen, E.T. and Watts, S. 2007. Understanding the Distinct Function of the Combatant Status Review Tribunals: A Response to Blocher. *Yale Law Journal Online*, 11 April. Available at: http://yalelawjournal.org/2007/04/11/corn_jensen_watts.html [accessed: 29 September 2012].

Department of Defense. *Dictionary of Military and Associated Terms.* Joint Publication 1-02, 12 April 2001 (amended 17 October 2008). Available at: http://www.bits.de/NRANEU/others/jp-doctrine/jp1_02(10-08).pdf [accessed: 29 September 2012].

Dörmann, K. 2003. The Legal Situation of 'Unlawful/Unprivileged Combatants'. *International Review of the Red Cross,* 85(849), 45–74.

Downes, C. 2004. 'Targeted Killings' in an Age of Terror: The Legality of the Yemen Strike. *Journal of Conflict and Security Law,* 9(2), 277–94.

Fenrick, W.J. 2009. ICRC Guidance on Direct Participation in Hostilities. *Yearbook of International Humanitarian Law,* 12, 287–300.

Garraway, C.H.B. 2007. 'Combatants' – Substance or Semantics?, in *International Law and Armed Conflict: Exploring the Faultlines: Essays in Honour of Yoram Dinstein,* ed. M.N. Schmitt and J. Pejic. Leiden: Martinus Nijhoff, 317–34.

Goldman, R.K. and Tittemore, B.D. 2002. Unprivileged Combatants and the Hostilities in Afghanistan: Their Status and Rights under International Humanitarian and Human Rights Law. American Society of International Law Terrorism Task Force Papers. Washington, DC: American Society of International Law.

Goodman, R. 2009. The Detention of Civilians in Armed Conflict. *American Journal of International Law,* 103(1), 48–74.

Henckaerts, J.-M. and Doswald-Beck, L. (eds) 2005. *Customary International Humanitarian Law: Volume II: Practice.* Cambridge: Cambridge University Press.

Henckaerts, J.-M. and Doswald-Beck, L. (eds) 2009. *Customary International Humanitarian Law: Volume I: Rules.* Cambridge: Cambridge University Press.

Inter-American Commission on Human Rights (IACmHR) 2002. Report on Terrorism and Human Rights. OEA/Ser.L/- V/II.116 Doc. 5 rev. 1 corr.

International Committee of the Red Cross (ICRC). Study on Customary International Humanitarian Law. Available at: http://www.icrc.org/customary-ihl/eng/docs/home [accessed: 29 September 2012].

International Institute of Humanitarian Law 2006. *The Manual on the Law of Non-International Armed Conflict, With Commentary.* San Remo: IIHL. Available at: http://www.iihl.org/iihl/Documents/The%20Manual%20on%20the%20Law%20of%20NIAC.pdf [accessed: 20 October 2012].

International Law Association 2000. Final Report of the Committee: Statement of Principles Applicable to the Formation of General Customary International Law, London. Available at: http://www.ila-hq.org/en/committees/index.cfm/cid/30 [accessed: 22 September 2012].

Matheson, M.J. 1987. Remarks: The United States Position on the Relation of Customary International Law to the 1977 Protocols Additional to the 1949 Geneva Conventions. *American University Journal of International Law and Policy,* 2(2), 419–31.

Mayer, J. 2009. The Predator War: What Are the Risks of the C.I.A.'s Covert Drone Program? *New Yorker,* 26 October.

Melzer, N. 2008a. Interpretive Guidance on the Notion of Direct Participation in Hostilities under International Humanitarian Law, Adopted by the Assembly of the International Committee of the Red Cross on 26 February 2009. *International Review of the Red Cross*, 90(872), 991–1047.

Melzer, N. 2008b. *Targeted Killings in International Law*. Oxford: Oxford University Press.

Military Juntas Case, Argentina: National Appeals Court (Criminal Division) Judgment on Human Rights Violations by Former Military Leaders (Excerpts) (1986) 1987. *International Legal Materials*, 26(1), 317–72.

New America Foundation 2012. The Year of the Drone: An Analysis of US Drone Strikes in Pakistan, 2004–2012, 11 October. Available at: http://counterterrorism.newamerica.net/drones [accessed: 20 October 2012].

Nowak Report 1995. Report Submitted By Mr. Manfred Nowak, Member of the Working Group on Enforced or Involuntary Disappearances, Pursuant to Paragraph 24 of Commission Resolution 1994/72, UN Doc. E/CN.4/1995/37.

O'Connell, M.E. 2009. Combatants and the Combat Zone. *University of Richmond Law Review*, 43(3), 845–64.

O'Connell, M.E. 2010. Unlawful Killing with Combat Drones: A Case Study of Pakistan, 2004–2009. Notre Dame Law School, Legal Studies Research Paper No. 09-43.

Ojeda, S. 2009. US Detention of Taliban Fighters: Some Legal Considerations, in *The War in Afghanistan: A Legal Analysis*, ed. M.N. Schmitt. Newport, RI: Naval War College, 357–69.

Paust, J.J. 2010. Self-Defense Targetings of Non-State Actors and Permissibility of U.S. Use of Drones in Pakistan. *Journal of Transnational Law and Policy*, 19(2), 237–80.

Plan of Operation Designed to Ascertain the Whereabouts or Fate of the Military and Civilian Missing, Annex to the Joint Commission to Trace Missing Persons and Mortal Remains, Rules of Procedure and Plan of Operation, Established on the Basis of a Memorandum of Understanding Between the Socialist Federal Republic of Yugoslavia, Republic of Croatia, Republic of Serbia, Yugoslav People's Army and the International Committee of the Red Cross, Pécs, 16 December 1991.

Reply of the Government of the United States of America to the Report of the Five UNCHR Special Rapporteurs on Detainees in Guantanamo Bay, Cuba. 2006. *International Legal Materials*, 45(3), 742–68.

Report of the Secretary-General's Panel of Inquiry on the 31 May 2010 Flotilla Incident 2011. Available at: http://www.un.org/News/dh/infocus/middle_east/Gaza_Flotilla_Panel_Report.pdf [accessed: 29 September 2012].

Roggio, B. and Mayer, A. 2012. Charting the Data for US Airstrikes in Pakistan, 2004–2012. *Long War Journal*, 1 October. Available at: http://www.longwarjournal.org/pakistan-strikes.php [accessed: 6 October 2012].

Schmitt, M.N. 2007. Targeting, in *Perspectives on the ICRC Study on Customary International Humanitarian Law*, ed. E. Wilmshurst and S. Breau. Cambridge: Cambridge University Press, 131–68.

Schmitt, M.N. 2010. Deconstructing Direct Participation in Hostilities: The Constitutive Elements. *New York University Journal of International Law and Politics*, 42(3), 697–740.

Secretary-General's Bulletin: Observance by United Nations Forces of International Humanitarian Law (1999), UN Doc ST/SGB/1999/13.

Shah, S.A. 2010. War on Terrorism: Self-Defense, Operation Enduring Freedom, and the Legality of U.S. Drone Attacks in Pakistan. *Washington University Global Studies Law Review*, 9(1), 77–130.

Siala, M.E. n.d. *Authentic Step By Step Illustrated Janazah Guide*. Available at: http://www.missionislam.com/knowledge/janazahstepbystep.htm [accessed: 20 September 2012].

UNCHR Res 2002/60 (2002), in Report of the Commission on Human Rights (2002), UN Doc E/2002/23, 253–5.

UNGA Res 3220 (XXIX) (1974), UN Doc. A/RES/3220.

United States 1997. *The Annotated Supplement to the Naval Handbook*, prepared by the Oceans Law and Policy Department, Center for Naval Studies. Newport, RI: Naval War College.

Watkin, K. 2010. Opportunity Lost: Organized Armed Groups and the ICRC 'Direct Participation in Hostilities' Interpretive Guidance. *New York University Journal of International Law and Politics*, 42(3), 641–96.

Wilmshurst, E. and Breau, S. (eds) 2007. *Perspectives on the ICRC Study on Customary International Humanitarian Law*. Cambridge: Cambridge University Press.

Wilson, S. 2011. In Gaza, Lives Shaped By Drones. *Washington Post*, 3 December. Available at: http://www.washingtonpost.com/world/national-security/in-gaza-lives-shaped-by-drones/2011/11/30/gIQAjaP6OO_print.html [accessed: 29 September 2012].

Chapter 6

The 'New Wars' of Children or on Children? International Humanitarian Law and the 'Underaged Combatant'

Noëlle Quénivet

The typical armed conflict of the last few decades has not been one in which such instruments of high technology as unmanned drones and guided missiles have been used (see de Berry 2001: 93); rather, it has been fought by young people with AK-47s and machetes, as in the Democratic Republic of Congo, Sierra Leone and Uganda. Beginning in the 1990s with Graça Machel's seminal report on the impact of armed conflict on children (1996), a coalition of non-governmental organisations and individual activists has strongly argued against the use of children in armed conflict, that is, the use of those under 18 years of age. A liberal society, it has been argued, cannot possibly approve of a child's involvement in an armed conflict: this would simply be contrary to the values of the civilised world (see Hughes 2000: 399). 'War is Not Child's Play!' is the title of a recent academic article that astutely reflects this view (Udombana 2006). From an historical perspective, however, children have often participated in armed conflicts, and in fact, such liberal states as the United Kingdom and the United States continue to recruit children to join their armed forces.[1]

Liberalism, which is based on the concepts of human dignity and universal human rights and contends that law is the best instrument for securing liberty, empowering humanity and bringing about social change (see Goodwin 2005: 41; Lee 2009: 7), sees children's involvement in armed conflict as a violation of human rights. Consequently, an international lobbying campaign has attempted to transform the moral value that children should not be involved in armed conflict into a legal norm that problematises their involvement. The main achievement of this campaign, which favours a 'universal approach [that] perceives all under-18 recruitment into armed groups as offensive, from under-18-year-olds enlisting in state armies with parental permission to young teenagers joining an armed group in order to defend their own social group to pre-teens abducted and desensitized to the act of killing' (Fox 2005: 42), has been the adoption of a series of hard and

---

1 'The majority of recent scholarly research relating to children and armed conflict has, quite rightly, been directed toward eliminating the use of child soldiers by rebel groups in developing nations' (Brosha 2005).

soft law instruments. Criticism of the view that child soldiering is unacceptable as such has sometimes been raised (see Rosen 2007), but it has not been welcome. Nonetheless, the mainstream view of child soldiering, that it is unacceptable as such, arguably fails to recognise and be sufficiently sensitive to local and regional cultures and traditions. A key underlying question remains: *why* should child soldiering *between 15 and 18 years of age in particular* be universally banned (see Lee 2009: 8)?

This chapter radically rethinks the notion of 'underaged combatant' in international humanitarian law in order to assess whether a change in the law is necessary. It begins by exploring how and why the phenomenon of child soldiering has gained prominence in recent years. It then examines the current legal framework in relation to the recruitment, conscription, enlistment and participation of children in armed conflict. The chapter ends by critically analysing international law in this area through the prism of two values that are essential to liberal thinkers: universality, the view that liberal values apply across cultures; and autonomy, the idea that each individual is able to take decisions independently. It concludes that the issue of child soldiering is more difficult to grasp than liberal thinkers present it and that the Zero Under 18 Campaign launched by the United Nations Special Representative for Children and Armed Conflict, which well reflects the current liberal approach, is unlikely to be successful because it fails to take into consideration the weight of history, politics and culture.

The Child Soldier Phenomenon: An Historical Approach to Childhood and Children in Armed Conflict

The definition of 'childhood' and how adults perceive 'little people' and their role in the world have changed over time (see McNeed 2004: 20; Lee 2009: 4). Until recently, the idea of children taking a direct and indirect part in armed conflicts was commonly accepted as an inevitable aspect of warfare. Social scientists contend that the concept of childhood did not exist during the Middle Ages (see James and James 2001: 26). The underlying belief was that as soon as a child's abilities grew, so his or her participation in society expanded. The idea that a person reached adulthood at a certain fixed age simply did not exist at that time, and young people were not granted any sort of special or distinctive social status (see James and James 2001: 26). By the fifteenth century, however, an awareness had developed to the effect that children should be afforded some special consideration (see James and James 2001: 26),[2] despite the fact that it remained quite common for them to

---

2   The first legal instrument to recognise this was the Geneva Declaration of the Rights of the Child of 1924, which was followed by the more comprehensive Declaration of the Rights of the Child of 1959 and then by the 1989 United Nations Convention on the Rights of the Child.

partake in armed conflicts.[3] Just as is the case today, military apprenticeship or military service was an attractive vocation, especially where a formal universal education system did not exist (see Jonasen 2009: 311).

Despite a growing awareness over the centuries of the difference between children and adults, little attention was devoted to actually defining who fell within the category of a child. It was only in the late 1990s that a consensus began to emerge that would unequivocally classify a child as anyone below 18 years of age (see Convention on the Rights of the Child 1989; Convention Concerning the Prohibition ... of Child Labor 1999). In 1999, the Council of Delegates of the International Red Cross and Red Crescent Movement stated that it was 'seriously alarmed by the increasing number of children involved in armed conflict and by the tremendous suffering endured by those children' (ICRC 1999: Resolution 8). Three years earlier, in 1996, Machel had published her report exposing the plight of children in armed conflict. As Lee summarises, 'the global discourse is that children have no place in war under any circumstance' (2009: 3).

Despite this growing consensus, however, no one has actually addressed the question of *why* child soldiering is, and should be, so widely and flatly condemned. To answer this question, one must investigate two key developments that have occurred in recent decades that have radically changed mainstream perceptions of child soldiering, namely the growing impact of liberal human rights ideology and the emergence of 'new wars'.

Liberal Human Rights Ideology

One key development in recent decades that has radically changed mainstream perceptions of child soldiering has been the growing impact of liberal human rights ideology. Liberalism is committed to a society in which individuals can freely and autonomously pursue and realise their interests (see Goodwin 2005: 37). Because liberals tend to view the individual as inviolable and human life as sacrosanct, liberalism prohibits violence except for in those rare cases in which society is threatened (see Goodwin 2005: 37). For liberals, individual human rights are fundamental in any given society. The advent of a human rights ideology that began with the adoption of the 1948 Universal Declaration of Human Rights and a range of universal and regional human rights treaties has solidified the liberal position in law.

As a result of liberalism's rights-based approach (see Lee 2009: 6), issues related to children have been entirely viewed through the prism of human rights. In fact, the first comprehensive report on the plight of children in armed conflict (Machel 1996) was based on a human rights framework, the 1989 Convention on

---

3 Examples in the American context include the drummer boys of the American Revolution and the powder monkeys of the War of 1812, the Mexican–American War and the Civil War, and in the German context include the Hitler Youth during the Second World War (see Gallagher 2010: 1).

the Rights of the Child (see Harvey 2003: 14). Machel's work led to a discourse in which 'child soldiering is an unambiguous violation of universal children's rights' (Lee 2009: 3). That being said, the fact that a different *corpus juris*, international humanitarian law, acts as *lex specialis* in situations of armed conflict[4] means that children are protected by international human rights law *and* international humanitarian law (see Harvey 2003: 6).

The Emergence of 'New Wars'

A second key development in recent decades that has radically changed mainstream perceptions of child soldiering has been the emergence of 'new wars'.[5] A link can arguably be drawn between the emergence of these armed conflicts in the 1980s and the proliferation of the recruitment and use of children in combat. As Kaldor summarises in *New and Old Wars: Organized Violence in a Global Era*, 'the new wars involve a blurring of the distinctions between war (usually defined as violence between states or organized political groups for political motives), organized crime (violence undertaken by privately organized groups for private purposes, usually financial gain), and endemic violations of human rights (violence undertaken by states or politically organized groups against individuals)' (1999: 2).

Three salient features of these 'new wars' contribute to the increased involvement of children in them. First, these conflicts are typically characterised by the abandonment of all moral standards and the lack of a clear delineation between war and peace (see Gallagher 2010: 2). Distinctions between fighters and civilians are generally not made (see Abbott 2000: 509; Harvey 2003: 5; Schauer 2009: 10) and, worse still, the civilian population becomes the target of systematic attacks carried out with extreme levels of brutality and violence (see Schauer 2009: 9–10). An increasing number of children have become the primary targets of armed forces and opposition groups in the 'new wars' and are abducted or forcibly recruited into military factions (see Singer 2005; Schauer 2009: 11, 41). Children are viewed as a ready and expandable commodity (see Jonasen 2009: 315), their objectification being illustrated by the fact that boys are sent to the front and, if killed, simply replaced by other boys (see Davison 2004: 137–8; Human Rights Watch 2004: 21). Children, who are known to be unaware of such concepts as mercy and sympathy until a later age (see Boyden 1994: 260; Waschefort 2010: 189), are often used to terrorise populations, thus increasing the overall level of violence and contributing to and reinforcing the cycle of violence.

---

4 See *Legality of the Threat or Use of Nuclear Weapons* (Advisory Opinion) [1996] ICJ Rep 226 and *Legal Consequences of the Construction of a Wall in the Occupied Palestinian Territory* (Advisory Opinion) [2004] ICJ Rep 136. For a discussion on the concept of *lex specialis*, see McCarthy 2008: 101.

5 It is argued that these armed conflicts stand in stark contrast to contemporary international armed conflicts or previous wars of national liberation.

A second salient feature of the 'new wars' that has contributed to the increasing involvement of children in them is that, since these conflicts tend to occur in poor countries, they are typically fought with light weapons that are cheap to buy. The increased accessibility of small arms since the end of the Cold War and technological improvements that have rendered such weapons easy to use (see Thompson 1999: 191; Davison 2004: 138) have led to a higher number of children taking a direct part in hostilities (see Harvey 2003: 25; Singer 2005) and a corresponding increase in the victimisation of women and children (see Harvey 2003: 60). Children using weapons against the civilian population has sadly become a common feature of these 'new wars'.

Finally, the fact that a wide range of actors, such as national liberation movements, insurgents, partisans, rebels, local militia, terrorist groups and corporations, are involved in the 'new wars' often makes it difficult to distinguish between these factions in practice. For example, an armed opposition group may use a local militia to 'recruit' individuals to work in mines. The natural resources are then sold to a corporation and the money received from the proceeds of the resources is used to buy weapons from a terrorist group. In this environment, children are an ideal weapon of war. Due to their young age, they 'can ... act relatively inconspicuously in conflict zones, observing troop deployments, dispositions of weapons and noting logistical arrangements without attracting undue attention' (Faulkner 2001: 494). As children are usually not suspected of participating in hostilities, they are often neither monitored nor stopped and searched while they are on duty. They are, therefore, an undeniable asset for these groups, notably because they can provide information on their movements and activities but also work as a communication bridge between them.

While such liberal states as the United Kingdom and the United States accept that children can be recruited into their own armed forces, they decry the use of children in the 'new wars'. Three main reasons seem to explain this seeming contradiction and why the international campaign against child soldiering has focused on conflicts waged in non-liberal states. First, there is the acknowledgment that the 'new wars' have fostered a culture of using and encouraging children to commit unspeakable acts of violence. In these conflicts, international humanitarian law is systematically violated, and war crimes are chronically perpetrated. Liberal states, however, tend to take a range of precautions to avoid such violations, or at least to lessen their occurrence (see Rogers 2000). Second, liberal states recognise that child soldiers, which are in large supply, both perpetuate the cycle of violence and lead to the escalation, prolongation and geographical expansion of conflict. Contemporary warfare as carried out by liberal states tends to adopt strategies that allow such conflicts to be geographically circumscribed and temporally limited, such as in Kosovo or Libya, and use technologies that require high levels of skills, thus providing no particular incentive for liberal states to use children. Finally, there is a fundamental distinction in the fact that the overwhelming majority of children who are entangled in such conflicts have not chosen a military path voluntarily and that those children who do choose careers as professional soldiers in the United Kingdom and the United States do so willingly.

The Legal Framework Related to Child Soldiering

International humanitarian law does not prohibit the recruitment and use of children in armed conflict who are between 15 and 18 years of age; rather, it is international human rights law that is at the forefront of the campaign against child soldiering. In order to understand the current movement towards banning child soldiers, one must examine the legal framework related to the recruitment, conscription, enlistment and participation of children in armed conflict (see Smith 2004: 1147).[6] Although this section examines these key issues by mostly concentrating on international humanitarian law, it also looks at international human rights law and, at times, international criminal law to provide a better understanding of the child soldier phenomenon.

Recruitment

Children are recruited into armed forces and armed opposition groups in various ways: some are abducted, others are forcibly recruited and some of them join voluntarily. Article 77 of the Protocol Additional to the Geneva Conventions of 12 August 1949, and Relating to the Protection of Victims of International Armed Conflicts, 8 June 1977 (Additional Protocol I), article 4(3) of the Protocol Additional to the Geneva Conventions of 12 August 1949, and Relating to the Protection of Victims of Non-International Armed Conflicts, 8 June 1977 (Additional Protocol II) and Rule 136 of the International Committee of the Red Cross Study on Customary International Humanitarian Law group under the single term 'recruitment' these different ways in which children join a group involved in hostilities.[7]

As the Commentary to article 77 of Additional Protocol I explains, while the obligation to refrain from recruiting children under 15 years of age is clear, the voluntary enrolment of children is neither explicitly mentioned nor prohibited (see Sandoz *et al.* 1987: ¶ 3184). As there is no express prohibition of the voluntary enrolment of children less than 15 years of age, this seems to indicate that voluntary enlistment is legally permissible. In other words, international humanitarian law distinguishes between two forms of recruitment, active recruitment by the armed forces (known as conscription) and voluntary enrolment, but only bans the former in international armed conflict. By

---

6   While recruitment relates to the manner in which a child becomes associated with an armed group, use relates to the way in which he or she is used and participates in the conflict (see Sivakumaran 2010: 1012).

7   The term 'recruitment' predates 'enlistment' and 'conscription' (see Waschefort 2010: 196).

contrast, the Commentary to article 4(3) of Additional Protocol II stipulates that '[t]he principle of non-recruitment also prohibits accepting voluntary enlistment' (Sandoz *et al.* 1987: ¶ 4557). Rule 136 of the Study on Customary International Humanitarian Law does not elaborate on this, though it does refer to the 1998 Rome Statute of the International Criminal Court, which distinguishes between two forms of recruitment, conscription and the enlistment of children under 15 years of age (arts. 8(2)(b)(xxvi) (for international armed conflicts) and 8(2)(e) (vii) (for non-international armed conflicts)). As the Commentary to the Rome Statute makes clear, '[c]onscription refers to the compulsory entry into the armed forces. Enlistment ... refers to the generally voluntary act of joining armed forces by enrolment, typically on the "list" of a military body or by engagement indicating membership and incorporation in the forces' (Triffterer 1999: 261).[8] A similar position was recently adopted by the Trial Chamber in *Lubanga*.[9] Again, a difference is made between compulsory and voluntary acts.

The distinction between compulsory and voluntary recruitment, of course, fails to account for abductions, which are one of the chief means used to recruit children (Legrand and Weissman 1995: 165; Madubuike-Ekwe 2005: 33).[10] The 2000 Statute of the Special Court for Sierra Leone, which distinguishes between two types of recruitment in article 4, has had its 'conscription' language interpreted to include acts of coercion for the purpose of using children in hostilities (AFRC: ¶ 734). Undoubtedly, this 'definition of conscription reflects its recognition of the changed nature of modern warfare' (United Nations Special Representative on Children and Armed Conflict 2008: ¶ 9, referring to AFRC: ¶ 734). The Special Court for Sierra Leone also explains that enlistment means accepting and enrolling individuals when they volunteer to join an armed force or group (AFRC: ¶¶ 734–5). In other words, enlistment does not involve an actual list of new recruits but also 'children enrolled by more informal means' (United Nations Special Representative on Children and Armed Conflict 2008: ¶ 9).

International human rights law instruments, such as article 38 of the Convention on the Rights of the Child, also impose restrictions upon states related to recruitment. The Convention on the Rights of the Child's prohibition of recruitment for those less than 15 years of age applies both in peacetime and in situations of armed

---

8   See also *Prosecutor* v. *Lubanga* (Confirmation of Charges), ICC-01/04-01/06, T Ch (2007): ¶ 246; *Prosecutor* v. *Brima, Kamara and Kanu* (Judgment), SCSL-2004-16-T SCSL, T Ch II (2007) (hereafter AFRC): ¶ 275. It must also be stressed that this provision applies not only to armed forces but also to armed opposition groups. The Optional Protocol to the Convention on the Rights of the Child on the involvement of children in armed conflict differentiates between state actors and non-state actors in this regard, and specifically recognises the duties of non-state armed groups.

9   *Prosecutor* v. *Lubanga* (Judgment), ICC-01/04-01/06, T Ch (2012) (hereafter *Lubanga*): ¶ 608.

10   See also *Prosecutor* v. *Sesay, Kallon and Gbao* (Judgment), SCSL-04-15-T, T Ch (2009): ¶ 1616 (hereafter RUF).

conflict, thus leaving aside difficult questions related to the classification of conflict. Moreover, it does not distinguish between compulsory and voluntary recruitment (see Breen 2007: 83). The 2000 Optional Protocol to the Convention on the Rights of the Child on the Involvement of Children in Armed Conflict (hereafter Optional Protocol) does make this distinction,[11] however, which means that the Optional Protocol's perspective is similar to the one in international humanitarian law and leaves open the definition of 'voluntary' (see Breen 2007: 89).

Conscription

Conscripting children under 15 years of age is clearly prohibited by international humanitarian law treaties, customary international humanitarian law (see ICRC Study on Customary International Humanitarian Law: Rule 136) and international criminal law (see Rome Statute 1998: arts. 8(2)(b)(xxvi), 8(2)(e)(vii)). By contrast, the Optional Protocol prohibits, pursuant to article 2, the compulsory recruitment of persons under 18 years of age. While conscription is clearly banned with regard to children under 15 years of age, the question is whether it is also so with regard to children between 15 and 18 years of age. Again, international human rights law raises the minimum age while other relevant branches of international law specify an age of 15.

Conscription is commonly viewed as the prerogative of the state to require its nationals to take part in some form of national service, in this case military service (see AFRC: ¶ 734). By definition, conscription is compulsory and, thus, coerced. The great majority of states do not conscript individuals under 18 years of age. Despite the existence of legal safeguards to combat forced recruitment, however, inefficiency, corruption and structural inadequacies mar the system (see Bald 2002: 548). One of the reasons for this is that many states do not properly document the age of people, which has the effect of facilitating the recruitment of minors because the state can always argue that it was not aware that the child was under 18 years of age.

In its contemporary understanding, conscription encompasses abductions and forced recruitment (see RUF: ¶¶ 1695, 1700, 1707). In general, it should be interpreted as 'encompass[ing] acts of coercion, such as abductions and forced recruitment ... committed for the purpose of using them to participate actively in hostilities' (AFRC: ¶ 734). Even if children are not actually used in a conflict, their abduction with the aim of using them is sufficient to sustain a conviction for conscription (see RUF: ¶ 1700). The law in this area has been interpreted such that it also applies to non-international armed conflict (see RUF: ¶ 194).

Although it is clear that no children under 15 years of age (under international humanitarian law) or under 18 years of age (according to the Optional Protocol) can be recruited, the reality is very different. Owing to the general lack of punishment

---

11   Article 3 of the Optional Protocol refers to voluntary recruitment.

in practice for armed groups when they recruit children, forced recruitment has become endemic in many of these conflicts (see Mitchell 2003–2004: 85–6).

Enlistment

On the other hand, international humanitarian law does not clearly ban enlistment, which can be understood as 'accepting and enrolling individuals when they volunteer to join an armed force or group' (AFRC: ¶ 735).[12] To some extent, this lack of prohibition caters to the fact that not all children are forced into soldiering. Many choose to join an armed group or a state's armed forces of their own volition.

According to international humanitarian law treaties, enlistment is only prohibited in non-international armed conflict.[13] The general prohibition of recruitment in non-international armed conflict is to be welcomed because the majority of cases of child recruitment today take place within the context of non-international armed conflicts. That being said, customary international humanitarian law bans enlistment in all conflicts (see ICRC Study on Customary International Humanitarian Law: Rule 136) while the Convention on the Rights of the Child and the Optional Protocol ban enlistment without referring to the type of conflict involved.[14] An important implication of this ban on enlistment in customary international humanitarian law is that it also binds armed forces and armed groups that are not affiliated with the state. By contrast, international human rights law only binds a state's armed forces.[15]

The bottom line is to determine what makes an enlistment 'voluntary' since this is the distinguishing factor between conscription and enlistment proper in international humanitarian law and international human rights law.[16] In Western states, a minor must make a willing and informed decision with the consent of his or her parent(s) or guardian(s).[17] Article 3(1) of the Optional Protocol requires

---

12   See also *Prosecutor* v. *Fofana and Kondewa* (Appeal Judgment), SCSL-04-14-A, App Ch (2008) (hereafter CDF): ¶ 140.

13   Article 77(2) of Additional Protocol I allows states to enlist children. In the context of Additional Protocol II, see article 4(3).

14   Article 38 of the Convention on the Rights of the Child and articles 1–4 of the Optional Protocol do not refer to the type of conflict involved.

15   See, however, Emmerson 2012. While a number of Security Council Resolutions, such as UNSC Res 1882 (2009) and UNSC Res 1998 (2011), refer to the obligations contained in the Optional Protocol to the Convention on the Rights of the Child, they stipulate that 'all parties to armed conflicts [should] comply with the obligations applicable to them under international law for the protection of children in armed conflict', thereby implicitly denying the universal applicability of the Optional Protocol.

16   However, the Rome Statute does not refer to the degree of voluntariness in joining an armed group. Thus, Smith argues that 'the forcible or voluntary nature of the recruitment is not an element of the crime' (2004: 1148). In other words, there is no defence to the recruitment of those under 15 years of age.

17   See section 328 of the Armed Forces Act 2006 of the United Kingdom.

states to raise the legal age for voluntary military recruitment to at least 16 years of age (see Harvey 2003: 28). Although this provision has been criticised for still allowing the recruitment of children between 16 and 18 years of age, states insisted upon it to keep the armed forces available as a source of employment, training and continuing education for those leaving school early (see Abbott 2000: 530–31; Breen 2007: 90, 92). Moreover, it would take a couple of years to train a soldier fully before sending him or her to a conflict theatre. During wars of national liberation, a number of children willingly and strategically joined armed groups. Undoubtedly, ideological attraction plays a significant role in wars of national liberation, and this is why Additional Protocol I allows the direct participation in hostilities of children less than 15 years of age (see Sandoz *et al.* 1987: ¶¶ 3184–5).

In the 'new wars', children join armed forces and armed groups for a range of reasons. The main push and pull factors include economic hardship and poverty, the lack of opportunities and access to education, a sense of belonging, ideological attraction, feelings of revenge, survival, the loss of parents and relatives able to protect them, the need to find a safer environment, the impression that one is in control and, thus, proactive rather than passive and victimised, and a willingness to defend the community.[18] In other cases, school curricula contain military elements, which contributes to the indoctrination of children who may wish to join 'willingly' yet are arguably not fully able to understand the ideological nature of their decision or to adequately assess the implications of their actions.

As a result, it is generally agreed that customary international law prohibits the recruitment of children less than 15 years of age into armed forces and armed groups, whether compulsory or voluntary, whether in international or non-international armed conflict. There might be an emerging norm barring the compulsory recruitment of children less than 18 years of age, but this does not seem to be universally accepted at the moment.

Participation

Besides the recruitment, conscription and enlistment of children, their participation in armed conflict is also regulated by international law. However, the legal framework that is used, whether it is international humanitarian law, international human rights law, international criminal law or a combination of these, will determine which kinds of participation are prohibited.

The 1977 Additional Protocols were the first international legal instruments to regulate the participation in hostilities of children less than 15 years of age. According to article 77(2) of Additional Protocol I, children are barred from

---

18   See Hughes 2000: 403; Happold 2005: 13–14; Singer 2005: 64; REDRESS 2006: 19; Taylor 2006; Wessells 2006: 49–50; Witness DRC-OTP-WWW-0046 2009: 18; Coomaraswamy 2010: 536; Rosen 2010: 51.

'tak[ing] a direct part in hostilities' in international armed conflict.[19] By contrast, article 4(3)(c) of Additional Protocol II does not use the adjective 'direct', thus encompassing such 'indirect' functions as 'gathering information, transmitting orders, transporting munitions or foodstuffs or committing acts of sabotage' (Dutli 1990). This distinction in terminology prompted the International Committee of the Red Cross to comment that, since '[t]he intention of the drafters of the article was clearly to keep children under fifteen outside armed conflict', indirect participation in *international* armed conflict should also be ruled out (see Sandoz *et al.* 1987: ¶ 3187). A resolution adopted at the 26th International Conference of the Red Cross and Red Crescent in 1995 reinforces this position inasmuch as it declares that 'parties to conflict take every feasible step to ensure that children under the age of 18 years do not take part in hostilities', thereby refraining from using any adjective before 'take part' (ICRC 1995b: Resolution 2C). The 1990 Declaration of Minimum Humanitarian Standards, which is considered to encapsulate minimum standards of humanity, also stresses that children should not take part in acts of violence, thereby setting a higher standard than the 'direct participation' expression enshrined in Additional Protocol I (see Declaration of Minimum Humanitarian Standards 1990; Meron and Rosas 1991). The Study on Customary International Humanitarian Law (Rule 137) confirms that the expression 'participat[ion] in hostilities' encompasses both direct and indirect acts that may affect enemy forces.

International human rights law also prohibits children's participation in armed conflict. Article 38 of the Convention on the Rights of the Child prohibits the *direct* participation of children (under 15 years of age) in hostilities.[20] The Optional Protocol (art. 1) uses similar wording but stipulates the age of 18 years. The wording used ('do not take a *direct* part in hostilities') seems to allow for, or at least does not preclude, indirect participation in hostilities. In this sense, there is congruence between the Convention on the Rights of the Child, the Optional Protocol and international humanitarian law instruments in the sense that they all forbid direct participation in hostilities. Arguably, the relevant provision in Additional Protocol I should be interpreted so as to align it with customary international humanitarian law. Therefore, it is argued that the *lex specialis*, namely Additional Protocol I and customary international humanitarian law, goes

---

19   The Commentary to Article 51(3) of Additional Protocol I explains that '"direct" participation means acts of war which by their nature or purpose are likely to cause actual harm to the personnel and equipment of the enemy armed forces' (Sandoz *et al.* 1987: ¶ 1944). This definition was reiterated verbatim in *Prosecutor* v. *Rutaganda* (Judgment and Sentence), ICTR-96-3-T, T Ch (1999): ¶ 100. In 2009, the International Committee of the Red Cross issued its Interpretive Guidance on the Notion of Direct Participation in Hostilities under International Humanitarian Law (see Melzer 2008). For a discussion, see Schmitt 2010.

20   As previously explained, the Convention on the Rights of the Child does not bind non-state entities such as armed opposition groups.

further than international human rights law in relation to the *types* of participation by children in armed conflict that it prohibits.

For cases of non-international armed conflict governed by Additional Protocol II, by virtue of the *lex specialis* character of international humanitarian law, Additional Protocol II supersedes the Convention on the Rights of the Child and its Optional Protocol, which means that all forms of participation are prohibited. Nevertheless, inasmuch as Additional Protocol II will not apply when a non-international armed conflict does not reach the threshold set by article 1(1), then article 38 of the Convention on the Rights of the Child and article 1 of the Optional Protocol will be the only legal instruments that will apply in a non-international armed conflict that only falls within the scope of common article 3 of the Four Geneva Conventions of 1949. Consequently, one must refer to the norms established in customary international humanitarian law that prohibit the (direct and indirect) participation by children in non-international armed conflict. Again, international human rights law is here less restrictive than international humanitarian law. However, the difference lies in the age set since the Optional Protocol prohibits the direct participation of children less than 18 years of age.

Non-binding instruments have broadened the definition of a child taking part in hostilities. Both the Paris Commitments adopted in February 2007 and the 1997 Cape Town Principles refer to children below 18 years of age in armed conflict. Yet, they differ in their approaches. Paragraph 6 of the Paris Commitments uses the expression 'used them to participate actively in hostilities', which again indicates that participation must take a direct form, though 'active' is considered as broader than 'direct'. The use of the word 'used' seems to indicate that the focus shifts away from the children and turns to those who make them take an active part in hostilities. Moreover, 'used' rather than 'participated' denotes an objectification of the child that clearly impacts upon how recruitment is perceived and reinforces the perspective of those recruiting children rather than of the children themselves. Going a step further, the Cape Town Principles concentrate on the concept of a child soldier, making no distinction between direct/active and indirect participation. A child is defined as '[a]ny person under 18 years of age who is part of any kind of regular or irregular armed force or armed group in any capacity, including but not limited to cooks, porters, messengers and anyone accompanying such groups, other than family members. It includes girls recruited for sexual purposes and forced marriage. It does not, therefore, only refer to a child who is carrying or has carried arms' (Cape Town Principles 1997: Definitions). Machel (2001: 7) also argues for such a definition in her 2001 follow-up book, and it does certainly seem to better reflect the myriad tasks in which children are involved.

A growing body of international criminal law deals with the use of children less than 15 years of age in armed conflict. The Special Court for Sierra Leone, for example, declared that the use of children under this age to participate actively in hostilities was unlawful as a matter of customary international law.[21] According to the Rome Statute, it is a crime to compel children to participate in armed conflict (see Rome Statute 1998: arts. 8(2)(b)(xxvi) (in the context of international armed conflict), 8(2)(e)(vii) (in the context of non-international armed conflict)). During the negotiation process, it was argued that the expression 'participate actively'[22] covers not only direct participation in combat activities but also military-related activities, such as scouting, spying, sabotage and the use of children as couriers (see Report of the Preparatory Committee 1998: 25, n. 12).[23] This also includes such activities as taking supplies to the frontline. The word 'using' in articles 8(2) (c)(xxvi) and 8(2)(e)(vii) of the Rome Statute reinforces the wish of the drafters of the Rome Statute to prohibit the participation of children in hostilities generally rather than in combat only. Activities 'unrelated to the hostilities such as food deliveries to an airbase [or] the use of domestic staff in an officer's married accommodation' (Report of the Preparatory Committee 1998: 25, n. 12), however, do not qualify as participation in hostilities.

An unintended consequence of broadly defining active participation in hostilities for children is that they then become legitimate targets for military operations, as the Special Court for Sierra Leone Trial Chamber stated in RUF (¶ 1723) and the International Criminal Court noted in *Lubanga*.[24] For this reason, one must be mindful not to give too broad an interpretation to the concept of 'active/direct participation in hostilities' since this would correspondingly reduce the number of children who would be legally protected from direct attack (see Waschefort 2010: 200). The Trial Chamber in *Lubanga* explains that '[t]he decisive factor, therefore, in deciding if an "indirect" role is to be treated as active participation in hostilities is whether the support provided by the child to the combatants exposed him or her to real danger as a potential target' (¶ 628). In other words, sweepingly stating that all activities carried out by a child actively contribute to hostilities turns the child into one who is 'used in hostilities' and is, therefore, ill-advised. As long as children are involved in armed conflict, it might not be sensible to broaden the concept of child soldiers in international humanitarian law too far.

---

21   See *Prosecutor* v. *Norman* (Decision on Preliminary Motion Based on Lack of Jurisdiction), SCSL-2004-14-AR72(E), App Ch (2004).

22   Note that in international criminal law the word 'actively' rather than 'directly' is used. In international humanitarian law, both 'directly' and 'actively' are used (see Waschefort 2010: 194–5, 197–8).

23   This interpretation was confirmed in 2012 by *Lubanga* (¶ 627).

24   'All of these activities, which cover either direct or indirect participation, have an underlying common feature: the child concerned is, at the very least, a potential target' (*Lubanga* 2012: ¶ 628).

The Liberal Discourse Condemning Child Soldiering: A 'Politics of Age'

Rosen argues that 'the "problem" of child soldiers ... derives not from any new phenomenon of young people being present on the battlefield but, rather, from an emerging transnational "politics of age" that shapes the concept of "childhood" in international law' (2007: 296; see also Lee 2009: 3). The key explanation for this seems to be the adoption of a human rights discourse, especially a discourse of children's rights, rather than an international humanitarian law framework. Moreover, by taking a human rights approach to child soldiering, the liberal discourse becomes a humanitarian one that instinctively strips children of their autonomy and, thus, their ability to be agents of their own lives, and portrays them as innocent victims.

Universality

The reconceptualisation of childhood and the current state of international law are based upon the assumption that childhood is different from adulthood and that it requires special protection (see McNeed 2004: 20; Breen 2007: 73; Kendall 2010: 27). International humanitarian law takes two seemingly contradictory approaches in this regard. On the one hand, it offers special protection to children,[25] but it does not differentiate between children and adults who take a direct part in hostilities. When children are involved in hostilities, they are considered combatants (in international armed conflict) or persons taking a direct part in hostilities (see Maslen 1999: 25) who can be targeted (see Cohn and Goodwin-Gill 1993: 45) and, if captured, benefit from prisoner of war status (in international armed conflict) (see Sandoz *et al.* 1987: ¶ 3194) or, in non-international armed conflict, be prosecuted. What international humanitarian law prohibits is the recruitment of children, thus pointing the finger at those who recruit them. While this seems to indicate that international humanitarian law is rather blind to the notion of childhood once children are participants, this position fails to acknowledge that international humanitarian law seeks to prevent the participation of children under 15 years of age in armed conflict in the first place and, thus, instinctively disapproves of their involvement in hostilities.[26] In other words, international humanitarian law distinguishes between childhood and adulthood and follows the international trend set by international human rights law in this regard.

---

25   See, for example, the protection that article 17 of the Fourth Geneva Convention offers in maternity cases and the stipulation in article 24 of the Fourth Geneva Convention that children under 12 years of age are required to wear some form of identity in case they are separated from their parents.

26   In terms of policy rather than law, the International Committee of the Red Cross wishes to prevent children from joining the military by offering them alternatives to enlistment (see ICRC 1995a: Commitment 1, Objective 1.2).

The key is to demarcate the Rubicon between childhood and adulthood. Technically, there are two ways to do this: either to set a specific age for adulthood or to link adulthood to certain skills and abilities. 'In liberal thought, chronological age draws a clear demarcating line between childhood and adulthood' (Schmidt 2007: 57), a position also found in the international legal and humanitarian discourse[27] that aims to set up a new cultural and legal international standard (see Rosen 2007: 297). The most common age for individuals to obtain special protections under international humanitarian law is 15 years of age (see ICRC Study on Customary International Humanitarian Law: Rule 135). A literal interpretation (see Helle 2000) of the relevant provisions demonstrates that international humanitarian law considers a child to be anyone under 18 years of age – 'persons under 18 years of age' and 'children under 15', thus implying that there are children above 15 years of age (see Fox 2005: 31). Rosen argues that this holds 'open the possibility that the concept of "childhood" could be extended beyond [the age of 15]' (2007: 301). Moreover, '[t]o adopt a general notion of "child" in the absence of a definition, as being relevant only [to] those under 15 years of age, would be detrimental to the interest of the child and thus not in conformity with the spirit underlying international humanitarian law' (Helle 2000: 804). Nevertheless, the Commentaries to the relevant treaty provisions do not seem to entirely support this view. The Commentaries to article 14 of the Fourth Geneva Convention and article 24 of Additional Protocol I explain, respectively, that the age of 15 was set to match the 'physical and mental development of a child' (Pictet *et al.* 1958: 126), though some flexibility might be appropriate (see Sandoz *et al.* 1987: ¶ 3179). Thus, it is difficult rigidly to conclude for purposes of international humanitarian law that a child is simply anyone who is under 18 years of age.

Furthermore, whereas international humanitarian law does not prohibit the recruitment and participation of children over 15 years of age, the International Committee of the Red Cross, together with National Red Cross and Red Crescent Societies, considers that no children under 18 years of age should be recruited or used in hostilities. This, of course, follows the Optional Protocol and the latest position in international human rights law (see ICRC 1995a: Commitment 1; ICRC 1999: ¶ 4). Should international humanitarian law follow a policy that is congruent with international human rights law? This would be difficult to achieve because, interestingly, such liberal states as the United States are among some of the most vehement opponents to the rigid 18 years of age approach.

Given that international human rights law is based upon universal ethical standards,[28] some claim that the rigid 18 years of age approach does not

---

27   '[I]nternational advocacy has now created a human rights framework, that raises the minimum age for recruitment and participation in hostilities from fifteen to eighteen' (Coomaraswamy 2010: 536).

28   As Kennedy explains, the human rights vocabulary 'offers answers rather than questions, answers that are not only outside political, ideological and cultural differences,

acknowledge local and regional cultures and traditions, including differing views as to who is a child and who is an adult. A contextual approach that pays heed to culturally constructed and developed ideas and practices of childhood versus adulthood (see Fox 2005: 43) might, therefore, be more appropriate in this area. Remarkably, this is also the approach taken by article 1 of the Convention on the Rights of the Child given that this provision states that adulthood can be reached before 18 years of age if majority is attained earlier in a specific state, thus allowing states to set an age for majority that is in line with cultural and social norms. Contextualists, that is, those who interpret the law by paying particular attention to the cultural and social context in which norms are applied, contend that the cut-off age between childhood and adulthood needs to be challenged. In their opinion, initiation rites, culturally scripted phenomena that are not determined by an abstract age, are the true markers of the passage into adulthood (see Rosen 2007: 297; Kendall 2010: 32). Anthropological research underwrites this assertion and suggests that 'there are a multiplicity of childhoods, each culturally codified and defined by age, ethnicity, gender, history, location, and so forth' (Rosen 2007: 297). Since law is applied within a specific context, ignoring such context while drafting universal norms inevitably leads to discrepancies between the state of the law and its application (see Jonasen 2009: 316).

While the efforts of non-governmental organisations to limit the extent and number of children in armed conflict must be praised, it should be stressed that these organisations and other political groups discount the 'more varied and complex local understandings of children and childhood found in anthropological research' (Rosen 2007: 296) that article 1 of the Convention on the Rights of the Child acknowledges. The definition of a child soldier clashes with local understandings of the involvement of young people in armed conflict (see Wessells and Davidson 2006: 30; Rosen 2007: 297). For example, anthropologists point out that '[i]t is a misnomer in many parts of Africa to call a 14-year-old carrying an AK-47 a child soldier since local people may regard that young person as an adult' (Wessels and Davidson 2006: 30) and childhood and military life are not necessarily understood as either incompatible or contradictory (see Rosen 2007: 297). Moreover, demography in many African states, where the population is disproportionately composed of children, helps to explain the fact that children there often take on adult responsibilities at an earlier age (see Zia-Mansoor 2005: 389) and are more politically and socially aware than their counterparts in the West. African children are also often entrusted with responsibilities that Western liberal culture would view as an abuse of their rights even though they are acceptable in the particular cultural and social context. For example, children may assist relatives at market stalls and in small family businesses. Street-vending and running errands are also common tasks given to children. Nonetheless, it must be borne in mind that the danger to which children are exposed as soldiers can hardly be 'justified

---

but also beyond the human experience of specificity' (2002: 101).

by arguments based on cultural and regional variations regarding the maturity of child soldiers' (Breen 2007: 79).

Interestingly, the approach adopted by international humanitarian law is one that seems to better toe the line of contextualists: it sets the age of childhood in relation to recruitment and participation in hostilities at 15 rather than 18 years of age. As the Commentary to Additional Protocol II explains, 'the moment at which a person ceases to be a child and becomes an adult is not judged in the same way everywhere in the world. Depending on the culture, the age may vary between about fifteen and eighteen years' (Sandoz *et al*. 1987: ¶ 4549). Aware of the significant cross-cultural variation in the age of childhood, the drafters of Additional Protocol II could not agree to raise the age of recruitment and participation to 18 years of age because some states argued that this would cause friction within their particular political and cultural environments (see Sandoz *et al*. 1987: ¶ 4556). Similarly, much of the discussions that took place during the negotiations leading up to the adoption of Additional Protocol I focused on cultural and regional variations in relation to child soldiering (see Breen 2007: 79).[29] The age of 15 was adopted as the lowest common denominator.

The Lack of Autonomy

When a rights-based approach is adopted in relation to child soldiers, one has to address the concept of autonomy upon which the liberal human rights enterprise is founded. In a modern world led by liberal thought, the individual is conceived of as someone who has the capacity and autonomy to act. The individual, who is viewed as independent and self-sufficient (see Fineman 1999: 17), is taken to be an essentially rational actor (see Goodwin 2005: 37), someone who is able to contribute to a society that values his or her capacity to act (see Soulet 2005: 49–50). Autonomy literally means living by one's own law; it is the ability to make certain decisions for oneself without undue interference from others. According to liberal thought, '[t]he individual is ... credited with knowledge of his own best interests and the ability to pursue them rationally' (Goodwin 2005: 37). This discourse is difficult to apply to children, who are viewed as not (yet) having full autonomy.[30]

It is at this point that the liberal discourse seems to contradict itself. On the one hand, liberals wish children to enjoy their autonomy and their rights (see Freeman 1992: 3), but on the other hand, probably influenced by a more humanitarian discourse, they regard children as innocent human beings who deserve protection and whose rights should be protected and promoted and whose needs must be

---

29 Moreover, the Commentary notes that '[t]he age of puberty varies, depending on climate, race and the individual' (Sandoz *et al*. 1987: ¶ 3179), thereby again taking into account the broader context.

30 'Typically, liberals assume quite minimal standards of "competence" to qualify for the rights associated with autonomy, standards that exclude young children' (Hill 1999: 852).

adequately addressed.[31] As Macdonald summarises, '[t]he emergence of individual agency threatens discourses of victimhood' (2008: 142). In practice, however, liberals have tempered their claims of autonomy and rights and emphasised the protection of children and the principle of the best interests of the child. This can be explained in the following manner. Liberals tend to believe that those 'who reject [the liberal] human-rights culture should change their ways' and that 'this culture is a morally superior way of life' (Evans 2003: 118). Thus, they wish to extend their ideas on a universal level, and this means engaging in a discourse of the 'other' that borders on paternalism and imperialism.[32]

In the eyes of liberals, children are not autonomous individuals endowed with the ability to make decisions. On the contrary, they are vulnerable individuals. First, a liberal approach tends to regard children as being unable to make conscious and informed decisions, especially when this concerns their participation in armed hostilities. It is widely understood that children have a limited capacity to understand the world. This inability plays against the child in this discourse inasmuch as he or she is coaxed into recruitment and used in hostilities because he or she is easy to manipulate, fearless and obedient (see Collmer 2004: 8). It is also relatively easy to indoctrinate a child (see Rosen 2010: 50) and convince him or her to take part in hostilities for the 'greater good' without understanding the consequences of his or her acts (see Sandoz *et al.* 1987: ¶ 4555). Does this mean that children are not able to make informed decisions? Perhaps, but at the very least, the liberal discourse seems to miss the point that with age and experience children acquire the ability to understand the world and become active agents of their own lives. 'It is generally accepted that from the age of 15 the development of a child's faculties is such that there is no longer the same need for special, systematic measures' (Dutli 1990). International humanitarian law appears to be more in line with this reality than international human rights law, which sets 18 years of age as the end of childhood.

Reverting to the issue of the 'new wars' and bearing in mind that it might indeed be difficult for children to understand the intricacies of such conflicts, one can reasonably ask whether international humanitarian law's approach is appropriate. International humanitarian law is principally built upon the idea of traditional armed forces, and the bulk of this body of law pertains to international armed conflicts and non-international armed conflicts between armed forces and armed opposition groups (see Harvey 2003: 8). Is international humanitarian law, particularly its provisions on child soldiers, outdated? It might be, but even though customary international humanitarian law covers additional types of conflicts, in

---

31   Schmidt explains that '[l]iberal views, which dominate at least the western, developed world, essentially see children as innocent, weak and in need of protection rather than as agents of their own and significant contributors to social and political life' (2007: 57).

32   As Goodwin explains 'the liberal desire to fuse political and human rights suggests an element of moral imperialism' (2005: 337; see also Schmidt 2007: 59).

particular non-international armed conflicts in which two armed opposition groups fight against each other, it still allows for the recruitment and use of children above 15 years of age. In fact, customary international humanitarian law cannot be altered unless those taking part in hostilities – both state and non-state actors – change their behaviour (practice) and also consider that by doing so they are bound by a legal norm (*opinio juris*) (see McCorquodale 2004: 498). As of now, there is simply no solid evidence that states and armed opposition groups consider the recruitment and participation of children between 15 and 18 years of age in armed conflict to be a violation of international humanitarian law.

A second reason why liberals have tempered their claims of autonomy and rights and emphasised the protection of children and the principle of the best interests of the child can be explained by the persistent and unceasing discourse of children as victims, especially within the context of armed conflict (see Brosha 2005). The mainstream view is that children cannot properly be considered perpetrators of violent acts and that their actions must be understood by looking at the wider social context. In fact, the reality is much grimmer. Indeed, children's participation ranges from helping out with cooking or managing the camp to committing atrocities. In many of these conflicts, after being forced to perform ritualistic killings, such as killing their family or relatives (see Human Rights Watch 2004: 27), children are provided with some rudimentary training on how to operate weapons (see Breen 2007: 73). They gradually enter a process of military socialisation that aims to transform them into killing machines (see Abbott 2000: 510; Legrand and Weissman 1995: 165; Thompson 1999: 193; Mischkowski 2005: 4; RUF: ¶¶ 1619–22, 1632, 1637). Generally, children who live in such an environment tend to lose their personality and identity (see Honwana 2005: 49), as well as any connection to the outside world (see Faulkner 2001: 495; Zia-Mansoor 2005: 397). They lose touch with any concepts of morality that may have been inculcated in them before they joined the armed groups (see Maslen 1999: 25; Alfredson 2001: 7). African conflicts show that many children, trapped in a world of sustained and orchestrated violence, turn into merciless killers (see Maslen 1999: 24; Honwana 2000: 65; Faulkner 2001: 499), becoming 'horde[s] of insensate killers' (Faulkner 2001: 495) that are still portrayed within liberal discourse as innocent individuals (see Brosha 2005).

Children should not only be seen as reluctant participants in armed conflict, however; they should also be viewed as active agents. One might question whether children who are trapped in such situations are genuinely free to consent to their participation in conflict or are simply means to an end for armed groups. It is reported that child soldiers often feel empowered through their experiences of fighting, bearing arms (see Lancaster *et al.* 2007: 13) and killing (see Twum-Danso 2003). Being in an armed group often means enhanced opportunities, autonomy and respect (see West 2000: 187). Are children agents of their own lives, that is, do they have the capacity to make informed choices?[33] The simple answer seems to be in the affirmative, at least to a large extent. For example, '[i]n all conflicts, children can take, and some choose to take, an active role in supporting violence. Children make calculated decisions during armed conflict about how to access shelter, food, medicine, and best ways to keep themselves and their family members safe' (Mazurana and Carlson 2006: 2). This shows that some children do in fact 'manipulate' situations in order to turn them into 'opportunities'. Honwana refers to 'tactical agency,' 'a specific type of agency that is devised to cope with the concrete, immediate conditions of their lives in order to maximise the circumstances created by their military and violent environment' (2005: 49).

Notwithstanding this, it could also be argued that a child soldier's actions are constrained by his or her weak position and that this means that he or she is in reality acting in relation to a specific event rather than looking at the long-term consequences of his or her actions (see Honwana 2000: 75–6). It might thus be argued that these children are indeed not autonomous. While children may exercise their agency (in the way that Honwana uses the term), furthermore, they do so without moral and ethical guidance. To illustrate the point, it is worth noting that child soldiers who attain positions of command in armed groups and become leaders often commit the worst atrocities (see Twum-Danso 2003: 146). The liberal approach to autonomy presupposes a conception of a morally autonomous agent (see Gaus 2005: 272). Again, this can hardly be applied to child soldiers. As such, in the context of child soldiers, it is indeed a fine line between victimhood, agency and autonomy. In other words, the reality is far more complex than the one portrayed in the liberal discourse.

Conclusions

Liberals seek to produce a social construction of childhood that reinforces a particular socio-legal order in which adults are autonomous individuals who protect innocent children, who are endowed with a range of rights, the most significant of which is the idea that all actions should take into account the child's best interests. This paternalistic stance ensures that children who willingly take part in hostilities will be viewed as having lost control of their (limited) agency. After all, fighting is only for adults.

The rise of a liberal human rights ideology, moreover, has led the world to look at child soldiering through the prism of children's rights rather than through the

---

33   Agency 'concerns events of which an individual is the perpetrator, in the sense that the individual could, at any phase in a given sequence of conduct, have acted differently. Whatever happened would not have happened if that individual had not intervened' (Honwana 2005: 48). Agency is a form of autonomy that focuses on the capacity to conceive and act upon projects and values, including projects and values that are 'about things other than one's own experiences' (Johnston 1994: 77).

lens of international humanitarian law. Broadly speaking, international law seeks to protect children from becoming child soldiers. The recruitment, conscription, enlistment and participation of children in armed conflict are clearly prohibited, but at the same time, international law does acknowledge that children can be full participants in hostilities. The current trend in international law is to try to remove all children from the battlefield, thus revealing international law's unwillingness to concede that children might be able to make autonomous decisions: 'Recruitment, whether enforced or voluntary, is always against the best interests of the child' (Coomaraswamy 2010: 542).

Of course, child soldiering is far from a positive experience. 'Young people shall be brought up in the spirit of peace, justice, freedom, mutual respect and understanding in order to promote equal rights for all human beings and all nations, economic and social progress, disarmament and the maintenance of international peace and security' (Declaration on the Promotion 1965: Principle 1). If they take part in hostilities, whether directly or indirectly, it is likely that once the conflict is over children will be unable to be viewed 'as active agents, as productive people in society' (Schauer 2009: 33). To ensure that fewer children take part in conflicts, a whole range of measures, preventive, educational, rehabilitative and others, must be enacted (see ICRC 2011: 5). And it will remain impossible to reduce the involvement of children in armed conflict if political leaders only focus on military strategies and pay scant attention to the welfare of the child.

References

Abbott, A.B. 2000. Child Soldiers – The Use of Children as Instruments of War. *Suffolk Transnational Law Review*, 23, 499–538.

Alfredson, L. 2001. *Sexual Exploitation of Child Soldiers: An Exploration and Analysis of Global Dimensions and Trends*. Coalition to Stop the Use of Child Soldiers. Available at: http://reliefweb.int/report/world/sexual-exploitation-child-soldiers-exploration-and-analysis-global-dimensions-and [accessed: 10 September 2012].

Bald, S. 2002. Searching for a Lost Childhood: Will the Special Court of Sierra Leone Find Justice for its Children? *American University International Law Review*, 18, 537–83.

Boyden, J. 1994. Children's Experience of Conflict Related Emergencies: Some Implications for Relief Policy and Practice. *Disasters*, 18, 254–67.

Breen, C. 2007. When is a Child not a Child? Child Soldiers in International Law. *Human Rights Review*, 8(2), 71–103.

Brosha, S. 2005. Children as Tools of War: Seeking Global Solutions through Theoretical Analysis, *Atlantic International Studies Journal*, 2. Available at: http://atlismta.org/online-journals/0506-journal-government-and-the-rights-of-individuals/children-as-tools-of-war/ [accessed: 10 September 2012].

Cape Town Principles and Best Practices on the Recruitment of Children into the Armed Forces and on Demobilization and Social Reintegration of Child Soldiers in Africa 1997. Available at: http://www.unicef.org/emerg/files/Cape_Town_Principles(1).pdf [accessed: 10 September 2012].

Cohn, I. and Goodwin-Gill, G.S. 1993. *Child Soldiers*. Geneva: Henry Dunant Institute.

Collmer, C. 2004. Child Soldiers – An Integral Element in New, Irregular Wars? *Connections. The Quarterly Journal of PfP Consortium of Defence Academics and Security Studies Institutes*, 3, 1–11.

Coomaraswamy, R. 2010. The Optional Protocol to the Convention on the Rights of the Child on the Involvement of Children in Armed Conflict – Towards Universal Ratification. *International Journal of Children's Rights*, 18, 535–49.

Davison, A. 2004. Child Soldiers: No Longer a Minor Incident. *Willamette Journal of International Law and Dispute Resolution*, 12, 124–57.

De Berry, J. 2001. Child Soldiers and the Convention on the Rights of the Child. *American Academy of Political and Social Science*, 575, 92–105.

Declaration of Minimum Humanitarian Standards (2 December 1990), reprinted in UN Doc E/CN.4/1995/116 (1995)

Declaration of the Rights of the Child, UNGA Res 1386 (XIV) (10 December 1959).

Declaration on the Promotion Among Youth of the Ideals of Peace, Mutual Respect and Understanding Between Peoples, UNGA Res 2037 (XX) (7 December 1965).

Dutli, M. 1990. Captured Child Combatants. *International Review of the Red Cross*, 278. Available at: http://www.icrc.org/eng/resources/documents/article/other/57jmea.htm [accessed: 10 September 2012].

Emmerson, B. 2012. Framework Principles for Securing the Human Rights of Victims of Terrorism, UN Doc A/HRC/20/14.

Evans, M. 2003. Liberalisms, in *Contemporary Political Thought: A Reader and Guide*, ed. A. Finlayson. Edinburgh: Edinburgh University Press, 113–25.

Faulkner, F. 2001. Kindergarten Killers: Morality, Murder and the Child Soldier Problem. *Third World Quarterly*, 22, 491–504.

Fineman, M. 1999. Cracking the Foundational Myths: Independence, Autonomy, and Self-Sufficiency. *American University Journal on Gender, Social Policy and Law*, 8, 13–29.

Fox, M.-J. 2005. Child Soldiers and International Law: Patchwork Gains and Conceptual Debates. *Human Rights Review*, 7, 27–48.

Freeman, M. 1992. Introduction: Rights, Ideology and Children, in *The Ideologies of Children's Rights*, ed. M. Freeman and P.E. Veerman. Dordrecht: Martinus Nijhoff, 3–6.

Gallagher, K. 2010. *Towards a Gender-Inclusive Definition of Child Soldiers: The Prosecutor v Thomas Lubanga Dyilo*. Available at: http://works.bepress.com/kristin_gallagher/1/ [accessed: 10 September 2012].

Gaus, G.F. 2005. The Place of Autonomy within Liberalism, in *Autonomy and the Challenges to Liberalism*, ed. J. Christman and J. Rogers. Cambridge: Cambridge University Press, 272–306.

Goodwin, B. 2005. *Using Political Ideas*. 4th edn. Chichester: Wiley.

Happold, M. 2005. *Child Soldiers in International Law*. Manchester: Manchester University Press.

Harvey, R. 2003. *Children and Armed Conflict: A Guide to International Humanitarian and Human Rights Law*. International Bureau for Children's Rights. Available at: http://www.essex.ac.uk/armedcon/story_id/000044.pdf [accessed: 10 September 2012].

Helle, H. 2000. Optional Protocol on the Involvement of Children in Armed Conflict to the Convention on the Rights of the Child. *International Review of the Red Cross*, 839, 797–809.

Hill, T. Jr. 1999. Autonomy and Agency. *William and Mary Law Review*, 40, 847–56.

Honwana, A. 2000. Innocents et coupables: Les enfants-soldats comme acteurs tactiques. *Politique Africaine*, 80, 58–78.

Honwana, A. 2005. The Pain of Agency, the Agency of Pain: Child-Soldiers as Interstitial and Tactical Agents, in *Makers & Breakers: Children & Youth in Postcolonial Africa*, ed. A. Honwana and F. De Boeck. Oxford: James Currey, 31–52.

Hughes, L. 2000. Can International Law Protect Child Soldiers? *Peace Review*, 12(3), 399–405.

Human Rights Watch 2004. *How to Fight, How to Kill: Child Soldiers in Liberia*. Available at: http://www.hrw.org/reports/2004/02/02/how-fight-how-kill-0 [accessed: 10 September 2012].

International Committee of the Red Cross (ICRC) 1995a. Council of Delegates. Plan of Action Concerning Children in Armed Conflict.

International Committee of the Red Cross (ICRC) 1995b. Council of Delegates. Resolution 2C.

International Committee of the Red Cross (ICRC) 1999. Council of Delegates. Resolution 8.

International Committee of the Red Cross (ICRC) 2011. Guiding Principles for the Domestic Implementation of a Comprehensive System of Protection for Children Associated With Armed Forces or Armed Groups.

International Committee of the Red Cross (ICRC). Study on Customary International Humanitarian Law. Available at: http://www.icrc.org/customary-ihl/eng/docs/home [accessed: 15 September 2012].

James, A. and James, A.L. 2001. Childhood: Toward a Theory of Continuity and Change. *American Academy of Political and Social Science*, 575, 25–37.

Johnston, D. 1994. *The Idea of a Liberal Theory: A Critique and Reconstruction*. Princeton: Princeton University Press.

Jonasen, M. 2009. Child Soldiers in Chad. *Intersections*, 10(1), 309–29.

Kaldor, M. 1999. *New and Old Wars: Organized Violence in a Global Era.* Cambridge: Polity.

Kendall, N. 2010. Gendered Moral Dimensions of Childhood Vulnerability. *Childhood in Africa*, 2(1), 26–37.

Kennedy, D. 2002. The International Human Rights Movement: Part of the Problem? *Harvard Human Rights Journal*, 15, 101–26.

Lancaster, P. *et al.* 2007. *Children in Conflict: Eradicating the Child Soldier Doctrine.* Research Report Prepared for the Carr Center for Human Rights and Supervised by Lieutenant-General the Honourable R.A. Dallaire. Available at: http://www.ksg.harvard.edu/cchrp/pdf/ChildSoldierReport.pdf [accessed: 10 September 2012].

Lee, A.-J. 2009. Understanding and Addressing the Phenomenon of 'Child Soldiers': The Gap Between the Global Humanitarian Discourse and the Local Understandings and Experiences of Young People's Military Recruitment. Refugee Studies Centre, Working Paper Series No. 52. Available at: http://www.rsc.ox.ac.uk/publications/working-papers-folder_contents/RSCworkingpaper52.pdf [accessed: 10 September 2012].

Legrand, J.-C. and Weissman, F. 1995. Les enfants soldats et usages de la violence au Mozambique. *Cultures et Conflits*, 18, 165–80.

McCarthy, C. 2008. Legal Conclusion or Interpretative Process? *Lex Specialis* and the Applicability of International Human Rights Standards, in *International Humanitarian Law and Human Rights Law: Towards a New Merger in International Law*, ed. R. Arnold and N. Quénivet. The Hague: Martinus Nijhoff, 101–21.

McCorquodale, R. 2004. An Inclusive International Legal System. *Leiden Journal of International Law*, 17, 477–504.

Macdonald, A. 2008. 'New Wars: Forgotten Warriors': Why Have Girl Fighters Been Excluded from Western Representations of Conflict in Sierra Leone? *Africa Development*, XXXIII(3), 135–45.

Machel, G. 1996. Impact of Armed Conflict on Children, UN Doc A/51/306.

Machel, G. 2001. *The Impact of War on Children: A Review of Progress Since the 1996 United Nations Report on the Impact of Armed Conflict on Children.* London: Hurst.

McNeed, L. 2004. The Languages of Childhood: The Discursive Construction of Childhood and Colonial Policy in French West Africa. *African Studies Quarterly*, 7(4), 20–32.

Madubuike-Ekwe, J. 2005. The International Legal Standards Adopted to Stop the Participation of Children in Armed Conflicts. *Annual Survey of International and Comparative Law*, 11, 29–48.

Maslen, S. 1999. *Kinder sind keine Soldaten – Politische und rechtliche Aspekte des Phänomens Kindersoldaten.* Konferenz, Kinder im Krieg, 25 August 1999, Friedrich-Ebert-Stiftung in Zusammenarbeit mit UNICEF. Available at: http://64.233.183.104/search?q=cache:JiacUbAOxmUJ:library.fes.de/pdf-files/iez/01374.pdf+Kinder+und+Krieg+%E2%80%93+eine+Bestandsaufnah me&hl=en&ct=clnk&cd=1&gl=uk [accessed: 10 September 2012].

Mazurana, D. and Carlson, K. 2006. *The Girl Child and Armed Conflict: Recognizing and Addressing Grave Violations of Girls' Human Rights.* United Nations Division for the Advancement of Women in Collaboration with UNICEF, EGM/DVGC/2006/EP.12. Available at: http://www.un.org/ womenwatch/daw/egm/elim-disc-viol-girlchild/ExpertPapers/EP.12%20 Mazurana.pdf [accessed: 10 September 2012].

Melzer, N. 2008. Interpretive Guidance on the Notion of Direct Participation in Hostilities under International Humanitarian Law, Adopted by the Assembly of the International Committee of the Red Cross on 26 February 2009. *International Review of the Red Cross*, 90(872), 991–1047.

Meron, T. and Rosas, A. 1991. A Declaration of Minimum Humanitarian Standards. *American Journal of International Law*, 85, 375–81.

Mischkowski, G. 2005. *Abducted, Raped, Enslaved: The Situation of Girl Soldiers in the Case of Uganda.* Medica Mondiale. Available at: http:// www.medicamondiale.org/download/doku_report/Mischkowski_ GirlSoldiersUganda.pdf [accessed: 6 August 2007].

Mitchell, A. 2003–2004. Sierra Leone: The Road to Childhood Ruination through Forced Recruitment of Child Soldiers and the World's Failure to Act. *Regent Journal of International Law*, 2, 81–114.

Paris Commitments to Protect Children Unlawfully Recruited or Used by Armed Forces or Armed Groups. 2007. Available at: http://www.icrc.org/eng/assets/ files/other/the-paris-commitments.pdf [accessed: 10 September 2012].

Pictet, J. *et al.* (eds) 1958. *Commentary on the Geneva Conventions of 12 August 1949: IV Geneva Convention Relative to the Protection of Civilian Persons in Time of War.* Geneva: International Committee of the Red Cross.

REDRESS 2006. *Victims, Perpetrators or Heroes? Child Soldiers before the International Criminal Court.* London: REDRESS Trust. Available at: http://www.iccnow.org/documents/Redress_childsoldiers_report_Sep06.pdf [accessed: 10 September 2012].

Report of the Preparatory Committee on the Establishment of an International Criminal Court, Draft Statute and Draft Final Act (14 April 1998), UN Doc A/ Conf.183/2/Add. 1.

Rogers, A. 2000. Zero-Casualty Warfare. *International Review of the Red Cross*, 837, 165–81.

Rosen, D. 2007. Child Soldiers, International Humanitarian Law, and the Globalization of Childhood. *American Anthropologist*, 109(2), 296–306.

Rosen, D. 2010. Social Change and the Legal Construction of Child Soldier Recruitment in the Special Court for Sierra Leone. *Childhood in Africa*, 2(1), 48–57.

Sandoz, Y., Swinarski, C. and Zimmermann, B. (eds) 1987. *Commentary on the Additional Protocols of 8 June 1977 to the Geneva Conventions of 12 August 1949.* Geneva: Martinus Nijhoff and International Committee of the Red Cross.

Schauer, S. 2009. Witness Statement, ICC-01/04-01/06-T-166-ENG CT WT (rev. dec. 1974). Available at: http://www.icc-cpi.int/iccdocs/doc/doc804068.pdf [accessed: 10 September 2012].

Schmidt, A. 2007. Volunteer Child Soldiers as Reality: A Development Issue for Africa. *New School Economic Review*, 2(1), 49–76.

Schmitt, M.N. 2010. Deconstructing Direct Participation in Hostilities: The Constitutive Elements. *New York University Journal of International Law and Policy*, 42(3), 697–740.

Singer, P.W. 2005. *Children at War*. New York: Pantheon Books.

Sivakumaran, S. 2010. War Crimes before the Special Court for Sierra Leone. *Journal of International Criminal Justice*, 8, 1009–34.

Smith, A. 2004. Child Recruitment and the Special Court for Sierra Leone. *Journal of International Criminal Justice*, 2, 1141–53.

Soulet, M.-H. 2005. La vulnérabilité comme catégorie de l'action publique. *Pensée Plurielle*, 2, 49–59.

Statute of the Special Court for Sierra Leone Established by an Agreement Between the United Nations and the Government of Sierra Leone Pursuant to SC Res 1315 (2000).

Taylor, D. 2006. I Wanted to Take Revenge. *Guardian*, 7 July. Available at: http://www.guardian.co.uk/guardianweekly/story/0,1824246,00.html [accessed: 10 September 2012].

Thompson, C. 1999. Beyond Civil Society: Child Soldiers as Citizens in Mozambique. *Review of African Political Economy*, 80, 190–206.

Triffterer, O. (ed.) 1999. *Commentary on the Rome Statute of the International Criminal Court*. Munich: C.H. Beck; Oxford: Hart; Baden-Baden: Nomos.

Twum-Danso, A. 2003. *Africa's Young Soldiers: The Co-Option of Childhood*. Institute of Security Studies, Monograph No. 82. Available at: http://www.issafrica.org/pgcontent.php?UID=1535 [accessed: 10 September 2012].

Udombana, N. 2006. War is Not Child's Play! International Law and the Prohibition of Children's Involvement in Armed Conflicts. *Temple International and Comparative Law Journal*, 20(1), 57–109.

United Nations Special Representative of the Secretary-General on Children and Armed Conflict, Written Submissions, Situation in the Democratic Republic of the Congo in the Case of *The Prosecutor v. Thomas Lubanga Dyilo*, Submitted in Application of Rule 103 of the Rules of Procedure and Evidence (2008), ICC-01/04-01/06-1229-AnxA 18-03-2008 2/10 CB T. Available at: http://childrenandarmedconflict.un.org/documents/AmicuscuriaeICCLubanga.pdf [accessed: 10 September 2012].

UNSC Res 1882 (2009), UN Doc S/RES/1882.

UNSC Res 1998 (2011), UN Doc S/RES/1998.

Waschefort, G. 2010. Justice for Child Soldiers? The RUF Trial of the Special Court of Sierra Leone. *Journal of International Humanitarian Legal Studies*, 1, 189–204.

Wessells, M. 2006. *Child Soldiers: From Violence to Protection.* Cambridge, MA: Harvard University Press.

Wessells, M. and Davidson, J. 2006. Recruitment and Reintegration of Former Youth Soldiers in Sierra Leone: Challenges of Reconciliation and Post-Accord Peace Building, in *Troublemakers or Peacemakers? Youth and Post-Accord Peace Building*, ed. S. McEvoy-Levy. Notre Dame: University of Notre Dame Press, 27–47.

West, H. 2000. Girls with Guns: Narrating the Experience of War of FRELIMO's 'Female Detachment'. *Anthropological Quarterly*, 73, 180–94.

Witness DRC-OTP-WWW-0046 2009. ICC-01/04-01/06-T-207-ENG WT 09/07-2009 6/65 NB T. Available at: http://212.159.242.181/iccdocs/doc/doc713215. pdf [accessed: 10 September 2012].

Zia-Mansoor, F. 2005. The Dilemma of Child Soldiers: Who is Responsible? *Kings College Law Journal*, 16, 388–99.

Chapter 7

Spatial Conceptions of the Law of Armed Conflict

Louise Arimatsu

In a 2002 article, Michael N. Schmitt predicted that twenty-first century warfare would differ dramatically from warfare in the twentieth century. Writing at a time when transnational terrorism was dominating the headlines, Schmitt nonetheless claimed that it was information warfare that would 'challenge existing doctrine on the waging of war, necessitate a revised concept of battle space and expand the available methods and means of warfare' (2002: 365). A decade on, few would disagree with Schmitt's analysis. The prospect of cyber warfare is necessitating a revised understanding of battle spaces. But what Schmitt could not have foreseen was that transnational terrorism, rather than cyber warfare, would first drive a rethinking of the battle space and the reconceptualisation of the spatial reach of the law of armed conflict. For the next decade, nearly every aspect of international law involving the use of force and the law of armed conflict was contested, dissected, reconstituted. Was transnational terrorism subject to the law of armed conflict or better governed by the law enforcement paradigm? Were terror suspects 'unlawful enemy combatants' or criminals? If the law of armed conflict applied, was the 'war on terror' an international or non-international armed conflict? As experts disagreed on these and other legal questions, there were increasing calls for new law to govern a new type of war (see Schondorf 2004; Corn and Talbot 2009). And at the root of all these questions was the geography question: where precisely is the battle space?

This chapter reflects upon the pattern of armed conflict over the last two decades and asks whether contemporary conflict has changed to such a fundamental degree that it compels us to re-evaluate the existing laws pertaining to armed conflict. In other words, has our spatial conception of the world – prompted by 'new' threats – altered to such an extent that the law can no longer function without a radical rethinking because its very foundations are grounded on an outmoded worldview? I position this investigation through a *re*consideration of the legacy of the traumatic attacks of 11 September 2001 and suggest that, rather than representing a defining moment warranting new laws to capture a new type of war, what we have witnessed is a reconstitution of the law of armed conflict's spatiality that has left untouched the fundamental rules and principles that comprise the law of armed conflict. In other words, transnational terrorism has served as a catalyst for how the law of armed conflict has been reconfigured, coded and framed, paving the way for engaging with contemporary and future conflicts through multiple lenses. This is not a claim about a new type of war but, rather, a *reawakening* prompted by the moment of rupture of 11 September that forced us to reflect upon the law, bringing into sharp relief its best and worst attributes. Some of the law's artificial constructs that had hitherto been hidden in plain view were exposed, as were the arbitrary foundations of the law, the 'gaps' and fault lines, its incoherence and limitations, fragility, malleability, rigidity. Yet that moment of critical introspection and reflection also revealed the common founding principles upon which the contemporary law of armed conflict is grounded. Not only did we *re*collect the values entrenched within the substantive rules, but we also observed, almost in wonder, the legal hurdles that had been embedded within the law's procedural make-up that functioned to agitate consciences.

This chapter opens with an overview of two distinct views that have emerged over the last two decades in response to the changing nature of warfare. Common to both is the anxiety that the modern state is ill-prepared to respond to the spatial reconceptualisation of the global order. In particular, this chapter explores how the law of armed conflict's spatial preconceptions have been radically challenged through state practice and the decisions of courts. I suggest that this reconstitution of space has engendered an angst that is as much about the *pace* of change as it is about the *outcomes* produced. The second part of this chapter considers the legal debates surrounding the use of unmanned aircraft systems, or drones, as a tactic in responding to transnational terrorism and suggests that the discomfort that many feel about this technology is symptomatic of a deep set of concerns related to the extended spatial, and temporal, reach of the law of armed conflict. I interrogate whether this reconfiguration of space is disrupting the divide between war and crime and between *jus in bello* and *jus ad bellum*. The final part of this chapter reflects upon whether the extended spatial scope of the law of armed conflict is to be welcomed or resisted.

'New Wars' and the Spatiality of the Law of Armed Conflict

The 'new wars' discourse has a bifurcated past in the sense that the body of work generated under its banner can be broadly divided into two schools of thought. The first of these schools comprises experts in the law of armed conflict. For these experts, the term 'new wars' is associated with two seemingly distinct topics. The first concerns technology's interface with war and, more specifically, implicates questions raised by the prospect of cyber warfare. The second topic, which has commanded considerable attention over the last decade, concerns the interface between the law of armed conflict and transnational terrorism. In their engagement with both the cyber project and transnational terrorism, legal experts like Schmitt have been governed by pragmatic concerns supplemented by partially utopian ambitions. The ostensible ambiguity of the law, whether in respect of transnational terrorism or rapid advances in technology coupled with the pace of globalisation, has demanded attention and clarification, not least to offer sound guidance to the armed forces.

A second constituency of the 'new wars' narrative adopts a far more expansive reading of the term. For these scholars, the disruption of the state-centric global order by the forces of globalisation has instituted fundamental changes in social relations that, in some situations, have spiralled into a 'new' type of conflict. These wars are marked by a wholly different variety of armed actors motivated by an array of aims. From the Balkans to the Democratic Republic of the Congo, the 'new wars' of today and tomorrow are 'criminal, depoliticised, private and predatory' in contrast to the 'old wars', which were 'ideological, political, collective, and even noble' (Kalyvas 2001: 100). As with the law of armed conflict experts, the objectives of these scholars are both pragmatic and utopian, though, in contrast to the former school, their temporal and subject matter focus has been wider. Committed to reshaping the thinking of decision-makers, their ambition has been to nurture a politics rooted in democracy and a cosmopolitan liberalism augmented by the international rule of law. But what also differentiates the two approaches is that while the former generally needs to assume that legal clarity will lead to improved compliance, the prevalence of non-compliance as a feature of 'new wars' is one of the primary concerns of the latter. Nonetheless, whether any of the more recent armed conflicts can be described as 'new', necessitating a radical rethinking of the relationship between war and law, remains contested.

In spite of the divergent methodological approaches, common to both schools is the question of how to 'rethink' both law and policy in a reconceptualised world space made *possible* with the end of the Cold War, *probable* with globalisation and *necessary* with law's ascendency and its interface with technology. With the collapse of the Cold War's crude binary worldview in which armed conflict was constituted for the most part through the political lens of the proxy war, a more attentive engagement with civil wars was made *possible*. What this revealed were alternative narratives that were far more complex and ones in which armed conflict was waged for a variety of reasons based on identities that transcended borders. What made the re-engagement with space more *probable* was the emergence of the political phenomena of 'global deterritorialisation' or the 'loss of space or of territorial markers' as a consequence of globalisation's accelerated temporal practices (see Debrix 1998: 829). In other words, the 'intensification of global inter-connectedness – political, economic, military and cultural – and the changing character of political authority' was seen to be eroding the autonomy of the territorial state and its monopoly on violence and thereby generating, and concurrently making more visible, armed conflict populated by a variety of global actors not yoked to the territorial state (see Kaldor 2008: 4). But what has *necessitated* a rethinking of the law of armed conflict's spatiality is the dominance of the legal lens through which contemporary conflict is viewed. Schmitt's analysis cited in the opening paragraph of this chapter indicates that both transnational terrorism and the recently resuscitated cyber warfare project require us to revise our concepts of the 'battle space'. In other words, critical scrutiny of our understanding of the law of armed conflict's spatiality is warranted because how today's wars are fought seems to challenge deeply held preconceptions about, and our fidelity towards, territory and boundaries. This has been made even more pressing with the increasing use of drones in the fight against transnational terrorism, a tactic that appears to 'redefine' the geography of war and leave legal experts grappling with the 'geography' or 'spatiality' of the law of armed conflict (see Anderson 2011).

Contemporary conflict thus seems to beckon us to – or rather *insist* that we – think past boundaries and territory in that these are conflicts fought in unfamiliar 'battle spaces'. In other words, some of today's conflicts are distinguishable from the paradigmatic 'traditional' armed conflict by virtue of their deterritorialised characteristics. By 'deterritorialised', I refer to those fought without any regard to territorial boundaries that may be global or regional in scope. Moreover, such conflicts involve non-state actors who are affiliated to an organised armed group by linkages other than that of territory. But if that is the case, what we have witnessed since the end of the Cold War is not the *emergence* of the deterritorialised conflict but its *re-emergence* in fact and visibility. Prior to the emergence of the territorial nation-state, armed conflicts were typically waged between parties united by culture, race, religion and nationality (albeit not linked to territory), and although the prevalence of such conflicts may have declined over time, they have always continued to fester, not least on the African continent. I do not, however, take the view that what we are glimpsing is the decay, erosion or decline of the territorial nation-state. Rather, territorialised conflicts, albeit in a reorganised shape,[1] will continue to subsist side-by-side with deterritorialised ones. The challenge for the law is to effectively capture both without losing sight of its overriding aims: to protect the victims of armed conflict and regulate the conduct of hostilities.

If the rules of armed conflict are indeed ancient in origin and deterritorialised conflicts are not unique to the twenty-first century, how do we account for the uneasy 'fit' between law and war? My claim is simple. A review of its ancient origins indicates that the law of armed conflict's rules and principles over the ages were always intended to bind the *parties* to the conflict rather than being conceptually linked to any notion of territory (see Arimatsu 2009). In other words, this body of law was originally simply agnostic to territorial boundaries. Nevertheless, through the codification of the law of armed conflict from the second half of the nineteenth century onwards, a territorial casing was superimposed upon the law that now struggles to navigate between its purpose and its form, the latter being dominated by international law's overarching goal: to regulate the relations between *territorial* nation-states. Codification situated the law within a territorialised legal apparatus that has functioned to constrain thinking by engendering a legal reasoning that is founded on territory. The

---

1   If the last decade offers us an indication of what the future might hold, multinational military operations that are confined to a pre-designated territorial location – in other words, within the boundaries of specific states – will continue to feature.

limitations of territorialised reasoning have become all too apparent in the face of the deterritorial dimensions of contemporary armed conflict, whether in the form of transnational terrorism or cyber warfare. Confronted by the deterritorialised conflict, the law of armed conflict has attempted to unshackle itself from the straitjacket imposed by territorialised legal reasoning, the edifice upon which public international law is constituted.

Embedded within the codified rules is a deep-seated fidelity to the border. This has led to some uncomfortable consequences as typified by the contorted reasoning of the International Criminal Tribunal for the former Yugoslavia in the Appeals Chamber's 1999 judgment in *Prosecutor* v. *Tadić*.[2] In that case, the Appeals Tribunal had to consider whether the defendant could rightly be charged with grave breaches of the Four Geneva Conventions of 1949. For the tribunal, the pivotal legal question was whether the victims were 'protected persons' as defined by the Geneva Conventions since the relevant offences only applied to 'those who, at a given moment and in any manner whatsoever, find themselves, in case of a conflict or occupation, in the hands of a Party to the conflict or Occupying Power of which they are not nationals' (Fourth Geneva Convention 1949: art. 4). The tribunal's predicament was that both defendant and victim were of the same nationality. Rejecting a literal reading of the text that was contingent upon satisfying a nationality requirement – *which is clearly nothing but the product of territorialised thinking* – the tribunal applied an 'allegiance' test that looked to the *relations* between the parties. In justifying its decision, the Appeals Chamber reasoned that, while 'previously wars were primarily between well-established States, in modern inter-ethnic armed conflicts such as that in the former Yugoslavia, new States are often created during the conflict and ethnicity rather than nationality may become the grounds for allegiance' (*Tadić* 1999: ¶ 166). While the outcome of this reasoning is welcome, the tribunal's attempt to explain the shortcomings of the law by referencing the changing nature of warfare risks conveying a misleading account of both warfare and the history of the laws of war.

The extent to which territorialised legal thinking permeates the law of armed conflict is most acutely revealed in the way in which the *ad hoc* tribunals have confronted questions involving the spatial scope of war and the law. For example, the tribunal's reasoning that some provisions of the Geneva Conventions extend to 'the entire territory of the Parties to the conflict, not just to the vicinity of actual hostilities'[3] exposes, above all, a mindset framed by territoriality. Likewise, on the question of the geographical scope of the law in respect of non-international armed conflict, the finding by the International Criminal Tribunal for Rwanda that common article 3 'must be applied in the whole territory of the State engaged in the conflict'[4] displays, above all, an unflinching commitment to the border.

---

2   *Prosecutor* v. *Tadić* (Judgment), IT-94-1/A, App Ch (1999) (hereafter *Tadić* 1999).

3   *Prosecutor* v. *Tadić* (Decision on the Defence Motion for Interlocutory Appeal on Jurisdiction), IT-94-1-AR72 (1995) (hereafter *Tadić* 1995): ¶ 67.

4   *Prosecutor* v. *Akayesu* (Judgment), ICTR-96-4-T, T Ch (1998): ¶¶ 635–6.

In 2006, the United States Supreme Court released its judgment in *Hamdan* v. *Rumsfeld*,[5] inadvertently bringing to the fore the geography question by resituating the law within a pre-territorialised landscape. In rejecting as 'erroneous' the government's argument that the armed conflict with Al Qaeda did not fall within the ambit of common article 3 because it was 'international in scope', the Court shifted the debate from the domain of territorialised legal reasoning to one rooted in a relationship (see *Hamdan*: 2795). With the simple statement that '[t]he term "conflict not of an international character" is used here [that is, in common article 3] in contradistinction to a conflict between nations' (*Hamdan*: 2795), it exposed the extent to which the material-institutional practices and conditions of a territorial viewpoint had permeated legal reasoning. That the classification of a conflict was determined by the parties to the conflict was widely accepted.[6] What remained 'fuzzy' were non-international armed conflicts, or those fought between states and non-state actors, that transcended borders. The Court's judgment was to follow the reasoning of classification to its logical conclusion. The geographical location of the conflict or whether a border was transgressed was irrelevant. In extending the spatial conception of the law further than that articulated by the *ad hoc* tribunals, the law of armed conflict was returned to its deterritorialised origins. Simply put, it is impossible to speak of the spatial scope of the law of armed conflict since the law governs a *relationship*. Transnational terrorism has been the catalyst for the law of armed conflict to negotiate and *re*claim a deterritorialised trajectory. And in the process, space has been reconstituted.

But does state practice tell us another story? There is no evidence to suggest that states view the spatial reach of the law of international armed conflict as any narrower than that articulated by the Appeals Chamber in *Tadić* 1999. Rather, the opposite is the case. State practice reveals that the spatial reach of the law of international armed conflict is potentially far more extensive, limited geographically by the law of neutrality complemented by the principle of territorial sovereignty. Insofar as non-international armed conflict is concerned, state practice supports a similar conclusion since the existence of such an armed conflict is a factual matter that is determined by the parties to the conflict, not their geographical location. To the extent that the overarching ambition of the law is humanitarian in objective, the border thus represents a point of negotiation rather than limitation. This understanding of how the law of armed conflict operates, particularly in regard to non-international armed conflict, has led, unavoidably, to the collision of two irreconcilable legal regimes.

In the following section, I examine how the law of armed conflict's agnosticism towards boundaries in respect of non-international armed conflict is disrupting the traditional divide between war and crime and between *jus in bello* and *jus ad bellum*. I suggest that it is the deterritorialised nature of perceived threats that has

---

5   *Hamdan* v. *Rumsfeld* [2006] 126 S. Ct. 2749 (hereafter *Hamdan*).

6   See *Military and Paramilitary Activities in and Against Nicaragua (Nicaragua* v. *United States)* [1986] ICJ Rep 14 (hereafter *Nicaragua*).

prompted states to increasingly turn to the *jus in bello*, which knows no borders, rather than the law enforcement paradigm that is founded on the preservation of the border. Disturbing though this trend is, what is far more problematic are the attempts to reinterpret the *jus ad bellum* edifice, constituted on the basis of regulating the relationship between territorially defined nation-states, to 'fit' with the deterritorialised conception of the *jus in bello*. These challenges are considered through the prism of the debates that surround the use of drones.

The Drone, Space and Law

Over a decade after the attack on the Twin Towers by Al Qaeda, the legal community remains divided on a number of questions that are of either a spatial or a temporal character, or a combination thereof.[7] There is considerable disagreement as to whether members of Al Qaeda (even those with operational or leadership roles) can be lawfully targeted – if at all – irrespective of where they are located. These disputes should not be misinterpreted as an *absence* of law but, rather, as an opportunity to reflect upon whether a state's response to transnational terrorism is more appropriately subject to the law of armed conflict or, alternatively, the criminal law model. If it *is* the former, the question that arises is on what basis a state may resort to force against an armed non-state actor located within the territory of another state without that state's consent. How these questions have been addressed has been deeply transformed and reframed by the revised spatial conceptions of the law pertaining to non-international armed conflict.

At the site of these two questions that form the core of current legal debate is the drone, a technologically advanced weapons system that has provoked heated exchanges among commentators both within and beyond the contours of the law. But is there anything unique about this particular piece of military technology to warrant such deep angst among liberals?[8] One explanation is that this technology forces us to confront a plethora of existential questions related to modernity itself. More than any previous means of warfare, the drone appears to threaten and obscure our ability to differentiate between the real and unreal, exposing our obsessive desire to control our environment, to institute order and discipline into the world and to reaffirm our agency. Yet, paradoxically, what the use of the drone most brutally and effectively does is to remind us of our mortality and our *inability* to discipline the world by situating us in an environment in which space and time are foreshortened. An alternative explanation for the unease engendered by the drone is that it appears to challenge the basic tenets of

---

7　The temporal scope of the law is not investigated in this chapter.

8　For the purposes of this chapter, the drone is treated as a remotely controlled armed weapons system. In other words, drones that are used for surveillance and intelligence gathering are excluded.

liberalism understood as a political doctrine. This concern inevitably raises the choice of law question (see Shklar 2004).

In the following subsections, I address both of the legal questions that have fuelled divisions among experts over the use of drones to target armed non-state actors. The law is at a critical juncture to the extent that the questions raised are not unique to transnational terrorism; the decisions made today are likely to affect warfare in both the physical and the cyber domains of tomorrow (see United Kingdom Ministry of Defence 2010: 76). I start with the choice of law question to suggest that at the moment when the spatial preconceptions of the non-international armed conflict were being challenged and the deterritorialised potential of the law was being embraced, the pull of the criminal law paradigm was partially severed; this led to a preference for the war paradigm, albeit only in respect of the deterritorialised non-international armed conflict. Hence, liberalism's anxiety is not necessarily with the drone as such but with what it signifies.

Rethinking the Choice of Law in the Context of Space

Although the legal regimes designed to apply in wartime and peacetime are rooted in divergent assumptions, the boundary between the two *conditions* is perpetually in flux, contested, uncertain. While there is greater certainty and clarity in respect of the two polar positions in the continuum of violence, the conviction that a line demarcating the divide between war and peace is universally recognisable is a testament to the law's proficiency at obscuring reality as much as it is an exposing of its internal limitations and bifurcated rigidity.[9] Thus, to accept the proposition that the relative clarity between war and peace, as evidenced by the codified rules of armed conflict, was replaced by 'confusion' in the course of the twentieth century is to receive, too readily, the narrative conveyed by the law's structure.[10] It is, therefore, hardly surprising that attempts to differentiate between warfare and criminal activity on the basis of actors,[11] geographical location, motive[12] or scale of violence all tend to collapse into themselves since the determination as to which of the two regimes most

---

9   See, for example, Lupi 1998: 379 (stating that 'it appears evident from the Report that it is truly difficult to ascertain whether the events reported can be set within a legal context of war or within that of a police operation aiming at restoring public order. Therefore, the Commission failed to express any legal evaluation of the facts, particularly from the perspective of international humanitarian law').

10   As Hobsbawm put it in 2003, '[i]t would be easier to write about war and peace in the 20th century if the difference between the two remained as clear-cut as it was supposed to be at the beginning of the century, in the days when the Hague conventions of 1899 and 1907 codified the rules of war.'

11   Both states and non-state actors can engage in what is regarded as 'criminal' behaviour and acts of warfare.

12   On the irrelevance of motive, see *Prosecutor* v. *Limaj et al.* (Judgment), IT-03-66-T, T Ch (2005): ¶ 170.

appropriately applies to any given situation of violence has been contingent, more often than not, on the arbitrary decision of the sovereign.

The right of the state to decide is, itself, founded on spatial assumptions constituted by the law. Short of armed conflict, how states respond to violence by non-state actors has traditionally been treated as a matter that rests primarily with the territorial state and, therefore, subject to its domestic law, though increasingly tempered by international human rights law. Domestic laws governing the relationship between the state and armed non-state actors are, for the most part, constituted on the basis that they apply *within* a particular space demarcated by international boundaries. This is evident in both treaty and customary international law, both of which consistently reaffirm the right of the state to decide how it governs within its territorial boundaries, not least in respect of matters pertaining to security. This right is also implicit in the law of armed conflict, which excludes 'situations of internal disturbances and tensions, such as riots, isolated and sporadic acts of violence and other acts of a similar nature' as falling *outside* its scope and, thus, not subject to the law of armed conflict (see Protocol Additional to the Geneva Conventions of 12 August 1949, and Relating to the Protection of Victims of Non-International Armed Conflicts 1977 (Additional Protocol II): art. 1(2)).

As a consequence, history is replete with examples of states refusing to concede that an outbreak of violence *within* its territory is a matter other than a temporary breakdown of law and order more properly governed by domestic criminal law. This has been the case even in situations of violence that go beyond those described above.[13] There are good reasons why states defiantly resist the existence of what is objectively a situation of armed conflict. First, to accept the factual existence of an armed conflict vis-à-vis an organised armed group is to admit to structural and systemic collapse and catastrophic political failure.[14] What is more, it is to allow for the intervention – legal and otherwise – of the *international* into the domain of the domestic and to voluntarily, albeit partially, relinquish sovereignty. Thus, time and again, for the dual purpose of excluding international scrutiny through the law and consolidating its internal authority through the reassertion of its monopoly on violence, states have consciously invoked the language of criminality and described the violence at issue as being on a par with rioting. The reflexive pull towards the conceptual domain of crime and law enforcement in responding to the violence of non-state actors is best demonstrated by the initial reaction of the United States to the 11 September attacks. In his address to the nation that evening,

---

13   See, for example, Abresch 2005 (discussing Russia's stance before the European Court of Human Rights in respect of the Chechnya conflict).

14   The argument often cited that conceding the existence of an armed conflict extends an element of status or legitimacy to the non-state actor is less compelling. However, 'although Common Article 3 specifically provides that its application does not affect the legal status of the parties to a conflict, states have been, and always will be, reluctant to admit that a state of armed conflict exists' (United Kingdom Ministry of Defence 2004: 384).

United States President George W. Bush situated transnational terrorism within the crime paradigm with the statement:

> Today, our fellow citizens, our way of life, our very freedom came under attack in a series of deliberate and deadly terrorist acts. The victims were in airplanes, or in their offices; secretaries, businessmen and women, military and federal workers; moms and dads, friends and neighbors. Thousands of lives were suddenly ended by evil, despicable acts of terror. The pictures of airplanes flying into buildings, fires burning, huge structures collapsing, have filled us with disbelief, terrible sadness, and a quiet, unyielding anger. These acts of mass murder were intended to frighten our nation into chaos and retreat. But they have failed; our country is strong. (The White House 2001a)

The United States was entitled to capture, prosecute and punish any and all alleged offenders for perpetrating what was unambiguously a series of criminal acts, not least murder, as defined in domestic law. The offences were perpetrated on American soil, within the United States' territorial jurisdiction. Yet, within twenty-four hours, President Bush was to radically transform the legal framework, announcing, 'I have just completed a meeting with my national security team, and we have received the latest intelligence updates. The deliberate and deadly attacks which were carried out yesterday against our country were more than acts of terror. They were acts of war' (The White House 2001b).

What factors motivated this paradigm shift is a matter of speculation. Clearly, in contrast to the criminal law, the law of armed conflict allows states far greater discretion in respect of the use of force and detention. States are permitted in armed conflict to use lethal force against their adversaries and armed non-state actors, while wartime detention rules allow far greater powers both in regard to the basis for and conditions of detention. That said, it is likely that it was the location of the armed non-state actor, Al Qaeda, which tipped the balance in favour of the war paradigm over the criminal law model since the effectiveness of the latter is contingent upon the ability of the state to enforce. Whereas the state's authority to enforce the criminal law within its territory is absolute, in situations in which the non-state actor is located in the territory of another state, it is a conditional right. Thus, the law enforcement model relies not only upon the unqualified collaboration between states but, crucially, a demonstrable capacity by states to control those within their territory. In the absence of a willingness and capacity to enforce by the state in which the armed non-state actor is located, the state that seeks to prosecute is left with no remedy since the law enforcement paradigm will not tolerate the crossing of a border.[15]

---

15   An indictment issued by a United States federal court against Osama bin Laden was all but ignored in the two years prior to 11 September. Requests to the Taliban to transfer bin Laden to American custody to face prosecution for the August 1998 bombings of the American embassies in Nairobi and Dar es Salaam, in which 224 persons lost their

As noted above, international law's deference to states when they decide upon the choice of law has never been unconditional. Both treaty and customary international law insist that where an armed conflict exists between a state and an organised armed group (or between such groups), the law of war applies (see Four Geneva Conventions 1949: common art. 3; Additional Protocol II: art. 1(2); see also *Tadić* 1995: ¶ 70). The choice of law question is one that has been addressed by the *ad hoc* tribunals, which have sought to inject some measure of objectivity into the question. Over the years, the tribunals have elaborated upon the requisite evidential criteria necessary to determine that the law of armed conflict applies in respect of both international and non-international armed conflict.[16] Experts disagree on whether the threshold for each is different since the codified law suggests that there is no requirement that violence of a certain level be demonstrated before the existence of an international armed conflict is recognised.[17] By contrast, there is now consensus that the existence of a non-international armed conflict is contingent upon satisfying two criteria – intensity of the hostilities and the involvement of an organised armed group.[18] These criteria, according to the tribunals, are meant to ensure that any determination as to the existence of an armed conflict will be a matter of objective analysis rather than the subjective judgment of either party. As the International Criminal Tribunal for Rwanda reasoned in *Prosecutor* v. *Akayesu*:

> It should be stressed that the ascertainment of the intensity of a non-international conflict does not depend on the subjective judgment of the parties to the conflict. It should be recalled that the four Geneva Conventions, as well as the two Protocols, were adopted primarily to protect the victims, as well as potential victims, of armed conflict. If the application of international humanitarian law depended solely on the discretionary judgment of the parties to the conflict, in most cases there would be a tendency for the conflict to be minimised by the parties thereto. Thus, on the basis of objective criteria, both Common Article 3 and Additional Protocol II will apply once it has been established there exists an internal armed conflict which fulfils their respective pre-determined criteria. (¶ 603)

---

lives and a further 4,500 were injured, were simply shunned (see UNSC Res 1267 (1999); see also Letter 1999).

16   For a useful summary, see ICRC Opinion Paper 2008.

17   This is because the treaty law envisages that an armed conflict can exist without recourse to hostilities, as, for example, in situations of occupation. Common article 2 states that the Four Geneva Conventions 'shall also apply to all cases of partial or total occupation of the territory of a High Contracting Party, even if the said occupation meets with no armed resistance'. For a different view, see International Law Association 2010.

18   This test has been consistently applied by international tribunals and domestic courts and used in reports of independent experts and commissions.

The tribunal's reasoning here, in 1998, must be understood within the context of a pre-11 September world in which the International Criminal Tribunal for Rwanda's primary motivation was to ensure that armed conflict was governed by laws subject to international scrutiny. That, three years later, states would *insist* upon being governed by the laws of war rather than law enforcement in their engagement with the non-state actor was simply not contemplated. This change in policy does not reflect a volte-face in state practice but simply a conceptual differentiation that states make in respect of non-international armed conflict that is waged primarily *within* their territory versus the deterritorialised non-international armed conflict that is waged primarily *outside* the state's territorial boundaries.

Until recent years, non-international armed conflicts were assumed to be conflicts waged between the state and an organised armed group that was situated *within* the state's territorial boundaries or, at least, with an armed group that was bound to the territory by virtue of a geopolitical construct, nationality. With the phrase 'occurring in the territory of one of the High Contracting Parties', the text of common article 3 had served to reinforce the view that non-international armed conflicts were confined to a space demarcated by lines on a map.[19] The state's need to avoid being tainted with catastrophic political failure from *within*, as already noted, functioned to explain the pull towards the criminal law paradigm. This reasoning continues to operate in situations of violence involving armed non-state actors linked to the territory by nationality and where the hostilities occur primarily, though not exclusively, within the territorial boundaries of the state. But in the case of violence emanating from non-state actors who possess no territorial connections with the state and are located *outside* its territory, in other words, where the conflict is *deterritorialised*, the 'political failure from within' reasoning has no traction and is simply irrelevant. Insofar as international scrutiny is concerned, there is little to separate the war law from the criminal law model since, because the armed non-state actor is located *outside* the state's territorial boundaries, the state's engagement with the international is unavoidable. Finally, that the law of armed conflict enables the state to claim the applicability of non-international armed conflict rules even though the conflict is waged extraterritorially means that the structural relationship between the parties can be preserved. In other words, the armed non-state actor remains the 'criminal' for the very act of resorting to violence. Thus, for the state, the *only* pertinent question is: '*which of the two models can most effectively facilitate its stated goals?*'[20] It is, therefore, hardly surprising that since 11 September states have adopted a

---

19   Those non-international armed conflicts that extended beyond the border were regarded as 'spill-over' conflicts in which the crossing was a temporary feature.

20   Although the very purpose of suppression conventions in respect of terrorism is to address the cross-border element of terrorism in the pursuit of common goals, their effectiveness is contingent upon the level of commitment to the shared objectives of each State party to the treaties. Thus, the effectiveness of such regimes depends upon whether, in practice, States parties enforce their treaty obligations within their own territories.

rhetoric that conveys a fractured ambiguity that oscillates between crime and war and is contingent, more often than not, upon the spaces and nature of the spaces inhabited by the armed non-state actor.

There are few who would challenge the view that the attacks of 11 September satisfied *Tadić*'s organisation and intensity criteria to operationalise the law of non-international armed conflict between the United States and Al Qaeda. If, as I have argued, the law of armed conflict is agnostic to boundaries because its aim is to regulate a *relationship*, the geographical locality of the hostilities between the two parties was, and remains for the duration of the armed conflict, irrelevant. Seen from this perspective, President Bush's declaration of 29 September 2001 that '[o]ur war on terror will be much broader than the battlefields and beachheads of the past. The war will be fought wherever terrorists hide, or run, or plan' is not entirely unreasonable (see Roth 2004: 2).

Since the spatial reconceptualisation of the law of non-international armed conflict appears to blur the divide between war and crime, does this mean that the choice of law question is once again confined to the domain of the sovereign's decision? Or should we ask at what point does a non-international armed conflict come to an end so as to preclude a state from asserting the right to be governed by the law of armed conflict? How do we recognise or objectively measure 'peace' or at least a situation of violence that is short of 'armed conflict'? Do the same criteria that determine the existence of an armed conflict – organisation and intensity – operate to signal the end of one? If non-international armed conflict rules become inapplicable once the organisational element of the armed group ceases to exist or when the intensity of the hostilities falls below a certain level, international human rights law by default applies. In such a scenario, targeted killings, irrespective of means, would amount to extrajudicial assassinations and, thus, be unlawful.

To accept that there is no 'geography' question in respect of non-international armed conflict and that to speak of the spatial scope of the law of armed conflict is an irrelevance is disquieting. For on this reading, non-international armed conflict rules appear too ready to assist states in their bid to legitimise the use of force against the armed non-state actor in the territory of another state in the absence of consent. In practice, however, this right is severely restricted by the internal structure of the law of armed conflict itself. In deploying force in such a situation, a state may be able to invoke the law of armed conflict vis-à-vis the armed non-state actor who directly participates in hostilities. Nevertheless, since force is being exercised without the authority of the territorial state, any and all persons who are not taking a direct part in hostilities continue to be fully protected by the domestic law of the territorial state and international human rights law. The consequence of this is that not only does the state that uses force risk violating international human rights law, but the state agents who act on its behalf will be subject to the domestic criminal law of the territorial state, irrespective of their status. This is for the simple reason that the right to use force within the territorial boundaries of a state resides *exclusively* with that state unless that force can otherwise be justified by *jus ad bellum* rules.

Self-Defence and the Deterritorialised Armed Conflict

The discourse that surrounds transnational terrorism is characterised by a tendency to conflate what has traditionally been treated as two separate and distinct bodies of law, *jus ad bellum* and *jus in bello*. Although the precise interaction between these two legal regimes continues to stoke disagreement, few experts would deny that there are good policy reasons for maintaining a distinction between the two (see Sassòli and Bouvier 2006: 102 and listed references; Schmitt 2007). What is more, a separation is necessary simply because the questions posed by each body of law are fundamentally different.[21] Transnational terrorism may be the catalyst that has unwittingly facilitated the fusion between the two regimes, but what has enabled, indeed prompted, the disruption of the conceptual boundary between the two legal regimes are the attempts to redefine the scope of self-defence to 'fit' with the deterritorialised conception of the *jus in bello* pertaining to non-international armed conflict.

The United States' use of the drone in Pakistan and Yemen[22] as a response to transnational terrorism has initiated a series of debates not only involving the geographical scope of *jus in bello* but whether, and under what circumstances, article 51 of the United Nations Charter can be invoked against non-state actors. On 30 April 2012, Assistant to the United States President for Homeland Security and Counter-terrorism John O. Brennan delivered a keynote speech in which he touched upon the Obama Administration's targeted killings policy using drones on foreign territory. The statement by Brennan that, '[a]s a matter of international law, the United States is in an armed conflict with al-Qa'ida, the Taliban, and associated forces, in response to the 9/11 attacks, and we may also use force consistent with our inherent right of national self-defense' (2012) raises more questions than it answers. Nevertheless, what is clear is that self-defence continues to be the legal basis for justifying the use of force. That said, the relentless assertions to invoke self-defence against non-state actors located in the territory of another state are both disturbing and puzzling in equal measure. This is a critical issue since the lawfulness of many of the drone strikes in foreign territories is contingent upon whether the crossing of a border and the subsequent use of force is lawful. Invoking self-defence enables states to both cross a border and use force lawfully, but there are fundamental problems, both legal and conceptual, with this claim.

The principal sources of *jus ad bellum* are the UN Charter and customary international law. Article 2(4) of the Charter sets forth the general prohibition on the use of force in providing that '[a]ll Members shall refrain in their international relations from the threat or use of force against the territorial integrity or political

---

21 *Jus ad bellum* sets forth the international law governing the resort to force by states as an instrument of national policy; *jus in bello* comprises the international law regulating the conduct of armed conflict.

22 The use of the drone has not been confined only to these two states, but it was its deployment in Pakistan and Yemen that first provoked public outcry.

independence of any State, or in any other manner inconsistent with the Purposes of the United Nations'. That the language of article 2(4) of the Charter evidences a spatial element is only to be expected since what public international law seeks to protect, above all, is the territorially constituted nation-state. While territoriality functions to delineate a geographical enclosure, it also operates as the foundational organisational principle upon which the entire geopolitical system rests. Contemporary international law has injected a spatial element into the principle of sovereignty such that this right, which belongs to all states, is understood principally as a claim over land and, with it, the right to exclude others from that particular space.

International law recognises a number of exceptional circumstances in which the use of force on the territory of another state is not unlawful. The two codified exceptions to the article 2(4) prohibition are uses of force authorized by the Security Council under Chapter VII and self-defence pursuant to article 51. Article 51, which recognises and reflects customary international law, provides that '[n]othing in the present Charter shall impair the inherent right of individual or collective self-defence if an armed attack occurs against a Member of the United Nations'. Prior to the attacks of 11 September, self-defence was regarded as an inter-state right that could be invoked only in the event of an 'armed attack' by another *state*. Although the provision was not intended to preclude armed attacks by non-state actors that were acting on behalf of a state, the Charter regime was not directly concerned with regulating the relations between states and armed non-state actors because such matters were assumed to fall 'essentially within the domestic jurisdiction of any state'.[23]

Invoked as an inter-state right, the use of defensive force by a state is necessarily subject to the law of international armed conflict and, importantly, geographically confined by the law of neutrality, which functions to protect the territorial sovereignty of neutral states (and their nationals) against the harmful effects of hostilities between the parties to the conflict. Although the scope of applicability of the law of neutrality may be modified by a decision of the Security Council under its Chapter VII mandate,[24] in the absence of such a decision, the

---

23 Article 2(7) reads: 'Nothing contained in the present Charter shall authorise the United Nations to intervene in matters which are essentially within the domestic jurisdiction of any state.' See, for example, Security Council resolution UNSC Res 688 (1991), which calls upon Iraq to end the repression of its civilian populations (Kurds and Shiites) while expressly recalling that article 2(7) prohibits the United Nations from intervening in matters within the domestic jurisdiction of states.

24 If, under article 39 of the UN Charter, the Security Council has determined 'the existence of any threat to the peace, breach of the peace, or act of aggression', it is entitled to decide what measures should be taken in accordance with articles 41 and 42 to maintain or restore international peace and security. Should the Security Council consider that measures provided for in article 41 would be inadequate or have proved to be inadequate, under article 42, 'it may take such action by air, sea, or land forces as may be necessary to maintain or restore international peace and security'.

traditional law of neutrality applies to international armed conflict. The law of neutrality prohibits the parties to an international armed conflict from conducting hostilities within 'neutral territory', which comprises the land territory of neutral states as well as waters subject to their territorial sovereignty and the airspace above these areas. The inviolability of neutral territory is set forth in article 1 of both the 1907 Hague Convention (V) Respecting the Rights and Duties of Neutral Powers and Persons in Case of War on Land and the 1907 Hague Convention (XIII) Concerning the Rights and Duties of Neutral Powers in Naval War and binds all parties by virtue of customary international law.[25]

It follows, therefore, that although a state's right to use force pursuant to article 51 may 'suspend' the obligation to respect the territorial sovereignty of the parties to the armed conflict, it does not alter in any manner the obligation owed by those parties to respect the territorial sovereignty of those states *not* involved in the hostilities. In a complex web of interconnected obligations, the law of neutrality, coupled with article 2(4) and the attendant customary international law obligations that uphold the territorial sovereignty of states, functions to curtail the geographical scope of a state's use of force. Simply put, although *jus ad bellum* contemplates that hostilities between the belligerent parties can potentially take place anywhere, the right to use force remains subject to the law of international armed conflict, and the unflinching caveat that the territorial integrity of those states *not* involved in the conflict remains intact. International law can withstand the self-defence exception as between territorially defined entities because the geographical scope of the conflict is contained by a body of supplementary rules that apply to international armed conflict. On the other hand, to extend the scope of article 51 in respect of non-state actors is troubling for the very reason that the law of neutrality does not apply to non-international armed conflict.

The view that article 51 applies to armed attacks by non-state actors is not shared by all.[26] Three views now dominate the discourse on the applicability of article 51 to armed attacks by such actors. The first insists that, as an inter-state right, article 51 can only be invoked in response to an 'armed attack' by a non-state actor where there is 'substantial involvement' of a state in the attack.[27] According to this view, the use of defensive force against a non-state actor based on the territory of another state without the consent of that state would violate its territorial sovereignty since article 51 does not apply to armed attacks by non-state actors. The second view attempts to extend to victim states a remedy in situations where there is little or

---

25   See *Legality of the Threat or Use of Nuclear Weapons* (Advisory Opinion) [1996] ICJ Rep 226: 260–61.

26   See *Legal Consequences of the Construction of a Wall in the Occupied Palestinian Territory* (Advisory Opinion) [2004] ICJ Rep 136 (hereafter *Wall*): 194; *Armed Activities on the Territory of the Congo (Democratic Republic of the Congo v. Uganda)* [2005] ICJ Rep 168 (hereafter *Congo*): 222–3.

27   This view corresponds with the International Court of Justice's judgment in *Nicaragua*: 64–5.

no evidence of the territorial state's involvement in the armed attack although it has allowed its territory to be used as a base from which the non-state actor is able to mount such an attack. Advocates of this view maintain that under such circumstances a victim state should be entitled to use force pursuant to article 51 against the state that harbours or gives sanctuary to the non-state actor. This view has traditionally been rejected by states on the basis that mere harbouring is insufficient to attribute the attack to the territorial state. Proponents of the third view simply claim that article 51 applies to armed attacks by non-state actors, though such attacks must meet the 'scale and effects' threshold test elaborated by the International Court of Justice (ICJ) in its 1986 judgment in *Nicaragua* (103–104).[28] The advantage of this view is that the question of attributing such attacks to a state is circumvented. Moreover, this view offers greater coherency since self-defence is a plea that is ordinarily invoked against the perpetrator of the attack rather than a third party for facilitating the attack. Advocates of this view further maintain that the state from which the attack has been facilitated cannot claim that its territorial integrity or sovereignty has been violated if the 'victim' state uses force in self-defence as long as the principle of necessity is strictly adhered to. Proponents of both last-mentioned views support their position by citing the practice of states in the immediate wake of 11 September.[29] There are intrinsic problems with all three views.[30] Nevertheless, my comments are restricted to the last view which, from the statement made by John Brennan, appears to be the basis upon which current American targeted killings rests.

If the legal effect of invoking self-defence against another state is to 'suspend' both the obligation to respect the territorial sovereignty and the prohibition on the use of force as between the parties, it is difficult to see how invoking self-defence

---

28   Although prior to 11 September there was some limited state practice coupled with assertions of a right to use force in self-defence against non-state actors, the evidence in support of such a norm was sparse, and such claims were met with resistance (see Schmitt 2008: 8–9). Those who support the view that article 51 provides the legal framework within which self-defence can be invoked against the non-state actor have maintained that the scale and effects of 11 September were such that there was instant, unambiguous and unanimous recognition among the international community that the United States and its coalition partners were entitled to resort to force based on the inherent right of self-defence. That the attack had been perpetrated by non-state actors was simply irrelevant since the language of article 51 did not expressly rule out the possibility of self-defence against an armed attack launched by a non-state actor. Proponents of this view maintain that a customary international law norm has 'crystallised', entitling states to respond with armed force in the face of an armed attack meeting the *Nicaragua* test by non-state actors.

29   On 12 September 2001, the Security Council adopted Resolution 1368, recognising the inherent right of individual and collective self-defence (see also UNSC Res 1373 (2001); North Atlantic Treaty Organization 2001; Organization of American States 2001; *Wall* (separate opinions of Judges Buergenthal, Higgins and Kooijmans); *Congo* (separate opinion of Judge Kooijmans)).

30   For a further criticism of the three views, see Arimatsu 2013.

against a non-state actor can 'suspend' those obligations which an attacking state owes to the state in which the non-state actor is located. Proponents of this view, therefore, maintain that it is through the principle of necessity that attaches to self-defence that the question is resolved. In effect, the state seeking to rely on self-defence can only do so if the territorial state is unable or unwilling to prevent further attacks from its territory by the non-state actor. On this reading, necessity is partially severed from the original self-defence claim invoked in response to the non-state actor since it is required to concurrently address the territorial state's failure in allowing its territory to be used as a base from which such attacks have been launched. The territorial state is in violation of its international obligations by allowing its territory to be used for such attacks, but whether such a failing is sufficient to deprive it of *its* right to territorial sovereignty and the right not to be attacked is highly questionable.

As noted, embedded in the inter-state conception of defensive force is a fidelity to the territorial border, which, through the law of neutrality, functions to geographically confine a state's use of force. Extending self-defence to armed attacks by non-state actors introduces the prospect of borderless wars since non-international armed conflict is not only agnostic to borders but unconfined by any geographical constraints. The deterritorialised organised armed group poses both practical and conceptual problems to the territorial nation-state because it operates in such a way as to maximise its deterritorialised attributes. Nevertheless, to embrace a deterritorialised understanding of self-defence – for that is the consequence of the claim that article 51 is capable of applying to non-state actors – is to dislodge the normative structure upon which the defence was originally conceived and to put at risk the *jus ad bellum* framework. The *jus in bello*, constituted on the basis of governing the parties to a conflict, cannot serve as the basis for extending the *jus ad bellum*, which, by contrast, was constituted on the basis of regulating the relations between territorially defined nation-states.

To concede that article 51 was designed exclusively to regulate relations between states and to return to the traditional inter-state understanding of self-defence as elaborated by the ICJ in *Nicaragua* does not necessarily deprive the state that has been the target of an armed attack by a non-state actor of a remedy. This is because the question that has not been answered adequately is why the relationship between the state and the non-state actor is fundamentally altered by the *geographical location* of the latter, requiring the former to justify its use of force in the first place. Since the only entity that possesses the lawful right to resort to force is the state, it is puzzling that states would choose to justify their use of force in response to an armed attack by a non-state actor. Clearly, this does not mean that the state seeking to use force can do so without surmounting the legal hurdles of crossing a border and using force lawfully within the territory of another state. In the absence of consent by the territorial state the doctrine of necessity may provide a far more coherent basis upon which to justify the use of force against the non-state actor located in the territory of another state that is unwilling or unable to prevent further attacks. That said, as with self-defence, the doctrine of necessity cannot resolve the spatial scope of the non-international armed conflict.[31]

The deterritorialised non-international armed conflict presents particular challenges for the liberal state that go beyond legal argument to policy choices. Thus, an executive decision, even *if* fully compliant with existing international law, will fail to persuade opinion for want of legitimacy.

From Transnational Terrorism to Cyber Warfare and the Law's Spatial Reach

Over the last two decades, the pattern of armed conflict *has* altered to the extent that, in parallel with the existence of the traditional territorial armed conflict, there has been a re-emergence of the deterritorialised armed conflict. The archetypal deterritorialised non-international armed conflict, transnational terrorism, has compelled the rethinking of the spatial scope of the law of non-international armed conflict beyond borders. In doing so, it has not only challenged the spatial assumptions embedded within the law itself but also exposed the extent to which conceptions of space frame the way in which we engage with the world. The re-emergence of such conflicts has, in part, been the outcome of globalisation, which fosters deterritorialised linkages and nurtures different understandings of the way in which space is constituted.

Our proclivity for thinking within spatial edifices is no better illustrated than in the discourse that surrounds cyberspace and cyber warfare. Partially constituted by geography's lexicon, electronic signals have been endowed with a material appearance in which spatial and territorial metaphors are used to depict what is nothing more than the flow of digital data through complex networks of interdependent information technology infrastructures and computer processing systems. Cyberspace is now commonly described as a 'new *domain* of warfare', of being militarily as critical as 'land, sea, air, and space' (Lynn 2010; see also United Kingdom Ministry of Defence 2010: 76). Despite imageries of borders that continue to insist on a distinction between the 'external' and the 'internal', cyberspace is borderless for the very reason that it is neither tangible nor a 'domain' or 'space'.[32] That said, cyberspace is founded on a 'physical architecture', and to that extent, it has some tangible attributes that can be regulated along with the conduct of those who operate within the domain.

---

31   The conditions attached to necessity function to severely restrict its availability, more so than self-defence. For these conditions, see Crawford 2002.

32   In his statement to the Council of Foreign Relations, United States Deputy Secretary of Defense William J. Lynn, III, commented that '[i]ntrusions will not always be caught at the boundary ... To find intruders once they are inside, we have to be able to hunt within our own networks' (2010).

For the territorial state, cyberspace represents both opportunity and unparalleled risk. Constituted for the purpose of reaching out to the widest possible global constituency, this technology has made geographical boundaries almost an irrelevance.[33] Thus, its core attribute is also its greatest vulnerability. It is a medium through which deterritorialised armed conflicts can evolve and thrive but, equally, one through which state identities can be nurtured and strengthened, thereby sustaining the prospect of territorially based armed conflict. For the law of war expert, cyberspace, as with transnational terrorism, demands a rethinking of space and law beyond borders. While there are questions that are specific to cyber warfare, there are few, if any, that this technology raises in respect of the law of armed conflict's spatiality that have not already been raised by transnational terrorism.

Globalisation and its attendant technologies are destabilising traditional conceptions of a global legal order founded exclusively on a territorialised sovereignty. Amid these transformations, the law of armed conflict is claiming a spatial scope that transcends borders since only then can it remain steadfast to its objectives, to protect the victims of armed conflict and regulate the conduct of hostilities. While doubts are always expressed as to resilience of the law of armed conflict in the face of the changing nature and means of warfare, there is no reason to think that the law cannot adequately respond to contemporary and future wars. The challenge for liberal states is not to rein in the law of armed conflict's spatial scope but, rather, to ensure that liberal values both guide and govern those who invoke the law beyond the border.

References

Abresch, W. 2005. A Human Rights Law of Internal Armed Conflict: The European Court of Human Rights in Chechnya. *European Journal of International Law*, 16(4), 741–67.

Anderson, K. 2011. Targeted Killing and Drone Warfare: How We Came to Debate Whether There is a 'Legal Geography of War'. American University Washington College of Law Research Paper No. 2011-16. Available at: http://papers.ssrn.com/sol3/papers.cfm?abstract_id=1824783 [accessed: 13 October 2012].

Arimatsu, L. 2009. Territory, Boundaries and the Law of Armed Conflict. *Yearbook of International Humanitarian Law*, 12, 157–92.

Arimatsu, L. 2013. The Law of State Responsibility in Relation to Border Crossing: An Ignored Legal Paradigm, in *The Influence of Geography on Law in Armed Conflict*, ed. A.E. Wall and M.R. Hover. International Law Studies 89. Newport, RI: United States Naval War College, 21–53.

---

33   '[G]lobal communications are almost seamlessly interconnected and virtually instantaneous, as a result of which distance and geographical boundaries have become essentially irrelevant to the conduct of computer network attacks' (United States Department of Defense 1999: 5).

Brennan, J.O. 2012. The Ethics and Efficacy of the President's Counter-terrorism Strategy, Wilson Center, 30 April. Available at: http://www.wilsoncenter. org/event/the-efficacy-and-ethics-us-counterterrorism-strategy [accessed: 13 October 2012].

Corn, G. and Talbot, E. 2009. Transnational Armed Conflict: A 'Principled' Approach to the Regulation of Counter-Terror Combat Operations. *Israel Law Review*, 42(1), 46–79.

Crawford, J. 2002. *The International Law Commission's Articles on State Responsibility: Introduction, Text and Commentaries*. Cambridge: Cambridge University Press.

Debrix, F. 1998. Deterritorialised Territories, Borderless Borders: The New Geography of International Medical Assistance. *Third World Quarterly*, 19(5), 827–46.

Hobsbawm, E. 2003. War and Peace. *Guardian*, 23 February.

International Committee of the Red Cross (ICRC) 2008. Opinion Paper, How Is the Term 'Armed Conflict' Defined in International Humanitarian Law? Available at: http://www.icrc.org/eng/resources/documents/article/other/armed-conflict-article-170308.htm [accessed: 17 October 2012].

International Law Association 2010. Final Report on the Meaning of Armed Conflict in International Law.

Kaldor, M. 2008. *New and Old Wars*. 2nd edn. Cambridge: Polity.

Kalyvas, S.N. 2001. 'New' and 'Old' Civil Wars: A Valid Distinction? *World Politics*, 54(1), 99–118.

Letter Dated 1 October 1999 From the Deputy Permanent Representative of the United States of America to the United Nations Addressed to the Secretary-General (1999), UN Doc S/1999/1021.

Lupi, N. 1998. Report by the Enquiry Commission on the Behaviour of Italian Peace-Keeping Troops in Somalia. *Yearbook of International Humanitarian Law*, 1, 375–9.

Lynn, W.J. III 2010. Remarks on Cyber at the Council on Foreign Relations, New York City, 30 September. Available at: http://www.defense.gov/speeches/ speech.aspx?speechid=1509 [accessed: 13 October 2012].

North Atlantic Treaty Organization 2001. Press Release: Statement by the North Atlantic Council, 12 September. Available at: http://www.nato.int/docu/ pr/2001/p01-124e.htm [accessed: 13 October 2012].

Organization of American States 2001. Res. 1: Terrorist Threat to the Americas, OAS Doc RC.24/RES.1/01 (21 September).

Roth, K. 2004. The Law of War in the War on Terror. *Foreign Affairs*, 83(1), 2–7.

Sassòli, M. and Bouvier, A.A. 2006. *How Does Law Protect in War?* 2nd edn. Geneva: International Committee of the Red Cross.

Schmitt, M.N. 2002. Wired Warfare: Computer Network Attack and Jus in Bello. *International Review of the Red Cross*, 84(846), 365–99.

Schmitt, M.N. 2007. 21st Century Conflict: Can the Law Survive? *Melbourne Journal of International Law*, 8(2), 443–76.

Schmitt, M.N. 2008. Responding to Transnational Terrorism under the Jus ad Bellum: A Normative Framework, *Naval Law Review*, 56, 1–42.

Schondorf, R. 2004. Extra-State Armed Conflicts: Is There a Need for a New Legal Regime? *New York University Journal of International Law and Politics*, 37(1), 1–78.

Shklar, J. 2004. The Liberalism of Fear, in *Political Liberalism: Variations on a Theme*, ed. S.P. Young. New York: State University of New York Press, 149–66.

United Kingdom Ministry of Defence 2004. *The Manual of the Law of Armed Conflict*. Oxford: Oxford University Press.

United Kingdom Ministry of Defence 2010. *Global Strategic Trends – Out to 2040*. 4th edn. Available at: http://www.mod.uk/NR/rdonlyres/6AAFA4FA-C1D3-4343-B46F-05EE80314382/0/GST4_v9_Feb10.pdf [accessed: 13 October 2012].

United States Department of Defense 1999. An Assessment of International Legal Issues in Information Operations. Available at: http://www.au.af.mil/au/awc/awcgate/dod-io-legal/dod-io-legal.pdf [accessed: 13 October 2012].

UNSC Res 688 (1991), UN Doc S/RES/688.

UNSC Res 1267 (1999), UN Doc S/RES/1267.

UNSC Res 1368 (2001), UN Doc S/RES/1368.

UNSC Res 1373 (2001), UN Doc S/RES/1373.

The White House 2001a. Statement by the President in His Address to the Nation, 11 September. Available at: http://georgewbush-whitehouse.archives.gov/news/releases/2001/09/20010911-16.html [accessed: 13 October 2012].

The White House 2001b. Remarks by the President in Photo Opportunity with the National Security Team, 12 September. Available at: http://georgewbush-whitehouse.archives.gov/news/releases/2001/09/20010912-4.html [accessed: 13 October 2012].

Chapter 8

An Assessment of Cyber Warfare Issues in Light of International Humanitarian Law

Kalliopi Chainoglou

Computer network attacks have become an increasing feature of international relations (see Independent International Fact-Finding Mission (Georgia) 2009: 217–19). Conducted on a regular basis, they have left states troubled as to the appropriate way to respond. As a result, the international community has progressively granted more comprehensive mandates to international organisations to regulate cyberspace, and international organisations, acting as norm-entrepreneurs under their respective mandates, have increasingly adopted more focused and ambitious instruments to regulate various aspects of cyberspace.[1] A mass of norms and rules on the maintenance of cyber security and the regulation of cyberspace has emerged that reflects emerging perceptions of what constitutes a threat to international peace and security and, just as importantly, what constitutes a threat to national security[2] on the eve of new technological possibilities for warfare.[3]

'Cyber warfare', 'cybercrime', 'computer network attacks', 'cyberterrorism', 'cyber hostilities' and 'informational warfare' are some of the terms that have been used to describe the malevolent use of cyberspace to threaten the security and

---

1   International organisations have adopted binding and non-binding instruments concerning cyber security and have held numerous workshops at regional level in order to create synergies with stakeholders, including other international organisations, in such areas of mutual interest as the creation of a safer internet and the elimination of cyber attacks.

2   For the most recent national cyber and information security doctrines (as of 21 November 2012) of Australia, Austria, Canada, the Czech Republic, Estonia, the European Union, Finland, France, Germany, India, Japan, Lithuania, Luxembourg, the Netherlands, New Zealand, Norway, Poland, Romania, Russia, Slovakia, South Africa, Switzerland, Uganda, the United Kingdom and the United States, see North Atlantic Treaty Organization Cooperative Cyber Defence Centre of Excellence 2012.

3   Identifying a state's critical infrastructure relates to what constitutes a threat to its national interests within the context of cyber warfare. The fact that states have different critical infrastructures has impeded efforts to find a common understanding of cyber security and the threat posed by cyber attacks (see Chainoglou 2010; Roscini 2010: 116).

national interests of states.[4] These terms appear vague and interchangeable in the normative instruments of international organisations, national security strategies of states and the contemporary international law and international relations literature (see Carr 2011: 45; Lindstrom 2012: 30). This underlines a feeling of frustration as to what exactly constitutes cyber warfare and whether cyber attacks occur in time of peace or during armed conflict; the unique characteristics of cyber attacks can hinder fact-specific and context-based assessments of the cyber activity in question and, thus, point (prematurely) to the application of international humanitarian law.[5] Uncertainty as to which parts of public international law apply to cyber attacks and cyber warfare point to difficulties in halting cyber attacks and allowing for legal remedies.[6]

During the last few decades, the use of computer network attacks in modern warfare has significantly increased. Computer network attacks are operations that, by targeting a data stream, aim to manipulate, disrupt, deny or destroy electronic information that is resident in computers or computer networks or gain control over a computer or computer network. In the contemporary battlefield, cyber attacks offer the possibility of attacking military objectives that would otherwise be inaccessible, for example due to the location of the military objective or the risk of disproportionate civilian injury or damage to civilian objects (see Jensen 2003; O'Donnell and Kraska 2003; Kelsey 2008: 1440–41). In certain circumstances, computer network attacks may reduce the humanitarian impact of military power and provide the kind of precise and tailored effects that a conventional military attack may not produce.

This chapter focuses on key aspects of computer network attacks and is based on *jus in bello* rules. In particular, it refers to two scholarly works on the application of international humanitarian law in this context: the 2010 Commentary on the Humanitarian Policy and Conflict Research (HPCR) Manual on International Law Applicable to Air and Missile Warfare (hereafter HPCR Manual and Commentary) (see Paust 2012) and the 2012 Tallinn Manual on the International Law Applicable to Cyber Warfare. The following discussion assumes that a state of armed conflict under common article 2 of the 1949 Four Geneva Conventions exists in order to

---

4   Of course, the applicable legal context points to the correct use of these terms. As such, 'cyber warfare', 'computer network attacks' and 'cyber hostilities' should only be used when the threshold of an armed conflict has been met as understood by international humanitarian law. For the purposes of this chapter, the above terms will be used interchangeably.

5   Only recently have scholars begun to recognise a legal 'grey area' in which a transnational cyber incident falls below the thresholds of *jus ad bellum* and *jus in bello* yet exceeds the traditional constructs of criminal law (see Tikk *et al.* 2010). Similarly, questions arise as to whether a cyber activity should be categorised as a cybercrime or a cyber attack. For example, can a cybercrime amount to a cyber attack if there is temporal proximity to ongoing hostilities (see Handler 2012: 232)?

6   For criticisms of the existing lack of a comprehensive legal framework to regulate cyber warfare, see *Cornish et al.* 2010: 21–2.

examine the applicability of international humanitarian law in the case of computer network attacks in international armed conflict.[7]

The Application of International Humanitarian Law

International humanitarian law has developed over many centuries, but most discussions of it begin with the 1863 Lieber Code (see United States War Department 1863). The rules of international humanitarian law are codified in, *inter alia*, the Four Geneva Conventions and the two Additional Protocols of 1977 and cover a wide spectrum of issues, including military necessity, humanity, the principle of distinction (see Additional Protocol I: arts. 48, 49, 51(2), 52(2)), proportionality (see Additional Protocol I: arts. 51(5)(b), 57(2)(a)(iii), 57(2)(b)) and the prohibition of perfidious methods of warfare (see Additional Protocol I: art. 37(1)). Parties to an armed conflict must take all feasible precautions in the choice of the methods and means of warfare with a view to avoiding or, in any event, minimising incidental loss of civilian life, injury to civilians and damage to civilian objects (see Additional Protocol I: arts. 57(1), 57(2)(a)(ii)). Combatants (other than those *hors de combat*) can be attacked. The use of weapons that are by their nature indiscriminate (see Additional Protocol I: art. 51(4)) and the use of methods and means of warfare that are of a nature to cause superfluous injury or unnecessary suffering are prohibited (see Additional Protocol I: art. 35(2)). Indiscriminate attacks are also prohibited (see Additional Protocol I: art. 51(5)). The right of parties to an armed conflict to choose methods or means of warfare is not unlimited, and they must seek to minimise collateral damage and incidental injury. Furthermore, attacks must be carried out outside neutral territory and cannot be carried out when a ceasefire is in effect (see Dinstein 2008: 184).

When considering modern weaponry and the methods and means of warfare, there has been a lot of criticism with regard to the adequacy of existing international humanitarian law instruments. For a number of scholars, practitioners and strategists, they seem outdated. They suggest that 'new wine cannot be put into old wineskins' and strongly contest the notion that existing international humanitarian law instruments can easily apply to cyber operations (see Schmitt 2002: 396; Brenner 2009: 9–10; Schaap 2009: 124; Dunlap 2011: 82). Arguably, cyber attacks and cyber weapons are *sui generis*, and their unique and evolving

---

7   On the classification of international and non-international armed conflicts within the context of cyber operations, see Schmitt 2012 and Tallinn Manual 2012: Commentary to Rules 21–2. Space constraints preclude this chapter from referring to international humanitarian law treaties other than the 1949 Four Geneva Conventions and the two Additional Protocols of 1977. Corresponding international humanitarian law rules also exist, but again, due to space constraints, they fall outside the scope of this chapter. On customary international humanitarian law, see ICRC Study on Customary International Humanitarian Law.

characteristics do not easily fit within the existing framework of legal norms. The characteristics of cyber operations can make it difficult to 'identify the existence of a cyber operation, its originator, its intended object of attack and its precise effects' (Tallinn Manual 2012: Commentary to Rule 20, ¶ 9). As a consequence, states have been pushed to design effective cyber operations as a response to the threat of hostile cyber activities (see United States 2011; see also Lobel 2012: 638).

International humanitarian law instruments are not restricted in their application to the methods and means of warfare that existed at the time of their adoption. The drafters of the Four Geneva Conventions and the two Additional Protocols of 1977 created a legal regime that anticipated the development of new weapons and methods and means of warfare. This is clear from article 36 of the 1977 Protocol Additional to the Geneva Conventions of 12 August 1949, and Relating to the Protection of Victims of International Armed Conflicts, (Additional Protocol I), which clearly stipulates that, 'in the study, development, acquisition or adoption of a new weapon, means or method of warfare, a High Contracting Party is under an obligation to determine whether its employment would, in some or all circumstances, be prohibited by [international law]'.[8] This issue has also been addressed, albeit in a different context, by the 1996 *Legality of the Threat or Use of Nuclear Weapons* advisory opinion, in which the International Court of Justice rejected the 'newness' of such unconventional weapons as nuclear weapons as a reason not to apply international humanitarian law.[9] Even though cyber attacks do not always physically damage life or property, international humanitarian law would apply to cyber operations as it would to any other operations within an armed conflict (see Dörmann 2004: 2; Tallinn Manual 2012: Commentary to Rule 20, ¶ 1).

Computer Network Attacks and Cyber Weapons

Within the context of cyber operations, methods of warfare include information technology, data collection and the infiltration of computerised systems to damage critical systems. Potential weapons, in the international humanitarian law sense of 'means of warfare', include computers and computer codes used to execute attacks, together with associated equipment (see HPCR Manual and Commentary

---

8   Even though new weaponry and means or method of warfare should be tested at an early stage, that is, during the study and development phase and prior to adoption, acquisition and deployment, few states have strictly complied with this obligation (see Daoust *et al.* 2002: 361–2). The fact that many states today take part in various cyber exercises within the context of cyber security and are members of international or regional organisations that adopt instruments on the regulation of cyberspace, however, could be understood as a form of informal assessment (compatible with the spirit of article 36) (see Ticehurst 1997; Geiss 2010; Hughes 2011).

9   *Legality of the Threat or Use of Nuclear Weapons* (Advisory Opinion) [1996] ICJ Rep 226: 259.

2010: 42), computer viruses, cyber data collection, wireless data communications jammers, compromised counterfeit computer software, electromagnetic pulse weapons, computer and networks reconnaissance tools and embedded Trojan time bombs (see Touré 2011: 10). The HPCR Manual and Commentary also lists as weapons those that do not necessarily involve the physical transfer of energy as long as they cause death, injury, destruction or damage: 'CNA [computer network attack] hardware, software and codes are weapons that can cause such effects through transmission of data streams' (2010: 55). Accordingly, if a computer network attack on an air traffic control system would result in an aircraft crashing or if a computer network attack on an operational train system would result in the collision of trains, then the equipment and computer codes used would qualify as weapons or, to put it more accurately, a 'weapon system' (HPCR Manual and Commentary 2010: 55).

Computer network attacks vary widely and can be directed against an individual computer or against an entire computer network. According to the HPCR Manual and Commentary, computer network attacks can include:

> gaining access to a computer system so as to acquire complete or partial control over it; transmitting viruses to destroy or alter data; using logic bombs that sit idle in a system until triggered on the occasion of a particular occurrence or at a set time; inserting worms that reproduce themselves upon entry to a system thereby overloading the network; employing sniffers to monitor and/or seize data; securing entry into a system in order to manipulate data, for instance by altering, deleting, or adding to it, and simply penetrating a system to observe data resident therein. (2010: 34, ¶ 2; see Rule 1(m))

However, not all computer network attacks will constitute an 'attack' within the context of *jus in bello*.

By applying international humanitarian law to cyber warfare, in other words, by applying it to cyber weapons and cyber weapons systems, any superfluous injury or unnecessary suffering caused will be deemed unlawful (see Tallinn Manual 2012: Commentary to Rules 41–2). Likewise, if the means of cyber warfare are used indiscriminately, that is, without a specific military objective and without taking into consideration the principles of distinction and proportionality, then this would amount to a violation of articles 51(4)(b) and (c) of Additional Protocol I (see Tallinn Manual 2012: Commentary to Rule 43).

Computer Network Attacks as 'Attacks'

The international humanitarian law principle of distinction protects civilians from 'attacks', which article 49 of Additional Protocol I defines as 'acts of violence against the adversary, whether in offence or in defence' (see HPCR Manual and Commentary 2010: Rule 1(e)). Although Additional Protocol I does not expressly define what an 'attack' entails, the Commentary to Additional Protocol I and military practice have filled this gap. According to these, the concept of 'attack' has a broad scope and comprises combat action that includes offensive or defensive measures, or a combination of these (see ICRC Study on Customary International Humanitarian Law; Sandoz *et al.* 1987: 603).[10] An 'attack' has traditionally been understood to be an act of violence that is part of land, sea or aerial warfare. The HPCR Manual and Commentary defines as 'attacks' certain non-kinetic acts that 'that do not involve the physical transfer of energy, such as certain CNAs [computer network attacks]' that result in death, injury, damage or destruction (HPCR Manual and Commentary 2010: 28, ¶ 7). Similarly, the Tallinn Manual defines a cyber attack as a cyber operation that is 'reasonably expected to cause injury or death to persons or damage or destruction to objects' (2012: Rule 30).[11]

A careful study of Additional Protocol I in conjunction with state practice reveals that only 'attacks' against civilians are forbidden (see Tallinn Manual 2012: Rule 32). While military operations that do not amount to an 'attack' can be directed against civilians and civilian objects (see Tallinn Manual 2012: Rule 37), 'attacks' cannot be carried out in violation of the prohibition against indiscriminate attacks: this would violate the principle of proportionality (see Additional Protocol I: arts. 51(5)(b), 57(2)(iii); Tallinn Manual 2012: Commentary to Rules 51 and 55).[12] Computer network operations that constitute 'attacks' and that do not distinguish between lawful and unlawful targets are prohibited (see Brown 2006: 195–7; Tallinn Manual 2012: Rule 49). This means that a cyber attack that would have an uncontrollable effect and that would not be directed against a specific military target would violate articles 51(4)(b) and (c) of Additional Protocol I, even if it were to be unsuccessful (see Tallinn Manual 2012: Commentary to Rule 59, ¶¶ 3, 4, 6).

In order to limit their impact upon civilians, computer network operations must be proportionate, target military assets and be justified on the basis of military advantage.[13] As such, computer network attacks that cause collateral damage at a level of harm in contravention of these principles will be unlawful. The United States' *Commander's Handbook on the Laws of Naval Operations* clearly stipulates that:

---

10   According to the Commentary to Additional Protocol I, the term 'attack' was meant to apply to all uses of the word throughout Additional Protocol I. However, it appears in the section on civilian protection to emphasise the principles of distinction and proportionality in the case of attacks against civilians.

11   Serious illness and severe mental suffering fall under the concept of injury (see Tallinn Manual 2012: Commentary to Rule 30, ¶ 8).

12   Interestingly, Rule 59 calls upon parties to take, to the maximum extent feasible, all necessary precautions to protect the civilian population and civilian objects, even by requiring them to physically remove them.

13   Military advantage can be achieved even by inflicting economic losses from attacks against military objectives (see *Eritrea-Ethiopia Claims Commission* [2005]: 335–6).

> In employing non-kinetic means of CNA [computer network attacks] against a military objective, factors involved in weighing anticipated incidental injury/death to protected persons can include, depending on the target, indirect effects (for example, the anticipated incidental injury/death that may occur from disrupting an electricity generating plant that supplies power to a military headquarters and to a hospital). (United States 2007: 8–17)

There is a clear distinction between 'attacks' and military operations that do not qualify as 'attacks': the latter constitute acts, including non-kinetic or non-forcible acts, that do not result in loss of life, physical or psychological injury or damage to property and, therefore, are not prohibited.[14] Military operations that do not amount to an 'attack' include information operations, cyber psychological operations,[15] intelligence-gathering operations, such as computer network attacks designed to exploit data resident in enemy computer networks, and surveillance operations, such as the use of unmanned drones.[16] While computer network attacks can manipulate electronically stored data, certain computer network attacks will not necessarily fall within the ambit of the kinetic effects of 'attacks'. Put simply, the latter will not amount to the integration of cyber and physical attacks in the theatre of operations.

Irrespective of the success of a purported 'attack', it is the intention of the attacker that matters in qualifying an act of violence as an 'attack'. Even intercepted cyber operations will be considered 'attacks' (see Tallinn Manual 2012: Commentary to Rule 30, ¶ 15). Furthermore, it is the nature of the act of violence along with the violent nature of its consequences that will trigger the threshold of an 'attack'. Even though Additional Protocol I does not refer to the actual consequences of an act of violence for it to qualify as an 'attack', such consequences are implied through such *jus in bello* principles as the protection of civilians. Rule 21 of the HPCR Manual and Commentary, for example, states that 'the application of the general rules prohibiting attacks directed against civilians or civilian objects, as well as indiscriminate attacks, is confined to air or missile attacks that entail violent effects, namely, acts resulting in death, injury, damage or destruction'. A military operation will only qualify as an 'attack' if it severely impacts upon civilians (death or physical or mental injury, or a combination of these), civilian objects (damage

---

14   For example, a computer network attack that targets air traffic control but does not result in death, injury, damage or destruction will not amount to an 'attack' (see HPCR Manual and Commentary 2010: Commentary to Rule 21, ¶ 3). Cyber espionage, however, does amount to an 'attack' (see Tallinn Manual 2012: Commentary to Rule 30, ¶ 2). The present chapter does not examine cyber espionage, but for a discussion of this, see Fidler 2012 and Melnitzky 2012.

15   For the legality of psychological operations and psychological warfare activities in *jus in bello*, see Chainoglou 2012.

16   For more on the international humanitarian law implications of drone attacks, with particular reference to civilian casualties, see Chapter 5 by Susan Breau in this volume.

or destruction) or both civilians and civilian objects;[17] and only these types of military operations can be considered unlawful. Anything short of this level of harm will not qualify as an 'attack'. Cyber operations that merely impact upon or cause inconvenience to a population, despite its suffering, irritation or fear, such as the unavailability of email communications in the state under attack or through the temporary denial of internet access, are not prohibited because they do not violate the principle of proportionality or involve 'incidental loss of civilian life, injury to civilians, damage to civilian objects' (see Tallinn Manual 2012: Commentary to Rule 30, ¶ 12 and Commentary to Rule 51, ¶ 5).[18]

If a planned attack, including a computer network attack, has as its primary purpose to spread terror among the civilian population, then it will violate article 51(2) of Additional Protocol I. A violation of article 51(2) neither necessitates the occurrence of any of the harms mentioned above, namely injury, death, damage or destruction, nor requires that the end result of the attack actually spreads terror among the civilian population. It is the *purpose* behind the 'attack' that matters (see Tallinn Manual 2012: Commentary to Rule 36, ¶¶ 2–5). The incidental spreading of terror among the civilian population is not unlawful when acts or threats of violence are pursued against lawful targets. Even 'shock and awe' operations that are designed to 'spread' terror among combatants and, thus, influence their morale are lawful as long as civilians are not themselves attacked and assuming that the primary purpose of the attack is not to spread terror among the civilians (see Dinstein 2010: 126; see also Official Records 1974–77: ¶ 51).

Given the fact that computer network attacks will often complement other military operations taking place within the context of an armed conflict, certain computer network attacks are more likely to cause functional damage than physical damage. Functional damage can involve damage to computer software.[19] The question is whether the computer software has been the object of an attack as international humanitarian law understands the concept. It would be premature to provide a definitive answer to this question at present (see Terry 2001: 90–91; Watts

---

17   The permanent loss of financial assets or a major disruption of the stock market that would result in widespread unemployment could qualify as an attack (see Schmitt 2002: 377).

18   It is important to stress, however, that Rule 52 in the Tallinn Manual provides the parties must take constant care of the population for the duration of cyber hostilities. According to one expert, '[c]yber warfare operations targeting local internet service or telecommunications providers may result in less collateral damage to the civilian population or civilian population surrounding the targeted object and, as a consequence, create more opportunities for targeting dual-use objects ... When the military advantage is compared to the collateral damage one can logically label this an appropriate targeting of a dual-use object' (Schaap 2009: 160).

19   In the case of the Georgian–Russian conflict, Georgian websites were targeted during the armed conflict, depriving the Georgian public of access to the news and interfering with the Georgian military's ability to coordinate its response to Russia (see Hollis 2011).

2010). However, if the functional damage requires the replacement of physical components of a damaged object, then this would amount to an 'attack' (see Tallinn Manual 2012: Commentary to Rule 30, ¶ 10).

International humanitarian law distinguishes between civilian objects and military objectives. Pursuant to article 52(1) of Additional Protocol I, civilian objects are 'all objects which are not military objectives'.[20] According to the Commentary to the Tallinn Manual, objects will qualify as military objectives by reference to their 'nature, location, purpose or use' (see Commentary to Rule 38, ¶¶ 6–11). For example, computers and computer infrastructure can be lawfully targeted with traditional weapons because they satisfy the criterion of 'nature'. In fact, if a state considers that targeting factories that produce computer hardware or software or computer components for military use would provide a military advantage, then it could, in principle, lawfully do so. Finally, civilian objects that once qualified as military objectives can potentially be classified once again as civilian objects if their military use ceases (see Tallinn Manual 2012: Commentary to Rule 38, ¶ 10).

Civilian Direct Participation in Hostilities

International humanitarian law has long accepted that civilians lose their protection from attack when and for such time as they directly participate in hostilities (see Additional Protocol I: art. 51(3); Additional Protocol II: art. 13(3); Tallinn Manual 2012: Rule 35). According to the Interpretive Guidance on the Notion of Direct Participation in Hostilities Under International Humanitarian Law, which the Assembly of the International Committee of the Red Cross adopted on 26 February 2009, for a specific act to qualify as direct participation in hostilities, the resulting harm must satisfy three elements (see Melzer 2008: 1016–31). First, the likelihood of the occurrence of harm must be evident; in other words, it must be reasonably expected that harm will result from the act in the prevailing circumstances (Melzer 2008: 1016–19). Second, a direct causal link must exist between the activity engaged in and the harm inflicted upon the enemy at the time and place where the activity takes place (direct causation) (Melzer 2008: 1019–25). Third, there must be a direct link between the act in question and the hostilities (belligerent nexus) (Melzer 2008: 1025–30). Clearly, participating in a computer network attack constitutes direct participation in hostilities if all the above criteria are met (see Dinstein 2012: 276; see also HPCR Manual and Commentary 2010: Rule 29(iii)). Direct participation in hostilities makes civilians susceptible to attacks, either by cyber or conventional means, for the duration of time that they are engaged in the qualifying act of direct participation, including immediately before and after the act in question (see Dinstein 2010: 147–9; Tallinn Manual 2012: Commentary to Rule 35, ¶ 8).

---

20 The Tallinn Manual considers all dual-use objects and facilities to be *a priori* military objectives (see Commentary to Rule 39, ¶ 1).

It is not unlikely that during hostilities civilians might engage in cyber warfare. States might even employ civilians in order to operate military information technology systems.[21] From a practical point of view, civilian information technology operators are more likely to have the most specialised training in computer systems and related developments in computer technology. A key question that arises is whether they can be said to take a direct part in hostilities. The International Committee of the Red Cross has determined that 'direct participation' by civilians in hostilities includes such cyber activities as '[i]nterfering electronically with military computer networks (computer network attacks) and transmitting tactical targeting intelligence for a specific attack' (ICRC 2009). Furthermore, according to the HPCR Manual and Commentary, engaging in electronic warfare or computer network attacks that target military objectives or combatants or civilians directly participating in hostilities or which are intended to cause death or injury to civilians or damage to or destruction of civilian objects constitutes direct participation in hostilities (see Rule 29). Computer network attacks can have a variety of effects, ranging from directly causing death, injury, destruction or damage to system shutdowns or systems malfunctions that affect the military capacity of the adversary but that do so indirectly. Clearly, when computer network attacks have such effects, any civilian information technology operators involved in such operations will be considered direct participants in hostilities (as long as the three criteria set out above are met).

One can argue that a civilian information technology operator's spatial distance from the military theatre of operations is irrelevant when determining whether he or she loses immunity from attack. It can also be said that, by its very nature, the 'maintenance of a weapons system is an act which has a direct causal relationship with the harm done to the enemy' (Schmitt *et al*. 2004: 13). On the other hand, when computer network attacks entail a lesser degree of harm, such as hacking into a military base's intranet, this will not, on its own, constitute direct participation in hostilities (see HPCR Manual and Commentary 2010: Rule 29(iii); Dinstein 2012: 276).

Another problematic issue concerns civilian information technology operators who maintain non-offensive military systems, such as security networks that protect personnel, infrastructure or material. Are they immune from attack or can they be targeted by computer network attacks? The question that arises is whether their civilian protection status is lost just for maintaining a non-offensive military network; in such a case, scholars consider these civilians to be directly participating in cyber hostilities (see Hathaway *et al*. 2012: 817).[22]

---

21   On the integration of civilian employees into states' cyber warfare structures and the civilianisation of certain functions in the armed forces, see Schmitt *et al*. 2004; Corn 2008: 286–7; Brenner and Clarke 2010; and Turns 2012: 291–2.

22   It is important to note that there are special repercussions for civilians who are not nationals of a State party to the conflict who are recruited for computer network attacks

A final point to be made concerns civilians who occasionally engage in cyber hostilities, that is, those who repeatedly launch cyber operations over a period of time but with brief pauses. In such cases, scholars have not reached agreement. Some argue that such a civilian loses his or her protection even 'in the intermediate time-frames punctuating military operations' (Dinstein 2012: 276); others argue that each act must be assessed under the 'direct participation scheme' on a case-by-case basis (see Tallinn Manual 2012: Commentary to Rule 35, ¶ 10).

Ruses of War and Perfidy

Ruses of war are legitimate acts of warfare that induce the adversary to act recklessly, but they neither infringe rules of law nor amount to inviting the confidence of the adversary such as to amount to perfidy. According to article 37(2) of Additional Protocol I, ruses of war are intended to mislead an adversary or to induce him to act recklessly but infringe no rule of international law applicable in armed conflict and are not perfidious because they do not invite the confidence of an adversary with respect to protection under that law. The following are examples of such ruses: the use of camouflage, decoys, mock operations and misinformation.

One way to assess the legality of various methods of computer warfare would be to determine whether they at least resemble or are analogous to ruses of war conducted in their traditional forms. Examples of lawful computer network attacks might include tampering with an adversary's computer database such that data relating to an enemy force's location, movement and composition is altered, transmitting messages and instructions to enemy subordinate units that appear to originate from enemy headquarters and vice versa, and relaying false orders or changing data as to an enemy's forces and activities.

Certain computer network attacks can overlap with psychological warfare activities given that the latter's purpose is to influence the mind of the adversary and undermine fighting morale. One such example might be the transmission through a cable news data stream to every television channel in enemy territory of false information about an enemy prime minister's personal conduct with regard to financial overspending (see Wingfield 2009: 525–6).

Perfidious acts, that is, acts that 'invit[e] the confidence of an adversary to lead him to believe that he is entitled to, or is obliged to accord, protection under the rules of international law applicable in armed conflict, with intent to betray that confidence' (Additional Protocol I: art. 37(1)), that are carried out with the intent to kill, injure or capture an adversary (see Bothe *et al.* 1982: 204; HPCR Manual and Commentary 2010: Rule 111; Tallinn Manual 2012: Commentary to Rule 60, ¶ 2) are prohibited. Under international humanitarian law, computer network attacks that are launched in bad faith will be unlawful on the condition that there is a nexus of proximity to the killing, injury or capture of the adversary (see Tallinn Manual

---

(see International Convention Against the Recruitment, Use, Financing and Training of Mercenaries: art. 3(1); see also Schmitt *et al.* 2004: 14).

2012: Commentary to Rule 60, ¶¶ 5–6). Furthermore, the use of computer network attacks to feign protected status, misuse a flag of truce (see Additional Protocol I: art. 38(1); Tallinn Manual 2012: Rule 62), the Geneva Conventions' distinctive emblems (see Additional Protocol I: art. 66) or the symbols of the United Nations or the International Committee of the Red Cross (see Additional Protocol I: arts. 38–39; Tallinn Manual 2012: Rule 63) or otherwise create the impression that hostilities have ended would be unlawful (see Dörmann 2004).[23] The improper use of codes and signals that have been granted by international organisations to medical units and vehicles would also be perfidious.

As explained above, the unique characteristics of computer network attacks challenge the application of international humanitarian law. One such example might involve routing attacks through several hosts, including civilian servers or computers, in order to obfuscate the source or origin of an attack. Such an operation would likely be lawful unless it breached the principle of distinction or crossed the threshold of perfidy (see HPCR Manual and Commentary 2010: Rule 116(e); Dinniss 2012: 261–2; Tallinn Manual 2012: Rules 31, 61, ¶ 4).

Another example that has intrigued international humanitarian law scholars concerns the use of a commercial email address, that is, one with a '.com' domain name extension, in order to camouflage a military computer or computer network; most scholars conclude that this would be lawful unless perfidious (see Shulman 1999; Wingfield 2009: 540). However, could the use of an international organisation's name as a domain name extension, such as 'icrc.org', in a computer network attack that aims at tampering with the enemy's network data be considered perfidious since this would invite the confidence of the enemy? According to the Tallinn Manual, 'an email from a Hotmail account to enemy forces that includes a bare assertion that the sender is a delegate of the International Committee of the Red Cross [does not breach the rule on the prohibition of the improper use of protective emblems and signs] because it does not misuse the organisation's emblem' (Rule 62, ¶ 4). Accordingly, in order to assess whether the rule would be breached, some of the experts in Tallinn suggested setting the threshold on the use of specified and recognised indicators (see Rule 62, ¶ 5). Others were of the opposite view, arguing that 'only cyber operations that employ electronic reproductions of the relevant graphic emblems, or which display the other protective indicators set forth in the law of armed conflict, are prohibited' (Rule 62, ¶ 6; see Dinniss 2012: 265). In other words, whether the use of 'icrc.org' would be unlawful remains unresolved.

---

23   Schmitt mentions that the 'US Department of Defense has also opined that using "computer 'morphing' techniques to create an image of the enemy's chief of state informing his troops that an armistice or cease-fire agreement had been signed" would be a war crime if false' (2002: 396).

Cyber/Computer Network Attacks and the Law of Neutrality

The law of neutrality regulates the interactions between states at war and states at peace. According to the law of neutrality, a neutral state must refrain from participating in a conflict to which it is not party, guarantee impartial treatment of belligerents and prevent belligerents from committing violations of the law of neutrality on its territory. Under the 1907 Hague Convention (V) Respecting the Rights and Duties of Neutral Powers and Persons in Case of War on Land, belligerents must respect the inviolability of a neutral state's territory, which means not transferring troops, munitions and other supplies for the conduct of war through its territory (see Hague Convention V: art. 2; see also Tallinn Manual 2012: Rule 92), and refrain from using any communication apparatus to communicate with belligerent forces on land or sea (see Hague Convention V: art. 3; see also Tallinn Manual 2012: Rule 93). It should be noted, however, that a neutral state is under no obligation to forbid or restrict the use of communication apparatuses belonging to belligerents (see Hague Convention V: art. 8; see also Tallinn Manual 2012: Rule 92, ¶¶ 4–5). A neutral state must also take measures to ensure and enforce the protection of its neutrality in relation to belligerent parties and, in particular, its armed forces. Moreover, it would violate a state's neutrality to place at the disposal of belligerents telecommunication installations not available to them under normal conditions, for example a neutral state's own military communications system, or provide belligerents with new information infrastructure or allow them to establish such facilities themselves (see Ryan and Ryan 2011).

These aspects of the law of neutrality, which one representative of the International Committee of the Red Cross recently characterised as having a 'slightly musty quality' (Carswell 2012), fail to address a number of pressing questions that arise within the context of cyber activities (see Tallinn Manual 2012: Rules 64, 91–5). For example, does the routing of attacks by a belligerent party through the internet nodes of a neutral state violate the law of neutrality? If a belligerent party acts within the territory of a neutral state by launching a cyber attack, will the neutral state lose its neutral status? If military personnel from a belligerent party are physically present on the territory of the belligerent party but launch a cyber attack through a neutral state's servers, will the neutral state lose its neutral status? In principle, it seems reasonable to argue that a cyber attack carried out through the use of cyber infrastructure located on the territory of a neutral state could amount to a violation of the law of neutrality.[24] Where a neutral state is unable or unwilling to impede an attack, then it could open itself to attack by the aggrieved

---

24 Theoretically, the use of cyber infrastructure in a neutral state's territory could violate article 1 of Hague Convention V. Moreover, based upon the design and nature of a cyber attack, the use of neutral cyber infrastructure could even fall within the meaning of 'munitions of war' moved across the territory of a neutral state under articles 2 and 5 or as 'erecting' or 'using' communication equipment established by the belligerents on a neutral state's territory under articles 3 and 5.

state.[25] The Commentary to the Tallinn Manual provides that where a neutral state has not halted cyber hostilities being conducted through its cyber infrastructure within a reasonable period of time that the 'aggrieved belligerent may lawfully launch a cyber operation to destroy the server's functionality' (Tallinn Manual 2012: Commentary to Rule 94, ¶ 6). On the other hand, a neutral state should not be deemed to have breached the law of neutrality when a belligerent uses its cyber infrastructure as a mere communication data stream. This is in line with the object and purpose of articles 8 and 9 of Hague Convention V. However, the transmission of cyber weapons across neutral territory will be deemed unlawful (see Tallinn Manual 2012: Rule 92, ¶ 5).

Moreover, due to the structure of contemporary internet communications, it is very unlikely that routing information will ever be available to the belligerent or the neutral state at the time of the attack.[26] From a practical point of view, Maurer is probably correct in concluding that '[n]eutral states can be expected to prevent belligerent states from conducting cyber hostilities from within their territory, but not the routing of belligerent cyber operations through their publicly accessible communications infrastructure' (2011: 20; see also Kelsey 2008: 1443–6; Kastenberg 2009: 52–3). Even if a neutral state could detect a cyber attack at the routing phase, a strict interpretation of the law of neutrality would suggest that it would have to shut down its information infrastructure entirely, but this would clearly be disproportionate. This would endanger the viability of a neutral state's infrastructure and fly in the face of its territorial sovereignty and inherent right to self-preservation (see Tallinn Manual 2012: ch. VII, ¶ 5).[27]

Conclusions

While certain aspects of cyber attacks can be reasonably dealt with within existing legal frameworks, it has been said more generally that the 'cyber domain generally falls to be regulated within the established framework of relevant parts of public international law' (Turns 2012: 283, n. 15; see also Addicott 2010: 550; Schmitt 2010: 153–4; Tikk 2011: 2–4). In particular, there is a sense of discomfort with the application of *jus ad bellum* and *jus in bello* rules to cyber attacks. As Turns (2012: 283–4) has pointed out, the phenomenon of cyber warfare and cyber attacks is

---

25   Interestingly, 'neutral cyber infrastructure located outside neutral territory, such as undersea cables, may be attacked if it constitutes a lawful military objective' (Tallinn Manual 2012: Commentary to Rule 91, ¶ 5).

26   Ryan *et al.* argue that 'the scope of the duties imposed on neutral nations with regard to information operations should change to require only that the neutral nation take no action favoring one belligerent over another. If it does favor one belligerent's information operations over another belligerent's information operations, its neutrality would be discontinued' (2011: 1190; see also Tallinn Manual 2012: ch. VII, ¶ 4).

27   On self-preservation, see Green 2012.

developing so fast that it tends to outpace existing public international law. In terms of customary international law, there seems to be insufficient state practice and *opinio juris* on cyber warfare.[28] Even though scholars have attempted to address the various dimensions of cyber warfare within the existing public international law framework by reflecting upon whether cyber warfare can be regulated by the *lex lata* of *jus ad bellum* and *jus in bello*, particular uncertainty exists with regard to the applicability of article 51 of the United Nations Charter.[29] At the moment, it is highly doubtful that a cyber attack could amount to a 'threat or use of force' under article 2(4) of the Charter (see Randelzhofer 2002: 117; Buchan 2012: 216; Tallinn Manual 2012: Rules 10, 11, 12) or an 'armed attack' under article 51 that would allow a state to exercise its inherent right to individual or collective self-defence (see Tallinn Manual 2012: Commentary to Rules 13 (self-defence), 14 (necessity and proportionality), 15 (immediacy), 16 (collective self-defence), 17 (reporting measures for self-defence)). There are also difficulties with respect to attribution and assessing the purpose and identity of perpetrators.[30] Moreover, there is no international jurisprudence on cyber warfare: international courts, in particular the International Court of Justice (see Handler 2012: 224; Turns 2012: 282), and international human rights bodies (see La Rue 2011: ¶ 81) have not adjudicated on the legality of cyber attacks.

Thus far, the international community has acted slowly and sceptically in setting up a normative framework to regulate the global cyber environment, with the instruments that international organisations have adopted to regulate cyber activities being of only limited scope. Although more and more international organisations are adopting instruments to govern the cyber domain and are expanding their agenda to tackle cyber security threats, there is a noticeable gap in transorganisational and transnational coordination of policies and measures within the existing international legal framework (see Organization for Security and Co-Operation in Europe; Tikk 2010; Noshiravani 2011). This stems from the fact that various international organisations are still struggling with the terms of cyber peace and cyber warfare within the context of the traditional international peace and security paradigm. States define cyber attacks differently and have developed their (offensive and defensive) strategies accordingly. To a certain extent, some states have fallen back on the Cold War *leitmotiv* of strategic stability and point to cyber attacks as increasing the 'fog of war' (see Bumiller and Shanker 2012). That the prospect of states adopting a comprehensive legal instrument on cyber warfare

---

28　See *Jurisdictional Immunities of the State (Germany* v. *Italy: Greece Intervening)* [2012] ICJ: ¶ 55.

29　According to Weneger, 'a cyber attack on another State or with effects in another State is such an "armed attack" or its equivalent, at least when entailing major destruction or loss of human lives' (2011: 83; see also Graham 2010: 96; O'Connell 2012: 190–91).

30　It is correctly pointed out that 'attribution of cyber attacks is a multifaceted process; it has technical, legal and political aspects, with each aspect feeding into the other' (Tsagourias 2012: 233; see also Lin 2010: 74; Koh 2012).

is not strong (see US News 2012)[31] further suggests that states have not yet reached a point of agreement on how cyber warfare should be regulated.[32] This explains concerns voiced about a cyber arms race that would be expected to provide the stability that nuclear arms control did during the Cold War (see Libicki 2011: 77). It seems that states have become entangled in a pointless race to develop offensive cyber weapons simply because other states are doing so. Because cyber attacks rely upon the exploitation of vulnerabilities that a hacker has traced and that the defending state has not, it is most likely that new vulnerabilities in computer network systems will always emerge, and it is difficult to appreciate the concept of deterrence and balancing cyber defence versus cyber offence in the current cyber strategic environment.

The present writer holds the view that the development of any new body of law to address computer network attacks should be a matter for negotiation within the United Nations following a rigorous assessment of state practice in the field of cyber warfare. If the quest for cyber peace remains a priority on the agenda of states and international organisations, then the only viable solution for cyber security might be to establish more transparent national policies on computer network attacks, for example to criminalise offensive cyber weapons and offensive cyber strategies, and adopt efficient measures to identify parties responsible for computer network attacks.

As the dust begins to settle, we should accept that many problems related to cyber attacks do not stem from the deficiencies of the existing public international law framework. In other words, they do not constitute legal challenges. Rather, they present undecided issues of policy with which policymakers and strategists must grapple.

References

Addicott, J.F. 2010. Cyberterrorism: Legal Policy Issues, in *Legal Issues in the Struggle Against Terrorism*, ed. J. Moore and R. Turner. Durham, NC: Carolina Academic Press, 519–66.

Bothe, M., Partsch, K.J. and Solf, W.A. 1982. *New Rules for Victims of Armed Conflicts: Commentary on the Two 1977 Protocols Additional to the Geneva Conventions of 1949*. Leiden: Martinus Nijhoff.

Brenner, S.W. 2009. *Cyberthreats: The Emerging Fault Lines of the Nation State*. Oxford: Oxford University Press.

---

31 A proposal for the creation of an international criminal tribunal for cyberspace has recently been submitted by Judge Stein Schjølberg (2012).

32 The International Court of Justice has noted that 'multilateral conventions may have an important role to play in recording and defining rules deriving from custom, or indeed in developing them' (*Continental Shelf (Libyan Arab Jamahiriya/Malta)* [1985] ICJ 13: 29–30).

Brenner, S.W. and Clarke, L.L. 2010. Civilians in Cyber Warfare: Conscripts. *Vanderbilt Journal of Transnational Law*, 43(4), 1011–76.

Brown, D. 2006. A Proposal for an International Convention to Regulate the Use of Information Systems in Armed Conflict. *Harvard International Law Journal*, 47(1), 179–221.

Buchan, R. 2012. Cyber Attacks: Unlawful Uses of Force or Prohibited Interventions? *Journal of Conflict and Security Law*, 17(2), 212–27.

Bumiller, E. and Shanker, T. 2012. Panetta Warns of Dire Threat of Cyberattack on U.S. *New York Times*, 11 October.

Carr, J. 2011. *Inside Cyber Warfare*. 2nd edn. Sebastopol: O'Reilly Media.

Carswell, A. 2012. Neutrality in Cyber War. Available at: www.law.berkeley.edu/files/Neutrality_in_Cyber_War_for_web.pdf [accessed: 18 November 2012].

Chainoglou, K. 2010. An Assessment of Jus in Bello Issues Concerning Computer Network Attacks: A Threat Reflected in National Security Agendas. *Romanian Journal of International Law*, 12, 25–63.

Chainoglou, K. 2012. Psychological Warfare, in *Max Planck Encyclopedia of Public International Law*, vol. 8, ed. R. Wolfrum. Oxford: Oxford University Press, 559–64.

Commentary on the Humanitarian Policy and Conflict Research Manual on International Law Applicable to Air and Missile Warfare 2010. Available at: http://ihlresearch.org/amw/Commentary%20on%20the%20HPCR%20Manual.pdf [accessed: 18 November 2012].

Corn, G.S. 2008. Unarmed But How Dangerous? Civilian Augmentees, the Law of Armed Conflict, and the Search for a More Effective Test for Permissible Civilian Battlefield Functions. *Journal of National Security Law and Policy*, 2(2), 257–95.

Cornish, P., Livingstone, D., Clements, D. and Yorke, C. 2010. *On Cyber Warfare*. London: Chatham House.

Daoust, I., Coupland, R. and Ishoey, R. 2002. New Wars, New Weapons? The Obligation of States to Assess the Legality of Means and Methods of Warfare. *International Review of the Red Cross*, 84(846), 345–63.

Dinniss, H.H. 2012. *Cyber Warfare and the Laws of War*. Cambridge: Cambridge University Press.

Dinstein, Y. 2008. Distinction and Loss of Civilian Protection in International Armed Conflicts, in *International Law and Military Operations*, ed. M.D. Carsten. International Law Studies, vol. 84. Newport, RI: United States Naval War College, 183–98.

Dinstein, Y. 2010. *The Conduct of Hostilities under the Law of International Armed Conflict*. 2nd edn. Cambridge: Cambridge University Press.

Dinstein, Y. 2012. The Principle of Distinction and Cyber War in International Armed Conflicts. *Journal of Conflict and Security Law*, 17(2), 261–77.

Dörmann, K. 2004. Applicability of the Additional Protocols to Computer Network Attacks. Available at: http://www.icrc.org/eng/assets/files/other/applicabilityofihltocna.pdf [accessed: 10 September 2012].

Dunlap, C.J. Jr. 2011. Perspectives for Cyber Strategists on Law for Cyberwar. *Strategic Studies Quarterly*, 5(1), 81–99.

Eritrea-Ethiopia Claims Commission: Partial Award: Western Front: Aerial Bombardment and Related Claims: Eritrea's Claims 1, 3, 5, 9-13, 14, 21, 25 and 26 [2005] 27 Reports of International Arbitral Awards 291.

Fidler, D.P. 2012. Recent Developments and Revelations Concerning Cybersecurity and Cyberspace: Implications for International Law. *ASIL Insights.* Available at: http://www.asil.org/insights120620.cfm [accessed: 21 June 2012].

Geiss, R. 2010. *The Legal Regulation of Cyber Attacks in Times of Armed Conflict.* Proceedings of the Bruges Colloquium: Technological Challenges for the Humanitarian Legal Framework, 21–22 October.

Graham, D. 2010. Cyber Threats and the Law of War. *Journal of National Security Law and Policy*, 4(1), 87–102.

Green, J.A. 2012. Self-Preservation, in *Max Planck Encyclopedia of Public International Law*, vol. 9, ed. R. Wolfrum. Oxford: Oxford University Press, 128–31.

Handler, S.G. 2012. The New Cyber Face of Battle: Developing a Legal Approach to Accommodate Emerging Trends in Warfare. *Stanford Journal of International Law*, 48(1), 209–38.

Hathaway, O.A., Crootof, R., Levitz, P., Nix, H., Nowlan, A., Perdue, W. and Spiegel, J. 2012. The Law of Cyber-Attack. *California Law Review*, 100(4), 817–86.

Hollis, D.M. 2011. Cyberwar Case Study: Georgia 2008. *Small Wars Journal.* Available at: http://smallwarsjournal.com/jrnl/art/cyberwar-case-study-georgia-2008 [accessed: 30 September 2012].

Hughes, R. 2011. Towards a Global Regime for Cyber Warfare. Available at: http://www.ccdcoe.org/publications/virtualbattlefield/07_HUGHES%20Cyber%20Regime.pdf [accessed: 30 September 2012].

Independent International Fact-Finding Mission on the Conflict in Georgia, vol. II, 2009. Available at: http://www.ceiig.ch/pdf/IIFFMCG_Volume_II.pdf [accessed: 17 November 2012].

International Committee of the Red Cross (ICRC) 2009. Direct Participation in Hostilities: Questions & Answers. Available at: http://www.icrc.org/eng/resources/documents/faq/direct-participation-ihl-faq-020609.htm [accessed: 18 November 2012].

International Committee of the Red Cross (ICRC). Study on Customary International Humanitarian Law. Available at: http://www.icrc.org/customary-ihl/eng/docs/home [accessed: 29 September 2012].

Jensen, E.T. 2003. Unexpected Consequences from Knock-on Effects: A Different Standard for Computer Network Operations? *American University International Law Review*, 18(5), 1145–88.

Kastenberg, J.E. 2009. Non-Intervention and Neutrality in Cyberspace: An Emerging Principle in the National Practice of International Law. *Air Force Law Review*, 63, 43–64.

Kelsey, J.T.G. 2008. Hacking into International Humanitarian Law: The Principles of Distinction and Neutrality in the Age of Cyber Warfare. *Michigan Law Review*, 106(7), 1428–51.

Koh, H. 2012. Harold Koh on Cyber Attacks, 19 September. Available at: http://www.liebercode.org/2012/09/harold-koh-on-cyber-attacks_19.html [accessed: 19 September 2012].

La Rue, F. 2011. Report of the Special Rapporteur on the Promotion and Protection of the Right to Freedom of Opinion and Expression, UN Doc A/HRC/17/27.

Libicki, M. 2011. The Nature of Strategic Instability in Cyberspace. *Brown Journal of World Affairs*, 18(1), 71–9.

Lin, H.S. 2010. Offensive Cyber Operations and the Use of Force. *Journal of National Security Law and Policy*, 4(1), 63–86.

Lindstrom, G. 2012. Meeting the Cyber Security Challenge. Research Series 7. Geneva: Geneva Centre for Security Policy.

Lobel, H. 2012. Cyber War Inc.: The Law of War Implications of the Private Sector's Role in Cyber Conflict. *Texas International Law Journal*, 47(3), 617–40.

Maurer, T. 2011. *Cyber Norm Emergence at the United Nations: An Analysis of the UN's Activities Regarding Cyber-Security*. Science, Technology, and Public Policy Program, Belfer Center for Science and International Affairs, Harvard Kennedy School. Available at: http://belfercenter.ksg.harvard.edu/publication/21445/cyber_norm_emergence_at_the_united_nationsan_analysis_of_the_uns_activities_regarding_cybersecurity.html [accessed: 12 October 2012].

Melnitzky, A. 2012. Defending America Against Chinese Cyber Espionage Through the Use of Active Defenses. *Cardozo Journal of International and Comparative Law*, 20(2), 537–70.

Melzer, N. 2008. Interpretive Guidance on the Notion of Direct Participation in Hostilities under International Humanitarian Law, Adopted by the Assembly of the International Committee of the Red Cross on 26 February 2009. *International Review of the Red Cross*, 90(872), 991–1047.

North Atlantic Treaty Organization Cooperative Cyber Defence Centre of Excellence 2012. National Strategies and Policies, 21 November. Available at: http://www.ccdcoe.org/328.html [accessed: 11 December 2012].

Noshiravani, R. 2011. Rapporteur Report on NATO and Cyber Security: Building on the Strategic Concept. London: Chatham House. Available at: http://www.chathamhouse.org/sites/default/files/public/Research/International%20Security/200511nato.pdf [accessed: 24 June 2012].

O'Connell, M.E. 2012. Cyber Security Without Cyber War. *Journal of Conflict and Security Law*, 17(2), 187–209.

O'Donnell, B.T. and Kraska, J.C. 2003. Humanitarian Law: Developing International Rules for the Digital Battlefield. *Journal of Conflict and Security Law*, 8(1), 133–60.

Official Records of the Diplomatic Conference on the Reaffirmation and Development of International Humanitarian Law Applicable in Armed Conflicts, Geneva 1974–77. Vol. 15, CDDH/215/Rev. 1.

Organization for Security and Co-Operation in Europe. *Cyber Security: Virtual Threats, Real Responses*. Available at: http://www.osce.org/home/76011 [accessed: 18 November 2012].

Paust, J.J. 2012. A Critical Appraisal of the Air and Missile Warfare Manual. *Texas International Law Journal*, 47(2), 277–91.

Randelzhofer, A. 2002. Article 2(4), in *The Charter of the United Nations: A Commentary*, vol. 1, ed. B. Simma. Oxford: Oxford University Press, 112–36.

Roscini, M. 2010. World Wide Warfare: *Jus ad Bellum* and the Use of Cyber Force. *Max Planck Yearbook of United Nations Law*, 14, 85–130.

Ryan, D.J., Dion, M., Tikk, E. and Ryan, J.J.C.H. 2011. International Cyberlaw: A Normative Approach. *Georgetown Journal of International Law*, 42(4), 1161–98.

Ryan, J. and Ryan, D. 2011. Neutrality in the Context of Cyberwar, in *Proceedings of the 6th International Conference on Informational Warfare and Security*, ed. L. Armistead. Reading: Academic Publishing International, 221–7.

Sandoz, Y., Swinarski, C. and Zimmermann, B. (eds) 1987. *Commentary on the Additional Protocols of 8 June 1977 to the Geneva Conventions of 12 August 1949*. Geneva: Martinus Nijhoff and International Committee of the Red Cross.

Schaap, A.J. 2009. Cyber Warfare Operations: Development and Use under International Law. *Air Force Law Review*, 64, 121–74.

Schjølberg, S. 2012. Recommendations for Potential New Global Legal Mechanisms Against Global Cyberattacks and Other Global Cybercrimes: An International Criminal Tribunal for Cyberspace (ICTC)-Prosecution for the Tribunal Police investigation for the Tribunal. EastWest Institute (EWI) Cybercrime Legal Working Group Papers. Available at: http://www.ewi.info/who-we-are [accessed: 6 December 2012].

Schmitt, M.N. 2002. Wired Warfare: Computer Network Attack and *Jus in Bello*. *International Review of the Red Cross*, 84(846), 365–99.

Schmitt, M.N. 2010. Cyber Operations in International Law: The Use of Force, Collective Security, Self-Defence, and Armed Conflicts, in *Proceedings of a Workshop on Deterring Cyberattacks: Informing Strategies and Developing Options for U.S. Policy*, Washington, DC: National Academies Press, 151–78. Available at: http://www.nap.edu/catalog/12997.html [accessed: 4 October 2012].

Schmitt, M.N. 2012. Classification of Cyber Conflict. *Journal of Conflict and Security Law*, 17(2), 245–60.

Schmitt, M.N., Dinniss, H. and Winfield, T. 2004. Computers and War: The Legal Battlespace. Background Paper Prepared for Informal High-Level Expert Meeting on Current Challenges to International Humanitarian Law, 25–27 June. Available at: www.hpcrresearch.org/sites/default/files/publications/schmittetal.pdf [accessed: 19 September 2012].

Shulman, M.R. 1999. Discrimination in the Laws of Information Warfare. *Columbia Journal of Transnational Law*, 37(3), 939–68.

Tallinn Manual on the International Law Applicable to Cyber Warfare 2012. Prepared by the International Group of Experts at the Invitation of the NATO Cooperative Cyber Defence Centre of Excellence. Available at: https://www.ccdcoe.org/249.html [accessed: 17 September 2012].

Terry, J.P. 2001. The Lawfulness of Attacking Computer Networks in Armed Conflict and in Self-Defense in Periods Short of Armed Conflict: What are the Targeting Constraints? *Military Law Review*, 169, 70–91.

Ticehurst, R. 1997. The Martens Clause and the Laws of Armed Conflict. *International Review of the Red Cross*, 37(317), 125–34. Available at: http://www.icrc.org/eng/resources/documents/misc/57jnhy.htm [accessed: 17 September 2012].

Tikk, E. 2010. Global Cyber Security: Thinking About the Niche for NATO. *SAIS Review of International Affairs*, 30(2), 105–19.

Tikk, E. 2011. *Ten Rules for Cyber Security*. Tallinn: Cooperative Cyber Defence Centre of Excellence.

Tikk, E., Kaska, K. and Vihul, L. 2010. *International Cyber Incidents: Legal Considerations*. Tallinn: Cooperative Cyber Defence Centre of Excellence.

Touré, H.I. 2011. Cyber Peace and the Threat of Cyber War, in *Quest for Cyber Peace*, ed. H.I. Touré and World Federation of Scientists Permanent Monitoring Panel on Information Security. Geneva: International Telecommunications Union, 7–13.

Tsagourias, N. 2012. Cyber Attacks, Self-Defence and the Problem of Attribution. *Journal of Conflict and Security Law*, 17(2), 229–44.

Turns, D. 2012. Cyber Warfare and the Notion of Direct Participation in Hostilities. *Journal of Conflict and Security Law*, 17(2), 279–97.

United States 2007. *The Commander's Handbook on the Laws of Naval Operations*. Available at: http://www.usnwc.edu/getattachment/a9b8e92d-2c8d-4779-9925-0defea93325c/1-14M_%28Jul_2007%29_%28NWP%29 [accessed: 4 October 2012].

United States 2011. International Strategy for Cyberspace: Prosperity, Security and Openness in a Networked World. Available at: http://www.whitehouse.gov/sites/default/files/rss_viewer/international_strategy_for_cyberspace.pdf [accessed: 16 May 2012].

United States War Department 1863. *Instructions for the Government of Armies of the United States in the Field, Gen. Orders No. 100*.

US News 2012. Should There be an International Treaty on Cyberwarfare? 8 June. Available at: http://www.usnews.com/debate-club/should-there-be-an-international-treaty-on-cyberwarfare [accessed: 9 June 2012].

Watts, S. 2010. Combatant Status and Computer Network Attacks. *Virginia Journal of International Law*, 50(2), 391–447.

Weneger, H. 2011. A Concept of Cyber Peace, in *Quest for Cyber Peace*, ed. H.I. Touré and World Federation of Scientists Permanent Monitoring Panel on Information Security. Geneva: International Telecommunications Union, 77–85.

Wingfield, T.C. 2009. International Law and Information Operations, in *Cyberpower and National Security*, ed. F.D. Kramer, Starr, S.H. and Wentz, L.K. Washington, DC: National Defense University Press, 525–42.

PART III
Islamic Law and its Interface with International Law

Chapter 9

The Islamic Law of *Qital* and the Law of Armed Conflict: A Comparison

Niaz A. Shah

Although the origin and history of the Islamic law of *qital*, that is, the Islamic *jus in bello*, and the law of armed conflict are different, both of these bodies of law share the ultimate aim and objective of minimising unnecessary human suffering.[1] Islamic law, furthermore, can complement the law of armed conflict at national and regional level. Although these two bodies of law are generally compatible, there are areas that are less clear, such as rules on naval warfare. These are the 'grey areas' of Islamic law. There are also aspects of the law of armed conflict that Islamic law does not cover at all, such as air warfare and the use of such weapons as nuclear weapons. These can be called the 'blind spots' of Islamic law.

This chapter seeks to demonstrate the broad compatibility between the Islamic law of *qital* and the law of armed conflict by examining the basic and general principles of both bodies of law. It does this in two parts. The first part discusses and compares the basic principles of the Islamic law of *qital* – military necessity, distinction, proportionality, humanity and an obligation to accept offers of peace – with similar basic principles of the law of armed conflict. The second part of this chapter discusses and compares some general principles of the Islamic law of *qital*, related to genocide, war crimes and crimes against humanity, the treatment of war captives, rape as a war crime, civilian immunity, individual criminal responsibility, mutilation, perfidy and ruses of war, child soldiers, safe passage and quarter, hostages and truces and armistices, with identical general principles of the law of armed conflict. Although not discussed in detail in this chapter, it should be pointed out that the grey areas and blind spots of the Islamic law of *qital* can also be clarified; they can be expanded upon and developed to ensure their compatibility with the law of armed conflict.

The purpose of this comparison is not to seek a parallel law of armed conflict or to argue that Islamic law should trump the law of armed conflict but to suggest that the Islamic law of *qital* can complement the law of armed conflict in those Muslim states where Islamic law is in force.

---

1 All forty-six of the Muslim majority states are parties to the Four Geneva Conventions of 1949, and unlike with international human rights treaties, not a single Muslim state has entered a reservation to any of these treaties.

The Basic Principles of the Islamic Law of *Qital* and the Law of Armed Conflict

Under the Islamic law of *qital* and the law of armed conflict, the parties to an armed conflict are not free to use violence without restriction. The Islamic law of *qital* has five basic principles, namely military necessity, distinction, proportionality, humanity and an obligation to accept offers of peace. The law of armed conflict shares all but the last of these. Let us compare these basic principles in both bodies of law in order to assess the extent of their compatibility.

Military Necessity

The Quran only permits the extent and degree of force necessary to achieve a legitimate military objective. Once this has been achieved, the Muslim army must cease its attacks. On several occasions, the Quran requires the Muslim army to fight its adversaries until they are defeated, choose peace instead of war and restrain itself from *fitna*, or 'mischief'. The following Quranic verses illustrate this point:

> Kill them wherever you find them, and drive them out from where they drove you out, as Fitnah ... is more severe than killing. However, do not fight them near Al-Masjid-ul-Haram (the Sacred Mosque in Makkah) unless they fight you there. However, if they fight you (there) you may kill them. (2:191)

> But if they desist, then indeed, Allah is Most-Forgiving, Very-Merciful. (2:192)

> Fight them until there is no Fitnah anymore, and obedience remains for Allah. But, if they desist, then aggression is not allowed except against the transgressors. (2:193)

> The holy month for the holy month, and the sanctities are subject to retribution. So when anyone commits aggression against you, be aggressive against him in the like manner as he did against you. (2:194)[2]

These verses impose different kinds of restraints upon the use of force. In verse 2:191, for example, the objective is to expel others from where the Muslims were expelled. The expulsion of Muslims from their homes is here regarded as *fitna*. Verses 2:192 and 2:193 both note that if 'they desist', military necessity ends and fighting will not be permitted. In verse 2:193, the objective is to end *fitna*, but if the other party desists from *fitna*, aggression will not be allowed. Verse 2:191

---

    2   This chapter uses Ali's translation of the Quran together with Usmani's 2008 translation.

imposes a limitation of place – the Sacred Mosque in Makkah – whereas verse 2:194 imposes a limitation of time, namely in its exclusion of the sacred months.

The practice of the Prophet Muhammad suggests that only force of a degree and kind that corresponds to what is necessary to achieve a legitimate military objective is permissible. For instance, when the tribe of Banu Qazagh, which had been camped outside Medina in order to attack it, fled when they saw the Muslim army approaching, they were not chased: the military objective, to prevent the impending attack on Medina, had been achieved (see Al-Bukhari 2008: 17). Another example of the basic principle of military necessity in the practice of the Prophet Muhammad involves the fleeing of the enemy on the occasion of the battle of Zeeqard due to a lack of water (see Al-Bukhari 2008: 408). The Muslim soldiers wanted to pursue the enemy, but the Prophet Muhammad did not allow them to do so and told them to show mercy once the enemy had been subdued. This also shows a concern for humanity (see Muslim 2008: 627).

Under the law of armed conflict, military necessity permits a party to an armed conflict to use the degree and kind of force that is required in order to achieve the legitimate purpose of the conflict, which is the complete or partial submission of the enemy as soon as possible with the minimum loss of life and resources. The use of force must also not be otherwise prohibited by the law of armed conflict (see United Kingdom Ministry of Defence 2005: 21–2). Military objectives 'are limited to those objects which by their nature, location, purpose or use make an effective contribution to military action and whose total or partial destruction, capture or neutralisation, in the circumstances ruling at the time, offers a definite military advantage' (Protocol Additional to the Geneva Conventions of 12 August 1949, and Relating to the Protection of Victims of International Armed Conflicts (Additional Protocol I): art. 52(2)). The contemporary law of armed conflict takes military necessity into account, which means that it cannot otherwise be pleaded as a justification for violations of law.

The basic principles of military necessity in the Islamic law of *qital* and the law of armed conflict are compatible.

Distinction

Distinction is one of the basic principles of the Islamic law of *qital*. The Quran says: 'fight in the way of Allah against those who fight you, and do not transgress' (2:190). This terse verse contains three important rules. First, Muslims are given permission to fight. Second, fighting is only permitted against those who fight Muslims, that is, combatants. Third, Muslims cannot transgress the limits set by Allah in verse 2:190, which means that they must only fight 'those who fight you'. The practice of the Prophet Muhammad clearly distinguishes between combatants and non-combatants. An example of this would be an incident at the time of the Prophet Muhammad during which the Muslim army's enemies used children as human shields by holding them outside of the walls of a fort so that the Muslim army would stop shooting them with arrows (see Shaybani 1966: 103; Hamidullah

1968: 202). The Muslim army asked the Prophet Muhammad about this, and he commanded them to only aim at the combatants (see Al-Mawardi 2005: 65). If it is absolutely necessary to hit a particular target and if it would be otherwise impossible to distinguish between military and non-military targets despite every reasonable effort having been made to do so, then any resulting collateral damage is acceptable under the Islamic law of *qital* (see Marghinani 2005: 446–7). Collateral damage is allowed, in other words, but distinction remains one of the basic principles of the Islamic law of *qital*.

Under the law of armed conflict, distinction is the second basic principle. Military objects are legitimate targets, but fighters must distinguish between military objectives and civilian objects and between fighters and civilians. 'In order to ensure respect for and protection of the civilian population and civilian objects, the Parties to the conflict shall at all times distinguish between the civilian population and combatants and between civilian objects and military objectives and accordingly shall direct their operations only against military objectives' (Additional Protocol I: art. 48).

The basic principles of distinction in the Islamic law of *qital* and the law of armed conflict are compatible.

Proportionality

Proportionality is the third basic principle of the Islamic law of *qital*. It is clearly laid down in the Quran. Several verses may be cited in support of it, such as:

> And if you were to harm (them) in retaliation, harm them to the measure you were harmed. And if you opt for patience, it is definitely much better for those who are patient. (16:126)

> The one who does something evil will not be punished but in its equal proportion. (40:40)

> The recompense of evil is evil like it. Then the one who forgives and opts for compromise has his reward undertaken by Allah. Surely, He does not like the unjust. (42:40)

All of these verses show that proportionality is a basic principle of the Islamic law of *qital*. Consider verse 16:126 in particular. This verse was revealed to prevent disproportionate harm in armed conflicts, thus making it the key Quranic verse on proportionality. It was revealed when Hamzah, the paternal uncle of the Prophet Muhammad, was killed in the Battle of Uhud (AD 625/AH 3). Abu Sufyan, who was leading the Quraysh army against the Muslims, was accompanied by his wife Hind bin Utbah. During the battle, Muhammad's uncle was killed, and Hind split Hamzah's belly and chewed off his liver. The Prophet Muhammad swore that he would kill, depending on the account, thirty or seventy people in revenge. When the Muslim fighters heard the Prophet Muhammad say this, they became very angry and swore to cut their enemies into pieces. On this occasion, verse 16:126 was revealed to prevent Muslims from committing such excesses (see Ibn Kathir 2005: 218–19; Al-Bukhari 2008: 499). On the day that Mecca was conquered, Hind was given amnesty together with others (see Tabari 2003: 345). Like many other verses, verse 16:126 can be interpreted in two ways: as laying down the principle of proportionality and as prohibiting mutilation. The occasion of its revelation makes it a classic example of both the principle of proportionality and the prohibition of mutilation.

The third basic principle of the law of armed conflict is proportionality. Proportionality requires that the anticipated civilian losses resulting from a military action should not be excessive in relation to the expected military advantage. The 1977 Protocol Additional to the Geneva Conventions of 12 August 1949, and Relating to the Protection of Victims of International Armed Conflicts (Additional Protocol I) refers to proportionality in two different places. In the first instance, it is mentioned in relation to indiscriminate attacks: 'an attack which may be expected to cause incidental loss of civilian life, injury to civilians, damage to civilian objects, or a combination thereof, which would be excessive in relation to the concrete and direct military advantage anticipated' (Additional Protocol I: art. 51(5)(b); see also Hague Convention (IV): art. 23(e)). It is mentioned in identical language in relation to precautions in attacks, in articles 57(2)(a)(iii) and (b).

The basic principles of proportionality in the Islamic law of *qital* and the law of armed conflict are compatible.

A Concern for Humanity

A concern for humanity lies at the heart of the Islamic law of *qital*. The most relevant verse, referred to above, is 16:126, which prohibits more harm than is necessary and outlaws mutilation. In some instances, the Muslim army set enemy forts on fire when enemy fighters were hiding in the forts (see Al-Bukhari 2008: 576). The Prophet Muhammad later prohibited this practice, saying that it was for Allah alone to punish by fire (see Marghinani 2005: 457). 'Fairness is prescribed by God in every matter, so if you kill, kill in a fair way' (Hamidullah 1968: 204 (citing Muslim)). Muslims are required to treat war captives humanely (see Tabari 2003: 182). The wounded shall be cared for and nursed. When Mecca was conquered in AD 629/AH 8, the Prophet Muhammad declared a general amnesty to Meccans despite the fact that they had persecuted him and forced him to migrate from Mecca to Medina (see Shafi 1974: 312).

This concern for humanity also runs through other Islamic principles. 'It does not ... [behove] Muslims to slay women or children, or men aged, bed-ridden, or blind, because opposition and fighting are the only occasions which make slaughter allowable ... and such persons are incapable of these' (Marghinani 2005: 448). This makes clear that non-combatants should not be harmed. Women and the elderly, however, will forfeit their protection if they give advice to those who fight

Muslims or help in the planning of war against Muslims since this will amount to direct participation in fighting under the Islamic law of *qital*. This concern for humanity in war should be shown by both parties, and this is why it is not obligatory for Muslim children and the aged and infirm to take part in conflict (see Marghinani 2005: 444). Preference must be given to unmarried men over married men in drafting soldiers (see Shaybani 1966: 85).

The fourth basic principle of the law of armed conflict is a concern for humanity. This forbids the infliction of suffering, injury or destruction that is not necessary to achieve legitimate military objectives. For instance, it is prohibited to attack a combatant who is out of action by being wounded or captured since no military advantage can be achieved by attacking him or her. The concern for humanity is at the heart of the law of armed conflict and can be found in several treaty provisions (see First Geneva Convention: arts. 3, 63(4); Second Geneva Convention: arts. 3, 62(4); Third Geneva Convention: arts. 3, 142(4); Fourth Geneva Convention: arts. 3, 158(4); Additional Protocol I: art. 1(2)).

The basic principles of humanity in the Islamic law of *qital* and the law of armed conflict are compatible.

Offers of Peace

In addition to the four basic principles of the Islamic law of *qital* just described, the Quran also emphasises an obligation to accept offers of peace. Verse 8:61 reads as follows: 'if they tilt towards peace, you too should tilt towards it'. The implication of this verse is that even if the enemy offers peace only with a view to deceive, this offer of peace must be accepted (see Asad 1997: 249). In other words, mere suspicion is not an excuse for rejecting an offer of peace (see Asad 1997: 249). While the Muslim army must always be ready for a 'good fight' lest it be forced upon it, even in the midst of fighting Muslims must always be ready for peace if there is any inclination towards peace from the other side. There is no merit merely in fighting by itself (see Ali 1989: 429). Ali contends that peace cannot be withheld when the enemy comes to terms (1989: 429). Put differently, Muslims cannot refuse an offer of peace because the Quran says: 'But if they cease, Allah is oft-forgiving, most Merciful' (2:192; see also 4:128). Since Allah is merciful and forgiving, so shall the Muslim army be merciful and forgiving. The verses dealing with the acceptance of peace are more relevant for a discussion of the use of force under Islamic law, but they can also be relied upon when discussing truces and armistices and collecting the wounded and burying the dead.

The law of armed conflict does not as such deal with the subjects of peace and peaceful relations among states, which are dealt with by, *inter alia*, article 2(4) of the United Nations Charter. As with the Charter, peace is the standard norm in Islamic law, and the use of force is an exception to this rule (see Shah 2008, 2013). The Islamic law of *qital* requires accepting offers of peace made by an opposing party during an armed conflict. By contrast, the law of armed conflict does not, and in this sense, it can be said that the Islamic law of *qital* is more progressive than the law of armed conflict.

To summarise, the four basic principles of the Islamic law of *qital* and the law of armed conflict are compatible. The Islamic law of *qital*, however, has an additional principle that requires Muslims to accept offers of peace during an armed conflict.

The General Principles of the Islamic Law of *Qital* and the Law of Armed Conflict

As alluded to above, the Islamic law of *qital* also has a set of general principles. Some of these are more clearly laid out than others. The following discussion of the Quranic rules and practices of the Prophet Muhammad demonstrates that, although not entirely comprehensive, there is a clear body of law that governs the conduct of *qital*. This body of law, however, needs to be further developed and expanded upon to cover all aspects of contemporary armed conflict. The following pages discuss and compare some general principles of the Islamic law of *qital*, related to genocide, war crimes and crimes against humanity, the treatment of war captives, rape as a war crime, civilian immunity, individual criminal responsibility, mutilation, perfidy and ruses of war, child soldiers, safe passage and quarter, hostages and truces and armistices, with identical general principles of the law of armed conflict.

Genocide

Some verses in the Quran, particularly verses 9:5 and 9:29, are sometimes interpreted in a way that suggests that the Quran permits the genocide of non-Muslims. The orthodox view is that the Quran did not allow *jihad* and favoured patience during the early years of Islam at Mecca (AD 610–22) (see Afsarudin 2008: 687; Al-Bukhari 2008: 17), and that *jihad* only became permissible in self-defence after the Prophet Muhammad migrated from Mecca to Medina and founded the first Muslim community there (AD 622–32/AH 1–10). The orthodox view continues by asserting that *jihad* became an ongoing duty for Muslims in perpetuity during the last year of the Medinan period, AD 631/AH 9, when verses 9:5 and 9:29 repealed all of the earlier revealed verses dealing with restraint. This view is sometimes referred to as the progression argument on the use of force because there is a very clear progression from a state of patience, or no use of force, in Mecca to permission to use force in self-defence in Medina to the licensing of the use of force against all non-Muslims at all times in perpetuity.

Let us closely analyse the progression argument. According to it, *jihad* was not allowed during the Meccan period. The following verses are usually cited to support this argument:

The one who defends himself after having been wronged; there is no blame on such people. (42:41)

Blame, in fact, is upon those who wrong people and make mischief on earth unjustly. (42:42)

And if one observes patience and forgives, it is, of course, one of the courageous conducts. (42:43)

(O Muslims,) many among the people of the Book desire to turn you, after your accepting the faith, back into disbelievers – all out of envy on their part, even after the truth has become clear to them. *So, forgive and overlook till Allah brings out His command.* (2:109; emphasis added)

Indeed, there is scholarly consensus that *jihad* was not allowed in Mecca.

In Medina, however, a new command was revealed that allowed force to be used in self-defence, a command to which verse 2:109 alludes. The following two verses are cited in support of this argument: 'Permission (to fight) is given to those against whom fighting is launched, because they have been wronged' (22:39); 'Fight in the way of Allah against those who fight you, and do not transgress. Verily, Allah does not like the transgressors' (2:190). There is scholarly consensus that these two verses allow the use of force in self-defence.

The progression argument continues by noting that this rule permitting *jihad* in self-defence remained in force for eight years. The Muslim community consolidated itself during this period, and in AD 631/AH 9, two separate commands were revealed regarding polytheists (pagans) and People of the Book (Jews, Christians and Sabians). Regarding polytheists, it is argued that verse 9:5 of the Quran sanctions the killing of this group of people unless they embrace Islam: 'So, when the sacred months expire, kill the Musriks [that is, polytheists] wherever you find them, and catch them and besiege them and sit in ambush for them everywhere. Then, if they repent and establish [prayer] and pay [poor due], leave their way.' The People of the Book were to be fought and killed but could be spared after being subdued and agreeing to pay the *jizya*, or 'protection tax'. Verse 9:29 is cited to support this argument: 'Fight those People of the Book who do not believe in Allah, nor in the Last Day, and do not take as unlawful what Allah and His Messenger have declared as unlawful, and do not profess the Faith of Truth; (fight them) until they pay the *jizya* with their own hands while they are subdued.'

The proponents of the progression argument contend that verses 9:5 and 9:29 repealed the earlier verses that permitted *jihad* only in self-defence. Thus, according to this view, one sees a progression from a state of patience, or no use of force, in Mecca to permission to use force in self-defence in Medina to the licensing of the use of force against all non-Muslims at all times in perpetuity. On this interpretation, given that verses 9:5 and 9:29 repealed the verses related to *jihad* in self-defence, Muslims are required to forcefully convert polytheists to

Islam or kill them. This, of course, would amount to a rule sanctioning genocide and requiring Muslims to subjugate the People of the Book.

A close study of verses 9:5 and 9:29 in their historical and Quranic context, however, suggests that the progression argument on the use of force is untenable. In fact, these two verses do not repeal the verses allowing for the use of force in self-defence. To show this, one must address the following questions: Has the Quran used the 'kill them [that is, polytheists]' language in other verses and in other contexts? What were the practices of the Prophet Muhammad and his immediate successors in dealing with polytheists and the People of the Book after verses 9:5 and 9:29 were revealed? Did they kill the people in question when they could have done so or did they treat them differently?

Verses 9:5 and 9:29
Chapters 8 and 9 of the Quran were revealed at Medina, and their subject matters are similar. Chapter 8 was revealed shortly after the Battle of Badr (AD 624/AH 2) and deals with the lessons of Badr: the question of war booty, the virtues necessary for good fighting, victory against the odds, clemency and consideration for one's own people and others in the hour of victory (see Ali 1989: 413). In other words, it addresses many of the large questions that arise at the outset of the life of a new organised community. Chapter 9 logically follows the argument in Chapter 8 and should be read within the context of Chapter 8 since a *Bismillah* ('in the name of Allah') is not written at the beginning of Chapter 9 (see Ali 1989: 413). Every chapter in the Quran begins with a *Bismillah* except Chapter 9, which suggests that the compilers of the Quran were not sure if they were separate chapters (Ibn Kathir 2005: 478).

Verses 1–29 of Chapter 9 were revealed before the Battle of Tabuk in October AD 631/AH 9 (see Ali 1989: 435). The subject matter of the chapter is 'what is to be done if the enemy breaks faith and is guilty of treachery' (Ali 1989: 435). It does not lay down new rules for the use of force. Chapter 9 discusses three kinds of people: polytheists, the People of the Book and hypocrites, that is, those who pretend to be Muslims but who never wholeheartedly embrace Islam. There were four kinds of polytheists in Medina in AD 630/AH 8. First, there were those with whom the Prophet Muhammad had concluded a peace treaty at Hudaybiyya in AD 628/AH 6, namely the Quraysh. One of the conditions of this treaty was that neither party would attack the other party or its allies. The treaty allowed other tribes to join any of the main parties to the treaty. Banu Bakr joined the Quraysh whereas Banu Khazagh joined the Muslims. Banu Bakr breached the terms of Hudaybiyya by attacking Banu Khazagh and so did the Quraysh by aiding its ally. The treaty having been violated, the Prophet Muhammad marched towards Mecca in AD 629/AH 8 to conquer it but ended up being able to do so without actual combat. The second group of polytheists were those with whom the Prophet Muhammad had peace treaties for fixed periods of time and who faithfully observed the terms of the treaties, such as Bani Zamrah and Bani Madlej. The third group of polytheists were those with whom the Prophet Muhammad had open-ended peace treaties with terms that were not fixed. The fourth group included those with whom the Prophet Muhammad had no treaty at all (see Al-Bukhari 2008: 179; Elahi 2008: 553). The first three verses in Chapter 9 address the first and second groups of polytheists, who had been given a four-month guarantee of *aman*, or 'safe passage':

> Here is a disavowal (proclaimed) by Allah and His Messenger against the [polytheists] with whom you have a treaty. (9:1)

> So, move in the land freely for four months, and be aware that you can never frustrate Allah, and that Allah is going to disgrace the disbelievers. (9:2)

> And here is an announcement, from Allah and His Messenger, to the people on the day of the greater Hajj, that Allah is free from (any commitment to) the [polytheists], and so is His Messenger. Now, if you repent, it is good for you. And if you turn away, then be aware that you can never frustrate Allah. And give those who disbelieve the good news of a painful punishment. (9:3)

Verse 9:4 was addressed to the third group, in particular Banu Zamrah and Banu Madlej: 'Except those of the Musriks [that is, polytheists] with whom you have a treaty, and they were not deficient (in fulfilling the treaty) with you, and did not back up any one against you. So fulfil the treaty with them up to their term.' Verse 9:7 was addressed to Banu Hamzah and Banu Kinana, who remained faithful to their treaties: 'How can the Musriks [that is, polytheists] have a treaty with Allah and His Messenger, except those with whom you made a treaty near Al-Masjid-ul-Haram? Then, as long as they remain straight with you, you too remain straight with them.' Verse 9:5 was addressed to the Quraysh (see Shafi 1974: 309–12), who broke the terms of Hudaybiyya: 'So, when the sacred months expire, kill the [polytheists] wherever you find them, and catch them and besiege them and sit in ambush for them everywhere. Then, if they repent and establish Salah and pay Zakah, leave their way.'

Verse 9:29 was revealed to address the People of the Book: 'Fight those People of the Book who do not believe in Allah, nor in the Last Day, and do not take as unlawful what Allah and His Messenger have declared as unlawful, and do not profess the Faith of Truth; (fight them) until they pay the *jizya* with their own hands while they are subdued.' The immediate context for this verse's revelation involved rumours that the Byzantines (Romans), who were People of the Book, were preparing to attack Arabia (see Ali 1989: 435). After verse 9:29 was revealed, the Prophet Muhammad gathered an army of 30,000 soldiers and marched in the direction of Syria, staying at Tabuk, a town bordering the Byzantine territory, in order to repel the imminent Byzantine attack. The Byzantine invasion did not materialise, but the Prophet Muhammad made treaties with some Christian and Jewish tribes near the Gulf of Aqabah (see Ali 1989: 435). Verses 9:30–129 were revealed after the Tabuk expedition and deal with the hypocrites who did not join the Tabuk expedition and other issues, such as who must participate in actual combat (see Ali 1989: 435).

Thus, a careful, contextual analysis of verses 9:1–29 indicates that they were revealed to address particular groups of people and their relationship with Muslims at a specific moment in history. The subject matter and intention of the verses were not meant to create new rules for the use of force by superseding previous verses as the progression argument would have it (see Shah 2008, 2011); rather, they were merely meant to address whether or not to dissolve specific treaties with particular tribes. The dissolution of treaties means an end to treaty obligations. This does not somehow create new rules for the use of force or repeal previous ones.

Elahi argues that verse 9:29 is not about spreading Islam through obligatory *jihad* and eliminating the People of the Book if they do not embrace Islam: rather, it is about the *jizya*, a symbol of political dominance and sovereignty (2008: 576). It is addressed to the Muslims of seventh-century Arabia and is not meant as an order to twenty-first-century Muslims to present the Quran to the People of the Book in one hand and a sword in the other and to kill them if they do not embrace Islam or pay the *jizya*. Verse 9:5 is about fighting specific polytheists, the Quraysh, who had broken their covenants with the Muslims. To reiterate, it is not meant as an order to twenty-first-century Muslims to kill polytheists on sight.

The 'kill them' language
In addition to this contextual analysis of verses 9:5 and 9:29, it is important to point out that the Quran does not use the 'kill them' language here for the first time. The same language was used in verses that were revealed earlier:

> *Kill them wherever you find them*, and drive them out from where they drove you out, as Fitnah (to create disorder) is more severe than killing. (2:191; emphasis added)

> They wish that you should disbelieve, as they have disbelieved, and thus you become all alike. So, do not take friends from among them unless they migrate in the way of Allah. Then, if they turn away, *seize them, and kill them* wherever you find them, and do not take from among them a friend or helper. (4:89; emphasis added)

> You will find others who want to be secure from you, and secure from their own people. (But) whenever they are called back to the mischief, they are plunged into it. So, if they do not stay away from you, and do not offer peace to you, and do not restrain their hands, then *seize them, and kill them* wherever you find them, and, we have given you an open authority against them. (4:91; emphasis added)

Whenever the Quran requires the killing of someone, be he or she Muslim or non-Muslim, this is always contingent upon the individual at issue having done or not done something. For instance, verse 2:191 focuses on expelling non-Muslims from territory that had previously been Muslim. In verse 4:89, killing is contingent upon 'if they turn away' language whereas in verse 4:91 it is contingent upon 'if they do not stay away from you' language. The 'kill them' language, in other words, is used on specific occasions for specific groups of people and is not meant to be extrapolated to the world at large. This is also the case with verses 9:5 and 9:29, which do not repeal or purport to repeal verses related to *jihad* in self-defence. The only normative value that verses 9:5 and 9:29 have today is that Muslims can choose to follow the course of action suggested in *but only in* similar contexts and conditions. The rule permitting killing for specific reasons is not confined to non-Muslims only; Islamic law also allows the killing of Muslims in certain cases, such as in cases of brigandage and *qisas*, or 'retribution' (see 5:32–3).

The practice of the Prophet Muhammad and Caliph Abu Bakr

As stated above, verses 9:1–29 were revealed before the Tabuk expedition in AD 631/AH 9. In fact, the Tabuk expedition began after permission was given by verse 9:29 to fight the People of the Book (see Shafi 1974: 358–62; Ali 1989: 35), thus making the verse the preface to the Battle of Tabuk in particular (see Shafi 1974: 358). When the Prophet Muhammad reached Tabuk, the governor of Aylah, Rubah, made a peace treaty with the Prophet Muhammad by agreeing to pay the *jizya*. The people of Jarba and Adhruh also agreed to pay the *jizya*, and the Prophet Muhammad wrote documents for each of them (see Tabari 2003: 58). The Prophet Muhammad did not kill them. After the death of the Prophet Muhammad in AD 632/AH 10, most of the former polytheist tribes who had embraced Islam during the life of the Prophet Muhammad renounced it and attempted to secede from the Muslim state. Some even tried to invade Medina (see Tabari 2003: 476), the capital of the Islamic state. Abu Bakr, the first caliph, sent forces to suppress the secessionist tribes and restore the writ of the Islamic government. He gave the following instructions to commander Muhajir before sending him to reinforce the expedition of Kindah: 'If this letter of mine reaches before you have achieved victory, then – if you conquer the enemy – kill the fighting men and take the offspring captive if you took them by force' (Tabari 2003: 185). If verse 9:5 truly sanctions the killing of all polytheists, then it seems logical to conclude that Caliph Abu Bakr would have given different instructions: 'kill them all when you capture them', or something to this effect. The practice of the Prophet Muhammad and Caliph Abu Bakr suggests that verses 9:5 and 9:29 did not repeal verses 22:39 and 2:190 or allow the genocide of polytheists.

Islamic law prohibits genocide in both times of war and times of peace. According to verse 5:32 of the Quran: 'Whoever kills a person not in retaliation for a person killed, nor (as a punishment) for spreading disorder on the earth, is as if he has killed the whole of humankind, and whoever saves the life of a person is as if he has saved the life of the whole of humankind.' This verse has two parts: a negative obligation to refrain from killing and a positive obligation to save the lives of innocents. The rule prohibiting the killing of innocents can be relied upon in the prevention and punishment of the crime of genocide, and the rule on saving innocent lives can be relied upon for humanitarian intervention. These rules apply to everyone, Muslim or non-Muslim, since the word used is the generic 'person'.

Genocide is a serious crime under international law, in both times of war and times of peace. Article 1 of the 1948 Convention on the Prevention and Punishment of the Crime of Genocide defines genocide as:

> any of the following acts committed with intent to destroy, in whole or in part, a national, ethnical, racial or religious group, as such:
> (a) killing members of the group;
> (b) causing serious bodily or mental harm to members of the group;
> (c) deliberately inflicting on the group conditions of life calculated to bring about its physical destruction in whole or in part;
> (d) imposing measures intended to prevent births within the group;
> (e) forcibly transferring children of the group to another group.

This definition has both mental and material elements and involves certain acts committed with certain intent.[3] This definition has been incorporated into the 1993 Statute of the International Tribunal for the Prosecution of Persons Responsible for Serious Violations of International Humanitarian Law Committed in the Territory of the Former Yugoslavia Since 1991 (hereafter ICTY Statute) (see Report of the Secretary-General (1993)), the 1994 Statute of the International Criminal Tribunal for the Prosecution of Persons Responsible for Genocide and Other Serious Violations of International Humanitarian Law Committed in the Territory of Rwanda and Rwandan Citizens Responsible for Genocide and Other Such Violations Committed in the Territory of Neighbouring States, Between 1 January 1994 and 31 December 1994 (hereafter ICTR Statute) and the 1998 Rome Statute of the International Criminal Court. Genocide is considered to be one of international law's most serious crimes.

The general principles prohibiting genocide in the Islamic law of *qital* and the law of armed conflict are compatible.

War Crimes and Crimes against Humanity

Criminal law is a highly developed branch of Islamic law. It applies in both times of war and times of peace. For example, two captives caught in the Battle of Badr (AD 624/AH 2), Nazer bin al-Haris and Aqba, were killed for their past crimes (see Al-Bukhari 2008: 69–72). Similarly, Ibn Khatal and Maqees bin Sababa were killed for their past crimes after Mecca was conquered in AD 629/AH 8 (see Al-Bukhari 2008: 504). After the Battle of Khyber, Zainab Bint Haris, the wife of

---

3   *Application of the Convention on the Prevention and Punishment of the Crime of Genocide (Bosnia and Herzegovina v. Serbia and Montenegro)* [2007] ICJ Rep 43: 121–2.

Salam, tried to kill the Prophet Muhammad and other fighters by sending him a roasted goat that had been poisoned. Bashir Bin Bara died after eating the poisoned meat. Zainab was handed over to the heirs of Bashir, who killed her in *qisas* (see Al-Bukhari 2008: 468). In the wake of the attack on Mecca, the Muslim commander Khalid bin Walid killed several individuals in fighting as a result of misunderstanding. The Prophet Muhammad sent Ali – his cousin and son-in-law – to pay compensation for their blood. Even compensation for a dog was paid (see Tabari 2003: 349). Islamic criminal law was applied in these instances, and it is in this sense justified to say that Islamic law punishes war crimes. Although the modern terminology of war crimes and crimes against humanity is not used in Islamic legal texts, these offences are certainly punishable under Islamic criminal law. For instance, murder is a crime under Islamic criminal law, and it does not matter whether the victim is killed during a time of war or time of peace.

The term 'crimes against humanity' originated from the term 'the laws of humanity' mentioned in the preamble of the 1907 Hague Convention (IV) Respecting the Laws and Customs of War on Land and its Annex: Regulations Concerning the Laws and Customs of War on Land (see Bassiouni 2007: 135–6), but it was first defined in the 1945 Agreement for the Prosecution and Punishment of the Major War Criminals of the European Axis, and Charter of the International Military Tribunal (hereafter Nuremberg Charter). Article 6(c) of the Nuremberg Charter defines crimes against humanity as:

> murder, extermination, enslavement, deportation, and other inhumane acts committed against any civilian population, before or during the war, or persecutions on political, racial or religious grounds in execution of or in connection with any crime within the jurisdiction of the Tribunal, whether or not in violation of the domestic law of the country where perpetuated.

International humanitarian law recognises that certain violations of the laws and customs of war, most of which were codified in the Hague Conventions of 1899 and 1907, are war crimes (see Ratner 2007: 420). The Nuremberg Charter defines war crimes as 'violations of the laws or customs of war' (art. 6(b)). The Four Geneva Conventions of 1949 and Additional Protocol I of 1977 contain lists of war crimes called 'grave breaches' and other violations of the laws of war. Grave breaches include wilful killing, torture or inhuman treatment (including medical experiments), wilfully causing great suffering or serious injury to body or health, extensive destruction and appropriation of property not justified by military necessity and carried out unlawfully and wantonly, compelling a prisoner of war or civilian to serve in the forces of the hostile power, wilfully depriving a prisoner of war or protected civilian of the right to a fair and regular trial, unlawful deportation or transfer of a protected civilian, unlawful confinement of a protected civilian, the taking of hostages, making civilians and non-defended localities the object or inevitable victims of attack, the perfidious use of the Red Cross or Red Crescent emblem, transfer of an occupying power of parts of its population to occupied territory, unjustifiable delays in repatriation of prisoners of war, apartheid, attacks on historical monuments and depriving protected persons of a fair trial (see First Geneva Convention: art. 50; Second Geneva Convention: art. 51; Third Geneva Convention: art. 130; Fourth Geneva Convention: art. 147; Additional Protocol I: art. 110). Other violations of the Geneva Conventions and Additional Protocols I and II are not grave breaches but are still regarded as war crimes.

The Rome Statute has added some violations of the laws and customs of war to the list of war crimes, such as the war crime of rape (art. 7(g)). States parties are obliged to penalise grave breaches, but it should be stressed that these provisions apply only in international armed conflicts. There is a separate and rather limited set of rules that applies to conflicts of a non-international character. This set of rules includes common article 3 of the Four Geneva Conventions and Protocol Additional to the Geneva Conventions of 12 August 1949, and Relating to the Protection of Victims of Non-International Armed Conflicts (Additional Protocol II), which prohibits, *inter alia*, torture, the taking of hostages, murder and ill-treatment. Article 8 of the Rome Statute also criminalises such acts as violence to life and person, outrages upon personal dignity, the taking of hostages and summary execution.

As stated above, Islamic criminal law punishes war crimes and crimes against humanity. The law of armed conflict categorises war crimes as grave breaches and other violations whereas Islamic criminal law does not make this distinction as such. Grave breaches exist in international armed conflicts but not in conflicts of a non-international character; by contrast, Islamic criminal law recognises war crimes in both types of conflicts. In this sense, the Islamic law of *qital* has a wider field of application than the law of armed conflict. Despite these differences, however, the Islamic law of *qital* and the law of armed conflict are essentially compatible on the question of war crimes and crimes against humanity.

War Captives

Islamic law requires humane treatment of war captives. A number of Quranic verses support this view. Verse 47:4 is particularly noteworthy: 'So, when you encounter those who disbelieve, then (aim at) smiting the necks, until when you have broken their strength thoroughly, then tie fast the bond, (by making them captives). Then choose (to release them) either (as a favour (shown to them), or (after receiving) ransom, until the war throws down its load of arms.' This is a key verse on taking captives and offers options for captives' eventual release. It encourages Muslim fighters to be steadfast during battle and fight until the enemy has been thoroughly routed. Enemy persons can be imprisoned and must not be released until the war is finally over. If there is a risk that captives might rejoin the enemy forces and attack Muslims again, then they must not be released. Verse 47:4 demonstrates two ways to deal with captives: they can be released as a favour shown or after the payment of a ransom (see Deoband 2009). It should also be noted that the Quran stipulates that captives must be treated humanely and fed well during their captivity: 'And they give food, out of their love for [God], to the needy, and the orphan, and the captive' (76:8).[4]

According to verse 8:67, '[i]t is not befitting a Prophet that he has captives with him unless he has subdued the enemy by shedding blood in the land. You intend to have the stuff of this world, while Allah intends the Hereafter (for you).' Abu Bakr Jasas argues that verse 8:67 repeals verse 47:4 (as cited in Elahi 2008: 43), and it has been interpreted by some to mean that every captured enemy fighter should be killed rather than held captive. According to this view, therefore, the rule of releasing captives for ransom or as a favour has been repealed, with the new rule being laid down in verse 8:67, to kill all non-Muslim captives. This argument, however, is untenable.

Chronologically speaking, verse 47:4 was revealed in AD 623/AH 1 whereas verse 8:67 was revealed in AD 624/AH 2 (see Usmani 2008: 219). The latter, however, does not seem to have repealed the former. Verses 8:67–71 were revealed when the Prophet Muhammad had consulted his companions as to how to deal with the seventy captives caught in the Battle of Badr (see Ali 1989: 432; Usmani 2008: 338). His companions offered different views. The advice of Caliph Abu Bakr and others was to release them after a ransom payment whereas Omer favoured killing them. The Prophet Muhammad acted on the advice of Caliph Abu Bakr and released the captives after they had paid a ransom (see Elahi 2008: 543). Thereafter, verse 8:67 was revealed, admonishing Muslims that *jihad* is not for such worldly gains as ransom but, rather, for the cause of Allah. As such, this verse does not prohibit the taking of ransom or repeal the existing rule on ransom. The following two verses support this interpretation: 'Had there not been a decree from Allah that came earlier, a great punishment would have overtaken you because of what you have taken' (8:68); 'So, eat of the spoils you have got, lawful and pure' (8:69). Verse 8:68 refers to a previous decree of ransom mentioned in verse 47:4 whereas verse 8:69 confirms the lawfulness of ransom. This is why the decision to demand ransom for the Battle of Badr captives was not overturned. Verse 8:67 aims to prevent situations in which enemy persons are arrested and released for financial gain rather than for genuine reasons related to the conflict. Such a situation is precisely what has happened in the current armed conflict in Pakistan given that Pakistani officials have arrested dozens of individuals and handed them over to the United States in return for huge bounties (see Musharraf 2006: 237).

The practice of the Prophet Muhammad also does not suggest that verse 8:67 has a repealing effect since he consistently released war captives after verse 8:67 was revealed (see Al-Bukhari 2008: 78–9, 580). The only exception to this was when captives were killed after the siege of Banu Qarayza in AD 627/AH 5 (see Hamidullah 1968: 217; Al-Bukhari 2008: 298). Banu Qarayza had an agreement with Muslims that they would not aid anyone against the Muslims, but during the Battle of Khandaq (AD 627/AH 5), Banu Qarayza sided with the Quraysh against the Muslims. After the Battle of Khandaq, the Muslim army laid siege to Banu

---

4   See *Khakhi* v. *The State* [2010] All Pakistan Legal Decisions, Federal Shariat Court 1.

Qarayza for about twenty-five days. Finally, Banu Qarayza asked the Prophet Muhammad to end the siege and decide their fate as he wished. The Prophet Muhammad appointed Sad bin Muadh as an arbitrator to decide the matter. He decided to kill all the males and take their wealth as war booty. Hundreds of men were killed as a result (see Al-Bukhari 2008: 298). Nomani argues that Banu Qarayza was a Jewish tribe and that Muadh's decision was according to Jewish law, specifically Deuteronomy 20:10–14 (see Hamidullah 1968: 217; Al-Bukhari 2008: 298). Nomani's argument seems convincing because the Quran, at verse 5:48, allows the application of Jewish law to Jews.

To sum up, captives must be treated humanely during their captivity. Their captivity can be terminated in three ways: they can be released as a favour shown, after payment of a ransom or in exchange for Muslim captives. It should also be stressed, however, that some war captives can be punished as *qisas* for their past crimes.

Admittedly, there are some differences of opinion among Sunni jurists on the issue of killing captives. Taken as a whole, however, these differences seem to only reflect the personal preferences of the various jurists as to how captives should be dealt with. Imam Abu Hanifa, for example, argues that the Muslim leader is allowed to kill or keep captives as *dhimmis*, or non-Muslim citizens who are under the protection of the Muslim state, but that they cannot be released for ransom (see Rushd 2006: 456). Imam Shafi says that captives may be exchanged for Muslim captives, but Abu Hanifa opposes this view (see Rushd 2006: 456). According to Shaybani (1966), captives can be released for ransom if Muslims need financial help. He also argues that captives can be released as a favour without ransom or in exchange for Muslim captives. Shaybani's view shows that verse 8:67 does not repeal verse 47:4. Ibn Rushd reports that a 'group of jurists maintained that it is not permitted to execute the prisoners' (Rushd 2006: 456).

Whatever the views of these various jurists on the issue of killing captives, juristic views do not create binding rules and because of this, they should not be confused with the obligatory rules of the Quran. The Quranic obligation on this matter appears in verse 47:4; and it is clear: to arrest and keep captives 'until the war throws down its load of arms' and then either to release them as a favour shown or after the payment of a ransom. War captives have the right to draw up wills regarding their property at home, and these must be communicated to the concerned person or persons. Among prisoners, a mother should not be separated from her child. The dignity of the prisoner should also be respected according to his or her position. 'Pay respect to the dignitary of a nation who is brought low', said the Prophet Muhammad (Hamidullah 1968: 215).

Article 4 of the Third Geneva Convention spells out the categories of persons entitled to prisoner of war status. The same treaty states that the detaining power is responsible for their treatment (art. 9) and maintenance free of charge (art. 15). 'Prisoners of war must at all times be humanely treated' (art. 13) and they 'are entitled in all circumstances to respect for their persons and their honour' (art. 14). A prisoner of war shall be subject to the laws of the detaining power, which shall take judicial or disciplinary measures in respect of any offence committed by a prisoner of war against such laws (art. 82), including for acts committed prior to capture (art. 85). Prisoners of war cannot be sentenced to penalties different than those specified for the forces of the detaining power for the same offences (art. 87). 'Prisoners of war shall be released and repatriated without delay after the cessation of active hostilities' (art. 118). The Third Geneva Convention is very elaborate and covers a wide range of other issues related to prisoners of war, such as medication, labour, external communications and the drawing up of wills. The Third Geneva Convention does not prohibit the death penalty (art. 100).

There are some differences in detail, but the general principles of the Islamic law of *qital* and the law of armed conflict on the treatment of war captives are compatible.

Rape as a War Crime

Islamic law prohibits sexual intercourse outside of marriage, be it consensual or non-consensual. This rule applies equally in both times of war and times of peace. Verse 24:2 of the Quran prescribes one hundred stripes for unlawful sexual intercourse, but the statutory law of some Muslim states, such as Pakistan, Iran and Saudi Arabia, punishes it by stoning to death. Under Islamic criminal law, rape is a serious offence punishable by death, both in times of war and times of peace.

The treatment of rape as a war crime has evolved over the years, but international law today recognises it as a crime against humanity. The Fourth Geneva Convention states that 'women shall be especially protected against any attack on their honour, in particular against rape, enforced prostitution, or any form of indecent assault' (art. 27; see Additional Protocol I: art. 76(1)). Articles 5(g) of the ICTY Statute and 3(g) of the ICTR Statute classify rape as a crime against humanity and a war crime. Article 7 of the Rome Statute recognises 'rape' and 'sexual enslavement' as crimes against humanity. Article 8(e)(vi) criminalises rape and sexual slavery committed in armed conflicts of a non-international character.

The Islamic law of *qital* and the law of armed conflict both treat rape as a war crime and are compatible in this regard.

Civilian Immunity

The Quran clearly states that only those individuals who are engaged in active combat can be targeted and that other persons or objects are immune from attack. The Islamic law of *qital* is based upon the premise that everything is immune from attack unless a rule explicitly permits it to be attacked. Consider verse 2:190: 'Fight in the way of Allah against those who fight you, and do not transgress. Verily, Allah does not like transgressors.' '[T]hose who fight you' may include those who contribute to the war effort, such as planning the war, but it certainly does not extend to non-combatants or objects that do not contribute to the war effort. Verse 2:190 does not prescribe specific punishment for transgressions except Allah's displeasure, but the Prophet Muhammad applied specific laws to specific transgressions. For instance, if a non-combatant was killed either by mistake or intentionally, compensation or punishment was awarded accordingly. As stated above, Walid killed some individuals in fighting as a result of a misunderstanding, so the Prophet Muhammad sent Ali to pay compensation for their blood (see Tabari 2003: 349).

Civilians and civilian objects are protected under the law of armed conflict. Parties to an armed conflict must always distinguish between combatants and civilians and between military objectives and civilian objects (see Additional Protocol I: art. 48). The civilian population also enjoys 'general protection against dangers arising from military operations' (Additional Protocol I: art. 51(1)), but collateral damage is permissible in certain circumstances (see Additional Protocol I: art. 51(5)(b)). The principle of civilian immunity is customary and applies to conflicts of both an international and a non-international character (see ICRC Study on Customary International Humanitarian Law: Rule 1). In addition, Additional Protocol II specifies that 'civilians shall enjoy general protection against the dangers arising from military operations' (art. 13(1)) 'unless and for such time as they take a direct part in hostilities' (art 13(3)). Collateral damage is not prohibited per se, but the principle of proportionality must not be breached.

The general principles in the Islamic law of *qital* and the law of armed conflict on civilian immunity are compatible.

Individual Criminal Responsibility

Islamic criminal law is based upon the concept of individual responsibility, and this applies equally in both times of war and times of peace. Anyone who commits an unlawful act has to bear its consequences (see Oudah 1999: 96). The principle of individual criminal responsibility is based upon the following verses of the Quran: 'No bearer will bear the burden of any other person' (35:18); 'if someone acts righteously, he does so for the benefit of his own soul, and if someone commits evil, he does so against it' (41:46); and 'whoever does evil shall be requited for it' (4:123).

Article 6 of the Nuremberg Charter recognises individual responsibility for crimes against humanity, war crimes and crimes against peace. Other international legal instruments recognise that individuals are responsible as individuals for any war crimes that they commit or which they order or assist others to commit. Article 7 of the ICTY Statute and article 6 of the ICTR Statute, for example, state that '[a] person who planned, instigated, ordered, committed or otherwise aided and abetted in the planning, preparation or execution of a crime ... shall be individually responsible for the crime'. Article 25 of the Rome Statute states that a person shall be individually responsible if he commits the crime himself or herself or orders, solicits or induces the commission of a crime, aids, abets or otherwise assists in its commission or its attempted commission or contributes to the commission or attempted commission of such a crime by a group of persons acting with a common purpose.

The general principles in the Islamic law of *qital* and the law of armed conflict on individual criminal responsibility are compatible.

Mutilation

The Quran prohibits mutilation, and as referred to above, verse 16:126, the most relevant verse on point, reads: 'and if you were to harm [them] in retaliation, harm them to the measure you were harmed. And if you opt for patience, it is definitely much better for those who are patient.' Verse 16:126 was revealed to prevent the mutilation of enemy persons. Mutilation and even the cruel treatment of beasts are not allowed (see Shaybani 1966: 99; Al-Mawardi 2005: 66).

The law of armed conflict prohibits mutilation in both international and non-international armed conflicts (see First Geneva Convention: arts. 3(1), 12(2); Second Geneva Convention: arts. 3(1), 12(2); Third Geneva Convention: arts. 3(1), 13; Fourth Geneva Convention: arts. 3(1), 32; Additional Protocol I: arts. 11(2)(a), 75(2)(a)).

The general principles in the Islamic law of *qital* and the law of armed conflict prohibiting mutilation are compatible.

Perfidy and Ruses of War

Islamic law forbids perfidy (see Shaybani 1966: 77). In fact, perfidious breaches of agreements justify the resumption of hostilities, and on several occasions the Prophet Muhammad resumed hostilities after the other party acted perfidiously. The example of Banu Nadir is an apt one of perfidy followed by an armed attack by Muslims. The Quran forbids treachery and all perfidious acts (8:58) and rewards those who are good in deed (5:13). The Quran (5:1) prohibits perfidious actions, and this is reinforced by Muslims' duty to fulfil their obligations (see Muslim 2008: 629).

On the other hand, the Islamic law of *qital* allows ruses of war and encourages them (see Muslim 2008: 630). According to the Quran, '[w]hoever turns his back to them on such a day – unless it is for a tactic in the battle, or to join a company – turns with wrath from Allah, and his abode is ... [Hell]' (8:16). Verse 8:16 sanctions punishment for those who show cowardice, but it permits ruses of war. The Prophet Muhammad used to say that war means deceiving one's enemy (see Al-Bukhari 2008: 277; Muslim 2008: 630). An example of this would be during the Battle of Khandaq when the Prophet Muhammad allowed for a campaign of misinformation that eventually undermined the enemy forces (see Tabari 2003: 284).

The law of armed conflict prohibits perfidy but allows ruse of war. Article 37(1) of Additional Protocol I states that 'acts inviting the confidence of an adversary to lead him to believe that he is entitled to, or is obliged to accord, protection under the rules of international law applicable in armed conflict, with intent to betray that confidence, shall constitute perfidy'. For instance, the feigning of intent to negotiate under a flag of surrender or of truce is perfidy. In contrast to perfidy, ruses of war are 'acts which are intended to mislead an adversary or to induce him to act recklessly but which infringe no rule of international law applicable in armed conflict and which are not perfidious because they do not invite the confidence of an adversary with respect to protection under that law' (Additional Protocol I: art. 37(2)). Some examples of these are the use of camouflage, mock operations, decoys and misinformation. Some perfidious acts, such as misusing the distinctive emblems of the Red Cross or Red Crescent, fall into the category of grave breaches of the law of armed conflict (see Additional Protocol I: art. 85(3)(f)).

The Islamic law of *qital* and the law of armed conflict are compatible on the prohibition of perfidious behaviour in armed conflicts.

Child Soldiers

Islamic law does not permit recruiting and sending child soldiers to the battlefield. The minimum age required to participate in *qital* is 15 years. This is the consensus view of Muslim jurists based upon the practice of the Prophet Muhammad (see Al-Bukhari 2008: 15, 281). Before starting the military expedition of the Battle of Badr (AD 624/AH 2), the Prophet Muhammad examined his army and sent the young ones back to Medina (see Al-Bukhari 2008: 51). A 14-year-old boy, Ibn Omer, asked permission from the Prophet Muhammad to participate in the Battle of Uhud (AD 625/AH 3), but he was not allowed to participate. He was given permission to participate in the Battle of Khandaq a year later (AD 626/AH 4), as by then he was 15 years of age (see Al-Bukhari 2008: 280–81). This practice was followed in later wars.

Article 77(2) of Additional Protocol I requires parties to an armed conflict to take 'all feasible measures' to prevent children below the age of 15 from directly participating in hostilities. States parties are also required to refrain from recruiting them into their armed forces. Article 8 of the Rome Statute classifies the conscription or enlistment of children under the age of 15 into a state's armed forces or using them to participate actively in hostilities as a war crime.[5] In Chapter 6 of this volume, Noëlle Quénivet discusses these and other aspects of 'underaged combatancy' in considerable detail.

In the sense that the Islamic law of *qital* is categorical in its prohibition of child soldiers and that the law of armed conflict, as described above, only requires taking 'all feasible measures', it can be said that the general tenor and purpose of the Islamic law of *qital* and the law of armed conflict are compatible, though not identical.

---

5   See *Prosecutor* v. *Lubanga* (Judgment), ICC-01/04-01/06, T Ch (2012).

Safe Passage and Quarter

Providing safe passage is one of the cardinal principles of the Islamic law of *qital*. *Aman* is defined as 'the practice of refraining from opposing them (i.e. the belligerents) through killing or capturing, for the sake of God' (Hamidullah 1968: 208 (citing Sarakhsi)). This is founded upon verse 9:6 of the Quran: 'And if any one of the Mushriks [that is, polytheists] seeks your protection, give him protection until he listens to the word of Allah, then let him reach his place of safety.' This verse was revealed when the Prophet Muhammad abrogated certain treaties with different tribes after they had violated the terms of the treaties (see Usmani 2008: 348). Verse 9:6 provides an exception in favour of those who seeks protection. '[L]et him reach his place of safety' means a non-Muslim's own place, where he or she can be safe (Qutb 2003: 69). *Aman* can be granted individually or en masse and can be conditional or unconditional (see Hamidullah 1968: 208).

At the time of the conquest of Mecca, the Prophet Muhammad said that those who entered the courtyard of Kaba or the house of their chief, Abu Sufyan, were safe. Those who closed the doors of their houses and did not fight were also given *aman* (see Al-Bukhari 2008: 485). *Aman* is available not only to active and potential combatants but also to those who are incapable of fighting, such as the infirm, women and infants (see Hamidullah 1968: 209 (citing Sarakhsi)). When a Muslim provides safe conduct, this will bind all Muslims, including the ruler (see Malik 1982: 198). Shaybani reports a saying from the Prophet Muhammad according to which 'the one lowest in status can bind others if he gives a pledge [of security]' (1966: 192). Muslims living outside of the Muslim state cannot give *aman*.

According to the law of armed conflict, the denial of quarter means 'refusing to spare the life of anybody, even of persons manifestly unable to defend themselves or who clearly express their intention to surrender' (Veri 1992: 93). Article 23(d) of the Hague Convention (IV) prohibits the denial of quarter. Article 40 of Additional Protocol I not only prohibits 'order[ing] that there shall be no survivors' but also prohibits 'threaten[ing] an adversary therewith' and 'conduct[ing] hostilities on this basis'. Article 4(1) of Additional Protocol II extends this rule to non-international armed conflicts.

Although not the same, the Islamic concept of *aman* is compatible with the tenor and purpose of quarter in the law of armed conflict.

Hostages

During the time of the Prophet Muhammad, hostages were customarily exchanged by parties as a pledge of good faith in carrying out the conditions of a treaty; killing them, however, was forbidden. This was the case even if the Muslim hostages had been treacherously killed by the enemy or if there had been a clear agreement that hostages could be beheaded as a form of collective punishment (see Hamidullah 1968: 205, 272 (citing Sarakhsi)). Several verses of the Quran, such as verses 6:165, 17:15 and 35:18, are cited for the view that no one should be punished for the wrongdoing of others; in other words, collective punishment is forbidden. During the reign of Amir Muawiyyah, the Byzantines broke their agreement when some of the Byzantines were being held hostage, but the Muslims did not kill them, saying that 'fulfilling ... a promise after treachery is better than responding with treachery' (Al-Mawardi 2005: 78). An enemy emissary carrying the message of his or her ruler cannot be turned into a hostage. The emissary is entitled to *aman* until he or she has delivered the message and returned to his or her country (see Shaybani 1966: 170; Hamidullah 1968: 145).

Common article 3 of the Four Geneva Conventions prohibits the taking of hostages (see also Fourth Geneva Convention: art. 34; Additional Protocol I: art. 75(2)(c)). Articles 147 of the Fourth Geneva Convention and 85(2) of Additional Protocol I both treat the taking of hostages as grave breaches.

The general principles in the Islamic law of *qital* and the law of armed conflict that prohibit the taking of hostages are compatible.

Truces and Armistices

The Islamic law of *qital* recognises both truces and armistices. There are four kinds of truces: those that are limited or unlimited by time and those that are limited or unlimited by place. Truces limited by time and place are fixed and generally occur during war on a battlefield in order to carry out such activities as parleys and burying the dead (see Hamidullah 1968: 263). A recent example of this would be the unilateral truce that the Pakistani Taliban declared during Ramadan 2009 in Waziristan, Pakistan, as a token of respect for the holy month of Ramadan, the month of obligatory fasting for Muslims. The group also said, however, that if it were to be attacked during Ramadan that it would respond in self-defence. The most important example of a truce for a fixed period of time was the Treaty of Hudaybiyya between the Prophet Muhammad and the Quraysh. It was fixed for ten years, and at the end of this period, each party was free of its treaty obligations. A truce unlimited in time and place usually takes place at the end of a war, when one party is defeated or both are exhausted (see Usmani 2008: 346 (commentary on verse 9:4)). The commander in charge may conclude a truce limited by time and place, but others may be concluded by the caliph or his authorised officials (see Hamidullah 1968: 264).

The law of armed conflict recognises armistices. Armistices are not peace treaties. Their main objective is to bring about a ceasefire. 'An armistice suspends military operations by mutual agreement between the belligerent parties. If its duration is not defined, the belligerent parties may resume operations at any time, provided always that the enemy is warned within the time agreed upon, in accordance with the terms of the armistice' (Hague Convention (IV): art. 36; see also arts. 37–41). The customary law of armed conflict allows for truces. Usually, a white flag is used to show a desire to communicate with the enemy (see United Kingdom Ministry of Defence 2005: 259; see also Solis 2010: 194).

The general principles related to truces and armistices in the Islamic law of *qital* and the law of armed conflict are compatible.

Conclusions

As this chapter has shown, the Islamic law of *qital* and the law of armed conflict are broadly compatible in their basic and general principles. Further compatibility can be achieved through a contextual approach to interpretation (see Shah 2006, 2008). This chapter has not discussed in detail the grey areas of Islamic law or its blind spots, but the former can be clarified and expanded, and new rules can be developed to cover the latter through *ijtihad*, a process of independent individual reasoning, by qualified Muslim jurists.

In closing, those who wish to maximise the application of the law of armed conflict in Muslim states must remember that the constitutions of most Muslim states give Islam the status of an official religion or prioritise Islamic law and only permit the adoption of laws that comply with Islamic standards. In some of these states, superior courts can invalidate existing laws that are found to be incompatible with Islamic standards. The primacy of Islamic law in Muslim states makes it all the more important to examine the compatibility between the law of armed conflict and the Islamic law of *qital*. Fortunately, as this chapter has shown, most of the basic and general principles of the Islamic law of *qital* and the law of armed conflict are compatible, and there is nothing in Islamic law to prevent Muslim states from adopting new laws to pave the way for the fuller application of the law of armed conflict in Muslim states.

References

Afsarudin, A. 2008. War and Violence, in *The Quran: An Encyclopedia*, ed. O. Leaman. Abingdon and New York: Routledge, 686–92.

Al-Bukhari, M.B.I. 2008. *Kashful Bari: Kitab Al-Maghazi (Book of Ghazqat)*, trans. S. Khan. Karachi: Maktaba Farooqia.

Al-Mawardi, A.H. 2005. *The Laws of Islamic Governance*, trans. A. Yate. London: Ta Ha.

Ali, A.Y. 1989. *The Meaning of the Holy Quran*. Brentwood, MD: Amana Corporation.

Asad, M. 1997. *The Message of the Quran*. Gibraltar: Dar Al-Andalus.

Bassiouni, C. 2007. Crimes Against Humanity, in *Crimes of War*, 2nd edn, ed. R. Gutman and D. Rieff. London and New York: W.W. Norton, 135–6.

Deoband, D. 2009. War Captives and Islamic Perspective. Available at: http://www.darululoom-deoband.com/urdu/current/jihad_e1.htm [accessed: 3 September 2009].

Elahi, A. 2008. *Anwarul Bayan*. Lahore: Maktabul Ulum.

Hamidullah, M. 1968. *Muslim Conduct of State*. Lahore: Ashraf.

Ibn Kathir, I. 2005. *Tafseer Ibn Kathir*, trans. M. Junagari. Lahore: Islamic Kutab Khana.

International Committee of the Red Cross (ICRC). Study on Customary International Humanitarian Law. Available at: http://www.icrc.org/customary-ihl/eng/docs/home [accessed: 3 October 2012].

Malik, I. 1982. *Al-Muwatta*, trans. A. Abdarahman and Y. Johnson. Cambridge: Diwan Press.

Marghinani, B. 2005. *The Hedaya*, trans. C. Hamilton, rev. Z. Baintner. Lahore: Darul Ishat.

Musharraf, P. 2006. *In the Line of Fire*. London: Simon & Schuster.

Muslim, A.H.H. 2008. *Muslim Shareef*, trans. A. Rehman. Karachi: Maktabah Rehmania.

Oudah, A.Q. 1999. *Criminal Law of Islam*, vol. II. New Delhi: Kitab Bhavan.

Qutb, S. 2003. *In the Shade of the Quran*, vol. 8, trans. A. Salahi. Leicester: The Islamic Foundation.

Ratner, S.R. 2007. War Crimes, Categories of, in *Crimes of War*, 2nd edn, ed. R. Gutman and D. Reiff. London and New York: W.W. Norton, 420–22.

Report of the Secretary-General Pursuant to Paragraph 2 of Security Council Resolution 808 (1993) (1993), UN Doc S/25704, Annex, Statute of the International Tribunal for the Prosecution of Persons Responsible for Serious Violations of International Humanitarian Law Committed in the Territory of the Former Yugoslavia Since 1991, 36–48

Rushd, I. 2006. *Bidayat al Mujtahid wa Nihayat al-Muqtasid*, trans. I.K. Nyazee. Reading: Garnet.

Shafi, M. 1974. *Maariful Quran*. Karachi: Darul Ulum.

Shah, N.A. 2006. *Women, the Koran and International Human Rights Law: The Experience of Pakistan*. Leiden: Martinus Nijhoff.

Shah, N.A. 2008. *Self-Defense in Islamic and International Law: Assessing Al-Qaeda and the Invasion of Iraq*. New York: Palgrave Macmillan.

Shah, N.A. 2013. The Use of Force under Islamic Law. *European Journal of International Law*, 24(1), 343–65.

Shaybani, M. 1966. The *Islamic Law of Nations: Shaybani's Siyar*, trans. M. Khadduri. Baltimore: Johns Hopkins University Press.

Solis, G.D. 2010. *The Law of Armed Conflict: International Humanitarian Law in War*. Cambridge: Cambridge University Press.

Statute of the International Criminal Tribunal for the Prosecution of Persons Responsible for Genocide and Other Serious Violations of International Humanitarian Law Committed in the Territory of Rwanda and Rwandan Citizens Responsible for Genocide and Other Such Violations Committed in the Territory of Neighbouring States, Between 1 January 1994 and 31 December 1994, UNSC Res 955 (1994), UN Doc S/RES/955.

Tabari, J.M.J. 2003. *Tarikh Al-Rusul Wal-Mumluk (History of Tabari)*, trans. M. Ibrahim. Karachi: Darul Ishaat.

United Kingdom Ministry of Defence 2005. *The Manual of the Law of Armed Conflict*. Oxford: Oxford University Press.

Usmani, M.T. 2008. *The Meaning of the Noble Quran*. Karachi: Maktaba Maariful Quran.

Veri, P. 1992. *Dictionary of the International Law of Armed Conflict*. Geneva: International Committee of the Red Cross.

Chapter 10

Islam as a Religion of Peace: An Articulated Reply to Terrorism

Anicée Van Engeland

Recent protests in the Muslim world about the video *Innocence of Muslims* (2012) followed by the killing of American citizens in Benghazi could convey the impression that Islam is a religion of violence. These events came after waves of terrorist attacks perpetrated around the world in the name of Islam. As a result, Islam has somehow emerged as a religion of war and death, a perception to which some scholars in both the West and the Muslim world have contributed. The media has also sometimes spread this view of Islam as being the root of all terror, and *jihad*, which comes from the Arabic 'to strive', as requiring perpetual wars of conquest and brutal Islamicisation. Alternative voices have often been misunderstood, sometimes deliberately, or drowned out entirely. Consequently, arguing that Islam is a religion of peace and that it regulates warfare in a way that resembles international humanitarian law is a difficult task.

This chapter seeks to demonstrate that the Quran and other Islamic sources of law can and should be interpreted in a way that stresses Islam's inner philosophy of peace.[1] Along with the Sunnah, which compiles what the Prophet Muhammad said or did, the Quran resonates with themes of peace, justice and solidarity. These legal sources, however, in both the Shia and Sunni traditions, also speak of war, *jihad al-qital* (the form of *jihad* that means warfare),[2] but it is crucial to recognise that they do so from the premise that war is an inescapable human reality. Islamic international law is composed of *siyar* that address warfare with a view to regulating it, not celebrating it, and it is the interpretations of these Islamic legal sources that matter. For example, *mojtahedin*, learned clerics versed in Islamic jurisprudence, can interpret Islam in a way that supports the view that it is

---

1   The main sources of Islamic law are the Quran, the Holy Book, the word of God as transmitted to the Prophet Muhammad; the Sunnah, which is a compilation of the deeds and sayings of the Prophet Muhammadas reported by his Companions through short stories called hadith; *ijma*, which is the consensus of the community on legal matters; and *qiyas*, a type of reasoning by analogy.

2   *Jihad al-qitalfi sabil Allah* is warfare 'in the way of Allah'. *Qatilu* means 'fighting' in Arabic. It can be distinguished from the spiritual form of *jihad* that each Muslim is expected to lead in his or her life in an effort to go beyond the temptations of Satan and selfish impulses.

inherently a religion of peace.[3] Others, by contrast, interpret Islamic legal sources in a way that justifies violent *jihad*. Although some interpretations of Islam convey the view that it promotes hatred and violence, it is important to recognise that these interpretations are distorted and typically put forward by either Islamic extremists who use Islam to justify a deadly agenda of terror (see Kepel 2005) or Western scholars who wave the flag of 'green peril' (see Haddar 1993).[4]

As Niaz A. Shah argues in Chapter 9 of this volume, there are many credible interpretations of Islam that reveal it to be a religion of peace. This chapter begins by analysing the discourses that legitimise the killing of civilians and looks at specific interpretations of Islamic legal sources and the rhetoric of Al Qaeda and some Western scholars. With a view to defeating the approach of Islamic extremists, it then presents interpretations of Islam that see it as a religion of peace. To do this, this chapter explores the limits set by Islam *in bello* and presents a series of humanitarian standards. It finishes by squarely addressing the existence of warmongering Islamic legal sources, in particular verse 9:5 of the Quran. This chapter is a call to interpret Islamic legal sources in a way that promotes peace. It is, after all, in the *maslahah*, or 'public interest', of all Muslims to do so.

Islam in the Eyes of Terror: The Killing of Civilians

Extremists' interpretations of Islam challenge Islamic law's traditional distinction between civilians and warriors (see Van Engeland 2010). Groups like Al Qaeda distort the Islamic law of war by twisting it, stripping it of its humanitarian content so that it fits a macabre ideological agenda. In addition to loosening

---

3   All of these sources of law need to be interpreted. The process of interpretations takes place through *ijtihad*, which is the exertion of a personal effort to interpret the sources of Islamic law. *Mojtahedin* carry this out, and given that Islamic legal sources need to be interpreted by human beings in order to be understood, it can be said that Islamic law is by its very nature vibrant: its sources need to be read, understood and given meaning to become law. This exertion allows for a dynamic approach to Islamic law, in opposition to *taqlid*, which is a rote process of unquestioning adherence to existing interpretations of Islamic legal sources. The practice of *ijtihad* was common in the early centuries of Islam but was discarded in Sunni Islam out of concern for the fallibility of human interpretations (see Weiss 1978: 204). This led to what is known as the closing of the *bab al-ijtihad*, or the closing of the gates of *ijtihad*. There is, however, a current debate as to whether or not the doors were actually closed. Many modern scholars argue that they were not or that they need to be reopened to allow Muslims to effectively respond to modern challenges. Shia Islam never closed the gates of interpretation, which means that *ijtihad* remains permitted in this school of law.

4   Islamic extremists, or fundamentalists, include groups that call for violent *jihad* and use terror to reach their aim of universalising Islam. Al Qaeda is the first group that comes to mind, but there are also others, such as Ansar al Islam, the Abu Sayyaf Group, Gama'a al Islamiyya and Jemaah Islamiya.

Islam's humanitarian imperatives, these groups also refuse to acknowledge the very existence of international humanitarian law. Unsurprisingly, their argument is that *jihad* aims to propagate Islam by all means, and this, of course, has practical consequences on the battlefield. Extremists frequently rely upon interpretations provided by Muslim classicist and neo-classicist scholars.[5] Some Western scholars also contribute, in their own way, to this depiction of Islam as a religion of war.

Extremists rely upon interpretations of Islam that favour violence. Shaykh Sulayman Abu-Ghayth, for example, a Kuwaiti spokesman for Al Qaeda, draws upon the Quran to justify *jihad* against the United States in the following manner:

> America knows only the language of force as the only way for putting a stop to it and making it take its hands off Muslims and their causes. America does not know the language of dialogue, or that of peaceful coexistence, appeals, or denunciation and condemnation! Only blood deters America. 'Fight them, and Allah will punish them by your hands, cover them with shame. Help you (to victory) over them, heal the breasts of believers' (9:14). (Center for Strategic Communication 2012: 7 (citing Abu-Ghayth))

The premise of such an understanding of *jihad* is that *jihadal-qital* is aggressive by its very essence: Muslims should attack (conquer, for example) in addition to defend. Because it is the interpretations of *jihad* by classicists and neo-classicists that contemporary groups like Al Qaeda rely upon to justify their warmongering discourse and attitude, it is critical to examine this scholarly inheritance.

The different schools of Islamic law take different approaches to *jihad* and humanitarian standards and understand them differently.[6] Some of the most important of these interpretations have been provided by classicists and neo-classicists (see Mir 1991: 114–19).

One thinker of critical importance is Sayyid Qutb, the former leader of the Egyptian Muslim Brotherhood. His interpretations of *jihad* transformed it into an obligation to wage a war of religion on a global scale to establish Islamic hegemony (see Qutb 1980). In this regard, Qutb's is a call for offensive *jihad*, not simply defensive *jihad*.[7] This, of course, furthers the argument that Islam promotes violence.

---

5 Classical Islam refers to the period when the doctrine of Islam matured, and a period of great scholarship took shape. Neo-classicism includes more recent scholars who revisit the work done during the classical period of Islam.

6 There are several schools of law in Islam, called *madhahib*.

7 The concept of *jihad* has been a source of much disagreement. One of the key debates relates to whether war should be defensive or offensive: should *jihad* only serve to protect Muslim territory and Muslims within the realm of Islam, or *Dar al-Islam*, or should it be an offensive enterprise to widen the territory of Islam, to *Dar al-Harb*, the territory of war? The division between *Dar al-Islam* and *Dar al-Harb* does not exist as such in the Quran or Sunnah: the existence of *Dar al-Islam* comes from verse 10:25 of the Quran, and the idea of *Dar al-Harb* was invented by classicists to justify a permanent state of war.

Ayman Al-Zawahiri, the current leader of Al Qaeda, relies upon Qutb's call for the global expansion of Islam and draws upon the Quran to support this propagation by the sword (see Musallam 2005: 189–90; Calvert 2010: 264). Al-Zawahiri and other extremists frequently refer to verse 9:5 of the Quran, the so-called 'Verse of the Sword'. This verse states:

> Then, when the sacred months have passed, slay the idolaters wherever ye find them, and take them (captive), and besiege them, and prepare for them each ambush. But if they repent and establish worship and pay the *jizyah* [that is, poll tax for non-Muslims] then leave their way free. Lo! Allah is Forgiving, Merciful.[8]

The aggressive nature of verse 9:5 can be explained by its context. Surah 9 was revealed when the Prophet Muhammad was nearing the end of his life and had to quell several insurrections. Consequently, it is not surprising to see him seeking to protect the realm he fought to acquire. Thus, verse 9:5 should be interpreted as a call for both defensive and offensive *jihad*, in other words, a call to protect the new territories of Islam while expanding through *jihad* against tribes that refused to be Islamicised. Classicists, who lived during the centuries immediately following the death of the Prophet Muhammad, when Islam was still expanding, adopted the same dual approach to *jihad*. They interpreted it as an imperative to both defend Muslims and Muslim territory and uphold and carry forward the Prophet Muhammad's message. Most neo-classicists, like the Pakistani theologian A. Al-Mawdudi and Qutb, revisited this approach in the twentieth century and chose to reinforce this understanding of *jihad* as both defensive *and* offensive in nature (see Al-Mawdudi 1976: 19; Qutb 1980).

More recently, however, a new debate has sprung to life. Given that the modern day context has changed and that Islam is no longer in a phase of expansion and conquest, should verse 9:5 still be understood as encouraging offensive *jihad*? A contextualised approach would suggest not, though extremists would disagree with this and argue that *jihad* of the sword is a permanent obligation for Muslims given the West's ongoing interference in Islam's affairs. Such extremists often invoke the Israeli–Palestinian conflict and the wars in Iraq and Afghanistan as examples of Muslim territories violated and Muslim populations under attack. The contemporary geopolitical environment, they argue, justifies defensive *jihad*, for example terrorist attacks in the Occupied Palestinian Territories, and offensive *jihad*, to proactively protect the interests of Islam. Al Qaeda takes this (offensive) approach to *jihad* and relies upon verse 9:5. Deceased leader of Al Qaeda Osama bin Laden, for example, made a clear, if selective, reference to the verse in his 1996 and 1998 *fatwas*, or 'legal opinions'.

There is, thus, a clear symmetry between the work of classicists, neo-classicists and Islamic extremists that is not altogether obvious at first sight. One development from this has been Qutbism, a school of thought that reinterprets Qutb's writings

---

8   The author uses the English translation of the Quran in Nikayin 2000.

to justify the deeds of extremist groups (see Boekhoff-van der Voort *et al.* 2011: 387). In 1981, for example, the Egyptian Islamist Muhammad abd-al-Salam released a book, *The Neglected Duty*, in which he states that *jihad* is the sixth pillar of Islam and that failing to embrace this demonstrates *kufr*, or 'disbelief' (see Faraj 1986). In his book, abd-al-Salam rejects the limitations that classicists and neo-classicists set on the killing of civilians, including children. Al Qaeda and other extremist groups rely upon such theoreticians and their theologically-distorted concepts of *jihad* to justify killing Unbelievers (see Van Engeland 2010). Qutbism now encompasses the basics of aggressive jihadism that Al-Zawahiri and others have embraced (see Al-Zawahiri 2005b: 245).

Let us consider Qutb's thinking in a bit more detail. Qutb articulated an offensive understanding of *jihad* that sought to universalise Islam and protect it against the West. As he put it, '[t]here is no room to say that the basic aim of the Islamic movement was "defensive" in the narrow sense which some people ascribe to it today, defeated by the attacks of the treacherous Orientalists' (Qutb 1981). For Qutbists, Muslims are commissioned to enter the battlefield, seize control of the institutions of political power and establish God's rule, and in furthering this offensive approach to *jihad*,they are told that they can legitimately rely upon verse 9:5 for support (see Qutb 1980, 1981). This analysis has obviously been used by extremists (see Singh 2007: 19). Abdullah Yusuf Azzam, for instance, the Palestinian theologian and mentor to bin Laden, was exposed to Qutbism and later taught it in Afghan training camps (see Azzam 1979; Singh 2007: 21–2). It is unsurprising that it has been inspirational for Al Qaeda.

Classicists and neo-classicists do not deny the existence of a law that governs warfare. Certainly, they encourage aggressive *jihad*, but they do accept minimal humanitarian standards *in bello*. For example, Muhammad Al-Shaybani, a jurist who is often considered to be the father of Islamic international law, argued that captives can be killed in certain circumstances but counselled that warriors must not 'behav[e] degradingly towards those who are defeated' (Al-Sarakhsi 1997: 250). Al-Mawdudi (1980: 39) also supports the existence of humanitarian standards, such as those laid down by the Prophet Muhammad. According to him, humanitarian principles are to be respected as long as the 'enemy' respects the same rules; if the other side does not respect the rules, then total war can be waged. Al-Mawdudi also calls for prisoners to be treated humanely and respects the distinction between civilians and warrior:

> Islam has first drawn a clear line of distinction between thecombatants and the non-combatants of the enemy country. As far as the non-combatant population is concerned such as women, children, the old and the infirm, etc., the instructions of the Prophet are as follows: 'Do not kill any old person, any child or any woman' (Abu Dawud). 'Do not kill the monks in monasteries' or 'Do not kill the people who are sitting in places of worship' (Musnad of Ibn Hanbal). (1980: 41)

Thus, while classicists and neo-classicists interpret *jihad* in a way that broadens the grounds for force *ad bellum*, they restrict the methods and means of warfare *in bello*. Many extremists, however, do not appreciate the restrictions that these scholars *do* acknowledge *in bello* and simplistically interpret aggressive *jihad* as a licence to propagate Islam by all means, including by deliberately targeting civilians. Such extremists frequently invoke, often unthinkingly, such Quranic verses as 8:12[9] and 2:193[10] and hadith[11] to support their behaviour, but in doing so, they contradict the teachings of classicists and neo-classicists.

Like the Islamic extremists, some Western scholars view Islam as a religion of violence and destruction. Many of these Western scholars have used texts written by classicists and neo-classicists to justify their view that Islam is the 'green peril' and that *jihad* threatens all Westerners. The American political scientist Amos Perlmutter (1992), for example, is one such scholar and clearly believes that Islam is not compatible with democracy. Streusand makes a similar point, stating that 'a new spectre is haunting America, one that some Americans consider more sinister than Marxism-Leninism … That spectre is Islam' (1989: 50).

Some such scholars go further and argue that the very idea of humanitarian principles in Islam is an invention of apologetic Islamic scholars. Such views rely upon the scholarly work of, in particular, Khadduri, who argued that *jihad* is a call for holy war that requires the propagation of the faith by the sword (see Stephens 1877: 98–9). For Khadduri (1966: 51), *jihad* seeks the universalisation of Islam through violence and the establishment of an imperial world state, with humanitarian principles being but just instruments that Muslims use to convert non-Muslims. Khadduri's views on *jihad* have been heavily relied upon by Westerners despite the cogent criticisms of them by many respected Muslims scholars, such as the renowned international jurist Zawati (2001).

Of course, Harvard political scientist Samuel Huntington contributed most prominently to this fear of Islam. His premise was a simple one: Islamic civilisation differs too greatly from Western civilisation and seeks, with China, to conquer the world, leading to a 'clash of civilizations' (Huntington 1997: 254). Huntington believed that Islam had 'bloody borders' (1993: 35) and that conflicts within the Muslim world and between it and the West might very well not be over. One of the great deceits of Huntington's thinking, of course, is that it looks exclusively at fundamentalists when speaking of Islam rather than appreciating the diversity of Muslims and their myriad experiences and ways of thinking.

---

9   'Remember when your Lord inspired to the angels, "I am with you, so strengthen those who have believed. I will cast terror into the hearts of those who disbelieved, so strike [them] upon the necks and strike from them every fingertip."'

10   'Fight them until there is no [more] fitnah and [until] worship is [acknowledged to be] for Allah. But if they cease, then there is to be no aggression except against the oppressors.'

11   'A single endeavour (of fighting) in Allah's cause in the forenoon or in the afternoon is better than the world and whatever is in it' (Bukhari 1944: vol. 4, bk. 52, no. 50).

On one level, the fears of Huntington and others that Islam might threaten the West seemed to materialise when Islamic-inspired terrorism began in the 1990s. Indeed, it is undeniable that the Islamic concept of *jihad* is central to the ideology of Al Qaeda and similar groups. These ideologues rely upon the work of Islamic scholars, classicists and neo-classicists alike, to broaden the permissible grounds of *jihad ad bellum*. Their aim is to defend Muslim territory and Muslims wherever they might be, and for them, this justifies an aggressive *jihad* that takes a proactive stance and seeks revenge against the enemy on its own territory. An illustration can be found in the World Islamic Front's *fatwa* from 1998, which lists the 'crimes' committed against Islam:

> First, for over seven years the United States has been occupying the lands of Islam in the holiest of places, the Arabian Peninsula, plundering its riches, dictating to its rulers, humiliating its people, terrorizing its neighbors, and turning its bases in the Peninsula into a spearhead through which to fight the neighboring Muslim peoples ...
>
> Second, despite the great devastation inflicted on the Iraqi people by the crusader-Zionist alliance ... So here they come to annihilate what is left of this people and to humiliate their Muslim neighbors.
>
> Third, if the Americans' aims behind these wars are religious and economic, the aim is also to serve the Jews' petty state and divert attention from its occupation of Jerusalem and murder of Muslims there. (World Islamic Front 1998)

These extremists justify the use of aggressive *jihad* to end foreign influence in Muslim-majority states and propel the creation of a new Islamic caliphate. Consequently, all actions that contribute to these twin aims are acceptable. A 1996 *fatwa* by bin Laden demonstrates this:

> The walls of oppression and humiliation cannot be demolished except in a rain of bullets.
>
> The freeman does not surrender leadership to infidels and sinners.
>
> Without shedding blood no degradation and branding can be removed from the forehead. (bin Laden 1996).

There are many other examples of deliberate distortions to fit the agenda of terror. Al-Mawdudi, for instance, saw Islam as:

> [a] comprehensive system which envisages to annihilate all tyrannical and evil systems in the world and enforces its own programme of reform which it deems best for the well-being of mankind. Islam addresses its call for effecting this programme of destruction and reconstruction, revolution and reform not just to one nation or a group of people, but to all humanity. (1976: 17)

Though he added a clear restriction:

> This system harbours no animosity against any human being. Our animosity
> is directed against tyranny, strife, immorality and against the attempt of an
> individual to transgress his natural limits and expropriate what is not apportioned
> to him by the natural law of God. (Al-Mawdudi 1976: 17)

Al Qaeda draws upon Al-Mawdudi's views and applies them to justify war against
the West. It has borrowed Al-Mawdudi's doctrine of Islam as a 'revolutionary
ideology and program which seeks to alter the social order of the whole world and
rebuild it in conformity with its own tenets and ideals' (Al-Mawdudi 1976: 5). For
Al Qaeda, this sufficiently justifies extending Islam through universal *jihad*.

Does this mean that Al-Mawdudi would have endorsed Al Qaeda's grounds
for going to war or indiscriminate killing? Certainly not. Al-Mawdudi was quite
clear in his writings that such actions could not be tolerated (see Al-Mawdudi
1980: 40). Indeed, he devotes an entire chapter in *Human Rights in Islam* to
'enemies at war' (see Al-Mawdudi 1980: 35–9). His argument is that 'rules
which have been framed by Islam to make war civilized and humane, are in the
nature of law, because they are the injunctions of God and His Prophet which are
followed by Muslims in all circumstances, irrespective of the behaviour of the
enemy' (Al-Mawdudi 1980: 35).

There have been some disagreements and ideological clashes within Al Qaeda
about *jihad* and the way in which it can be waged. Famously, Al-Zawahiri, who
at the time was Al Qaeda's second-in-command, criticised Abou Moussab Al-
Zarqawi's strategy in 2005 of targeting Shia in Iraq. Al-Zawahiri thought that
attacks on Shia targets would give a negative image of jihadists because it would
encourage attacks against other Muslims and distract from the real mission of
'taking down' the United States (see Fishman 2006: 23). Furthermore, Sayyed
Imam Al-Sharif, a theoretician who is part of Al Qaeda's Shura Council and whose
ideas influence the movement, has supported war against enemy soldiers but
rejected the deliberate targeting of civilians. Indeed, he has criticised Al-Zawahiri
for supporting the deliberate targeting of civilians, stating:

> I say it is not honorable to reside with people – even if they were nonbelievers
> and not part of a treaty, if they gave you permission to enter their homes and live
> with them, and if they gave you security for yourself and your money, and if they
> gave you the opportunity to work or study, or they granted you political asylum
> with a decent life and other acts of kindness – and then betray them, through
> killing and destruction. This was not in the manners and practices of the Prophet.
> (Gerges 2011: 122 (citing Al-Sharif 2007))

Still, Al Qaeda and similar groups seem to have no ethical dilemma when it
comes to killing civilians (see Al-Zawahiri 2005a). They pay no heed to the
cornerstone of Islamic law that distinguishes between those who fight and those

who do not, much less several interpretations of Islamic legal sources that prohibit indiscriminate attacks, massive killings, bloodbaths and other such sufferings (see Hashmi 1999; Van Engeland 2008). This prohibition is based upon the Quran, which states: 'Do not take life, which Allah has forbidden, unless it be by right; if anyone, is slain unjustly, we indeed have given his heir the right of retribution' (17:33). By contrast, Al-Zarqawi declared it acceptable to kill civilians 'as long as they are infidels' (Cordesman and Davies 2008: 153 (citing Al-Zarqawi)). He added that 'Islam does not differentiate between civilians and military (targets) but rather distinguishes between Muslims and infidels' (Cordesman and Davies 2008: 153 (citing Al-Zarqawi)).

Theologically-unconvincing *fatwas* have also been circulated, such as one by Saudi cleric Ali Al-Khudairi, who justified 11 September as follows:

> It is legitimate to kill all infidel Americans ... it is astonishing to mourn the [American] victims as being innocent. Those victims may be classified as infidel Americans which do not deserve being mourned, because each American is either a warrior or, a supporter in money or opinion, of the American government. It is legitimate to kill all of them, be they combatants or non-combatant like the old, the blind, or non-Muslims. (2002)

These statements and actions contradict the Islamic ethic of saving lives. The Quran and other sources of Islamic law set up humanitarian standards and limitations to war, and warriors are expected to follow them. Extremists, however, pay no heed to this and regularly violate humanitarian standards *in bello*.

The World Islamic Front's 1998 *fatwa* is yet another example of this. It states that it is the duty of all Muslims to kill American citizens, both civilian and military, and their allies everywhere:

> The ruling to kill the Americans and their allies – civilians and military – is an individual duty for every Muslim who can do it in any country in which it is possible to do it, in order to liberate the al-Aqsa Mosque and the holy mosque [that is, Mecca] from their grip, and in order for their armies to move out of all the lands of Islam, defeated and unable to threaten any Muslim. This is in accordance with the words of Almighty Allah, 'and fight the pagans all together as they fight you all together,' and 'fight them until there is no more tumult or oppression, and there prevail justice and faith in Allah'. (World Islamic Front 1998)

The fact that the text of this *fatwa* relies upon excerpts from the Quran, which are quoted without any clear sense of context, demonstrates how Al Qaeda uses and (mis)interprets Islamic legal sources for instrumental gain. For example, the *fatwa* orders Muslims to 'fight the pagans all together as they fight you all together', which is from verse 9:36 of the Quran, but this is a clear distortion of Quranic meaning. This is so because this verse actually attests to the need for humanitarian standards in that it also imposes restraints upon warriors: 'But know that Allah is with those who restrain themselves.' This distorted use of the Quran to justify offensive *jihad* rests on a flimsy basis indeed.

It is important to stress that there are alternative readings of Islam and that not all Islamist groups encourage an expanded interpretation of *jihad* or the indiscriminate killing of civilians. For example, the Muslim Brotherhood released the following statement after 11 September: '[We] strongly condemn such activities that are against all humanist and Islamic morals ... [We] condemn and oppose all aggression on human life, freedom and dignity anywhere in the world' (2001).

The True Face of Islam: The Regulation of Warfare and the Promotion of Peace

Arguing that Islam is a religion of peace does not mean that it is pacifist: it is not. Although the Quran devotes more than a hundred verses to peace, Islam acknowledges the human reality of warfare and seeks to regulate it. The distinction between civilians and warriors lies at the core of this philosophy, which has been described as an ethic for saving lives. Approaching Islam as a religion of peace and respecting the inner philosophy of Islam and the message of the Prophet Muhammad clearly contradicts the interpretations and practices of *jihad* surveyed above. Islam is a religion of peace that regulates warfare and sets limitations to it.

Islam as a Religion of Peace that Regulates Warfare

Extremists too often discard the many peaceful verses in the Quran and hadith (see Boisard 1988: 5). Hassan Al-Banna (1948), the Egyptian founder of the Muslim Brotherhood, reminded us that Islam is first a religion of love and peace, of solidarity and social justice. His writings are even more important in today's world in which Islam is so often misquoted and misused to spread terror and hatred. Peace, freedom (especially freedom of religion), security, equity and social justice lie at the core of Islam (2:190, 2:194).

Many verses in the Quran and Sunnah support this view. According to verse 60:8 of the Quran, 'God does not forbid you from showing kindness and dealing justly with those who have not fought you about religion and have not driven you out of your homes. God loves just dealers.' Verse 5:32 states:

> Because of that, We decreed upon the Children of Israel that whoever kills a soul unless for a soul or for corruption [done] in the land – it is as if he had slain mankind entirely. And whoever saves one – it is as if he had saved mankind entirely.

It is said that the following words were inscribed upon the hilt of the Prophet Muhammad's sword: 'Forgive him who wrongs you; join him who cuts you off; do good to him who does evil to you, and speak the truth although it be against yourself' (Bennett 1998: 60–61).

There is also a series of hadith that insist upon peace and humanity: 'The Messenger of God said: when God created the creation, God inscribed upon the Throne, "My compassion overpowers My wrath"' (Bukhari: bk. 37, no. 6628). Another hadith reported by Muslim tells the story of prisoners brought to the Prophet Muhammad. Among them was a mother with her child held fast against her chest. The Prophet Muhammad said: 'Do you think this woman could ever manage to throw her child into the fire?' The Prophet Muhammad's companions replied: 'By God, so far as it lies in her power, she would never throw her child into the fire!' The Prophet Muhammad then said: 'God has more compassion for God's servants than this woman does for her child' (Muslim: bk. 37, no. 6635).

These values sustain a *jihad* of peace, a joined-up effort of the *Ummah*, the 'community of Believers', to live in a fair and stable society in which war, if it must happen, is strictly regulated. The propagation of the peaceful message of Islam is a priority for all Muslims and Islam as a whole. This philosophy also influences the way in which Islam approaches war. It teaches that everything feasible must be done to maintain peace and that war can only be resorted to as a last resort. If there is a pact, treaty or covenant, Islam imposes strict rules to honour it, and the Quran states that those who disrespect these rules will be punished (8:72). Consider the following verse:

> And fulfil the covenant of Allah you have covenanted, and break not the oaths after you have confirmed them, and indeed you have appointed Allah your surety. Verily! Allah knows what you do. And be not like her who undoes the thread which she spun after it has become strong, by taking your oaths a means of deception among yourselves, lest one party be more numerous than another. Allah only tests you by this. And on the Day of Resurrection, he will certainly make clear to you that wherein you used to differ. (16:09)

Besides this inner philosophy of peace, Islam also sets clear limitations to how *jihad* should be waged.

Limitations to War: Defensive Jihad *and Humanitarian Standards*

Reformist Muslims view peace as the normal state of life. For them, *jihad al-qital* is to be avoided since it is no good in itself. One cannot go to war for the sole purpose of fighting. Consequently, *jihad* can only be waged for good reasons (see Khan 1978: 210). These reasons are self-defence and protection. For example, war can be justified on self-defence grounds, to defend Muslims or Muslim territory under attack. Violent *jihad* can only be justified to protect Islam and the oppressed. These are Islam's *ad bellum* rules, that *jihad* is only defensive.

As far as humanitarian standards are concerned, it is unsurprising that the Quran contains such standards given that the Prophet Muhammad fought several wars against tribes to get them to submit to Islam and in defence of his followers (see Mottahari 1998: iii–x). These form the Quranic rules on the conduct of hostilities, such as: 'Fight in the cause of God with those who fight against you, but do not commit transgression; for God dislikes those who transgress' (2:190). According to another verse:

> Permission is given to those who fight because they have been wronged, and God is indeed able to give them victory; those who have been driven from their homes unjustly only because they said, 'Our Lord is God' - for had it not been for God's repelling some men by means of others, monasteries, churches, synagogues and mosques, in which the name of God is much mentioned, would certainly have been destroyed. Verily God helps those that help Him – lo! God is Strong, Almighty – those who, if they are given power in the land, establish worship and pay the poor-due and enjoin what is good and forbid iniquity. (22:39–41)

Like the Quran, hadith also frame war. 'Do not be eager to meet the enemy but ask God for safety; yet, if you meet them, persevere and have patience; and know that Paradise is under the Shadow of Swords' (Khan 1978: 210 (citing hadith reported by Bukhari)). These two sources of law and the process of *ijtihad* shape today's Islamic humanitarian standards (see Hashmi 2002).

Because the Quran and hadith are sometimes difficult to understand, interpreters must grapple with the text using *ijtihad*. The role of the interpreter, the *mojtahed*, is crucial because he or she gives meaning to the legal sources of Islam, though it is also true that the decentralised nature of the interpretive process in Islam means that extremists can interpret verse 9:5 as encouraging the slaughter of Unbelievers while other Muslims can interpret it more faithfully to the specific historical context that it was meant to address. The verse addresses a situation that does not exist nowadays and, therefore, is no longer applicable. Given the context in which we live, a defensive approach to *jihad* should be stressed because it respects the peaceful orientation of the Quran better than the concept of aggressive *jihad*. Defensive *jihad* is also very similar to the United Nations Charter in its restrictive understanding of the grounds to go to war and to the Geneva Conventions from a *jus in bello* perspective (see Van Engeland 2008: 87; Van Engeland 2010: 141).

This brief analysis demonstrates that defensive *jihad* exists and that it has been adequately theorised by many scholars. While it is true that arguing that Islam is a religion of peace is based upon a selection of interpretations, it should also be acknowledged that interpreting Islam in this way also respects the deeply rooted message of Islam in which warmongering verses and hadith are limited by their historical context and peaceful verses apply throughout history, today and for all time.

The Notion and Protection of Civilians in Islamic Humanitarian Law

The peaceful approach of Islam is supported by a multiplicity of peaceful Quranic verses and hadith that have a permanent application rather than by a focus on those verses that address a discrete period of time during which the Prophet Muhammad had to deal with rebellions. As demonstrated above, defensive *jihad* does not contradict this. Let us explore some of Islam's humanitarian standards in some more detail.

Islamic humanitarian law does not significantly differ from international humanitarian law (see Van Engeland 2008: 95). Both bodies of law regulate the conduct of hostilities and contain certain restrictions on weapons, the methods and means of warfare and indiscriminate attacks. The distinction between those who fight and those who do not lies at the very core of Islamic law (see Zawati 2001: 89), though classicists and neo-classicists find exceptions, or rather limitations (see Belkhodja 1992: 136).

Islam requires that war be waged *fi sabil Allah*, or 'in the way of Allah', which means that divine principles and duties must be respected (see Abdel-Haleem *et al.* 1998: 67). As Ayatollah Damad states, the 'requirements of war should give way to humanitarian imperatives' (2003: 86). This means that the following humanitarian principles in the Quran apply: proportionality (16:126–8), humanity (5:32), compassion, non-discrimination, dignity, equality and fraternity (4:1) and justice (16:90). Islam also recognises many other humanitarian standards, such as the prohibition of torture and unnecessary suffering, the prohibition of excess and wickedness, non-combatant immunity, the prohibition of the mutilation of men and animals, as well as the destruction of trees and crops, the prohibition of the destruction of religious symbols and the destruction of houses and other private property, the prohibition of expulsion from one's homeland, the prohibition of rape and weapons of mass destruction, limitations on the battlefield in time and space, respect for the right to surrender and the prohibition of massacres and acts of revenge against civilians (see El-Dakkak 2000: 93). A good example of a humanitarian standard can be found in the following hadith: 'Do not kill an old person, a child, a woman; do not cheat on the booty, do well: God likes the ones who act right' (Sultan 1986: 57). Another hadith reports that the Prophet Muhammad said that '[p]risoners are your brothers and companions. It is because of God's compassion that they are in your hands. They are at your mercy, so treat them well as if you were treating yourself, with food, clothes and housing' (Ereksoussi 1960: 650).

These humanitarian standards are divine orders that cannot be disrespected. To violate these rules would be *haram*, or 'forbidden', and would show *kufr* (see Abdel-Haleem *et al.* 1998: 69). As stated above, the foundation of Islamic humanitarian law is the simple yet demanding principle 'do not transgress'. All wars must be waged according to these key divine principles as a matter of Islamic legal obligation.

Most Muslim jurists, classicists, neo-classicists and modern scholars agree upon the fundamental distinction between civilians and warriors. For example, the Syrian scholar Wahbah Al-Zuhayli (1992: 500–501) notes that the *illah*, or '(legal) rationale', for not killing civilians in wartime is that they are not able to fight or harm Muslims. To reinforce this key difference between civilians and warriors, Al-Zuhayli explains that the verb *qatilu*, 'to fight', is reciprocal: someone who does not enter a fight and is without arms cannot be attacked. Therefore, we can more accurately speak of the existence of an Islamic ethic of saving lives rather than, as extremist groups would have it, an Islamic ethic of killing. This ethic operates in different degrees and at different levels according to different scholars. Most scholars of Islam accept the reality of war and the unfortunate likelihood of civilian casualties given that it is almost impossible to wage warfare without risk to civilians. Al-Zuhayli (1992: 406), for instance, states that fortresses can sometimes be brought down even if this would cause some risk to civilians. When civilians seek the protection of the enemy by hiding inside an enemy fortress, they risk certain consequences. It should also not be forgotten that the enemy may also bear some responsibility for civilian casualties in such situations given its duty to protect its own population (see Al-Shaybani 1966: 101–2).

Since the rise of such extremist groups as Al Qaeda, Muslim intellectuals have made a considerable effort to respect this distinction. These same voices have condemned terrorist attacks by reminding the world that civilians are not legitimate targets under Islamic law. As Saudi Shaikh Abdulaziz Al-Ashaikh put it in his Eid Al-Adha sermon on 1 February 2004:

> You must know Islam's firm position against all these terrible crimes. The world must know that Islam is a religion of peace and mercy and goodness; it is a religion of justice and guidance … Islam has forbidden violence in all its forms. It forbids the hijacking [of] airplanes, ships and other means of transport, and it forbids all acts that undermine the security of the innocent. (Kingdom of Saudi Arabia 2011: 9)

And the Guide of the Islamic Republic of Iran, Ayatollah Khamenei, reacted to 11 September by stating:

> Killing of people, in any place and with any kind of weapons, including atomic bombs, long-range missiles, biological or chemical weapons, passenger or war planes, carried out by any organization, country or individuals is condemned …
> It makes no difference whether such massacres happen in Hiroshima, Nagasaki, Qana, Sabra, Shatila, Deir Yassin, Bosnia, Kosovo, Iraq or in New York and Washington. (Gregorian 2003: 104 (citing Ayatollah Khamenei 2001))

These and other words and deeds demonstrate that respected religious authorities within the Muslim world have indeed consistently condemned extremists' distorted interpretations of Islam and the terrorism that they have unleashed.

Although there has been a discernible congruence over time between Islamic humanitarian law and international humanitarian law, differences *do* exist. Most of these differences are the result of different interpretations of Islamic legal sources. As noted above with regard to verse 9:5, the same verse can lead to different interpretations, and it seems reasonable to conclude from this that the extent to which such verses can be interpreted in very different ways will impact upon the way in which Islam is practised during war and which rules are respected on the ground.

In approaching the language of Islam, one of the first questions to ask is whether a particular verse in the Quran has been abrogated, or nullified.[12] Consider the Verse of the Sword. As to whether it has abrogated peaceful verses in the Quran, some Muslim jurists advocate restraint and argue that war can only be sanctioned as a last resort. Others believe that Quranic verses have to be understood contextually, by taking into account the historical background. At the time that the Verse of the Sword was revealed, there were several assassination attempts against the Prophet Muhammad and tribes in rebellion against Islam. Verse 9:5 speaks with hostility about some of these tribes because of their violent behaviour towards the rule of Islam at the time. In this light, it becomes quite clear that the Verse of the Sword does not give carte blanche to kill all Unbelievers: it applies to the context of the time only.

Besides the context, verse 9:5 applies to *mushrikun*, or 'polytheists': the verse focuses on those polytheistic tribes that the Prophet Muhammad had to defeat in the past and those still challenging him at the time that the verse was revealed. To this, extremists respond that in situations in which verses contradict one another, later verses override earlier ones, and since the warmongering verses were written in Medina, when the Prophet Muhammad and Islam had been established and were relatively secure, they override the Meccan verses that are far more peaceful. Others would counter this timeline approach by contrasting the Verse of the Sword with the following verse from the Quran:

> There is no compulsion in religion, for the right way is clearly distinct from the wrong way. Whoever therefore rejects the forces of evil and believes in God, he has taken hold of a support most unfailing, which shall never give way, for God is All Hearing and Knowing. (2:256)

This verse means that no violence can justify expansive *jihad*. Only defensive *jihad*, which aims at protecting Muslims and Muslim territory, is tolerated in Islamic law.

The essential point in all of this is that individual Muslims have the power to decide for themselves to follow particular religious rulings and a corresponding duty

---

12 *Naskh*, or 'abrogation', is the process that is used when approaching contradictory verses in the Quran and hadith, as well as between the Quran and hadith. Applying *naskh* is very controversial and is rarely even applied: it is seen as an act of heresy that seeks to effectively 'cut off' parts of the Quran.

to distinguish the good from the bad. Although this empowers individual Muslims, this is somewhat problematic because interpretive debates become endless and inconclusive. There is no hierarchy to tell us which interpretation is 'right'. This means that fundamentalists can still then be 'in the right' in their interpretations.

One possible way to put an end to these debates is by making greater use of the concept of *maslahah*, an Islamic legal tool that can be roughly translated as 'public utility'. *Maslahah* strives for what is best for society and the *Ummah*. Clearly, killing civilians, even if they are Unbelievers, should be argued to be illicit, especially given that much of the Quran understands Islam as a religion of peace and stresses its ethic of saving lives. It is in the interest of society to acknowledge limitations to war and humanitarian standards, furthermore, because this will reduce the differences between Islamic humanitarian law and international humanitarian law. It will also mean that humanitarian standards will more likely be respected in wars with Unbelievers and that, when captured, Muslim warriors can expect decent treatment, if not in accordance with Islamic humanitarian law, then in accordance with international humanitarian law. In fact, the Iran–Iraq War in the 1980s illustrates this in the sense that Iran referred to Islamic law in making its *ad bellum* and *in bello* arguments, and Iraq drew upon international law rules.

Conclusions

The novel interpretations of Islam provided by Islamic extremists and some Western scholars are not faithful to the spirit of the Quran and hadith. There are certainly some warmongering verses in the Quran and hadith, but they should be interpreted in their proper context and yield to the considerable Islamic legal sources that advocate peace and regulate war as an exceptional occurrence. Interpretations of the Quran that encourage war should be deconstructed using different interpretative techniques and the concept of *maslahah*. It is only when this is done that extremists will be defeated, on their own terms, using their own instruments. As a hadith states:

> Fighting is of two kinds: the one who seeks Allah's favour, obeys the leader, given the property he values, treats his associates gently and avoids mischief, will have the reward for all the time whether he is asleep or awake; but the one who fights in a boasting spirit, for the sake of display or to gain a reputation, who disobeys the leader and does mischief in the earth will not return with credit or without blame. (Abu Dawud: bk. 8, no. 2509 (narrated by Mu'adh ibn Jabal))

Unfortunately, these calls for reason are hardly heard in a post-11 September world that is divided between extremists who use Islam to fulfil a maddening ideological scheme and analysts in the West who present Islam as a threat to Western civilisation.

It has been said that extremists work outside the structure of Islam by distorting it and its basic tenets to fit their agenda. It has also been said that Islamic extremists act as the plaintiff, judge and executioner, and execute innocents. One has to remember that the Quran advocates justice, proportionality and compassion. The main issue for the time being is that extremists hold a megaphone, and insignificant attention is being paid to those who argue for Islam as a religion of peace.

References

Abdel-Haleem, H., Sherif, A.O. and Daniels, K. (eds) 1998. *The Crescent and the Cross: Muslim and Christian Approaches to War and Peace.* New York: Palgrave Macmillan.

Abu Dawud. Hadith. Available at: http://www.hadithcollection.com/abudawud.html [accessed: 14 November 2012].

Al-Banna, H. 1948. *Peace in Islam.* Available at: http://web.youngmuslims.ca/online_library/books/peace_in_islam/index.htm [accessed: 25 September 2012].

Al-Khudairi, A. 2002. Fatwa.*Al-Hayat*, 13 February.

Al-Mawdudi, A. 1976. Jihad *in Islam.* Lahore: Islamic Publications.

Al-Mawdudi, A. 1980. *Human Rights in Islam.* Leicester: Islamic Foundation.

Al-Sarakhasi 1997. *Dar Al-Kutub*, vol. 4. Elmiya: Beirut.

Al-Shaybani, M. 1966. Kitab al-Siyar al Kabir, in *The Islamic Law of Nations*, trans. M. Khadduri. Baltimore: Johns Hopkins University Press.

Al-Zawahiri, A. 2005a. Cavaliers sous l'étendard du Prophète, in *Al Qaida dans le texte*, ed. G. Kepel. Paris: Presses Universitaires de France, 289–94.

Al-Zawahiri, A. 2005b. La Moissonamère: Les soixanteans des Frères musulmans, in *Al Qaida dans le texte*, ed. G. Kepel. Paris: Presses Universitaires de France, 245–61.

Al-Zuhayli, W. 1992. *Athar al-Harb fi al-Fiqh al-Islami.* Bayreuth: Dar al-Fikr.

Azzam, A.Y. 1979. *Defence of the Muslim Lands: The First Obligation after Iman.* Medina: Maktabah Publications. Available at: http://www.kalamullah.com/Books/defence.pdf [accessed: 14 November 2012].

Belkhodja, H. 1992. La conception islamique de la guerre, in *Religion et Guerre*, ed. M. Torelli *et al.* Paris: MAME, 135–42.

Bennett, C. 1998. *In Search of Muhammad.* Washington, DC: Cassell.

Bin Laden, O. 1996. Declaration of War against the Americans Occupying the Land of the Two Holy Places.PBS. Available at: http://www.pbs.org/newshour/updates/military/july-dec96/fatwa_1996.html[accessed: 14 November 2012].

Boekhoff-van der Voort, N., Versteegh, C. and Wagemakers, J. (eds) 2011. *The Transmission and Dynamics of the Textual Sources of Islam: Essays in Honour of Harald Motzki.* Leiden: Brill.

Boisard, M. 1988. *Jihad: A Commitment to Universal Peace.* Indianapolis: American Trust.

Bukhari 1944. *Hadith of Bukhari.* Charleston: Forgotten Books.

Bukhari.Hadith. Available at: http://www.hadithcollection.com/sahihmuslim.html [accessed: 14 November 2012].

Calvert, J. 2010. *Sayyid Qutb and the Origins of Radical Islamism*. London: Hurst.

Center for Strategic Communication 2012. *How Islamist Extremists Quote the Qur'an*. Available at: http://csc.asu.edu/wp-content/uploads/pdf/csc1202-quran-verses.pdf [accessed: 25 September 2012].

Cordesman, A.H. and Davies, E.R. 2008. *Iraq's Insurgency and the Road to Civil Conflict*. Santa Barbara, CA: Praeger.

Damad, M. 2003. International Humanitarian Law in Islam and Contemporary International Law, in *Islamic Views on Human Rights: Viewpoints of Iranian Scholars*, ed. H. Salimi. New Delhi: Kanishka.

El-Dakkak, M.S. 2000. *State's Crimes Against Humanity: Genocide, Deportation and Torture from the Perspectives of International and Islamic Laws*. Kuala Lumpur: A.S. Doordeen.

Ereksoussi, M.K. 1960. Le Coranet les conventions humanitaires. *Revue Internationale de la Croix Rouge*, 503, 641–50.

Faraj, A. 1986. *The Neglected Duty*. New York: Macmillan.

Fishman, B. 2006. After Zarqawi: The Dilemmas and Future of Al Qaeda in Iraq. *Washington Quarterly*, 29(4), 19–32.

Gerges, F.A. 2011. *The Rise and Fall of Al-Qaeda*. Oxford: Oxford University Press.

Gregorian, V. 2003. *Islam: A Mosaic, Not a Monolith*. Washington, DC: Brookings Institution Press.

Haddar, L.T. 1993. What Green Peril? *Foreign Affairs*, 72(2), 27–42.

Hashmi, S. 1999. Saving and Taking Life in War: Three Modern Muslim Views. *Muslim World*, 89(2), 158–80.

Hashmi, S. 2002. Interpreting the Islamic Ethics of War and Peace, in *Islamic Political Ethics: Civil Society, Pluralism and Conflict*, ed. S. Hashmi. Princeton: Princeton University Press, 194–215.

Huntington, S. 1993. The Clash of Civilizations? *Foreign Affairs*, 72(3), 22–49.

Huntington, S. 1997. *The Clash of Civilizations and the Remaking of World Order*. New York: Touchstone.

Kepel, G. (ed.) 2005. *Al Qaida dans le texte*. Paris: Presses Universitaires de France.

Khadduri, M. 1966. *The Islamic Law of Nations*. Baltimore: Johns Hopkins University Press.

Khan, M.R.A. 1978. *Islamic Jurisprudence*. Lahore: S.H. Muhammad Ashraf.

Kingdom of Saudi Arabia 2011. Condemning Extremism and Promoting Moderation: Public Statements of Senior Saudi Officials and Religious Scholars Condemning Extremism and Promoting Moderation. Washington, DC: Royal Embassy of Saudi Arabia. Available at: http://www.saudiembassy.net/files/PDF/Reports/Condemning_Extremism.pdf [accessed: 16 October 2012].

Mir, M. 1991. *Jihad* in Islam, in *The Jihad and its Times*, ed. H. Dajani-Shakeel and R.A. Messier. Ann Arbor: Center for Near Eastern and North African Studies, University of Michigan, 113–26.

Mottahari, M. 1998. *Jihad va Movared-e Mashruyiat-e an Dar Quran*. Tehran: Islamic Culture and Relations Organization.

Musallam, A. 2005.*From Secularism to* Jihad*: Sayyid Qutb and the Foundations of Radical Islamism*. Westport, CT: Praeger.

Muslim. Hadith. Available at: http://muttaqun.com/files/PDF/Sahih-Muslim.pdf [accessed: 30 October 2012].

Muslim Brotherhood 2001. *Al-Ahram Weekly Online*, 13–19 September. Available at: http://kurzman.unc.edu/islamic-statements-against-terrorism/ [accessed: 25 September 2012].

Nikayin, F. 2000. *Quran: A Poetic Translation from the Original*. Skokie: The Ultimate Book.

Perlmutter, A. 1992. Islam and Democracy Simply Aren't Compatible. *International Herald Tribune*, 21 January.

Qutb, S. 1980. *In the Shade of the Qu'ran*. Available at: http://www.kalamullah.com/shade-of-the-quran.html [accessed: 29 October 2012].

Qutb, S. 1981. *Milestones*. Available at: http://www.izharudeen.com/uploads/4/1/2/2/4122615/milestones_www.izharudeen.com.pdf [accessed: 29 October 2012].

Singh, B. 2007.*TheTalibanizationof Southeast Asia: Losing the War on Terror to Islamist Extremists.*Westport, CT: Praeger.

Stephens, M. 1877. *Christianity and Islam: The Bible and the Koran*. New York: Scribner.

Streusand, D.E. 1989. Abraham's Other Children: Is Islam an Enemy of the West? *Policy Review*, 50, 50–54.

Sultan, H. 1986. La conception islamique, in *Les dimensions internationales du droithumanitaire*, ed. Institut Henry Dunant. Paris: Pedone, 47–60.

Van Engeland, A. 2008. The Differences and Similarities Between International Humanitarian Law and Islamic Humanitarian Law: Is There Ground for Reconciliation? *Journal of Islamic Law and Culture*, 10(1), 81–99.

Van Engeland, A. 2010. The Challenge of Fragmentation of International Humanitarian Law Regarding the Protection of Civilians: An Islamic Perspective, in Jihad *and its Challenges to International and Domestic Law*, ed. M.C. Bassiouni and A. Guellali. The Hague: Hague Academic Press, 139–68.

Weiss, B. 1978.Interpretation in Islamic Law. The Theory of *Ijtihād*. *American Journal of Comparative Law*, 26(2), 199–212.

World Islamic Front 1998. *Jihad* Against Jews and Crusaders, 23 February. Available at: http://www.fas.org/irp/world/para/docs/980223-fatwa.htm [accessed: 25 September 2012].

Zawati, H.M. 2001. *Is Jihad a Just War? War, Peace and Human Rights under Islamic and Public International Law*. Lewiston, NY: Edwin Mellen Press.

Chapter 11

Islamic Law after the Arab Spring: The Challenges of Islamism and Modernity

John Strawson

'[T]his program is founded on four fundamental principles, which represent the great purposes of Sharia (Islamic law), namely: Freedom ... Justice ... Development ... Leadership.'

Freedom and Justice Party Election Program (2011: 3)

The Arab Spring has transformed the political and legal landscape of North Africa and the Middle East. The greatest beneficiaries of the new dispensation have been Islamist parties, who have triumphed in elections across the region. In opposition, Islamists argued for a state based upon Islamic law. Now in power, the test for Islamists will be how they will implement their agenda in practice and use it to shape their societies.[1] The new political situation has created huge expectations among the peoples of the region for clean government, an end to corruption and for a fair economy. Having put an end to authoritarian regimes, the pressure is on the Islamists to deliver a genuine alternative order at the heart of which lies the dignity of the citizen.

This chapter reflects upon current Islamist attitudes to Islamic law, political pluralism and human rights in the wake of the Arab Spring. It focuses upon Egypt in particular because that state occupies a position of great influence in the Arab world, not only due to its size but also due to its centrality in culture, the media and religion; and what happens in Egypt will have significant implications for the region at large. In Egypt, the Freedom and Justice Party, which the Muslim Brotherhood created,[2] became the largest party in the subsequently dissolved parliament, the Constituent Assembly, and its candidate, Mohammed Morsi, has become Egypt's first freely elected president. The chapter will reflect upon the character of the 25 January Revolution and its implications for the Muslim Brotherhood. It will then consider the constitutional and legal aspects of the Freedom and Justice Party Election Program (hereafter Election Program). This chapter suggests that the

---

1   There is an emerging literature on the Arab Spring (see Goldstone 2011; Pollack 2011; West 2011; Wright 2011; Ajami 2012; Dabashi 2012; Darwish 2012; Prashad 2012).

2   For authoritative accounts of the history of the Muslim Brotherhood, see Mitchell 1993 and Lia 1998. On its contemporary politics, see Tadros 2012.

picture is far more complex than Tibi's conclusion that the 'fall of authoritarian regimes ... seems not to fulfill the promise of democratization but rather portends the empowerment of Islamism' (2012: xiii). This issue is not so much the question of democratisation itself but, rather, the highly populist form of democracy that is taking shape under Islamist influence in Egypt, and the conditions that this has created for governments to manipulate shari'a for their own ends.

Islamists and the Revolts

The drama and scale of the Arab Spring shocked both the region and outside powers. In a matter of days, longstanding authoritarian regimes were swept aside, and popular mass demonstrations in Tunisia, Egypt, Bahrain, Libya, Yemen and Syria between December 2010 and April 2011 placed the rule of law, democracy, human rights and political pluralism on the Arab agenda as never before (see Chase 2012). In a matter of months, decades of intimidation and repression were swept away as millions of people defied the police and security forces to demand their rightful role in running their own societies.

During these five months, the protests were decidedly peaceful. Although the protestors were sometimes met with a fierce response from the regimes then in power, the former did not resort to arms. In Tunisia, the regime quickly gave way, and President Zine El-Abidine Ben Ali fled into exile. In Egypt, an eighteen-day revolt forced President Hosni Mubarak to resign. In Libya and Syria, weeks of peaceful protests were met by military responses from the government, and both states soon descended into civil war. The government in Bahrain sought the support of Saudi Arabia to smother the opposition; in nearby Yemen, it took months to sideline President Ali Abdullah Saleh and transfer power within the regime. While it is true that these protests unfolded in different ways throughout the region, they shared a number of features: demands for free elections, political accountability and social justice. Within eighteen months, elections had taken place in Tunisia and Egypt, and Islamist parties gained pluralities or majorities.[3]

Although the street protests in North Africa and the Middle East triggered these electoral successes, the Islamist wave was already well-established before 2011. Since the beginning of the 1990s, Islamists had scored victories or secured significant representation in a number of free or partially free elections that had taken place. The Algerian Islamic Salvation Front, for example, was clearly on course to victory in 1992 when the military intervened, and across the region, Islamists gained seats in parliaments in Morocco, Jordan and the Gulf States. Hamas won demonstrably free elections in Palestine in 2006, and Islamist parties continue to dominate the governments of post-Saddam Iraq. At the same time,

---

3   In the elections in Libya, the Muslim Brotherhood did not do as well. The coalition of forces that had led the National Transitional Council and dominated the parliamentary elections were, however, already well-versed in the language of political Islam.

outside the Arab world, the Islamists of the Justice and Development Party have governed Turkey since 2002.

Electoral participation has been something that Islamist organisations have traditionally eschewed. Their electoral successes bring with them the paradox that, while still subscribing to the idea of an Islamic state that espouses God's sovereignty, Islamists today owe their power to a democratic mandate. In articulating their vision of Islamic law, Islamists are caught between the conflicting pressures of their popular mandate and what they understand to be divine will.

Islamic law encompasses two broad elements: *usul al-fiqh*, which is the juristic methodology that develops the law, and shari'a, which is its product and forms the basis of the normative system that is Islamic law. The origins of Islamic law lie in the Quran and the prophetic period, when the Prophet Mohammed established the first Islamic-led societies in Medina and Mecca in the seventh century of the Common Era (CE). While the Quran and the practice of the Prophet Mohammed, the sunnah, are the origins of Islamic law, as a juristic methodology and normative system, Islamic law continued to evolve over the next two hundred years and critically matured in the eighth century CE as the Umayyad Empire gave way to the Abbasid (see Hallaq 2009: 27–124).

Although Islam boasts a rich jurisprudence that stretches back over 1,400 years, political Islam, since its beginnings in the 1920s, has been very reluctant to draw upon this heritage. Indeed, one of the most notable and radical characteristics of today's Islamist movements has been their utter rejection of the history of Islamic civilisation, including its jurisprudence. In the main, this stems from the view that rulers and even religious authorities in the Muslim world have been corrupted to such an extent that they lie outside Islam altogether. It is for this reason, for example, that very few Islamist movements engage with the classical Islamic international relations and rarely demonstrate a familiarity with the *siyar* and discussion shown by Niaz A. Shah in Chapter 9 of this volume. Islamist thinkers tend to argue that official accounts of Islamic history have been (mis)used, merely to serve those in power. As a result, Islamism sets out to rescue Islamic civilisation by re-narrating it. The result has been the reconstitution of a flexible version of Islamic law that is tied to the requirements of power and, thus, has a dirigiste feel to it.

The Revolution in Egypt

In the case of Egypt, Islamists have had to respond not merely to their democratic mandate but also, of course, to the popular revolutionary events that made the free elections possible in the first case. However, the Muslim Brotherhood's relationship to the events in Tahrir Square was very ambivalent. President Morsi has described revolutionary Egypt as the 'cornerstone in the Arab Spring movement' (2012c). In the eighteen days of revolution in Egypt, Tahrir Square did indeed come to symbolise the values of the Arab Spring.

One of the most popular slogans of the demonstrators in Cairo, 'bread, freedom and social justice', brought together their economic, social and political demands (see El-Menawy 2012: 57). The slogan, of course, is reminiscent of the slogan 'bread, peace and land' that the Bolsheviks used when they seized power in Russia in October 1917, and this similarity perhaps gives a clue as to the secular and leftist orientation of many of the demonstrators in Egypt. Indeed, it is a paradox that what many in the media dubbed the 'Facebook revolution' was, in fact, a quite classical revolution (see El-Menawy 2012; Ghonim 2012; Soueif 2012). However, the other paradox is that while Egypt's first democratically elected president celebrates the revolution, his own organisation, the Muslim Brotherhood, was largely absent from the mass movement in those critical eighteen days (see Brown 2012: 206–8): While sections of its youth movement and some individuals did participate in the protests, they did so without the support of the main organisation (see Tadros 2012: 37–40). Significantly, the main slogans of the demonstrators rarely invoked Islam and never raised the programmatic demand of the Muslim Brotherhood for *al-nizam Islami*, an Islamic regime, in other words, an Islamic state. Indeed, these slogans were only raised after the overthrow of President Mubarak (see Tadros 2012: 40–42).

Throughout the uprising against President Mubarak, it was clear that, while there were leading figures, there was no common leadership or ideology behind the demonstrations. The formation of the Revolution Youth Coalition was the nearest the movement for change came to having some form of recognisable leadership. Although the Revolution Youth Coalition continued to exert considerable influence in the period immediately following President Mubarak's fall from power, it lacked ideological cohesion and was unable to offer any clear vision for a new Egypt. On the whole, its component parts were fairly small organisations that had their roots in the far left, which is extremely marginal in Egyptian society (see Cook 2012: 298–9). The Revolution Youth Council certainly had no settled position on the contours of an alternative constitution or position on the rule of law. Moreover, it was ill-equipped to deal with the way in which the armed forces moved to remove President Mubarak and establish a government.

While it was certainly a popular movement that forced President Mubarak from power, it was the military, with the slogan 'the people and the army are one hand', that actually seized power. This was less a revolution than a coup from within the regime, as it was General Mohammed Hussein Tantawi, President Mubarak's long-serving defence minister, who essentially took charge. The Supreme Council of the Armed Forces proceeded to act with great speed in clothing its rule with the cloak of law by issuing a constitutional decree and plan for parliamentary and presidential elections.[4] For the revolutionaries of Tahrir Square, the fact that the transitional period in Egypt was firmly under the control of those who had been in

---

4   Beginning on 13 February 2011, there were a series of constitutional declarations following the overthrow of President Mubarak. The main instrument dates from 23 March 2011.

power alongside the unpopular President Mubarak placed them in a quandary: how were they to press for democracy? Were they to be with the military or against it?

The regime carried out several highly skilful manoeuvres with the Revolution Youth Coalition, including using it as a sounding board to gauge public opinion. For example, it was the Revolution Youth Coalition's repeated agitation to bring criminal charges against President Mubarak for ordering the killing of civilians during the revolution that forced the hand of the Supreme Council of the Armed Forces, which then proceeded to arrest President Mubarak and put him on trial. Rather like many other secular and leftist parties, the Revolution Youth Coalition tended to look back rather than to argue for a new political order. Instead of focusing upon developing a new agenda for a new Egypt, the Revolution Youth Coalition tended, as with the arrest of President Mubarak, to concentrate on the crimes of the *ancien régime*. Indeed, the secular and leftist forces sometimes appeared to see the military as a protective shield that could hold off the Islamists while they gathered their strength. When the military proposed elections within six months of its having taken power from President Mubarak, secular and leftist groups opposed this on the ground that such elections would unfairly assist the well-organised Muslim Brotherhood and should be postponed for some time (see Cook 2012: 301). There was some truth to this assessment, but therein was also the irony: arguing over the timing of the elections found secular and leftist forces supporting a longer period of military rule and the Muslim Brotherhood emerging as the standard bearers of democracy.

The Muslim Brotherhood had been participating in elections albeit under various guises for decades and could now publicly and clearly offer its agenda for the first time. The Egyptian Muslim Brotherhood, it will be recalled, is a well-organised movement that has deep roots in Egyptian society stretching back to 1928, when Hassan Al-Banna founded the movement (see Mitchell 1993). This long history and experience surviving a pro-British monarchy, the Free Officers Revolution in 1952 and the regimes of Gamal Abdel Nasser, Anwar Sadat and Mubarak[5] meant that the Muslim Brotherhood was not only administratively very strong but also had a great deal of strategic flexibility. In addition, while the secular and leftist opposition had largely been outside politics under the *ancien régime*, the Muslim Brotherhood, despite its formal illegality, had carefully built itself as an opposition force within the People's Assembly (the lower house of parliament), numbering eighty-eight members in 2005 (see Brown and Hamzawy 2011: 9–46). During the 2005–10 Parliament, the Muslim Brotherhood claimed that its priories were defending freedom, the constitution and human rights and fighting corruption. This meant that it could credibly say that it had been 'exposing the shameful crimes of the regime and revealing its ugly secrets, thus playing a major role in breaking the barrier of fear and increasing public awareness, which were the most important reasons for the blessed revolution and its great success' (Election Program 2011: 4). Thus, whatever the actual role of the Muslim Brotherhood

---

5   On the modern history of Egypt, see Baker 1978 and Cook 2012.

in Tahrir Square, it cast itself as the major catalyst for the revolution. Although Ghonim (2012) and Tadros (2012: 37–46) have argued that this is a highly dubious view, the Muslim Brotherhood's record of parliamentary opposition to President Mubarak was undeniable.

As noted above, the forces that brought the masses onto the streets of Egypt were recently formed groups (see El-Menawy 2012; Ghonim 2012; Soueif 2012) that lacked a common organisational past and, unlike the Muslim Brotherhood, did not have a record of political activism upon which to draw. In the immediate euphoria following President Mubarak's fall, the protesting masses, along with secularists and leftists, concentrated their efforts upon organising large demonstrations to pressure the military government to allow civilian rule; in other words, they did not use this time to develop a clear political agenda or build grassroots organisations. The Muslim Brotherhood, on the other hand, formed the Freedom and Justice Party and began to project a political agenda for the future.

The result was that when much-delayed parliamentary elections were held, the Freedom and Justice Party easily became the largest party (to the surprise of many), and to the chagrin of the Muslim Brotherhood, the Salafi Al-Nour Party came in second, with 24 per cent of the vote compared with the Freedom and Justice Party's 36 per cent share. From the time of the final results of parliamentary elections in January 2012 until the presidential election run-off in June 2012, the Muslim Brotherhood presented itself as the democratic alternative to the military. This was made all the more dramatic in the presidential run-off when Morsi faced Ahmed Shafik, who had been President Mubarak's last prime minister and was very much seen as the military's preferred candidate. While the latter organised his campaign around calls for order, the Freedom and Justice Party argued for change. President Morsi narrowly won, and many thought that this would make him a weak president who would necessarily be in the pocket of the military. However, he very quickly asserted his authority and soon removed the head of the Supreme Council of the Armed Forces, General Tantawi, along with a whole layer of senior military officers. With this accomplished, President Morsi could credibly say that he had vanquished both the old Mubarak government and, at least temporarily, the entrenched military regime. He was able, in other words, to claim the mantle of the Arab Spring.

When President Mubarak was overthrown and the Supreme Council of the Armed Forces issued Constitutional Declaration 2011, which was to act as a temporary constitution during the transitional period, the scene was set for holding elections and drafting a new (permanent) constitution. Arguments over the composition of the Constituent Assembly, however, meant that there was to be no draft constitution at the end of the period of military rule. Despite some legal challenges, the new Constituent Assembly has now adopted at least two draft constitutions for public consultation (see Coleman 2012).[6] The military had

---

6   The consultation process has been well-organised through a government website available at: http://www.dostour.eg [accessed: 29 October 2012].

intended the constitution to be a fait accompli whereas, in fact, President Morsi now has a major influence over the process. He issued a new Constitutional Declaration that gave himself the power to reconstitute the Constituent Assembly in the event that it failed to produce an acceptable draft (see Morsi 2012b). In a later declaration, he extended the life of the assembly and made it immune to legal challenges (see Morsi 2012a). All of this, of course, has created a political environment very different than the one the military had been planning for Egypt and has turned the spotlight not merely on President Morsi but also on the Muslim Brotherhood and its platform for action more generally.

Having passed from opposition to government and now having a dominant position within the Constituent Assembly, the Muslim Brotherhood had to make concrete what 'implementing shari'a' means in practice. Article 2 of the 1971 Constitution states that the '[p]rinciples of Islamic law (Shari'a) are the principal source of legislation', though the text is silent as to who or what has the competence to interpret this language. The term 'principles of Islamic law (Shari'a)' is admittedly quite ambiguous and in practice it has been left to the high courts, including the Supreme Constitutional Court, to interpret this language. As Lombardi notes, the 'result is a situation in which there is a broad desire for Islamization in the abstract, but violent disagreement about what form Islamization should take – disagreement that is rooted in very different ideas about how to interpret the shari'a' (2006: 7). Today's concentration of power in the hands of the Muslim Brotherhood means that it can now inject its own interpretation of shari'a into the political process. Drafts of the new constitution have retained the 1971 language, but new provisions would allow the president to appoint judges and give Al-Azhar University a role in the interpretation of shari'a (see Afify 2012). Effectively, this would mean that the Muslim Brotherhood, through its control of the courts and Al-Azhar, would be able to shape the relationship between Islam and the state for some time to come.

The role of shari'a and the relationship between Islam and the state have been central issues in Egypt's formation as a modern state. As Hallaq observes, Egypt encapsulates 'the longest experiment in jural modernization and, simultaneously, perhaps one of the fiercest tendencies to contest jural secularization in the name of one Islamic ideology or another' (2009: 476–7). What is particularly fascinating about the current period is the way in which the process that Hallaq describes has been turned upside down, with the Islamists now in power being forced to confront two centuries of legal modernisation.

There are many layers to this complex legal history, which stretches back to the establishment of the rule of Mohammad Ali (see Vatikiotis 1969) through the great legal reforms of the Ottomans and encompasses British rule after 1882 (see Mansfield 1971), the 1952 Revolution and the Nasser period (see Mansfield 1969), subsequent Soviet influence (see Ginat 1993) and the role of the West again with the period of the *infitah*, or 'opening', under Sadat (see Hinnebusch 1985). This long period of legal transformation involved modernising trends within Islamic law as well as the influences of colonialism, a Soviet alliance and globalisation.

The Ottoman reforms focused upon the codification of law, which by the end of the nineteenth century had produced codes in almost all areas of law (see Gerber 1994), and it is noteworthy that, in the main, these influences on the Egyptian legal system came from outside. Furthermore, it is significant that whatever the ideological coloration of these influences, they all had in common the view that the state should be the dominant force within the legal system. As a result, the Egyptian legal system moved in significant measure into a state-run system with, *inter alia*, the state taking charge of legal education (see Zubaida 2003). This also included Islamic legal education after Nasser brought Al-Azhar under government control (see Rubin 1990: 80–83).

The Egyptian Muslim Brotherhood in Historical Context

This history of two centuries of legal modernisation frames contemporary debates about law in Egypt and is the environment in which the Muslim Brotherhood has formed its view about the role of Islamic law in society. In general, it has always identified the corrupting influence of power and been particularly keen to conflate corruption with foreign influences. Within Islamist circles, this has led to the mantra that 'shari'a is the alternative to imported solutions' (Tibi 2012: 97 (citing Al-Qaradawi)). According to the writings of Sayyid Qutb in the 1950s and 1960s, these corrupting foreign influences were said to have reached the highest echelons of Islamic authority. Indeed, Qutb frequently used the term *Jahiliyyah*, which refers to the period of ignorance before Islam, and branded most of what appeared to be Islamic as, actually, *Jahiliyyah*. Consider the following passage from *Milestones*:

> We are surrounded by Jahiliyyah today, which is of the same nature as it was during the first period of Islam, perhaps a little deeper. Our whole environment, people's beliefs and ideas, habits and art, rules and laws – is Jahiliyyah, even to the extent that what we consider to be Islamic culture, Islamic sources, Islamic philosophy and Islamic thought, are also constructs of Jahiliyyah. (Qutb 1991: 32)

Qutb's view that power has corrupted Muslim societies to the point that Islam has itself lost its content and that those claiming authority are actually charlatans is widespread among Islamists. This is especially so within the field of Islamic legal authority, and the Muslim Brotherhood holds particular contempt for Al-Azhar and its leading scholars, including the Grand Sheikh of Al-Azhar. In Egypt, as we have noted, Al-Azhar is effectively under state control through the Ministry of Waqf and Al-Azhar Affairs, meaning that for years the Muslim Brotherhood has been able to draw attention to Al-Azhar and its entanglement with the government as proof that Islam has been subjugated to the whims of those (corrupt officials) in power. As a result, even the *fatwas*, or 'legal opinions', of the Grand Sheikh of Al-Azhar have been seen as questionable in that they have been, it is argued, issued in the interests of *Jahiliyyah*. Thus, in this account, the entire structure of legal authority has been placed outside of Islam. For the Muslim Brotherhood, two centuries of legal modernisation were two centuries too many of collusion between foreign (often colonial) intruders and a dissolute Egyptian elite, with an increasing divorce between Islamic law and the authentic values of Islam being the result. Having dismissed the foremost Islamic legal authority, Al-Azhar, as being un-Islamic, the Muslim Brotherhood is then forced to make the case for a new authority. As Qutb (1991: 21–35) explains, this requires building a new Islamic society that will see the Muslim Brotherhood as the nucleus.

While the Muslim Brotherhood may reject the *form* of two centuries of legal modernisation in Egypt, it would be incorrect to suggest that it rejects modernisation as such. The Muslim Brotherhood, Hallaq notes, has 'a wider view of juridical possibilities allowing for an Islamic law that could be modified to reflect the changing realities of the world, in ways comparatively far more open to the interpretative possibilities' (2009: 477). The Muslim Brotherhood places this task firmly within the structure of the state, a feature that it shares with other modernising forces in Egyptian history, be they Ottoman, British or Nasserite. The difference lies in the *quality* of the relationship between the state and religion (*din wa-dawlah*), the rationale of Islamism (see Tibi 2012). Having criticised the way in which previous regimes used the state to undermine Islam, today's Muslim Brotherhood seeks to reverse this process and use the state as an instrument to Islamicise the constitution and the legal system.

As many theorists have pointed out, while Islamism is often portrayed as a movement that recalls the past and seeks to return to a pure point of Islamic origin, it is a quintessentially modern movement. Islamists engage in a radical reconstruction of the prophetic period in an attempt to caste the Prophet as the architect of their agenda for an Islamic state (see Ajami 1992; Ayubi 1993; Tibi 2012). While Islamism is a broad worldwide movement, with colorations that range from violent to moderate, the Egyptian Muslim Brotherhood has both the longest history and strongest organisational structure of any contemporary Islamist movement (see Mitchell 1993; Lia 1998). Because of this, it has a great influence over many organisations outside of Egypt. Al-Banna remains venerated, and its best-known ideologue, Qutb, who Nasser executed in 1966, remains a bestselling author internationally. And one of the Muslim Brotherhood's most popular exponents today, Sheikh Yusuf Al-Qaradawi (see Baker 2003: 47–8, 142–4; Soage 2010), has a massive following through his Al-Jazeera television show and well-run website.

The Muslim Brotherhood was founded at the height of secularisation in the Arab world between the First and Second World Wars. This was a period that saw the rise of Arab nationalism and more narrow nationalist currents demanding independence from European colonial powers. These currents were overwhelmingly secular and were often influenced by modernist ideological movements from Europe, including liberalism, communism and fascism. In Egypt, the main political forces focused upon removing the British, who had occupied the country in 1882 and set up a *de facto* colony.

After the First World War, the Middle East experienced popular movements not unlike the Arab Spring of recent years when nationalist sentiment swept through French- and British-ruled North Africa (see Anderson 2011). Seething resentment that despite playing their part in the defeat of the Ottomans the peoples of the Middle East were rewarded not with independence but with a League of Nations mandate system covering Mesopotamia (now Iraq), Syria, Lebanon and Palestine (including present-day Jordan) sparked major revolts in the Arab world. The high point came with the General Syrian Congress's declaration of independence in July 1920, though this was crushed by the French with British support. In the same period, the British had set about crushing the Kurdish revolt in Iraq and, in the wake of the events in Syria, installed the failed King of Syria, the Hashemite Faisal, as king of Mesopotamia under British mandate. The nationalist movement in Egypt fared no better, and the British were able to reassert control. All of this meant that the 1920s saw the defeat of protest movements and the secular nationalist politics that had led them, and it was within this context that the Muslim Brotherhood and Islamism were born.

The combined collapse of the Ottoman Empire and the failure of secular nationalist politics created a fertile environment for Islamism, which from its very beginning offered a vision not so much of an Islamic revival, as Afghani and Abduh had done in the late nineteenth century, but, rather, a new politics that would be simultaneously rooted in Islam and oriented towards the remoulding of society through the creation of an Islamic regime to 'implement' Islamic law.[7] Islamism would confront the colonial West and offer an alternative vision to the failed secular nationalist forces in Egyptian society. These latter forces were failing miserably, according to the Islamist narrative, because they lacked commitment to Islam. Today's wave of Islamist politics was also initiated by yet another defeat of secular nationalist forces, this time with the defeat of the Arabs in the 1967 Arab–Israeli War. For Islamists, this humiliating defeat was a warning from 'on high' that a non-Islamic regime had no future. In order to convert defeat into victory, the 'only solution' was Islam, an Islam that was not a return to the faith as such or, indeed, its revival but, rather, the projection of an Islamic state authentically rooted in Islamic law.

The Freedom and Justice Party's Election Program (2011)

In order to understand Islamist attitudes to Islamic law, political pluralism and human rights in the wake of the Arab Spring, it is helpful to turn to the Freedom and Justice Party's 2011 Election Program. In engaging with these questions, it is important to bear in mind the distinction that Tibi makes between Islam and

---

7   This view has been controversially challenged by Tariq Ramadan (2002).

Islamism in his book *Islamism and Islam* (2012). There is often a tendency in some accounts of the Muslim Brotherhood's views to conflate Islamism with Islam (see Cohen 2012), but this is unhelpful. While Tibi's basic thesis that Islamism is a form of religious politics rather than religious faith as such is sound, his view that Islamism is inherently homogeneous and totalitarian is more questionable.

Clearly, today's Muslim Brotherhood is not the same movement as Al-Banna's and Qutb's. Nor has it followed the trajectory of violent extremist groups such as Al Qaeda who also draw on Qutb, as can be seen in Anicée Van Engeland's arguments in Chapter 10 of this volume. While both Al-Banna and Qutb regularly denounced democracy, the Election Program announced that the 'State envisaged in our program is the national constitutional Islamic modern democracy, based on Sharia (Islamic law) as a frame of reference' (2011: 10). No doubt, Tibi would argue that framing the nature of the state within shari'a effectively means subjecting the constitutional and democratic elements of it to predetermined Islamic legal norms that are inherently anti-democratic. The Election Program goes on to explain each of these terms, however. As far as shari'a is concerned:

> Sharia nurtures aspects of faith, worship, and morality, and also regulates various aspects of life for Muslims and their non-Muslim partners in the homeland. However, in some (few) cases, Sharia regulates these aspects through definitive texts with direct relevance and significance. It can also regulate through general rules and principles, leaving details for interpretation and legislation as suits different times and environments, in the service of justice, righteousness and the interests of the homeland and citizens. (Election Program 2011: 10–11)

While this is a highly ambivalent statement, it nonetheless represents an important shift in the Islamist discourse from the time of Al-Banna and Qutb. During their time, shari'a was seen as a completed and perfected system of law, and the function of the Islamic state was simply to implement it. The Election Program, however, understands shari'a in much more limited and conditional terms. For the Freedom and Justice Party, the general principles of shari'a can only be given shape within particular circumstances. As with any election manifesto, this formula was undoubtedly the result of a compromise between many different positions.

The indeterminate nature of the language in the Election Program needs to be further scrutinised within the context of what follows, and here, the text outlines the four key characteristics of the state:

> A. The State is based on the principle of citizenship, where all citizens enjoy equal rights and duties guaranteed by law in accordance with the principles of equality and equal opportunities without discrimination because of religion or race.
> B. The State is a constitutional one ... This constitutional State must preserve the rule of law by extending and strengthening the rule of the judiciary, safeguarding its independence ...

C. The State is Democratic, based on the Shura (consultation) principles, which the FJP believes are essential for the foundation of the state with all its institutions ... it is a pattern of behaviour and a general approach to managing the various aspects of life in the State, in addition to being a frame of work for faith and a moral guide for the behaviour of individuals and their social relations, instilled in the hearts and minds of individuals, families, societies and the rulers, in order for it to become part and parcel of the patriotic character ... and to engage all citizens.

D. The State is civil and civilian, for the Islamic State is civilian in nature. It is not a military state ruled by armed forces who get power by military coups, and it is not ruled like a dictatorship, nor is it a police state controlled by the security forces, nor is it a theocracy – governed by the clergy or by Divine Right. There are no infallible people who can monopolise the interpretation of the Holy Koran and have exclusive right to legislation for the nation and are characterised by Holiness. In fact, the rulers in the Islamic state are citizens elected according to the will of the people; and the nation is the source of authority. The basis of appointment to all positions and functions in the State is competence, experience and the [sic] honesty. And just as it is the nation's right to choose its ruler, legislators and representatives, it also has the right to question them and hold them accountable, to dismiss and replace them. (Election Program 2011: 11)

This lengthy description of the type of state that the Freedom and Justice Party imagines contains many different elements, and many problematic formulations. It is noteworthy that when referring to the equality of citizens, the Election Program refers to discrimination in relation to race and religion but does not mention gender, though it is also true that in explaining the principle of equality later on the document explains that non-discrimination principles also extend to grounds of sex. This is followed by another ambiguous clause, however, which seeks to 'ensure women's equal access to all their rights, consistent with the values of Islamic law, maintaining a balance between their duties and their rights' (Election Program 2011: 12). This leaves unanswered questions such as the extent to which women will actually have 'equal access to all their rights' since this is quite clearly conditioned upon consistency with the 'values of Islamic law' and a balance between rights and duties. What is meant by the values of Islamic law is naturally elusive, and one assumes that a distinction must be made between values and norms of Islamic law. Article 68 of Egypt's 2012 Draft Constitution includes a form of this proposal except that it replaces the 'values of Islamic Law' with the 'provisions of Islamic law' (see Afify 2012), which, it is suggested, implies a more conservative interpretation. While some commentators, such as Amr Adly of the Egyptian Initiative for Personal Rights, suggest that this latter formula is the work of Salafis in the Constituent Assembly (see Afify 2012), as we shall see, the Muslim Brotherhood's position on gender equality is itself highly problematic.

The Election Program devotes an entire section to women's policies. After a formal statement that 'the basic principle of Islamic law is equality between women and men in rights and duties' (Election Program 2011: 24), this section continues by explaining that the party has 'the greatest respect, appreciation and support for women's role as wives, mothers and makers of men; and aims to better prepare them for this role' (Election Program 2011: 24). These highly problematic formulations are compounded when the Election Program turns to Egypt's obligations to protect women's rights under international human rights law. At this point, it sees the international human rights law project itself as being a foreign imposition. In particular, it asserts that the family has been undermined by 'a whole list of civil society organisations that receive foreign funds from suspicious sources' (Election Program 2011: 24). The Election Program continues:

> Those were helped along down that slimy slope with a package of corrupt laws passed not due to public demand, but were the result of international dictates imposed on us by international conventions signed under the previous regime.
>
> Thirty years ago, Egypt joined an international convention for women called the 'Convention on the Elimination of all forms of Discrimination Against Women (CEDAW)' although this Convention controls the most private of the marital relationship details.
>
> Do any members of our great public know that Egypt is a party to the Convention on the Rights of the Child (CRC), which allows a child to choose the family to live with? Do Egyptians realise that they are obliged to accept homosexuals and treat them in the best and kindest way possible, in compliance with these agreements?? Not to mention the legalisation of adoption in ways strictly forbidden in Islamic law?! (Election Program 2011: 24)

This commentary is instructive in that it reveals one of the main hallmarks of Islamism, namely the notion that outside influences have penetrated the land of Islam and seek to undermine Islamic purity and violate the Islamic homeland. Worse still, so the Islamist argument continues, this has been facilitated by corrupt Egyptians who either have been acting as part of the *ancien régime* or, in the case of non-governmental organisations, are able to raise money from abroad in order to finance their activities. Although it is true that Mubarak was also suspicious of non-governmental organisations and introduced laws that severely restricted the ability of such groups, in particular human rights groups, to raise funds from abroad (Law on Non-Governmental Societies and Organisations, Law 84, 2002), the *ancien régime* did have some positive policies on the topic of gender equality and supported a series of initiatives that promoted the rights of women and girls. Yet, according to the Muslim Brotherhood's worldview, the very fact that the past authoritarian government supported some progressive policies means that these policies must of necessity be corrupt.

The Freedom and Justice Party has reserved particular ire for two non-governmental organisations in particular. Consider the following call for the:

> Abolition of the National Council for Women and the National Council for Childhood and Motherhood, which acted as the intelligence arm of the international players in Egypt, and replacing them with a national council for the family intent on providing a healthy climate for making good balanced families and takes into account family affairs and security. (Election Program 2011: 25)

Just to make sure that this does not go unnoticed, this passage is printed in bold type in the Election Program.

The two organisations in question have different missions. Established in 2000, the National Council for Women campaigns to advance the rights of women generally. More recently, it has been prominent in protesting the composition of the Constituent Assembly on the basis that only seven of its one hundred members are women. It has also objected to the fact that nearly half of the Constituent Assembly is in the hands of Islamist parties. This has been typical of the National Council for Women's campaigning work, which has attempted to mobilise people from all walks of life to challenge conservative views towards women. Interestingly, the Supreme Council of the Armed Forces renewed the National Council for Women's mandate by military decree in February 2012 after the publication of the Election Program.

In contrast to the National Council for Women, the National Council for Childhood and Motherhood was established by the Ministry of State for Family and Population in 1988 and has been responsible for recommending policies for the government on childhood and motherhood issues and running various educational initiatives. It has worked in collaboration with the United Nations Children's Fund, the World Health Organization and a number of French and Dutch non-governmental organisations, and was supported by Suzanne Mubarak, the wife of former President Mubarak. The mere fact that these institutions date back to the time of the *ancien régime* and were supported by Suzanne Mubarak is seen as evidence enough for Islamists of a corrupting influence, and it is extraordinary that this suspicion also extends to the United Nations Children's Fund and the World Health Organization, which are seen as acting 'as the intelligence arm of the international players'. Although unfortunate from a women's rights perspective, this is not altogether surprising; rather, it is emblematic of the Islamist penchant to distinguish between Islamic and imported solutions (see Tibi 2012: 96).

The Freedom and Justice Party sees gender equality policies in international instruments and as promoted by non-governmental organisations as imported solutions that seek to undermine Egyptian traditions. Running throughout this discourse of suspicion is the sense that not only does corruption stem from the *ancien régime* but that, by acting as a conduit for foreign infiltration, the *ancien régime* weakened the social, economic and moral fabric of the country. The association of President Mubarak with the 'foreigner' reinforces the notion that the Freedom and Justice Party is not just Egypt's leading Islamist party but also its most patriotic party. In this way, the flag and Islam become intertwined, and the defence of Islam becomes the defence of country. At the same time, this narrative rejects outside impurities and recovers Egypt from corrupting influences to secure its independence.

As far as gender equality and the family are concerned, it is clear that, despite frequent references to equality in the Election Program, this is conditioned by several policy goals, including the integration of 'traditional family values in education curricula' and the consolidation of 'the values of chastity and modesty in the media, in education curricula, and in street advertisements' (Election Program 2011: 25). In the long term, the Freedom and Justice Party has committed itself to reviewing the 1979 Convention on the Elimination of All Forms of Discrimination Against Women and the 1989 Convention on the Rights of the Child and has placed this goal within the context of developing a 'road map to achieve complete independence for the Egyptian state, in all matters pertaining to family, women and children' (Election Program 2011: 25). Once a review of these conventions has taken place, the Freedom and Justice Party promises a 'popular decision ... so that Egyptian policy, in this regard, stems from the inherent pure values of the Egyptian people, not from some international agenda' (Election Program 2011: 25).

Thus, one sees very clearly that questions of international human rights law, and especially the human rights of women, are viewed in decidedly Islamic and national terms. The slippage between 'Islamic' and 'national' is highly instructive. The nation and the people are constructed as 'pure', with international obligations only having been imposed by the corrupt and authoritarian *ancien régime*. The argument appears to be that if there had been a truly democratic system, the Egyptian people would never have accepted many aspects of treaty-based international human rights law. In order to reverse this process, the Freedom and Justice Party pledges itself to allowing the people a vote in rejecting these human rights norms. It is interesting that this is seen as a long-term goal since this suggests that there is a plan to shift public opinion away from the gender equality policies of the past. The abolition of the National Council for Women and the National Council for Childhood and Motherhood would, of course, remove important advocacy organisations for women's rights from the political arena. Once removed, this would undoubtedly make it easier to implement policies in education that would reinforce 'traditional family values', chastity and modesty. Then, once these policies had had their effect, there could be a vote on the Convention on the Elimination of All Forms of Discrimination Against Women and the Convention on the Rights of the Child.

This is revealing not merely because of what it says about the Freedom and Justice Party's views on gender issues and human rights generally but also because of what it suggests about the party's attitude to democracy. It seems that Egypt's new system can be most accurately characterised as a populist democracy. One should recall that referenda are popular ploys that authoritarian governments use when attempting to recruit popular opinion to bolster their legitimacy. In this type of 'democracy', majorities tend to be celebrated and minorities repressed, and human rights are often seen as inconvenient impediments to the will of the people. The logical end of this position is that democracy should necessarily be unfettered from restraints, thus allowing those in government to wield great power. Still, while the Election Program refers to the rule of law and shari'a, it is clear that both of these terms are used rhetorically rather than normatively. The few references to shari'a as such – the 'enlightened principles of Sharia' (10), shari'a 'as frame of reference' (10), the 'greatest objectives of sharia' (12) and the 'values of Islamic law' (Election Program 2011: 12) – indicate that a rather indeterminate character has been assigned to Islamic law. It is also evident that this indeterminacy is not to be disturbed by Islamic legal authorities outside of the government since, as the election manifesto stipulates, there are 'no infallible people who can monopolise the interpretation of the Holy Koran' (Election Program 2011: 11). While this language can be read as evidence that the Muslim Brotherhood does not seek to transform Egypt into an Arab Iran, that is, an Islamic theocracy in the Arab world, when read within the context of the election manifesto as a whole, it can take on a quite different meaning. Essentially, it can be read as giving the government the ability to declare what Islamic law is without reference to Islamic legal authorities. As the Presidential Declaration of 22 November 2012 indicates, President Morsi sees his government as outside any form of legal regulation.

Thus, in power, the Muslim Brotherhood appears to be using its popular mandate to craft a constitution that lacks many of the checks and balances just as under President Mubarak's regime. The Egyptian Social Democratic Party's Tamer al-Meehy has argued that the 'revolution didn't happen to amend the 1971 Constitution, it happened to make a new constitution and a new political system … But it's becoming clear that they want to rule with the same mechanisms with little improvements' (quoted in Afify 2012). This assessment has been reinforced by Morsi's November 2012 Declaration (Morsi 2012a) that has seen the President concentrate more powers into his hands than previously possessed by Mubarak. The Supreme Constitutional Court has become so concerned that it issued a statement attacking the draft constitution for undermining its judicial authority (see Afify 2012), and the president of the court, Maher El-Beheriri, has said that the current draft will 'threaten judiciary independence' (Egypt Court Rejects Constitutional Draft 2012).

Conclusions

The Egyptian Constituent Assembly saw battles between Islamists and secularists over the constitution and the role of shari'a and its position within the state. In the end, the Islamists prevailed, and the 2012 constitution reflected their views. However, it is evident that these remain the central issues of continuing political strife in Egypt as the Islamists begin to consolidate their new found power. As the Egyptian Constituent Assembly deals with the conflicting views of Islamists and secularists over the constitution, the role of shari'a and the position of Islamic law within the state lie at the centre of the debate. For the Islamists of the Muslim Brotherhood and the Salafi Al-Nour Party, the state is central to the implementation of Islamic law. What is at stake is how the institutions and force of the state should be used to compel adherence to Islamic law. The very idea of compulsion, however, may undermine the force of shari'a itself. As An-Na'im (2008) has argued, it is questionable whether the state can replace a Muslim's conscience with enforced adherence to its version of Islam, especially given the Quranic injunction that there can be no compulsion in religion. Once state compulsion is used, the Muslim citizen loses his or her free will to act in accordance with conscience. Thus, a constitutionally enforced Islam would actually undermine Islam's basic tenet of no compulsion in religion. Elsewhere in North Africa and the Middle East, of course, the dangers of religious compulsion are perhaps best exemplified by the Islamic Republic of Iran (see Martin 2003; Mirsepassi 2010), where state control by jurists has undermined the ability of Muslim citizens to act according to their understanding of Islam's requirements. Given that Islamic jurisprudence has many different schools and many different trends, the idea that there is a singular Islamic legal voice is highly problematic.

The Arab Spring has ushered in the elements of democracy in several North African and Middle Eastern states through the popular will of citizens no longer willing to accept authoritarian rule. The revolutions have profoundly transformed the societies in the region and have created certain conditions of pluralism that have allowed citizens to speak more freely today than they have been able to do for a generation. Although Islamists have experienced great successes at the polls, it is clear that their democratic mandates do not allow them to implement shari'a according to Qutb's simplistic formulation of half a century ago. Islamic law is now squarely discussed within the context of democracy and human rights, and as we have seen, as far as the Muslim Brotherhood is concerned, these concepts are not incompatible with Islam. It may well be that the Islamists' adherence to a populist version of democracy might prove as troubling as their view of shari'a. Indeed, the events surrounding the rushed adoption of the 2012 constitution by the Constituent Assembly and the swift calling of a referendum by President Morsi confirm these fears.

Baker (2003) argues that the suffering that Islamists underwent at the hands of President Mubarak meant that they forged a common alliance with other dissidents and developed an appreciation for human rights. The next period of the Arab Spring will reveal whether shari'a's flexibility will be an asset in the solidification of democracy in the region or, rather, a weapon for a new authoritarianism.

References

Afify, H. 2012. Principles and Precedents: Is the Draft Constitution an Evolution – Or a Revolution? *Al Masry al Yom*, 18 October. Available at: http://www.egyptindependent.com/node/1185011 [accessed: 19 October 2012].

Ajami, F. 1992. *The Arab Predicament: Arab Political Thought and Practice Since 1967*. Cambridge: Cambridge University Press.

Ajami, F. 2012. The Arab Spring at One. *Foreign Affairs*, 91(2), 56–65.

Anderson, L. 2011. Demystifying the Arab Spring. *International Affairs*, 90(3), 2–7.

An-Na'im, A.A. 2008. *Islam and the Secular State: Negotiating the Future of Shari'a.* Cambridge, MA: Harvard University Press.

Ayubi, N. 1993. *Political Islam: Religion and Politics in the Arab World.* London: Routledge.

Baker, R.W. 1978. *Egypt's Uncertain Revolution under Nasser and Sadat.* Cambridge, MA: Harvard University Press.

Baker, R.W. 2003. *Islam Without Fear: Egypt and the New Islamists.* Cambridge, MA: Harvard University Press.

Brown, N.J. 2012. *When Victory is not an Option: Islamist Movements in the Arab World.* Ithaca: Cornell University Press.

Brown, N.J. and Hamzawy, A. 2011. *Between Religion and Politics.* Washington, DC: Carnegie Endowment for International Peace.

Chase, A.T. 2012. *Human Rights, Revolution and Reform in the Muslim World.* Boulder, CO: Lynne Rienner.

Cohen, R. 2012. Shari'ah's Limits. *New York Times*, 18 October.

Coleman, I. 2012. Debate Over Egypt's Draft Constitution. Council on Foreign Relations, 18 October. Available at: http://blogs.cfr/coleman/2010/10/18/debate-over-egypts-draft-constitution/ [accessed: 19 October 2012].

Constitution of the Arab Republic of Egypt 1971. Available at: http://www.sis.gov.eg/en/LastPage.aspx?Category_ID=208 [accessed: 31 October 2012].

Constitutional Declaration 2011. Available at: http://www.sis.gov.eg/en/lastpage.aspx?category_id=1155 [accessed: 19 October 2012].

Cook, S.A. 2012. *The Struggle for Egypt: From Nasser to Tahrir Square.* Oxford: Oxford University Press.

Dabashi, H. 2012. *The Arab Spring: The End of Postcolonialism.* London: Zed Press.

Darwish, N. 2012. *The Devil We Do Not Know: The Dark Side of the Revolutions in the Middle East.* Hoboken, NJ: John Wiley & Sons.

Egypt Court Rejects Constitutional Draft Articles Spelling Out Its Powers. 2012. *Al-Ahram*, 16 October.

Egypt's Draft Constitution 2012. Available at: http://www.egypt_draft_constitution_unofficial_translation_dri_pdf [accessed: 1 November 2012].

El-Menawy, A.L. 2012. *Tahrir: The Last Days of Mubarak.* London: Gilgamesh.

Freedom and Justice Party Election Program 2011. Available at: http://www.fjponline.com/uploads/FJPprogram.pdf [accessed: 29 October 2012].

Gerber, H. 1994. *State, Society and Law in Islam: Ottoman Law in Comparative Perspective.* Albany: State University of New York Press.

Ghonim, W. 2012. *Revolution 2.0: The Power of the People is Greater than the People in Power.* London: Fourth Estate.

Ginat, R. 1993. *The Soviet Union and Egypt.* London: Frank Cass.

Goldstone, J. 2011. Understanding the Revolutions of 2011. *Foreign Affairs*, 90(2), 8–16.

Hallaq, W.B. 2009. *Shari'a: Theory, Practice, Transformations*. Cambridge: Cambridge University Press.

Hinnebusch, R.A. 1985. *Egyptian Politics under Sadat: Post-Populist Development of an Authoritarian-Modernizing State*. Cambridge: Cambridge University Press.

Law on Non-Governmental Societies and Organisations, Law 84, 2002

Lia, B. 1998. *The Society of Muslim Bothers in Egypt: The Rise of an Islamic Mass Movement 1928–1942*. Reading: Ithaca Press.

Lombardi, C.B. 2006. *State Law as Islamic Law in Modern Egypt: The Incorporation of Shari'a into Egyptian Constitutional Law*. Leiden: Brill.

Mansfield, P. 1969. *Nasser's Egypt*. Harmondsworth: Penguin.

Mansfield, P. 1971. *The British in Egypt*. London: Weidenfeld and Nicolson.

Martin, V. 2003, *Creating an Islamic State: Khomeini and the Making of the New Iran*. London: I.B. Tauris.

Mirsepassi, A. 2010. *Democracy in Iran: Islam, Culture and Political Change*. New York: New York University Press.

Mitchell, R.P. 1993. *The Society of the Muslim Brothers*. New York: Oxford University Press.

Morsi, M. 2012a. English Text of Morsi's Constitutional Declaration. *Al-Ahram*, 22 November. Available at: http://English.ahram.org.eg/News/58947.aspx [accessed: 22 November 2012].

Morsi, M. 2012b. English Text of President Morsi's New Egypt Constitutional Declaration. *Al-Ahram*, 12 August. Available at: http://english.ahram.org.eg/news/50248.aspx [accessed: 22 September 2012].

Morsi, M. 2012c. Selected Excerpts of Morsi's Speech. *New York Times*, 30 August.

National Council for Childhood and Motherhood. Available at: http://www.nccm-egypt.org [accessed: 29 October 2012].

National Council for Women Egypt. Available at: http://www.ncwegypt.com [accessed: 29 October 2012].

Pollack, K.M. 2011. *The Arab Awakening: America and the Transformation of the Middle East*. Washington, DC: Brookings Institution Press.

Prashad, V. 2012. *The Arab Spring, Libyan Winter*. Edinburgh: A.K. Press.

Qutb, S. 1991. *Milestones*. Delhi: Markazi Maktaba Islami.

Ramadan, T. 2002. *Aux sources du renouveau musulman: D'al-Alfghani à Hassan al-Banna un siècle de réformisme islamique*. Lyon: Tawhid.

Rubin, B. 1990. *Islamic Fundamentalism in Egyptian Politics*. London: Macmillan.

Soage, A.B. 2010. Yusuf Al-Qaradawi: The Muslim Brothers' Favorite Ideological Guide, in *The Muslim Brotherhood: The Organization and Politics of a Global Islamist Movement*, ed. B. Rubin. New York: Palgrave Macmillan, 19–37.

Soueif, A. 2012. *Cairo: My City, Our Revolution*. London: Bloomsbury.

Tadros, M. 2012. *The Muslim Brotherhood in Contemporary Egypt: Democracy Refined or Confined?* London: Routledge.

Tibi, B. 2012. *Islamism and Islam*. New Haven: Yale University Press.

Vatikiotis, P.J. 1969. *Modern History of Egypt*. London: Weidenfeld and Nicolson.

West, J. 2011. *Karama! Journeys Through the Arab Spring*. London: Heron Books.

Wright, R. 2011. *Rock the Casbah: Rage and Rebellion Across the Islamic World*. New York: Simon & Schuster.

Zubaida, S. 2003. *Law and Power in the Islamic World*. London: I.B. Tauris.

Afterword

A Liberal Way to War? International Law and Two Centuries of 'Benevolent Aggression'

David Turns[1]

The legality of the use of force in international law has not been thematically integrated into any of the three parts of the present volume, and its connection with any notion of liberalism may seem tenuous in the extreme. Nevertheless, the history of the last two centuries shows that liberal states, far from being inherently 'peace-loving', display a distinct tendency to engage in 'imprudent aggression' against weaker, non-liberal states, by which they feel profoundly threatened.[2] While in the past such threats were felt above all in the sense of negative effects upon liberal states' tangible imperial-commercial interests, today's threats are perceived more as being in the nature of challenges to intangible liberal values, principally democracy (see Buchan 2010). The international legal concept of 'humanitarian intervention', which the North Atlantic Treaty Organization-led intervention in the Libyan Civil War in 2011 illustrated most recently, demonstrates liberal states' use of the *jus ad bellum* ostensibly in the service of such values.

The notion of humanitarian intervention, which is often said to exist putatively as a right in customary international law (see Zifcak 2010: esp. authorities cited at 505–7), has since 1945 found itself legally circumscribed by the general prohibition in the United Nations Charter of the use of force (see art. 2(4)), except in the very limited circumstances of self-defence (see art. 51) and collective security enforcement measures authorised by the United Nations Security Council acting under Chapter VII of the Charter (see art. 42). The United Nations' adoption of a doctrine of 'responsibility to protect' in 2005 (see UNGA Res 60/1 (2005): ¶¶ 138–9) has almost certainly contributed to a notion of 'liberal [humanitarian] interventions', of which Libya may yet prove to have been the high-water mark. At the time of writing this chapter, controversies over whether or not to

---

1   The views expressed herein are entirely personal to the author and do not represent any policies or opinions held by Her Majesty's Government, the Ministry of Defence or the British Armed Forces.

2   This pattern of behaviour is not contradicted by liberal states' consistent maintenance of a special, separate 'zone of peace' among themselves (see Doyle 1997: 258–65).

intervene militarily in Syria in response to President Bashar al-Assad's systematic attacks upon parts of Syria's own civilian population illustrate the contemporary difficulties; operational constraints imposed under the *jus in bello* also need to be borne in mind.

This Afterword begins by setting out the contemporary context that lends this subject its current topicality, in terms of both a specific case study, Libya, and its reflection of certain trends in international law. Some historical comparisons with selected similar cases from the last two centuries will then be made in order to show that any liberal conundrums in respect of the use of force in international relations are nothing new. Finally, the contemporary context of the uprising in Syria and the extent to which the notion of responsibility to protect has been adopted as a norm of international law will be considered. It will be suggested that the evidence to that effect is tenuous at best and that purportedly 'humanitarian' interventions remain circumscribed by a host of extra-legal practical considerations, although the rhetoric continues to be couched in a legal form.

Liberalism and Liberal States

As Michael Doyle has written, '[t]here is no canonical description of Liberalism' (1997: 206). The concept can mean different things to different people, at different times and in different contexts. Domestically in the United Kingdom, for example, people tend to associate the term primarily with a particular moderate, centrist[3] political tradition – since 1988 in the incarnation of the Liberal Democrats – that was formed in the mid-nineteenth century and descended from the Whig Party of the late seventeenth and eighteenth centuries, has been influenced by the ideas of John Locke and Jeremy Bentham and promotes progressive social, electoral and welfare reform and the freedom of the individual from excessive interference by the state, particularly in matters of civil liberties and human rights (see Doyle 1997: 213–29). In the economic sense, the 'commercial pacifism' of Adam Smith and Joseph Schumpeter has long advocated the triumph of free trade and unrestrained mercantilism as vehicles for the creation of wealth and the discouragement of war (see Doyle 1997: 230–50). In the context of international relations and international law, Immanuel Kant's internationalism suggests a 'state of peace' between liberal states, which willingly work together for the common good and, ultimately, the good of all humanity (see Doyle 1997: 251–300).

The use of 'liberal state' herein is meant in essence to refer to 'a state that demonstrates respect for democracy, human rights and the rule of law' (Buchan

---

3 Note that in some states, the title 'liberal' is nevertheless used in the political context to denote parties that do not correspond to the essentially Western concept of liberalism herein considered: a typical example is the Liberal Democratic Party of Russia, which is led by the nationalist-populist anti-Semite Vladimir Zhirinovsky and is generally agreed to be neither liberal nor democratic.

2010: 414), one that typically, but not invariably, espouses the capitalist principles of the free market and generally seeks to respect or at least invoke international law as the basic framework for its dealings with other states. The concept is by no means necessarily restricted culturally to Western or Christian states; rather, it embraces states to be found, in varying numbers to be sure, on all continents and in every region of the world, with many different religious faiths and none in particular – although it is true that in terms of both numbers and historical tradition, this concept of liberalism finds most support in Europe and the Americas.

An important caveat should be noted, however, one that is of great importance to the topic at hand: liberal states exhibit a tendency to engage in 'imprudent aggression' against weaker, non-liberal states, by which they feel profoundly threatened. It might be said that they are internally liberal, while being externally aggressive, although they are generally not aggressive towards each other. It is noticeable that, by and large, liberal states do not go to war with other liberal states. This has not always necessarily been the case, however: one need only think of the War of 1812 between the United States and the United Kingdom, for example (see Borneman 2005). However, around the time of the so-called 'Year of Revolution' in 1848 in European societies, the distinction between liberal democracies such as the United Kingdom, Belgium and Switzerland, and despotic autocracies such as Prussia, Austria and Russia, began to become apparent, and it has become even more marked in the post-Second World War era. A discussion of the modern concept and use of humanitarian intervention and responsibility to protect will help to elucidate the place of this tendency in the international legal framework, though it is first necessary to consider the contemporary aspects of liberal interventionism.

Libya: A Case Study

The time seems curiously ripe for a consideration of the way in which liberal societies relate to war. The death of former Libyan dictator Colonel Muammar Gaddafi in October 2011, after he was taken into custody by rebel militia, heralded the end of military operations that had been conducted in the skies above Libya since March 2011 by a 'Coalition of the Willing' under the leadership of the North Atlantic Treaty Organization (NATO) (see UNSC Res 2016 (2011)).[4] Those operations, which the Security Council had authorised under Chapter VII of the UN Charter (see UNSC Res 1973 (2011)), were hailed in certain quarters as the epitome of disinterested humanitarian liberalism at work in the name of saving human lives and ridding a long-suffering people of an oppressive and unstable dictator who had ruled over them with considerable brutality for more than four

---

4 Although the Coalition was led and dominated by NATO states, it included such non-alliance partners as Jordan, Morocco, Qatar, Sweden and the United Arab Emirates.

decades.[5] The intervention in Libya was undertaken, at least if one chooses to believe the rhetoric deployed in the Security Council debates at the time of the adoption of Resolution 1973[6] and repeated subsequently by NATO (see NATO and Libya), solely in order to secure the protection of human life. That original humanitarian motivation, coupled with the restraints strongly urged by, *inter alia*, a very active human rights and non-governmental organisation community and increasingly exposed and promoted by a twenty-four hour media, had a distinct effect on the conduct of military operations (*jus in bello*) by the Coalition forces and influenced the decision to use only aerial operations (no 'boots on the ground')[7] and to have restrictive targeting directives and limited Rules of Engagement (see Laird 2011).

In its *jus ad bellum* aspects, Operation Unified Protector – as the combination of naval interdiction operations in application of the arms embargo, no-fly zone enforcement and air strikes to protect Libyan civilians from attack by Colonel Gaddafi's forces was codenamed – clearly benefited from a relatively high level of international consensus[8] and perceived international legality and legitimacy that similar NATO operations directed unilaterally against the then-Federal Republic of Yugoslavia in 1999 lacked – notwithstanding increasing criticism by some states, which accused the alliance of exceeding its mandate in the prosecution of some aspects of the operation (see UNSC (2011) UN Doc S/PV.6528: 9 (Russia); UNSC (2011) UN Doc S/PV.6566: 4 (South Africa); UNSC (2011) UN Doc S/PV.6595: 4–5 (South Africa); UNSC (2011) UN Doc S/PV.6620: 3 (Russia)). Some commentators, predictably perhaps, have hailed the Libyan case as the first example of a truly *humanitarian* intervention (see Western and Goldstein 2011); others, perhaps more significantly, have suggested that it is the first actual illustration of responsibility to protect in practice since the United Nations adopted that much-lauded doctrine in 2005 (see Axworthy and Rock 2011; Ban 2012).

If we consider the rationale that was advanced diplomatically for the intervention in Libya in light of the express language of Resolution 1973,[9] then Libya seems to

---

5   Such coverage in the *Guardian* (24 March 2011), *Toronto Star* (25 March 2011) and *Los Angeles Times* (28 September 2011) was typical.

6   Although the ambassadors of the ten states that voted in favour of Resolution 1973 did not expressly cite responsibility to protect as such in their statements following the Security Council vote, the tenor of the language used clearly indicated that it was essentially what they had in mind (see UNSC (2011) UN Doc S/PV.6498).

7   The use of force was authorised, 'while excluding a foreign occupation force of any form on any part of Libyan territory' (UNSC Res 1973 (2011): ¶ 4).

8   Nevertheless, it should be remembered that Resolution 1973 was adopted over the abstaining votes of five states (Brazil, China, Germany, India and Russia). The consensus – such as it was – that enabled the two permanent members on this list to abstain in respect of Libya was to evaporate when the Security Council found itself confronted with the situation in Syria in late 2011 and early 2012.

9   The protection of the Libyan civilian population is a leitmotiv that recurs through much of the text of Resolution 1973, especially operative paragraphs one through eight.

represent a clear case of humanitarianism in action, accepted as such by much of the international community – and, thus, possibly a case of a genuine humanitarian intervention carried out in accordance with the responsibility to protect doctrine. Some have even seen the Libyan case as a vindication for British Prime Minister Tony Blair's famous speech to the Chicago Economic Club in 1999, in which he proclaimed the virtues of liberal interventionism in order to protect the human rights of populations oppressed by their own governments (see Blair 1999).

The fact that Resolution 1973 was adopted over the abstentions of five members of the Security Council, however, including two of its permanent members, should serve as a warning that the notion of responsibility to protect is by no means universally accepted. Although certain states in General Assembly debates have spoken out against the acceptance of responsibility to protect as a doctrine of international law, these states are not exactly established members of the community of liberal states (see UNGA (2009) UN Doc A/63/PV.105: 3 (Venezuela), 4 (Cuba), 5–6 (Sudan), 6 (Iran), 7 (Nicaragua)). Furthermore, the fact that such states as Brazil, Germany and India refused to vote in favour of Resolution 1973 clearly demonstrates that the jealous guarding of national sovereignty remains a powerful cornerstone of international law for many states, including those that in many other respects conform to liberal ideas. In particular, Germany's abstention illustrates the fact that not even all NATO states were initially persuaded that military intervention was the correct response to the Libyan situation.

Humanitarian Intervention in International Law: Some Nineteenth-Century Precedents

It is instructive to recall that there is nothing very new about the notion of humanitarian intervention as such. From at least the early nineteenth century, it was generally accepted that those states that had interests to protect elsewhere, and the capability with which to protect them, were unrestrained by any legal considerations in so doing. One of the earliest acknowledged examples of humanitarian intervention is said to have been the Anglo-Franco-Russian intervention in the Greek War of Independence (1821–32), which led to the conclusive defeat of the Turco-Egyptian forces and the creation of the independent Kingdom of the Hellenes.

In 1827, alarmed by reports of massacres committed by Ottoman troops in Greece almost as much as by increasing dangers to maritime commerce in the Eastern Mediterranean Sea, and under increasing popular pressure to save a gallant Christian people fighting for liberation against a corrupt and cruel Muslim tyranny, the British, French and Russian governments concluded the Treaty of

London.[10] According to this treaty, they proposed a mediated settlement to the Sultan which would peacefully resolve the disputes between him and his Greek subjects. After proposing that Greece become a tribute-paying dependency of the Ottoman Empire, the treaty stated:

> If, within the said term of one month, the Porte [the Imperial Ottoman Government] does not accept the Armistice proposed in Article I of the patent Treaty, or if the Greeks refuse to carry it into execution, the High Contracting Powers shall declare to either of the Contending Parties which may be disposed to continue hostilities, or to both of them, if necessary, that the said High Powers intend to exert all the means which circumstances may suggest to their prudence, for the purpose of obtaining the immediate effects of the Armistice of which they desire the execution, by preventing, as far as possible, all collision between the Contending Parties; and in consequence, immediately after the above-mentioned declaration, the High Powers will, jointly, exert all their efforts to accomplish the object of such Armistice, without, however, taking any part in the hostilities between the Two Contending Parties. Immediately after the signature of the present Additional Article, the High Contracting Powers will, consequently, transmit to the Admirals commanding their respective squadrons in the Levant, conditional Instructions in conformity to the arrangements above declared.

Although the disclaimer of any intention of 'taking any part in the hostilities' gives the impression that the Allied Powers were not contemplating armed intervention in the conflict, the language actually referred only to involvement in the hostilities 'between the Two Contending Parties', that is, between the Turks and the Greeks. Since the Allied Powers had in fact already resolved to intervene on the side of the Greeks, as well as predetermined the outcome of the proposed mediation, the Ottoman rejection thereof did not in any way preclude the legitimacy of an Allied naval confrontation with the Ottoman fleet. On the contrary, such rejection, coupled with the envisaged Greek acceptance of an armistice, all but guaranteed armed intervention: this was the real meaning of the last sentence in the text just quoted. When the Commander-in-Chief of the British Mediterranean Fleet, Admiral Sir Edward Codrington, sailed into Navarino Bay on 20 October 1827 to coerce the Turco-Egyptian fleet at anchor to comply with the Allies' policy, the consequent battle – the last major fleet engagement fought wholly under sail – led to the complete destruction of the Turco-Egyptian fleet. This deprived the Sultan of command of the sea and, with it, maritime supply routes to his armies fighting in Greece. By 1832, the Greeks had their independent kingdom, complete with an imported German king (Otto, of the Bavarian Wittelsbach dynasty), under the protection of the Great Powers.

---

10   Treaty Between Great Britain, France, and Russia, for the Pacification of Greece, London, 6 July 1827 (hereafter Treaty of London).

From among several other examples of humanitarian intervention during the 'Age of Empire' in the nineteenth century, two further instances may be selected for consideration here: the cases of Egypt and Cuba. In 1882, British forces intervened in Egypt, which was nominally a province of the Ottoman Empire at the time but actually independent in all but name, after rioting in Alexandria had caused the deaths of a number of nationals of various European states. Western representations of the unrest at the time emphasised the brutality and slaughter that the mutinous Egyptian Army of Colonel Ahmed Arabi Pasha had perpetrated (see The Ruined Egyptian City 1882) and which had claimed up to 2,000 European deaths. These same Western accounts, however, omitted to explain that Arabi Pasha was in fact attempting to overthrow the government of the Khedive Tewfik, who was popularly seen as being excessively compliant with the Anglo-French Condominium over the Suez Canal Zone. After the 1869 opening of the Canal, British shareholders had acquired a majority stake in the Canal by buying out the Egyptian share of bonds in response to Egypt's failure to repay the loans that Tewfik's predecessor, the Khedive Ismail (1863–79), had incurred in his attempts to modernise the country and in his unsuccessful 1875 war with Emperor Yohannes IV of Ethiopia. The Caisse de la Dette Publique (Commission of Public Debt) had been established by Ismail in 1876 in order to regulate the Egyptian government's repayment of its debts to the United Kingdom and France, which states effectively used the Commission to control Egyptian public policy.

Context aside and notwithstanding the inconvenient fact that Arabi Pasha had actually ordered his troops to suppress the riots in Alexandria, the Western rhetoric of the day bears a striking resemblance to what we hear in the twenty-first century with regard to dictatorships:

> By this last outrage [the massacre in Alexandria] Arabi Pasha has put himself outside the pale of humanity. He must be followed and his army dispersed. It is satisfactory to know that the British preparations are complete, and that we are ready to carry out the will of Europe if no other nation can be found to do the work. Should the Porte still hold back, Lord Dufferin [the British Commissioner to Egypt] will state in the conference that England is prepared to undertake the task, but will welcome the co-operation of any other Government. (The Ruined Egyptian City 1882)

Egypt was subsequently to be ruled indirectly by the United Kingdom, initially as the so-called 'veiled protectorate' and after 1914 as a nominally independent kingdom, until 1952. The presence in Egypt of the Suez Canal and its strategic importance to the security of the British Empire exposed the professed concern to protect human life as little more than a facade in this case.

In 1898, the United States declared war on Spain, partly out of sympathy for the rebels in Cuba, who were fighting for their independence and had been the victims of the first examples of what were later to be termed 'concentration camps',[11] and partly in response to the mysterious destruction of the *USS Maine*, which had previously been sent to Havana Harbour to provide a show of force in order to deter harassment of American and other foreign nationals, particularly journalists, by the Spanish authorities in Cuba (see Traxel 1999: 92–106).[12] Controversy continues to this day as to the exact cause of the explosion that sank the *Maine*: the initial United States Naval Court of Inquiry blamed a submarine mine, without being able to determine who had been responsible for it (see Official Report of the Naval Court (Sampson Board Report)), but more recent investigations, with the benefit of modern technology, have thrown considerable doubt on this conclusion.[13] A little over two months before the sinking of the *Maine*, United States President William McKinley had dismissed the growing clamour for a military 'humanitarian' intervention to protect the Cuban population from Spanish repression, in light of conciliatory moves by a new government in Spain. He did so in the following terms:

> Not a single American citizen is now in arrest or confinement in Cuba of whom this Government has any knowledge. The near future will demonstrate whether the indispensable condition of a righteous peace, just alike to the Cubans and to Spain as well as equitable to all our interests so intimately involved in the welfare of Cuba, is likely to be attained. If not, the exigency of further and other action by the United States will remain to be taken ... If it shall hereafter appear to be a duty imposed by our obligations to ourselves, to civilization and humanity to intervene with force, it shall be without fault on our part and *only because the necessity for such action will be so clear as to command the support and approval of the civilized world*. (McKinley 1897: 6263; emphasis added)

Although the American intervention was clearly not entirely altruistic, and the geographical location of Cuba a mere 90 miles south of Florida undoubtedly played a part in the United States' interest in the island in light of the Monroe Doctrine, it is noteworthy that the United States Congress, in voting to declare war

---

11 The policy of so-called *reconcentración* (literally meaning the 're-concentration' of civilians away from their villages into camps 'protected' by Spanish troops) was invented by the Spanish Captain-General of Cuba, General Valeriano Weyler y Nicolau, in 1896 as a way of segregating Cuban insurgents and civilians in order to make it harder for the former to operate. Although the policy was substantively successful within these parameters and helped to achieve Spain's military objectives vis-à-vis the insurgents for a time, Weyler's failure to provide adequately for the 'reconcentrated' Cuban civilians' needs led to the deaths of thousands from disease and starvation, which in turn backfired politically by arousing American liberal opposition to Spain's policy.

12 For contemporary criticism of the *reconcentración* policy from the American perspective, see McKinley 1897: 6255–6.

13 For a summary of the various reports and investigations, see Fisher 2009.

on Spain, passed the Teller Amendment (see Joint Resolution for the Recognition of the Independence of the People of Cuba 1898):

> Resolved ... That the United States hereby disclaims any disposition or intention to exercise sovereignty, jurisdiction or control over said Island except for the pacification thereof, and asserts its determination, when that is accomplished, to leave the government and control of the Island to its people.

This language contains advance shades of the terms of Resolution 1973 in that the latter explicitly rejects the possibility of 'any foreign occupation force on Libyan territory'. Democratic Senator Henry M. Teller apparently proposed the amendment because of congressional fears that the increasingly expansionist Republican administration of President McKinley – which had refrained from formally recognising a state of belligerency in Cuba – was preparing the outright annexation of the island (as was actually being done at the same time in respect of the Republic of Hawai'i). It is equally clear that Spanish Captain-General of Cuba General Valeriano Weyler y Nicolau's policy of *reconcentración*, although reversed by his successor, Brigadier Ramón Blanco y Erenas, was sufficiently brutal to have earned him the sobriquet 'The Butcher' and was the main public impulse justifying the United States' intervention in Cuba.[14] The fact that the so-called 'yellow journalism' of the *New York World* and *New York Journal* deliberately fanned American popular indignation against the Spanish atrocities, although initially peculiar to the place and time, also pointed the way to the pressures that liberal governments face from modern mass media coverage of atrocities abroad.

(British) Liberalism and Humanitarian Intervention

Perhaps the most interesting reaction to a situation of internal atrocities for the purposes of this Afterword and the most revealing in terms of positing a theoretical rationale for armed 'humanitarian' intervention in the nineteenth century occurred in a case in which, for all the international condemnation, no actual military action took place: the so-called 'Bulgarian Atrocities' of 1876. These occurred in the context of the April Uprising of that year, in which Bulgarian insurgents, seeing the success that their South Slav brothers in Serbia and Montenegro had already achieved, rebelled against Ottoman rule. In suppressing the Uprising, Ottoman irregular troops – the infamous *Bashi-bazouks* – committed atrocities against the Bulgarian civilian population on such a scale that when reports of what was going on reached Western Europe and the United States (see MacGahan 1876),[15] they

---

14   See n. 11 above.

15   Some 5,000 Bulgarians, many of them women and children, were massacred by Ottoman irregulars at the south Bulgarian town of Batak, an atrocity that acquired particular notoriety at the time.

caused a huge popular outcry and the complete evaporation of support for the Ottoman Empire, on whose behalf the United Kingdom had gone to war against Russia in the Crimea just two decades earlier. As a result, when another Russo-Turkish War ensued in 1877, Turkish appeals for British help fell on deaf ears in London, leading to Turkey's military defeat and the eventual recognition of Bulgarian independence, as well as the Austro-Hungarian pre-emptive occupation of Bosnia and Herzegovina.

One of the most influential reactions to the reports of the Bulgarian Atrocities was a famous pamphlet published in 1876 by William Ewart Gladstone, then Leader of the Opposition and head of the British Liberal Party. Although it was largely a political tract aimed at lambasting his Tory opponents – then in government under Benjamin Disraeli – for their anaemic reaction to the crisis, in it Gladstone laid out his view of what the United Kingdom should do:

> My hope ... is twofold. First, that ... [the British government] may be led to declare distinctly, that it is for purposes of humanity alone that we have a fleet in Turkish waters. Secondly, that that fleet will be so distributed as to enable that force to be most promptly and efficiently applied, in case of need, on Turkish soil, in concert with the other Powers, for the defence of innocent lives. (Gladstone 1876: 43)

He then set out in the pamphlet what ought to be the 'three great objects' of British policy in respect of the crisis in Bulgaria:

> 1.) To put a stop to the anarchical misrule ... the plundering, the murdering, which ... still desolate Bulgaria
> 2.) To make effectual provision against the recurrence of the outrages recently perpetrated under the sanction of the Ottoman Government, by excluding its administrative action for the future ... from Bulgaria
> 3.) To redeem by these measures the honour of the British name. (Gladstone 1876: 49–50)

He went on to consider whether there ought to be a fourth aim, namely, 'the maintenance of the "territorial integrity of Turkey"'. Gladstone was careful to distinguish Turkey's 'integrity' from her 'independence', reviving a phrase which had been used to justify British intervention in the Crimean War: integrity he described as 'territorial integrity', and by independence, he meant the 'actual, daily and free administration of all the provinces of [Turkey's] vast domain' (1876: 50–51). He concluded that the 'integrity of Turkey' should be preserved but that this was not to mean 'immunity for her unbounded savagery, her unbridled and bestial lust' (Gladstone 1876: 53). It is interesting to note the parallels between the language used by Gladstone in the 1870s and that contained in article 2(4) of the UN Charter, nearly seventy years later, with its prohibition of the threat or use of force against the 'territorial integrity or political independence of any state'.

For all the overheated rhetoric, neither the United Kingdom nor any of the other, equally outraged, Western powers actually intervened by force in response to the Bulgarian Atrocities. It was left to Russia – then, as now, hardly a standard bearer for freedom and the values of enlightened liberalism – to declare war on the Ottoman Empire in 1877; through their victories at Plevna and the Shipka Pass, as well as at Beyazit and Kars in the Caucasus, the Russians forced the Turks to grant the Bulgarians autonomy at the Treaty of San Stefano, and subsequently full independence at the Congress of Berlin in 1878.

Three years after the publication of his famous pamphlet on the Bulgarian Atrocities, Gladstone, seeking re-election to parliament in a Scottish seat, developed a more comprehensive view of how British foreign policy should be conducted, in the form of his six 'right principles' of foreign policy. They were that the aims of British foreign policy should be:

1.) 'to foster the strength of the Empire by just legislation and economy at home ... and to reserve the strength of the Empire, to reserve the expenditure of that strength, for great and worthy occasions abroad.'

2) 'to preserve to the nations of the world and especially ... to the Christian nations of the world – the blessings of peace.'

3) '[t]o strive to cultivate and maintain ... what is called the Concert of Europe; to keep the powers of Europe in union together.'

4) 'to avoid needless and entangling engagements', such as unnecessary annexations of territory which would overstretch the military and human resources of the Empire without adding to British strength.

5) 'to acknowledge the equal rights of all nations'.

6) 'the foreign policy of England should always be inspired by the love of freedom'.
(Biagini 2004: 9 (citing Gladstone's Third Midlothian Speech, 27 November 1879))

It is worth noting that these 'right principles' were rather limited in scope, particularly as regards the other nations that might benefit from their application. They applied to Christian nations and non-Christian nations with stable governments with which the United Kingdom could make formal treaties which would be honoured, such as the Emperors of China and Japan, the Emir of Afghanistan and the King of Zululand. They did not apply to countries that had 'long forfeited' their independence and were thus no longer considered 'nations'[16]

---

16 An example in the mindset of the day would have been Egypt, which in 1879 had been an autonomous tributary vassal state of the Ottoman Empire since 1805 and before that a province of the same Empire since 1517. Sir Robert Phillimore in the High Court of Admiralty recognised as much, denying the Khedive of Egypt a claim to sovereign immunity in respect of a maritime collision involving an Egyptian government ship (see *The Charkieh* [1873] 4 A. & E. 59: 75–86). The last independent Egyptian state prior to Ottoman rule had been the Mamluk Sultanate (1250–1517).

and regions within which there was no established or recognised government, where 'anarchy' reigned.

It is tempting to think that this description, which is tantamount to what we would today call a 'failed state', would apply perfectly to Somalia since the overthrow of General Mohamed Siad Barre in 1991. On that basis, out would go any notion of a 'right' foreign policy in respect of Somalia. Yet the international community has continued to persist in attempting to improve the situation in that state, from the disastrous interventions ordered by the Security Council in the early 1990s[17] to the rather more successful operations to combat piracy off the Somali coast since 2008 (see UNSC Res 1816 (2008)). The latter, it should be noted, were undertaken with the consent of the Transitional Federal Government of Somalia – a factor that may account for their comparative success.

Despite the very Euro- and Christian-centric conception of Gladstone's approach to foreign policy in general, when it came to what we would now call human rights, he was altogether more universalist in his perspective. In another of his Scottish election campaign speeches, he said:

> Remember the rights of the savage, as we call him. Remember that the happiness of his humble house, remember that the sanctity of life in the hill villages of Afghanistan among the winter snows, is as inviolable in the eye of Almighty God as can be your own. Remember that He who has united you together as human beings in the same flesh and blood, has bound you by the laws of mutual love; that that mutual love is not limited by the shores of this island, it is not limited by the boundaries of Christian civilisation; that it passes over the whole surface of the earth, and embraces the meanest along with the greatest in its unmeasured scope. (Biagini 2004: 8 (citing Gladstone's Second Midlothian Speech, 26 November 1879))

The reference to Afghanistan might be thought of as remarkably prescient for 1879, until we recall that by then the United Kingdom had already fought one

---

17 There were two United Nations Operations in Somalia (UNOSOM I and II), separated by a Unified Task Force (UNITAF) under American command. The first of these, a limited peace-keeping operation authorised by Security Council Resolution 751 (1992), was wound down when it became apparent that more robust military force would need to be deployed to secure the situation in Somalia; the more aggressive UNITAF, which was sanctioned by the Council to replace UNOSOM I on 3 December 1992 (see UNSC Res 794 (1992)), was a comparative success and was notable both for being the first time that the Security Council used its Chapter VII powers to assure the provision of humanitarian assistance and for representing the high-water mark of American engagement with the concept of 'state-building' – something that was to be explicitly disavowed by the next Administration to occupy the White House (see Turns 2009: 387–88). Security Council Resolution 814 (1993) gave UNOSOM II a hopelessly broad mandate, and UNOSOM II collapsed after coming under sustained attack from Somali militias, particularly those loyal to the Mogadishu warlord Mohamed Farrah Aidid.

(unsuccessful) Anglo-Afghan War (1839–42) and was at that very time engaged in fighting a second one (1878–80). Moreover, every British government that had held office since 1843 had sent at least one military expedition overseas. It was the 'Age of Empire' and intervention was an integral part of the imperial arsenal. Speaking in the House of Lords during a debate in which forcible intervention in the American Civil War was proposed, the Foreign Secretary, Earl Russell, put it thus:

> If we have taken part in interventions, it has been in [sic] behalf of the independence, freedom, and welfare of a great portion of mankind. I should be sorry, indeed, if there should be any intervention on the part of this country which could bear another character, I trust that this will not be the case ... but that when we feel ourselves bound to interfere ... it will be an interference in the cause of liberty and to promote the freedom of mankind, as we have hitherto done in these cases. (*Hansard* HL Debs, 23 March 1863, vol. 169, c. 1740)

Humanitarian Intervention and Chapter VII of the United Nations Charter: 'Liberal Enforcement Action'?

In the context of the protection of national interests, humanitarian intervention has long been considered permissible in order to protect a state's own citizens from danger abroad. One may recall the Belgian operation at Stanleyville in 1964 (see Odom 1988) or the Israeli raid on Entebbe in 1976 (see UNSC (1976) UN Doc S/PV.1941: 8 (United States)). Occasionally, it is true, armed interventions may be sanctioned by either the invitation of the target state or the United Nations,[18] without formal adoption of a resolution to that effect.[19] On the other hand, there is clearly a general principle of non-intervention in customary international law, in the sense that states – whether acting individually or in concert – are prohibited from intervening in the affairs of other states without their consent (see UNGA Res 2131 (1965)).[20] Moreover, the notion of intervening abroad to protect *foreign*

---

18 Thus, the 2011 Saudi military intervention in Bahrain was entirely consistent with international law because it was undertaken at the express request of the Bahraini government (see Bronner and Slackman 2011).

19 In 2011, for example, France used its military forces already stationed in Côte d'Ivoire under a bilateral defence agreement to intervene directly for the protection of civilians in the civil war between the forces of displaced former President Laurent Gbagbo and his elected successor Alassane Dramane Ouattara. This had the effect of defeating the former and taking him into custody for eventual trial by the International Criminal Court (see Côte d'Ivoire, Letter from Sarkozy 2011).

20 Although the terms of the resolution strongly reflect the then-prevalent context of decolonisation and anti-imperialism in international relations, the fact that it was adopted with 109 votes in favour and none against, with only one abstention, supports its status as

nationals has been much more dubious since 1945, as the general prohibition of the use of force under the UN Charter admits of only two exceptions: self-defence and collective security enforcement operations authorised by the Security Council acting under Chapter VII. It is worth recalling that the British Foreign and Commonwealth Office was content as late as 1986 to publicise its formal opinion that there was no such thing as a *right* of humanitarian intervention in international law (see Roberts 2000: 14). NATO's unilateral intervention in the Kosovo War in 1999, far from unequivocally crystallising a 'right' to humanitarian intervention in international law, merely served to emphasise the philosophical and doctrinal gulf between liberal states, which broadly advocate such interventions, and others, which are highly suspicious of them.

Among other things, the UN Charter preserves for the Security Council the right to order military enforcement actions in article 42. The Cold War, which effectively crippled the Council's work in the sphere of international peace and security, was bracketed by two uses of this power in situations in which there was a clear case of inter-state transgression: the North Korean invasion of South Korea in 1950 and the Iraqi invasion and annexation of Kuwait in 1990. The wording of the UN Charter, however, while enshrining the principle of non-intervention in internal affairs, has always made it clear that Chapter VII can override state sovereignty in this respect:

> Nothing contained in the present Charter shall authorize the United Nations to intervene in matters which are essentially within the domestic jurisdiction of any state or shall require the members to submit such matters to settlement under the present Charter; but this principle shall not prejudice the application of enforcement measures under Chapter VII. (art. 2(7))

What is particularly interesting for purposes of the present analysis is the way in which the evolving practice of the Council over the last twenty years has coincided with the rise of humanitarian motives as a trigger for enforcement action. One may consider the following examples, all precedents, despite often being disclaimed as such by the Council itself, which occurred prior to the operation in Libya:

1. In Somalia, the Unified Task Force was authorised to use 'all necessary means' to secure humanitarian assistance operations (see UNSC Res 794 (1992); see also n. 17 above).
2. In Bosnia and Herzegovina, the United Nations Protection Force was allowed to use force in self-defence to protect United Nations 'safe areas' and humanitarian aid convoys (see UNSC Res 836 (1993)).

---

declaratory of a norm of customary international law (see also UNGA Res 2625 (1970); *Military and Paramilitary Activities in and Against Nicaragua (Nicaragua* v. *United States)* [1986] ICJ Rep 14: 106–108; *Armed Activities on the Territory of the Congo (Democratic Republic of the Congo* v. *Uganda)* [2005] ICJ Rep 168: 226–7).

3. In Sierra Leone, the United Nations Mission in Sierra Leone was set up to protect civilians and assist in the full implementation of the peace agreement that had ended the civil war (see UNSC Res 1270 (1999)).
4. In Liberia, a temporary multinational force was created to stabilise the post-conflict situation and prepare the ground for a full-scale peace-keeping force, which was deployed later in 2003 (see UNSC Res 1497 (2003)).
5. In Sudan, a hybrid United Nations/African Union force was created to support the African Union force already deployed in the Darfur region to deter violence and protect civilians against the Janjaweed militia (see UNSC Res 1769 (2007); see also Barnidge 2009).

Viewed in light of this trajectory and the fact that it is the first operation of its kind since the adoption of responsibility to protect as doctrine, Operation Unified Protector against the Gaddafi regime in Libya seems to represent a clear and natural progression. The big question that remains is: why intervene only in certain states and not in others? One can think of various states that are notorious for their brutality towards large sections of their own populations but in respect of which one hears no call for liberal intervention: Belarus, Zimbabwe, Burma (Myanmar), North Korea, for example, and there are, of course, many others. China's policies in Tibet and Russia's in Chechnya are equally contentious. How are liberal states to choose? Should all transgressor states be subject to interventions? Or, because we cannot do something about all of them, should we do nothing about any of them?

Back to the Future: The Case of Syria

The situation in Syria poses the main controversy for liberal interventionism at the time of writing. The Assad regime is no less brutal – indeed, it is arguably more so – than the Gaddafi regime was in Libya, yet the pro-sovereignty, anti-intervention movement has reasserted itself with a vengeance in the wake of the NATO-led intervention in Libya. With operations in Libya winding down but not yet quite concluded, a draft resolution on Syria (proposed by France, Germany, Portugal and the United Kingdom) (see UNSC Draft Resolution (2011)) was vetoed by China and Russia.[21] Although the draft made no reference to any military intervention in Syria, it did refer to the possibility of considering economic sanctions under article 41 of the UN Charter in the event of Syrian non-compliance (see ¶ 11). As the British Ambassador stated in the debate following the veto, 'The text we voted on today contained nothing that any member of this Council should have felt the need to oppose. Yet two members chose to veto' (UNSC (2011) UN Doc S/PV.6627: 7). The American Ambassador went further in her disavowals that Syria represented a

---

21 Four other members of the Council abstained in the vote (Brazil, India, Lebanon and South Africa).

repeat of Libya: 'Others [on the Council] claim that strong Security Council action on Syria would merely be a pretext for military intervention. Let there be no doubt: this is not about military intervention; this is not about Libya' (UNSC (2011) UN Doc S/PV.6627: 8). But the Libya precedent undeniably cast a long shadow over the Council's deliberations, and those states that are perennially suspicious of the West had ample opportunity to state their concerns. Thus, the South African Ambassador explained his state's abstention from the vote as follows:

> We believe that [the reference to economic sanctions was] designed as a prelude to further actions. We are concerned that this draft resolution not be part of a hidden agenda aimed at once again instituting regime change, which has been an objective clearly stated by some. We are thus concerned about the fact that the sponsors of this draft resolution rejected language that clearly excluded the possibility of military intervention. (UNSC (2011) UN Doc S/PV.6627: 11)

Russia, as expected, went the furthest in drawing a parallel between the Libyan and Syrian scenarios and in expressing unhappiness with the very idea of military intervention in such circumstances:

> Our proposals for wording on the non-acceptability of foreign military intervention were not taken into account, and based on the well-known events in North Africa, that can only put us on our guard ... The situation in Syria cannot be considered in the Council separately from the Libyan experience. The international community is alarmed by statements that *compliance with Security Council resolutions on Libya in the NATO interpretation is a model for the future actions of NATO in implementing the responsibility to protect.* It is easy to see that today's 'Unified Protector' model could happen in Syria ... For us, Members of the United Nations, including in terms of a precedent, it is very important to know how the resolution [on Libya] was implemented and how a Security Council resolution turned into its opposite. The demand for a quick ceasefire turned into a full-fledged civil war, the humanitarian, social, economic and military consequences of which transcend Libyan borders. The situation in connection with the no-fly zone has morphed into the bombing of oil refineries, television stations and other civilian sites. The arms embargo has morphed into a naval blockade in western Libya, including a blockade of humanitarian goods ... These types of models should be excluded from global practices once and for all. (UNSC (2011) UN Doc S/PV.6627: 4; emphasis added)

Syria, in an entirely predictable broadside against the West, nevertheless made the not ineffective accusation of hypocrisy that underlies much of the unease about a policy of liberal interventionism:

> Certain Council members have tried of late to intervene in our domestic affairs under the pretext of the protection of civilians. We only wonder here where they

have been and why they have not protected civilians in Palestine, the occupied Syrian Golan, Southern Lebanon, Iraq, Afghanistan and Libya, when the citizens of those countries were beleaguered by crimes against humanity and war crimes … Through such conduct, they undermine international legitimacy and seek to lead the entire world into a new colonial era and military adventures in various places that are bound and doomed to fail. Those very states led the whole world into two world wars that claimed millions of lives on our planet. With their colonial behaviour, their enslavement and their attitude, they caused the untold suffering of hundreds of millions in Asia, Africa and Latin America. (UNSC (2011) UN Doc S/PV.6627: 13–14)

A further draft resolution tabled four months later by a broader cross-section of states including notably several Arab states was, if anything, even more unexceptionable but was again vetoed by China and Russia, this time without any abstentions (see UNSC Draft Resolution (2012)). The Council debates surrounding that vote (see UNSC (2012) UN Doc S/PV.6710; UNSC (2012) UN Doc S/PV.6711), however, do not reveal any further insights as to the position of humanitarian intervention or the responsibility to protect doctrine in international law.

The general flavour of the objections to authorising action against Syria, however, is clear enough: the NATO-led action in Libya has scared off those states that are chronically nervous or suspicious of Western motives, thereby confirming the view that liberal interventionism remains a fundamentally Western, liberal democratic concept. States with more authoritarian tendencies, principally Russia and China, have been very explicit in their invocation of state sovereignty as an absolute principle of international law. What is perhaps more interesting is the fact that democracies from the developing world – Brazil, India and South Africa – have been equally wary of the rush to intervene. The resulting spectacle is an unedifying one, and it is difficult to take entirely seriously, for example, Russian protestations that the violence in Syria is unacceptable and must cease, while Russia simultaneously prevents the adoption of resolutions that are framed far more in terms of Chapter VI than Chapter VII.

Where, then, does this leave the notions of liberal interventionism and responsibility to protect? It might be said that Libya was an 'easy target' compared to Syria: just across the Mediterranean from Europe and with European Union members Malta, Italy and France fearing a flood of refugees from the conflict, with state armed forces of dubious proficiency (although that assumption was to some extent undermined by eight months of ferocious resistance to the rebels and NATO) and last, but probably not least, with oil. But the Libyan oil reserves are actually among the smallest in the region in relative terms, and Syria also is 'just across the Mediterranean' (albeit a different part of it). What probably makes the real difference is the fact that the Syrian armed forces are much more powerful and professional than their Libyan counterparts, as has been amply demonstrated, and that Syria – unlike Libya – is not a vast isolated desert state. It is relatively small, and its neighbours include Turkey, Iran, Iraq, Israel and Lebanon – a volatile position indeed! The consequences of a military intervention in Syria would likely not be as neatly self-contained as in Libya. Thus, we seem to return, inexorably, to a fundamentally self-serving doctrine: states that believe in intervention will intervene, but only when it suits their own national strategic interests. The brave new dawn of unilateral interventions, irrespective of world opinion and United Nations approval, is already – a mere thirteen years after NATO's apparent success in Kosovo – becoming but a memory.

At this juncture, it is pertinent to recall some of Prime Minister Blair's words from his 1999 Chicago speech, flush with the confidence of the Kosovo operation. In setting out his vision of liberal interventionism, this is what he had to say about the criteria to be applied in deciding whether or not to intervene:

> This [NATO's Kosovo campaign] is a just war, based not on territorial ambitions but on values ... We cannot turn our backs on conflicts and the violation of human rights within other countries if we want still to be secure ... No longer is our existence as states under threat. Now our actions are guided by a more subtle blend of mutual self-interest and moral purpose in defending the values we cherish. In the end values and interests merge. If we can establish and spread the values of liberty, the rule of law, human rights and an open society then that is in our national interests too. The spread of our values makes us safer ... The most pressing foreign policy problem we face is to identify the circumstances in which we should get actively involved in other people's conflicts. Non-interference has long been considered an important principle of international order. And it is not one we would want to jettison too readily. One state should not feel it has the right to change the political system of another or foment subversion or seize pieces of territory to which it feels it should have some claim. But the principle of non-interference must be qualified in important respects. Acts of genocide can never be a purely internal matter. When oppression produces massive flows of refugees which unsettle neighbouring countries then they can properly be described as 'threats to international peace and security'. When regimes are based on minority rule they lose legitimacy – look at South Africa.
>
> Looking around the world there are many regimes that are undemocratic and engaged in barbarous acts. If we wanted to right every wrong that we see in the modern world then we would do little else than intervene in the affairs of other countries. We would not be able to cope. So how do we decide when and whether to intervene? I think we need to bear in mind five major considerations. First, are we sure of our case? War is an imperfect instrument for righting humanitarian distress; but armed force is sometimes the only means of dealing with dictators. Second, have we exhausted all diplomatic options? We should always give peace every chance, as we have in the case of Kosovo. Third, on the basis of a practical assessment of the situation, are there military operations we can sensibly and prudently undertake? Fourth, are we prepared for the long term? In the past we talked too much of exit strategies. But having made a commitment we cannot simply walk away once the fight is over; better to stay with moderate numbers of

troops than return for repeat performances with large numbers. And finally, do we have national interests involved? The mass expulsion of ethnic Albanians from Kosovo demanded the notice of the rest of the world. But it does make a difference that this is taking place in such a combustible part of Europe. (Blair 1999)

Of his five criteria, it is perhaps Blair's second criterion – the need to exhaust all available diplomatic options – that is becoming the most significant in the multi-polar world of the second decade of the twenty-first century. The reality now is that no state can afford to fight unilaterally unless it is clearly acting either in self-defence or in execution of a very specific mandate from the Security Council under Chapter VII of the UN Charter. Interventions for such 'intangible' purposes as the protection of humanity or human rights are becoming all but impossible to justify to the international community at large unless they are done in coalitions and with United Nations sanction.

Conclusions

Just as the age of responsibility to protect is apparently dawning, there is a risk that we may be returning to the nineteenth-century paradigm of intervention: it is likely only when the national interest is *directly* implicated. There are other factors at work, too:

1. In an age of recessions, economic crises and budget cuts – not least to the armed forces – can Western liberal states financially afford to carry out liberal interventions? Wars, after all, are expensive. It was said that every missile fired by the Royal Air Force in Libya cost the British taxpayer £500,000 (see Jackson 2011). Is this financially sustainable?
2. Is there the physical capability to project the force necessary to execute successful interventions? This is linked to the previous point.
3. Is there popular and media support for liberal interventions abroad? The tradition of isolationism remains strong, not least in the United States – as seen by the extreme reluctance on display in the United States at the start of the operation in Libya, which in fact led to the United States quickly handing over operational command and control of the mission to NATO.
4. In an 'internally liberal' state, does the national law – particularly at a constitutional level – make for 'easy interventions'? Again, it is worth remembering the uproar in the United States over whether President Barack Obama's decision to engage in Libya without congressional consent was legally valid under the United States Constitution.

On balance, the debates in the United Nations surrounding the notion of responsibility to protect have revealed much in the way of rhetoric and very little in the way of concrete action. The one arguable example of responsibility to protect in action to date has been Operation Unified Protector in Libya in 2011, and its claim to have established responsibility to protect in practice is fatally undermined, in the opinion of the present author, by the failure of the sponsoring states and of the Security Council expressly to invoke the doctrine as the basis for action, coupled with the strong backlash on the part of other, less liberal, states. The situation in international law with regard to 'humanitarian interventions', in other words, seems to remain much as it was before: that there is no treaty-based rule or norm of customary international law that unequivocally permits such interventions, unless they are done with the consent of either the target state or the United Nations.

The 'benevolent aggression' of Western liberal democracies may remain, in principle, benevolent. But it is becoming less and less aggressive in the face of political, diplomatic, economic and operational realities.

References

Axworthy, L. and Rock, A. 2011. A Victory for the Responsibility to Protect, November. Available at: http://www.uottawa.ca/articles/a-victory-for-the-responsibility-to-protect [accessed: 19 December 2012].

Ban, K.-M. 2012. Address to the Stanley Foundation Conference on the Responsibility to Protect, 18 January. Available at: http://www.un.org/apps/news/infocus/sgspeeches/statments_full.asp?statID=1433 [accessed: 18 December 2012].

Barnidge, R.P. Jr 2009. The United Nations and the African Union: Assessing a Partnership for Peace in Darfur. *Journal of Conflict and Security Law*, 14(1), 93–113.

Biagini, E.F. 2004. Gladstone's Midlothian Campaign of 1879 – The *Realpolitik* of Christian Humanitarianism. *Journal of Liberal Democrat History*, 42, 6–12.

Blair, T. 1999. *PBS Online Focus – The Blair Doctrine*, 22 April. Available at: http://www.pbs.org/newshour/bb/international/jan-june99/blair_doctrine4-23.html [accessed: 18 December 2012].

Borneman, W.R. 2005. *1812: The War that Forged a Nation*. New York: HarperCollins.

Bronner, E. and Slackman, M. 2011. Saudi Troops Enter Bahrain to Help Put Down Unrest. *New York Times*, 14 March.

Buchan, R. 2010. Explaining Liberal Aggression: The International Community and Threat Perception. *International Community Law Review*, 12(4), 413–36.

Côte d'Ivoire, Letter from Nicolas Sarkozy, President of the Republic, to Ban Ki-moon, United Nations Secretary-General, Paris, 4 April 2011. Available at: https://pastel.diplomatie.gouv.fr/editorial/actual/ael2/bulletin.gb.asp?liste=20110406.gb.html&submit=consulter [accessed: 18 December 2012].

Doyle, M.W. 1997. *Ways of War and Peace: Realism, Liberalism and Socialism*. New York: W.W. Norton.

Fisher, L. 2009. Destruction of the *Maine* (1898). Law Library of Congress, 4 August. Available at: http://loc.gov/law/help/usconlaw/pdf/Maine.1898.pdf [accessed: 18 December 2012].

Gladstone, W.E. 1876. *Bulgarian Horrors and the Question of the East*. London: John Murray.

Jackson, P. 2011. Libya: Is Cost of Military Mission Sustainable? *BBC News*, 22 March. Available at: http://www.bbc.co.uk/news/uk-12806709 [accessed: 19 December 2012].

Joint Resolution for the Recognition of the Independence of the People of Cuba, Demanding that the Government of Spain Relinquish its Authority and Government in the Island of Cuba, and to Withdraw its Land and Naval Forces from Cuba and Cuban Waters, and Directing the President of the United States to Use the Land and Naval Forces of the United States to Carry These Resolutions into Effect, 20 April 1898, 30 Stat. 738 (Teller Amendment).

Laird, R. 2011. *French Libya Lessons Learned: Better Targeting, Flexible ROEs, Limits to Armed UAVs*, 23 September. Available at: http://defense.aol.com/2011/09/23/french-libya-lessons-learned-better-targeting-flexible-roes-l/ [accessed: 18 December 2012].

MacGahan, J.A. 1876. The Turkish Atrocities in Bulgaria: Horrible Scenes at Batak. *The Daily News*, 22 August. Available at: http://www.attackingthedevil.co.uk/related/macgahan.php [accessed: 18 December 2012].

McKinley, W. 1897. First Annual Message to the Senate and House of Representatives, 6 December, in *A Supplement to a Compilation of the Messages and Papers of the Presidents*, vol. 13, ed. J.D. Richardson. New York: Bureau of National Literature, 6251–75.

North Atlantic Treaty Organization. NATO and Libya. Available at: http://www.nato.int/cps/en/natolive/topics_71652.htm [accessed: 18 December 2012].

Odom, T.P. 1988. Dragon Operations: Hostage Rescues in the Congo, 1964–1965. Leavenworth Papers 14. US Army Combat Studies Institute. Available at: http://www.dtic.mil/cgi-bin/GetTRDoc?Location=U2&doc=GetTRDoc.pdf&AD=ADA211790 [accessed: 18 December 2012].

Official Report of the Naval Court of Inquiry into the Loss of the Battleship MAINE (Sampson Board), 21 March 1898. Available at: http://www.spanamwar.com/mainerpt.htm [accessed: 18 December 2012].

Roberts, A. 2000. The So-Called 'Right' of Humanitarian Intervention. *Yearbook of International Humanitarian Law*, 3, 3–51.

The Ruined Egyptian City. 1882. *New York Times*, 15 July.

Traxel, D. 1999. *1898: The Birth of the American Century*. New York: Vintage.

Treaty Between Great Britain, France, and Russia, for the Pacification of Greece, London, 6 July 1827 (Treaty of London). Available at: http://www.fordham.edu/halsall/mod/1827gktreaty.asp [accessed: 18 December 2012].

Turns, D. 2009. *Jus ad Pacem in Bello*? Afghanistan, Stability Operations and the
    International Laws Relating to Armed Conflict, in *The War in Afghanistan: A
    Legal Analysis*, ed. M.N. Schmitt. International Law Studies 85. Newport, RI:
    United States Naval War College, 387–410.
UNGA (2009), UN Doc A/63/PV.105.
UNGA Res 2131 (1965), UN Doc 2131(XX).
UNGA Res 2625 (1970), UN Doc 2625(XXV).
UNGA Res 60/1 (2005), UN Doc A/RES/60/1.
UNSC (1976), UN Doc S/PV.1941.
UNSC (2011), UN Doc S/PV.6498.
UNSC (2011), UN Doc S/PV.6528.
UNSC (2011), UN Doc S/PV.6566.
UNSC (2011), UN Doc S/PV.6595.
UNSC (2011), UN Doc S/PV.6620.
UNSC (2011), UN Doc S/PV.6627.
UNSC (2012), UN Doc S/PV.6710.
UNSC (2012), UN Doc S/PV.6711.
UNSC Draft Resolution [On Situation of Human Rights in the Syrian Arab
    Republic] (2011), UN Doc S/2011/612.
UNSC Draft Resolution [On Situation of Human Rights in the Syrian Arab
    Republic] (2012), UN Doc S/2012/77.
UNSC Res 751 (1992), UN Doc S/RES/751.
UNSC Res 794 (1992), UN Doc S/RES/794.
UNSC Res 814 (1993), UN Doc S/RES/814.
UNSC Res 836 (1993), UN Doc S/RES/836.
UNSC Res 1270 (1999), UN Doc S/RES/1270.
UNSC Res 1497 (2003), UN Doc S/RES/1497.
UNSC Res 1769 (2007), UN Doc S/RES/1769.
UNSC Res 1816 (2008), UN Doc S/RES/1816.
UNSC Res 1973 (2011), UN Doc S/RES/1973.
UNSC Res 2016 (2011), UN Doc S/RES/2016.
Western, J. and Goldstein, J.S. 2011. Humanitarian Intervention Comes of Age:
    Lessons from Somalia to Libya. *Foreign Affairs*, 90(6), 48–59.
Zifcak, S. 2010. The Responsibility to Protect, in *International Law*, 3rd edn, ed.
    M.D. Evans. Oxford: Oxford University Press, 504–27.

Index

www.ingramcontent.com/pod-product-compliance
Ingram Content Group UK Ltd.
Pitfield, Milton Keynes, MK11 3LW, UK
UKHW020400010325
455677UK00021B/551